Begum Khaleda Zia:
Portrait of a People's Leader of Bangladesh

Edited By:

Q. M. Jalal Khan

K. M. A. Malik

Begum Khaleda Zia:
Portrait of a People's Leader of Bangladesh

Edited By:

Q.M. Jalal Khan, PhD (New York)

K. M. A. Malik, PhD (London)

Academica Press
Washington~London

Library of Congress Cataloging-in-Publication Data

Names: Khan, Q. M. Jalal (editor) | Malik, K. M. A (editor).
Title: Begum Khaleda Zia : portrait of a people's leader of Bangladesh / Q. M. Jalal Khan | K. M. A. Malik
Description: Washington : Academica Press, 2021. | Includes references.
Identifiers: LCCN 2020951639 | ISBN 9781680531046 (hardcover) | ISBN 9781680531053 (paperback) | ISBN 9781680538953 (ebook)

Copyright 2021 Q. M. Jalal Khan

Contents

Advance Praise for the Book xi

Begum Khaleda Zia:
Portrait of a People's Leader of Bangladesh xv

Preface and Acknowledgement xvii

জ্যোতির্ময়ী **(Luminous Khaleda)** 1

Chapter 1
Begum Khaleda Zia:
Her Battles for a Democratic and Prosperous Bangladesh 5

K M A Malik

Chapter 2
Begum Khaleda Zia:
Her Patriotic Politics and Its Historical Context 37

Zoglul Husain

Chapter 3
Begum Khaleda Zia:
A Tale of Courage, Patriotism, Betrayal and Tragedy 61

Mahmudur Rahman

Chapter 4
Begum Khaleda Zia:
The Pragmatic and Patriotic Leader That She Is 85

Jasim Uddin Ahmad

Chapter 5
Begum Khaleda Zia:
The Shining Light of Political,
Economic, and Educational Reforms in Bangladesh 93

A N M Ehsanul Hoque Milan

Chapter 6
**Begum Khaleda Zia: Her Eviction from Home
and Imprisonment -- Hasina's Ugly Exposure of Zia-Phobia!** 109

R Chowdhury

Chapter 7
Begum Khaleda Zia: Her State-Building Strategies and Policies .. 115

Syed Serajul Islam

Chapter 8
**Begum Khaleda Zia: The Greatest Political Phenomenon
of Bangladesh and the Hasina Regime's Smallest-Minded
Semi-Release of Her from Long and Unjust Imprisonment** 127

Q M Jalal Khan

Chapter 9
Begum Khaleda Zia—Her Life, Her Story **by Mahfuz Ullah:
My Speech at the Launch of the Book, November 18, 2018** 163

Asif Nazrul (Translated by Ahmad U Shihab)

Chapter 10
**Begum Khaleda Zia: A Beloved Icon of Patriotism,
Fighter for Democracy, and Victim of Fascist Injustice** 171

Nazma Mustafa

Chapter 11
**Begum Khaleda Zia: Mother of Democracy, Bangladesh's
Most Popular, Yet Most Tormented Political Leader** 193

Mohammad Zainal Abedin

Chapter 12
**Begum Khaleda Zia: Never One of
the "Two Begums" in Bangladesh Politics** 207

Abid Bahar

Chapter 13
Begum Khaleda Zia: Personal Recollections and Beyond 221

R Chowdhury

Chapter 14
Begum Khaleda Zia: Her Long Walk, In and Out of Bondage and Freedom, to Save the Nation—No End in Sight 237

Q M Jalal Khan

Appendix A
(Authentic Counter Narrative to the Disturbingly Distorting Hasina-Awami Story) 295

Appendix B
(Corruption and Awami BAKSAL Propaganda Development Under the Regime) 301

Appendix C
(More Corruption Under the Regime) 331

Appendix D
(The regime's failure to face the corona virus disease) 333

Appendix E
(There Is No Freedom of Speech Under the Regime) 337

Appendix F
(Conspiracies Behind the BDR Massacre) 339

Appendix G
(The Regime's Controversial ICT) 343

Appendix H
(New and reconstituted BNP under the leadership of the Zia family) 345

Authors' Short Bios 351

Advance Praise for the Book

"This book--a highly engaging collection of essays featuring the political life of Begum Khaleda Zia--fills a void in the political analysis of Bangladesh. The book rightly portrays her as a democrat at heart and political practice. If she wanted, she could have stayed in power, but she gave up power voluntarily, believing she would return to power in a fair election. Unfortunately, the political party that succeeded hers in power in late 2008 didn't hold a free and fair election ever since. Additionally, in a fascist fashion, it jailed her on trumped up charges and sham trials. The book thus rightly highlights the fact that Khaleda Zia has been immensely victimized under the current undemocratic regime. The contributors to the book are well-known for their writings on the politics and development issues of Bangladesh. They point out the former Prime Minister's achievements and sufferings objectively and credibly. I am pleased to see that the book is a depiction of her patriotism, popularity, sincerity, and struggle for democratic rule in the country. Begum Khaleda Zia's political contributions as featured in this volume will inspire generations of academics and politicians to study and fight for restoration of democracy in Bangladesh." – Dr Mohammad A Auwal, Professor of Communication Studies, California State University, Los Angeles.

"The subject of this book, Begum Khaleda Zia, is truly a people's leader, incredible and exemplary. Both in and out of power, she proved it again and again since she entered politics following the assassination of her husband and highly popular President Ziaur Rahman in 1981. Both are/were extremely popular, legendary, and phenomenal, so much so that they are exampled by themselves in successfully leading the nation out of critical times with an admirable sense of mission and vision. No other leader of Bangladesh has so far been able to reach their sky-rocketing popularity, which they earned by virtue of their lasting achievements and legacy in all the fields of state building endeavor that great democratic leaders of a new third world country are expected to strive for. President Zia's and Begum Zia's patriotic and nationalist goals and ideals, their efforts to unify the nation and define the idea of Bangladesh nationhood, their selfless sacrifice for the cause of the nation, their sincere commitment to political, economic, and educational reforms, and their struggles in the face of endless odds and oppression made them an inspiring model and embodiment of noble and lofty aspirations of a whole new people of Bangladesh. This book is a worthy record of the challenges and accomplishments of the three-time former Prime Minister Begum Zia in particular, and the historic 'President-Prime Minister' couple together in general." --- Dr M Saidul Islam, Associate Professor of Sociology, Nanyang Technological University, Singapore.

"A very welcome publication, which would breathe the essential elixir and vitality of a new life among the people of Bangladesh. It is going to be a fresh, cooling breeze blowing in the sultry, choking and suffocating political atmosphere in our beloved country. This book has been contributed to by authors well-known for their writings on the political chains and shackles of Bangladesh—a country which for the last twelve years has unbearably become Awami-ridden, corruption-ridden, police-ridden, partisan judiciary-ridden, looter-and-cheater-ridden, rape-and-yaba-and-murder-and-casino-and-enforceddisappearances-ridden, Hindutva-ridden, and Indian RAW-ridden. It has become a country that has completely gone down politically, institutionally, ethically, morally, and culturally. The authors describe, in fine authentic details, Begum Zia's democratically-enlightened and patriotically-imbued achievements in power and her sufferings, challenges and sacrifices, out of power, especially in the face of Hasina's authoritarian rule, as deadly and dangerous as it is. In her popularity, patriotism, and struggle for a democratic system that has gone completely missing in Bangladesh since 2009, a free Begum Zia, who is now in bondage at the age of seventy-five, is what the country mostly needs. Her track records demonstrate that she deserves to be portrayed the way the writers in this volume have attempted to do. In the context of the recent history of Bangladesh, especially the Awami autocratic rule and the state-sponsored totalitarian terror and tyranny it has put the country through, Khaleda Zia has become a noble icon of democratic and patriotic politics the legacy of which will last long." ---Dr Kanak Sarwar, New York-based journalist in exile

Begum Khaleda Zia:
Portrait of a People's Leader of Bangladesh

This book is dedicated to:

All the Founding Fathers of Bangladesh as mentioned with respect and objective evaluative comment (that history will judge one's good deeds and bad) by Begum Khaleda Zia in her memorably unifying speech in the Parliament on 29 June 2013 (www.youtube.com/watch?v= 0aP7wuBCxRA).

The memories of those whose legacies for Muslim empowerment in Colonial Bengal are still alive and well in modern Bangladesh.

Nawab Sir Khawaja Salimullah Bahadur, the fourth Nawab of Dhaka and one of the leading Muslim politicians during the British Raj, who was the most pioneering key figure in the political resurgence of the people of Muslim (East) Bengal, especially in the establishment of Dhaka University for their educational improvement and intellectual enlightenment (and who died an early death in Kolkata, allegedly conspiratorial, at the age of only less than forty-four in early 1915).

Sir Khawaja Nazimuddin, former Governor-General and Prime Minister of Pakistan and Chief Minister of East Bengal, who, along with the other members of Dhaka's noble and lofty Nawab family, was instrumental in effectively following through the hopes, dreams and promises of Nawab Sir Salimullah in terms of his/their historic and generous landed contributions in the field of education and culture in East Bengal (now Bangladesh) during the 1920s and onwards.

Sher-e-Bangla A K Fazlul Huq, a Bengali statesman and jurist who served as the first Prime Minister of undivided Bengal and later as the Home Minister of Pakistan, who also moved the famous Pakistan resolution in 1940, who was the first to seek East Bengal's autonomy in

1954, and who took the first legislative moves to liberate the Bengal peasantry from the curse of the Zamindari system.

Maulana Abdul Hamid Khan Bhasani, politician, activist, Islamic ideologist, a life-long fighter for peasants and workers' rights, and the first to seek separation of East Bengal from Pakistan as early as in 1957.

Ziaur Rahman, declarer and proclaimer of the independence of Bangladesh in March 1971, who was at the forefront of the liberation war throughout the year, and who again came forward to save the nation during the difficult times in 1975. Leading the nation most successfully through the ideal of Bangladeshi Nationalism and the policy of multi-party democracy until early 1981 (when he was assassinated, most tragically and conspiratorially, on May 30), he remains one of the brightest luminaries in the political sky of Bangladesh to provide direction and inspiration to the nation in all its circumstances—good or bad, rain or shine, dog days or heydays. And,

All the Shaheeds (Martyrs) of the War of Liberation in 1971.
All the fighters for Justice and Democracy in Bangladesh.
All the victims of extra-judicial killings, enforced disappearances, and fascist party and police brutalities.

Preface and Acknowledgement

The idea of coming up with a 'Thank You' volume in tribute to Begum Khaleda Zia (for her honest valor and virtues, her patriotic and state-building commitment and contributions, and her determined and persistent standing up against the continued oppression and repression in Bangladesh under Awami police control and occupation since 2009) first occurred to Dr K M A Malik, a UK-based professor, scholar, author, and political activist. He offered his inspiring guidance as he proposed to me to bring out a book on the former prime minister and opposition leader, who has been one of the greatest and most phenomenal political figures of Bangladesh. Picking up on Dr Khalifa Malik's suggestion, both he and I contacted potential contributors, whose response was immediate and spontaneous. That speaks of the place Begum Zia, 75 years of age, holds in the hearts and minds of the people of Bangladesh now turned into a fascist police and prison state of fear, coercion, and intimidation with hundreds of thousands harassed, humiliated, haunted, and hounded by countless false and fictitious cases against them, including Khaleda Zia herself. I thought of the project to be highly worthwhile and immediately got started with it.

After much discussion among us, we decided to call the book, *Begum Khaleda Zia: Portrait of A People's Leader of Bangladesh*. It is a title that echoes what Dr Lawrence Ziring, who was a Professor of Government and Politics at Western Michigan University and a leading expert on South Asia, aptly calls Begum Zia's husband Ziaur Rahman, "A People's President."[1] The couple—Zia and Khaleda—has indeed been unprecedentedly popular with the people of Bangladesh in their overwhelming majority. On 24 May 2011, the New Jersey State Senate honored Begum Zia as a "Fighter for Democracy." It was the first time the state Senate had so honored any foreign leader, from South Asia or any other part of the world.

I am glad that I was able to complete the work within a short period of time with contributions by several eminent writers and from different perspectives. While some of the contributions are colored with somewhat personal touch, they are all, however, unified and held in uniformity in terms of certain themes and ideas. All chapters are in conversation with each other amounting to a general estimate of Begum Zia's politics, achievements, sufferings and her overcoming or still fighting against the tremendous odds and difficulties created by BAKSAL-India conspiracies. Written by people of recognized credentials, the book is an independent and historical evaluation of her career, successes, struggles, sufferings and contributions towards Bangladesh and its people and her stand against Indian hegemonism for national sovereignty.

Being human, Begum Zia may have her own share of faults and miscalculations. All politicians have theirs. However, we believe that, for Begum Zia, her faults have been few and far between when we note that there are countless of them, horrible and heinous, being constantly committed for years by many of her contemporaries in political leadership. That is why she is regarded to be dauntingly greater and more superior to her peers and counterparts. Her accomplishments far outweigh her (and her party BNP's) lapses, as do her great words, actions and speeches, be they in the parliament, party anniversaries, or public meetings. Unfortunately, since 2009 or so, according to Dr Malik, the BNP in all its wings, including the media, publicity, research and communication, has lost the capacity to capitalize on the good works by its great leader. "But we are hundred percent right," he claims, "to go ahead with a book on her politics, challenges and accomplishments."

Begum Zia does not have to be angelically innocent and flawless to be a living legend as she already is in the eyes of her country people, all Bangladeshis, as one nation, one community. In fact, we believe that, in her mythic popularity of the proportion of the Pied Piper of Hamelin, her political wisdom and sagacity, and her continuous uphill battle against the autocratic forces, Begum Zia, so to speak, has surpassed all other political leaders in South Asia or the entire Indian subcontinent, as a matter of fact. While she successfully overcame the authoritarian forces that were unleashed by H M Ershad in the 1980s, she is still suffering from the more fatal and fascist forces that have been strangulating her own person, her party, the BNP, and the entire Bangladesh, all reeling under the tyrannical Hasina regime since 2009.

Starting from her young age to her latest statement regarding the BNP being wrong about joining the so-called Jatiya Oikya Front (National United Front) with Dr Kamal Hossain as the leader in 2018 during her imprisonment, Begum Zia, even in her ailing health, remains a great guiding and leading force—to the envy of her critics and to the popular support of the masses and millions of her followers. Currently semi-free but virtually still in bondage (sort of house arrest), yet calm and composed, and also firm and far-sighted, Begum Zia's stand as expressed in the same statement that the BNP should give more thought before leaving Jamaat-e-Islam is also absolutely politically correct, to the approval of the vast majority of her supporters.

In completing the book, I must add here that I had the benefit of kind cooperation from two dynamic and very reliable hands: (1) R Chowdhury, a US-based former decorated soldier and diplomat (who has also authored several books of autobiography and political commentary and dozens of incisive and insightful articles of political analysis); and (2) Zoglul Husain, a UK-based organizer and campaigner of the liberation war of Bangladesh in 1971 and author of numerous articles of penetrating political analysis. It is the latter who thinks that the volume is a collection of excellent articles all of which have a great mass or a wealth of information and references to show the great achievements of Khaleda Zia. They also suggest, he thinks, the rough and rugged road she had to and is still having to traverse, and the pitfalls in which her husband President Ziaur Rahman's glorious life came to an abrupt end in 1981 in a supposed India-orchestrated plot which had then army chief General H M Ershad and Sheikh Hasina in the loop (ref: Matiur Rahman Rentu's historically important book).

Dr Malik, Mr Chowdhury, and Mr Husain, all three are men of depth and wisdom, armed with an amazing knowledge of history and political developments in Bangladesh. In possession of an impressive ability to describe the political scenarios in fine authentic and analytical details, they took their valuable time to give an eagle-eyed second or sometimes even a third look at most of the contributions, some of which required extensive editing. It would not have been possible to put the volume together without their assistance and cooperation.

In addition to the above three contributors, we have a chapter from the incredibly bold and brilliant Mahmudur Rahman, former Adviser to the Government, Editor of the popular daily Amar Desh, and an eminent author and public intellectual. His presence with us is to be acknowledged with pride and pleasure. A nationally and internationally well-known political dissident who immensely suffered under the yoke of the fascist Hasina -- from imprisonment to incarceration in police custody to physical torture in the court premises by the Hasina goons--, Mahmudur Rahman is a household name loved by all Bangladeshis. There are other contributors-- former State Minister of Education, Bangladesh, Dr A N M Ehsanul Hoque Milan (also a victim of fraud and falsehood of the totalitarian police regime of Sheikh Hasina); former Jahangirnagar University Bangladesh Vice Chancellor Professor Jasim Uddin Ahmad, Dr Asif Nazrul of Dhaka University, Lakehead University Canada Professor Syed Serajul Islam, New York-based senior journalist Mohammad Zainal Abedin, Dawson College of Canada faculty Dr Abid Bahar and New York-based blogger Nazma Mustafa. I thankfully acknowledge their excellent contributions which have already been acclaimed by readers who had the opportunity of access to their writings.

One name I would like to make a special mention of, that is, Poet Abdul Hye Sikder, who, also a victim of Awami hoodlums and hooligans, has contributed a nice poem on the subject and title figure of the volume— Begum Zia. Placed at the very beginning, the poem provides an aesthetically and spiritually refreshing variety to the volume's contexture. I should also like to mention Dr M Kamrul Ahsan, Professor of Philosophy, Jahangirnagar University; Nasrullah Khan Jonaid, educationist and ex-Senate Member, Dhaka University; Saleh Shibly, journalist (London); and Oliullah Noman (journalist-in-exile in London) for their help and cooperation. Together, as a group, we feel strong and committed, united in a common cause.

Our book, *Begum Khaleda Zia: Portrait of A People's Leader of Bangladesh*, is possibly the fifth of its kind in recent years. Earlier, well-known author, journalist and media personality of great knowledge and intellect, Shafik Rehman (currently exiled in London, following the Hasina regime's atrocious persecution of him at home on fictitious cases), published *Democratic Leader Khaleda Zia* (2012, in English), which is a collection of essays originally published in the world press praising the leader. The same year he also did a Bengali version of the above, সংগ্রামী নেত্রী খালেদা জিয়া (2012). (Now late) Mahfuz Ullah, a great writer and intellectual, wrote *Begum Khaleda Zia—Her Life, Her Story* (Dhaka: The Universal Academy, 2018); Dr Emajuddin Ahmad (who also recently passed away) and Poet Abdul Hye Sikder had a volume in Bangla, named খালেদা জিয়া- তৃতীয় বিশ্বের কণ্ঠস্বর *(Khaleda Zia, Voice of the Third World (2019)*; and there is S. Abdul Hakim's *Begum Khaleda Zia of Bangladesh: A Political Biography* (South Asia Books/Vikas Publishing House, 1992).

In addition, there are other works of note, such as "Conversations: Khaleda Zia; A Woman Leader for a Land That Defies Islamic Stereotypes" (1993) by Barbara Crossette; and "New Premier in Bangladesh Vows to Stamp Out Corruption" (2001) by Celia W. Dugger. There was a cover story on Begum Zia by Time magazine's Alex Perry in April 2006, a rare feat to be achieved by a Bangladesh politician.[2] All those also are great works.

However, this present publication, in drawing together some intellectual and analytical minds writing from different angles and approaches, is a scholarly contribution with a qualitative difference from the other works mentioned above. One of this book's overarching highlights is Khaleda Zia's and particularly her (late) husband President Ziaur Rahman's history-making framework of Bangladesh nationalism, which "in the context of modern identity politics," as one political science scholar puts it, "has recently attracted a global resonance." The historic ideal of Bangladeshi nationalism has been singled out from among President Zia's manifold landmark measures to be thematized and privileged in different chapters (such as, Chapters. 1, 2, 3, and 14, with significant elaboration and references towards the middle of Chapter 8).

It deserves to be reiterated that the great majority of the people of Bangladesh think President Ziaur Rahman and Begum Khaleda Zia are the two best, finest and noblest leaders Bangladesh is/was blessed with. By virtue of their struggle, success, suffering and sacrifice for democracy, peace, national unity, identity, integrity, sovereignty and harmonious development, they were and remain the two greatest and most phenomenal political leaders Bangladesh has ever produced. Legends of undying name and fame in the history of the country, they were and remain the most popular and fantastic politicians the nation has so far witnessed. Political pied pipers as they are/were, both reached the height of popularity through their selfless state building measures and their patriotic love for the country.

To conclude, we have attempted to capture in this book different aspects of Begum Zia's life, background, challenges, struggles, and achievements, both political as well as personal. Notwithstanding the possible repetition of some factual details, each contributor wrote in his/her own style and expertise. That makes each chapter unique, of its own distinctive hue. Readers are expected to engage and identify with the protagonist (Begum Zia) as they proceed reading through the book. They will discover the broad vista and vast aura about her and will invariably come to the conclusion that she surpassed many subcontinental leaders in terms of leadership, suffering, sacrifice and achievement for the cause of her nation and her country. If they agree to what the authors tried to convey, their modest and humble efforts at bringing Begum Khaldea Zia, as the other volumes did, to the national and international attention and awareness will be paid for.[3]

Dr Q M Jalal Khan
20 November 2020

---

[1] *Bangladesh: From Mujib to Ershad, An Interpretive Study* (Oxford University Press, 1986; University Press Limited, Dhaka, 1992).

[2] http://content.time.com/time/covers/asia/0,16641,20060410,00.html
Perry is also the author of *Rebuilding Bangladesh.*

[3] For a few glimpses, as a memory lane, into the life of Begum Khaleda Zia, see:
- https://youtu.be/voXPd0p1IFw Khaleda in prison, behind bars
- https://youtu.be/10IiwKp4jdA (Zia and Khaleda visiting an African country)

- www.youtube.com/watch?v=WaEWS9QCgy8 (Khaleda casting her vote)
- www.youtube.com/watch?v=dm4FS_ZopqM (Khaleda exchanging Eid greetings)
- www.youtube.com/watch?v=0aP7wuBCxRA (Khaleda giving a memorable speech in the parliament as the opposition leader in 2013)
- www.facebook.com/photo.php?fbid=10216294378863741&set=gm.767645134067549&type=3&theater Begum Zia's fantastic address on the occasion of the founding anniversary of the BNP in 2015.
- www.youtube.com/watch?v=uXdEO1BrX54 (President Zia along with Mrs Zia visiting Malaysia)
- www.youtube.com/watch?v=iBdzm31zba4&list=PLExHoCI_4SUvTdjqejJA50HC-ilJQb-n7&index=80&app=desktop (watch Khaleda addressing a crowd) www.youtube.com/watch?v=iBdzm31zba4&list=PLExHoCI_4SUvTdjqejJA50HC-ilJQb-n7&index=80&app=desktop (watch Khaleda resigning and addressing a crowd)
- https://youtu.be/HVgx5w0RKvM "কোথাও আমার হারিয়ে যেতে নেই বাধা || ১৯৯৪ সালের স্কুল বিতর্ক || তৎকালীন প্রধানমন্ত্রী খালেদা জিয়া" (Great debate to watch with interesting comments from Prof Emajuddin Ahmed in presence of Prime Minister Begum Zia)
- President Zia arriving in Egypt www.youtube.com/watch?v=AVDDLSFxP-4
- President Zia arriving in his treacherous mortal enemy India:www.youtube.com/watch?v=U-B46TaUOz8
- https://youtu.be/x_a8WW7KKF0"টকশোতে শহীদ জিয়াউর রহমানের জীবনী নিয়ে ঝড় তুলল"
- www.youtube.com/watch?v=MhqJK4pit24 Honest, smart and brilliant President Zia
- ঢাকার শাহীন স্কুলে তারেক জিয়া গেছিলো ভর্তি পরীক্ষা দিতে https://www.facebook.com/photo.php?fbid=1495707290631195&set=a.100794310122507&type=3&theater
- http://everything.explained.today/Khaleda_Zia/

জ্যোতির্ময়ী (Luminous Khaleda)

আব্দুল হাই শিকদার/Abdul Hye Sikder

তুমি আমার ধূলিকে করেছো পবিত্র মৃত্তিকা।
বেদনা করেছো সঙ্গীতময়,
নদীকে দিয়েছো গতি,
জাতির জন্য স্বৈরশাসনমুক্ত প্রথম ভোর।

তোমার জন্য লিখলাম আমি পদ্মা কর্ণফুলী।

তুমি আমার আকাশ থেকে সরিয়ে দিয়েছো মেঘ।
বারুদ এবং আগ্রাসনের অন্ধ করেছো চোখ।
বৃক্ষকে তুমি সবুজ করেছো
সবুজ পেয়েছে দেশ,
দেশজুড়ে আজ মহিমান্বিত তোমার জয়ধ্বনি।

তোমার নামের পাশে রাখলাম এশিয়ার সব ফুল।

তুমি আমাকে ফিরিয়ে দিয়েছো বলবার অধিকার।
কষ্টের জ্বালা মুছিয়ে দিয়েছো পরম মমতা নিয়ে।
কর্দমে তুমি ফুটিয়ে তুলেছো শপথের শতদল,
সেই শতদলে সকল কালের ব্যথিতজনের আশা,
হাতে নিয়ে তুমি এসেছো জ্যোতির্ময়ী।

তোমাকে দিলাম পৃথিবীর সব পাখিদের কলরব।

যুদ্ধ তোমার শেষ হয়নি কো

ফিরতে পারোনি ঘরে,
ক্ষুধাতুর শিশু তোমার জন্য দুয়ারে দাঁড়িয়ে আছো
এশিয়ার এক মজলুম দেশে তোমার নীলাম্বরী
তাইতো প্রাণের পতাকার মতো ওড়ে।
হাজেরা জননী তাই মাঠে মাঠে পানির অন্বেষণে,
ক্লান্তিবিহীন ছুটে যাও তুমি প্রান্তরে জনপদে।
দু'চোখে তোমার স্বপ্নের রেনু,
স্বপ্নের পাশে প্রশিথিউসের আগুন,
সে আগুনে হবে পাবলিক দেশে জীবনের জাগরণ।

তোমার হাতে দিলাম তুলে আমার বাংলাদেশ।

English Translation, by:
Saleh Mahmud Riyad and Q M Jalal Khan

Khaleda the Luminous

You have transformed my poor dust into the sacred earth
My pains into the music of feeling warmth
Flowing rivers gather speed by your benign blessings
You brought the first dawn to your people
Free from the autocratic rule of the nineteen eighties.

I inscribe for you the Padma, the Karnaphuli.

You cleared the dark cloud from my sky.
Blinded the odious eyes of arms and aggression
Greened my pale trees; and
Deepened the greenery further everywhere
An overwhelming chant of your majestic victory
Resounds all over,

I place all the flowers of Asia before you,
For the sake of your name, your beauty.

জ্যোতিৰ্ময়ী (Luminous Khaleda)

You returned my rights to speak;
Blotted out my unbearable pains
Through your compassion and care
You made possible a hundred buds of our oaths
To blossom in the mud and mire
All the hopes and dreams of all battered souls
Lying in those leaves and fronds,
You are bearing in your hands;
Oh, the glittering soul!

I place the twittering of all birds of the world before you.

You are now in the middle of another long war
Yet to return home as the burden of more battles you bear
Hungry child awaits you at the door
The fringe of your clothes flies in the sky
As the flag of heart of the masses in an oppressed land
Mother Hajar looking for water from field to field arid,
And you running from the crowded cities to the countryside
Tireless, breathless, relentless---
Your eyes embower the pollens of dreams,
That contain the fire of Prometheus
The fire that would usher in the waking of life in this alluvial soil.

I bestow my motherland upon your honored hands.
****

Editor's Note: A good, *literal* translation, close to the original text, may be likened to remaining faithful in an adult relationship in human life. But the notion of fidelity in art is different. A better, *literary* translation may not be exactly faithful to the original, which may be viewed as a Mona Lisa or Cleopatra with an elusive beauty and variety that never age or stale. The above poem in translation may at times seem to be slightly removed from the original Bengali text. However, it is only understandably and reasonably so. When a text, especially an imaginative poem of figurative language, is rendered into a second language, it is neither easy nor necessary, with exceptions, of course, to stick fully and completely to the original form and structure in the source language.

The target (second) language version, if it drifts at all, may gain or lose some little text in order to be better understood and more interesting. That happens not only in terms of the cultural connotations and suggestiveness of the figures of speech—images, metaphors, and idioms--, but also rhyme, half-rhyme, alliteration, and assonance, of which there may still be room within the original free verse in which this poem already is. What is more important, however, is to keep faithful to the tone of voice of the poetic persona and the spirit of the letter, not necessarily to the letter itself in the word for word composition in the original. In the process, the translation exercise becomes something of a creative or *literary* rendering or adaptation, rather than merely *literal* or mechanical imitation.

There is a vast body of critical literature on the art of translation (অনুবাদ শিল্প) by writers and scholars with translation studies courses being offered at the academia. As far as creative literature is concerned, one may wish to compare Jibanananda Das's *Banalata Sen* and Nazrul Islam's *Bidrohi*, perhaps the two most famous Bengali poems done into more languages than any other Bengali poems, to their respective translations, including those in English. One may also like to see Charles Kingsley's "The Sands of Dee" ("O Mary, go and call the cattle home") in the great Indian Bengali poet-politician Humayun Kabir's "মেঘনায় বান" ("শোন মা আমিনা রেখে দেরে কাজ ত্বরা করে মাঠে চল/এল মেঘনায় জোয়ারের বেলা এখনি নামিবে ঢলা"); Shakespeare's sonnets in the Bengali translations by Sudhindranath Dutt and others; a number of Wordsworth's sonnets in their Bengali translations; and T S Eliot's "Journey of the Magi" in Rabindranath Tagore's তীর্থযাত্রী (included in his পুনশ্চ volume). I used to know a 3rd year English major student who rendered Eliot's The Waste Land as পোড়ো জমি in about 1978/79.

Chapter 1

Begum Khaleda Zia: Her Battles for a Democratic and Prosperous Bangladesh

K M A Malik

"Some are born great, some achieve greatness, and some have greatness thrust upon them." ---- Shakespeare's Twelfth Night, Act 2 Scene 5

Introduction

Begum Khaleda Zia is a name already established as a great leader and stateswoman of Bangladesh, both nationally and internationally. In the present essay, I shall try to explore the pathways she had to travel to attain this status. It did not happen in a day or two; it took nearly four decades of dedication and hard struggles against many odds. But how exactly has she arrived at her present position? As one of greatest fighters of the last century, Muhammad Ali said, "It isn't the mountains ahead to climb that wear you out; it's the pebble in your shoe." Begum Zia reached the pinnacle of political power and earned the love and respect of the whole of Bangladesh, but there were many pebbles (and needles) in the shoe that also caused her great suffering and pain.

The question is: how did Begum Zia's difficult and very tortuous "Long March" to "greatness" all begin? What were the challenges she had to face, what were the main obstacles she had to overcome, what battles she had to fight against her enemies and win, when did she retreat for tactical reasons, who were her main enemies and what were their weapons, and, above all, how did she conduct herself in victory and retreat? Finally, what are the legacies she is leaving behind for the people of Bangladesh after such a long political career? Obviously, this is such a vast subject that is impossible to cover in a short essay. I shall, therefore, try to discuss and analyze some selected aspects of the political career of this great leader of Bangladesh.

Begum Zia became active in politics not by any pre-conceived plan, but as a consequence of the tragic assassination of her husband President Ziaur Rahman in 1981. She started from a simple housewife with no direct organizational and political experience and assumed the top leadership of Bangladesh Nationalist Party (BNP) only to fill up the vacuum created after her husband's death. The BNP was not only the ruling party then but it was also the most popular mass organization. She led a coalition of several political parties for about 8 years against a military dictatorship to usher in a democratic dawn in the country. Then since 1991 she has run the country's administration as prime minister during three terms and also as the leader of the opposition. She became the embodiment of democracy, freedom and justice in a country that has remained embroiled in feudal, corrupt and mercenary culture under both military and civilian administrations. However, there were also the patriotic spirits and practices built from the Pakistan movement and later the freedom war and a glorious example set by Zia and his government.

Khaleda Zia is undoubtedly the most popular and dignified (only next to President Zia), but persecuted political leader in Bangladesh. She achieved "greatness" not by virtue of birth nor by paying for the services of lobby groups, but by relentless struggles against tyranny, authoritarianism and foreign domination, and by her own constructive contributions to the people of Bangladesh. Unfortunately, like many other historical figures, her journey has never been easy; she became target of vicious disinformation and propaganda campaign by her local and foreign enemies and became a victim of a new style "regime change" in 2007. She was made to suffer both mentally and physically, not only during the military regimes of General Hussain Muhammad Ershad and General Moeen U Ahmed but also during the highly controversial, conspiratorial, and authoritarian rule of Sheikh Hasina Wazed (2009--).

Bangladesh: the Indian embrace at birth

The new state of Bangladesh came into being in 1971 as a result of an armed liberation war but there was a serious lack of policy decisions and concrete actions necessary for consolidation of the state and protection of its sovereign interests against external encroachments. Talks of vague ideals of the spirit of liberation, fake promises, hollow sloganeering, and exaggerated expectations gave rise to extreme frustrations, discontent, dissent, discord; theft of state assets and unbridled corruption at high places, misrule, mismanagement, abolition of democracy in favor of a one-party authoritarian rule, repression of all opposition forces and suppression of all dissenting voices, armed activities by some underground leftist parties (as well as of government party elements), brutal methods of "enforced disappearances" and unlawful killings (30-35,000 patriots) by the ruling party gangs and various allied groups (Rakkhi Bahini, Lal Bahini, Mujib Bahini, etc.), the devastating death tolls (500,000 in direct effects and about 1,000,000 in after effects) during the 1973-74 man-made famine and. above all, the closure of all methods for peaceful change of power, all created the conditions for the military coup that overthrew the Mujib regime on 15 August 1975. All members of the Mujib family, except his two daughters, Hasina and Rehana, lost their lives during the coup. The two sisters survived the mini-massacre because they were on a European holiday at the time. At a later date, they were given shelter by India where they lived under India's security protection until they returned to Bangladesh in May 1981. The Awami League has marked 15th August as the 'Mujib Killing Day' but, in reality, that was a successful military uprising to overthrow an authoritarian regime, in which, very unfortunately, President Mujibur Rahman and his family also lost their lives.

After the violent overthrow of Sheikh Mujibur Rahman on the 15th August, 1975, Bangladesh was going through a political vacuum and a phase of uncertainty and destabilization. It also saw itself under the threat of foreign intervention. This was precipitated by some politically ambitious elements, both outside and within the army, allegedly for a so-called "scientific socialist revolution and classless army."[1] This section known as Jatiya Samajtantrik Dal ("National Socialist Party of

Bangladesh") (JSD) was led by a group of youth leaders and had a secret network within the lower ranks of the armed forces. They believed in the overthrow of the existing regime by "armed insurrection" (probably under the spell of a Cuban-style "romantic revolution"). Due to the circumstances of their birth, members being selectively recruited from pro-Mujib Students League and some cadres trained by an Indian army officer, it was widely believed that they had important connections with the external agencies of some foreign countries.

The changes brought about by the August uprising bore historic significance for Bangladesh and its foreign relations. The new regime was led by Khondakar Mushtaq Ahmed, a prominent Awami League leader and colleague of Sheikh Mujibur Rahman since 1949. It was driven by the military officers who staged the coup. They proclaimed a "non-aligned" foreign policy, sought to build up "friendly" relations with the Islamic world and China, and improve the relations with the USA and other western countries, and reduce their dependence on Indian "advice and help" to run the newly formed state. Due to historical and geographical reasons, India's own imperial ambitions as originally visualised in the Nehru Doctrine,[2] and also due to India's support to Bangladesh during the 1971 liberation war, it could see the new country only as a client state and not as a fully-fledged independent state with its own sovereign rights in expanding foreign relations and developing economic, cultural and strategic policies according to the will of its citizens.

India must have been alerted by Sheikh Mujib's attempt at projecting Bangladesh on an international stage by joining the NAM summit in Algiers (6 September 1973) and, more significantly, by attending the OIC summit in Lahore (22-24 February 1974) without any prior discussion with the Indian authorities.[3] At that time, Sheikh Mujib was not only failing to stabilize the political, economic and social system of his new country, but he was also perceived to defy or ignore the terms of seven-point agreement and twenty-five year treaty signed earlier (in November 1971 and March 1972 respectively) with India.[4] It was irritating toIndia, but there was no way it could intervene militarily in Bangladesh without risking a long drawn out armed resistance and ruining whatever political capital it gained by "helping" the Bangladeshi refugees and the liberation war efforts in 1971. The Indian authorities would, therefore, be reviewing their strategy and strengthening their "soft power" and "covert operations" capabilities.

During the Lahore visit of Sheikh Mujibur Rahman, Pakistan's prime minister Zulfikar Ali Bhutto accorded a hero's welcome to the Bangladesh leader. In a return visit to Bangladesh (28-29 June 1974), Mr Bhutto was also given a grand reception. A photograph of the two leaders' emotionally charged embrace and the attempts at reconciliation were celebrated in a positive way in both Pakistan and Bangladesh. The event was also covered in many international media. India did not show any reaction officially but they were not very pleased with the prospect of a possible Bangladesh-Pakistan rapprochement either.

It is well known to the public, but not highlighted in the biased Indian and pro-Indian Bangladeshi media, that the most important reason why India intervened directly in the 1971 Bangladesh war was to serve its own long-term political, economic, cultural and strategic interests by dismembering its arch-enemy Pakistan and creating a nominally independent "satellite" entity in the erstwhile East Pakistan. So, any policy decision by Dhaka, independent of India's "advice" and to have good relations with India's "enemies," was seen as a serious threat to India's national interests and regional hegemony. Bangladesh, a Muslim majority country, having good and friendly relations with another Muslim country like Pakistan, and even with a non-Muslim country like Nepal or China has always been considered as having committed acts of "treachery" and "unpardonable sin" by the Indian chauvinists and policy makers.

So, any attempt at Bangladesh improving relations with Pakistan or China has raised eyebrows in the neighbouring country. Two such recent examples are: (a) the telephone conversation between Sheikh Hasina and Imran Khan on the COVID-19 and Kashmir issues, and (b) the involvement of Bangladesh in China's Belt and Road Initiative (BRI) megaproject with proposed investments, over a decade, of more than US$ 50 billion in Bangladesh economy. As of the current year, China has already committed $31 billion to Bangladesh for funding projects in roads, railways, bridge and tunnel construction, power plants, water treatment facilities and also for defence cooperation. All these developments are said to be detrimental to Indian interests, for which the Indian media and their Bangladeshi affiliates have been conducting a vicious anti-Bangladesh propaganda.

It was well known that Mr Bhutto was a prominent actor in inciting the 25th March military crackdown in Dhaka, and that under no circumstances could he be absolved of his arrogance and genocidal crimes in Bangladesh. However, during his visit to Dhaka as the prime minister of Pakistan, Mr Bhutto publicly apologized for what he called the "shameful repression and unspeakable crimes" committed in Bangladesh by the Pakistani Army in 1971.[5]

Since the small sections of the pro-Indian elements within Bangladesh establishment were not happy about the August 15, 1975 changeover, they organized a counter coup on November 3, 1975 under the leadership of Brigadier Khaled Mosharraf. They put the Army Chief General Ziaur Rahman under house arrest and sent the August 15 coup leaders into exile (offering them immunity from future prosecutions). But they failed to gain the complete trust and support from the army "sepoys and junior officers" and also from the general public. They were also perceived to be India-sponsored. As a result, the army personnel and general people, including the underground Jatiya Samajtantrik Dal (JSD) militants, staged a counter-counter uprising on 7th November against the four-day old Khaled Mosharraf takeover and freed Ziaur Rahman from captivity.[6]

Ziaur Rahman was the most popular army officer in independent Bangladesh and had the trust of the army rank and file as well as of the young people wishing for a qualitative change in the political and economic landscape of the new nation. But a section of the rebels, mostly in the ranks and files, led by Colonel Abu Taher (retired, freedom fighter) behaved as unruly anarchists and raised slogans for a classless army. This infantile attitude was probably due to their misguided urge for a quick and instantaneous "socialist" revolution. History brought the young General Zia again to the vanguard of Bangladesh struggle. Within the shortest possible time, he united the army and the people, subdued the hot headed civil and armed rebels, restored public order and opened up a new horizon of hope and success but failed to stop the anti-Bangladesh activities from across the border by India-sponsored elements like Kader Siddiqi and the tribal rebels in the Chittagong Hill Districts. He saved the nation at this critical stage from the impending disaster of civil war and potential external armed intervention, as he did five years before by valiantly coming forward and making the crucial declaration of independence and successfully fighting throughout 1971.

Legacies of Ziaur Rahman

Ziaur Rahman was a military man but unlike other "generals in politics," he arranged for a return to a multi-party democracy, made defunct by Sheikh Mujibur Rahman in 1975. Sheikh Mujib buried the last vestiges of multi-party democracy by introducing a one-party BAKSAL system with himself as the "President for Life." The life of Ziaur Rahman was cut short by assassin's bullets on 30 May 1981. He was in power, first as Deputy Martial Law Administrator and then as elected President (with President Abu Sadat Mohammad Sayem as CMLA, even though it was Zia who ran the show). He was in power for about five and a half years (1976-81) but made historic contributions to the story of Bangladesh. His legacies include the following contributions for which his name would be written in golden letters in the history of Bangladesh:

> 1. Major Zia was the first Bengali army officer to revolt against the Pakistan army on the 25th March night (02:15 hrs on 26th March) of 1971, immediately after the enemies had launched a crackdown on the Bengali army, police and general people, and organized whatever forces were available or could be mobilized.
>
> 2. Major Zia made the first radio broadcast on 26th March evening 1971 from the Kalurghat Radio Station near Chittagong and declared the independence of the "People's Republic of Bangladesh" with himself as the head of the provisional government. To give it more credibility and legitimacy he made a second broadcast next day in the name of Sheikh Mujibur Rahman. "This is Swadhin Bangla Betar Kendra. I, Major Ziaur Rahman, do hereby declare the independence of the People's Republic of Bangladesh on behalf of our great national leader, Bangabandhu Sheikh

Mujibur Rahman. [...] We shall fight to the last to free our motherland. By the grace of Allah, victory would be ours."[7]

Zia made the clarion call to the whole country to join the liberation war and solicited international recognition for the new republic. At that moment of our existential crisis, with Sheikh Mujib under Pakistani detention and rest of the top political leadership hiding or escaping to safety in India, Ziaur Rahman's voice galvanized the nation.[8] Whatever his detractors may say, it was Ziaur Rahman who ignited the first spark of the armed resistance that would gradually engulf the whole prairie of Bangladesh, and that led, ultimately, to the defeat of the Pakistani occupation army and victory of the Bangladeshi people on 16th December 1971. When in power, one can revise/rewrite history even using a loyal court to deny the honor and recognition due to this great hero, which Sheikh Hasina has done in a very shameful, Machiavellian way, but the truth can never be erased from history. I myself read the headline in the London Evening Standard on 27th March 1971, "East Pakistan Cut-off from the World; Major Zia Declares the Independence of Bangladesh." And from that moment, I have remained an unashamed and unabashed admirer of Ziaur Rahman.

3. After the tumultuous events of 1975 for the control of the soul of Bangladesh, Ziaur Rahman brought back discipline and re-established the chain of command in the armed forces; he also strengthened the defence and security capacities of the country.

4. Ziaur Rahman was very conscious about the need to save the "rivers" of Bangladesh and get a fair share of the waters of the 53 trans-boundary rivers from India. However, the upper riparian India was reluctant to negotiate any water sharing arrangement with the lower riparian Bangladesh. Bangladesh took the issue to the UN for international arbitration, but India resisted the move; it has since been withdrawing waters, unilaterally, from these rivers. By raising this issue in the UN, Zia became a target of Indian propaganda.

5. India has been inspiring, abetting, organizing, helping and arming the tribal insurgents in Chittagong Hill Districts from the Pakistan period. This they have been doing since 1960s in

order to maintain pressure on the Dhaka authorities. Ziaur Rahman understood the nature of this game; so he formulated and implemented the required policies not to the liking of the Delhi authorities.[9]

6. Ziaur Rahman wanted to negotiate all problems between India and Bangladesh, including issues like enclaves, Talpatti island, sea boundaries, border, trade, security, transport, etc., but India always adopted coercive and/or deceptive diplomacy in order to extract one-sided benefits from Bangladesh.

7. Ziaur Rahman abolished the much hated Rakkhi Bahini and other pro-Mujib militia groups, and stopped various excesses carried out by them. The activities of various underground opposition groups were also reduced or curtailed.

8. Ziaur Rahman enhanced closer diplomatic, security and trade contacts with many countries (including Pakistan, China, Saudi Arabia, etc.) in defiance of the India-Bangladesh treaties (1971 and 1972) signed earlier. This was done despite serious reservations of India.

9. Ziaur Rahman reorganized the regular armed forces and started a modernization program. He raised the strength of the army from one division to four divisions and took all initiatives to equip the armed forces with weapons procured from China and other sources. He refused to get arms and training from the Indian army -- an act of unpardonable offence to India's hegemonic ambitions.

10. President Ziaur Rahman took the initiative to form SAARC comprising of all the states in the South Asian region. This was an excellent forum for discussion and resolution of any outstanding issues/disputes involving the member states. This forum, however, could not fulfil all its objectives mainly because of the mutual distrust and bitter rivalry between two member states (India and Pakistan).

11. President Zia launched an all-out program for making Bangladesh self- sufficient in food (which he achieved after Mujib's famine-stricken Bangladesh of 1974-75, and he even exported rice). He initiated a "canal digging" programme for rural development and irrigation purposes.

12. Zia encouraged the patriotic, honest and capable professionals, academics, lawyers, accountants and others to get involved in the political process and running of the country.

13. Zia opened up the labour markets of Saudi Arabia and other Middle Eastern countries for Bangladeshi workers and professionals to work there.

14. The greatest impact Zia made on the political landscape of Bangladesh was to define a new identity for his country. He introduced "Bangladeshi Nationalism" as opposed to "Bungalee/Bengali Nationalism" adopted by Sheikh Mujib's Bangladesh Awami League. According to Ziaur Rahman and the party he founded, Bangladesh Nationalist Party (BNP), "Bangladeshi Nationalism" emphasizes the central role of Islam in the national life, recognises equal rights and social justice for all citizens of the country irrespective of religious faiths, ethnicity and cultural traditions. In contrast, "Bungalee/Bengali Nationalism" is based on a corrupt version of "secularism." It denies any political role Islam may play in the affairs of the state but it has no problem in accepting the supremacy of the Hindutva ideology in India. Q M Jalal Khan and Mahmudur Rahman have discussed the issues of "Bungalee" vs "Bangladeshi" Nationalism in greater details in their books.[10]

Begum Khaleda Zia has always remained faithful to the above legacies of her husband and political icon, President Ziaur Rahman, and upheld the causes for which her husband died.

Khaleda Zia enters the political arena

After the assassination of President Ziaur Rahman on 30th May 1981, the country was thrown into a terrible crisis and uncertainty. As per Constitutional Provisions, Vice President Justice Abdus Satter became the acting president and in a free and fair election held in November the same year he got duly elected as President (wining 65.5% of the votes against the Awami League candidate Dr Kamal Hossain who polled 26%). But the Army Chief of Staff General H M Ershad, widely suspected as the mastermind behind Zia's killing, had other plans. He deposed President Sattar and his BNP government in a bloodless coup on 23rd March 1982 and initiated a military regime that lasted for about nine years, until he was overthrown by a massive popular movement in 1990, led By Begum Khaleda Zia.

On being deposed, President Sattar retired from all political activities and resigned from the BNP leadership. It was at this critical time that Begum Khaleda Zia stepped into national politics (5 January, 1982), assumed the leadership of the BNP (1983), and within a very short span of time emerged as the most popular and trusted political leader of the country. As the elected Chairperson and top leader of the most popular political party (BNP), she has been an integral part of the political process of Bangladesh for the last 38 years. During this long period, she has served the country both as the head of government (1991-96, February-June 1996, 2001-06) and as the leader of the opposition not only inside the parliament (1997-2001, 2009-2014) but also on the streets (1983-1990, 2007-2008, 2014-2020 (a lot of times in jail).

Fighting for Democracy

Khaleda Zia faced the greatest challenge of her life soon after being elected the leader of the BNP in 1982. General Ershad was consolidating his power through a military-civil bureaucratic regime with support from India and a section of the political class in Bangladesh. His main target was to discredit and demolish the BNP and form a tactical understanding and working alliance with Sheikh Hasina Wazed, the other important political leader of Bangladesh. Sheikh Hasina was the leader of the Bangladesh Awami League (AL), the second largest political party of the country. The party talked about democracy when convenient but did never hesitate to act in a dictatorial way using violence and other unethical methods to achieve its goal. Ershad and Hasina joined forces together since early 1980s in a political alliance against Khaleda Zia and her party, the BNP. The purpose was to eliminate the Khaleda-led nationalist forces and re-establish the hegemony of the pro-Awami League forces. Both General Ershad and Sheikh Hasina were diabolical characters, politically speaking, and tried to outsmart and outmaneuver each other, but always united in their efforts to destroy the BNP and Khaleda Zia. Even after the death of General Ershad, his political successors, Mrs Rowshan Ershad and Ghulam Muhammed Quader, have continued their "collaborative" politics with Sheikh Hasina.

Khaleda Zia had to wade through the existing political swamp in order to re-establish the democratic system of governance in the country. She waged a relentless struggle and led popular protests throughout the period of the Ershad regime until the autocratic regime was overthrown in 1990. Sheikh Hasina played a "hide and seek" game during the Ershad regime, sometimes joining the mass movement, sometimes ***encouraging sabotage, and sometimes collaborating with the regime***.[11] On several occasions, Hasina pretended to fight for democracy and participated in the anti-Ershad mass movement, but at convenient moments she collaborated with the autocratic Ershad regime. For example, the anti-Ershad mass movement reached a high peak at the beginning of 1986 and the fall of the discredited regime seemed to be quite close. All the opposition political parties including BNP and Awami League agreed to boycott the elections scheduled for 7th May. Sheikh Hasina announced in a public meeting in Chittagong only a few days before that those who would participate in the proposed elctions under Ershad would be marked as "national traitors." Khaleda Zia was the main leader of the anti-Ershad movement and it was quite evident that she would win handsomely in any "free and fair" election, a prospect totally abhorrent to Hasina.

After the Chittagong declaration, Hasina returned to Dhaka and without consulting anyone else or offering any reasonable explanation she announced next day that she and her party would participate in the elections "for the sake of democracy." This was like stabbing the nation-wide united "pro-democracy" movement from the back. Despite condemnation by other anti-Ershad parties and groups, Hasina's Awami League party along a few other smaller parties participated in the elections and legitimised the Ershad regime. Ershad's Jatiyo party took 153 (simple majority) of the 300 parliamentary seats and gave 76 seats to Awami League. It was this act of her treachery to democratic mass movement that prolonged the life of Ershad's pseudo-democratic regime for another four years until 1990 when it was finally overthrown. The exact reason for Hasina's sudden volte-face was never known, but one could relate this to an undisclosed amount of benefits in cash or kind from Ershad, RAW advice and/or purely personal hatred for Khaleda Zia. Hasina acted in a diabolical manner, with her eyes firmly fixed on: (i) preventing BNP and Khaleda Zia from getting elected in a free and fair election; (ii) failing in the 1st objective, dislodging the BNP and Khaleda Zia from power by hook or by crook; (iii) gaining absolute power for herself and her family through a "one-party" dictatorship. Hasina's two other main objectives were to take revenge and hang the alleged killers (all freedom fighters) of her father and also some prominent leaders of the anti-India, pro-Islamic forces accused of committing war crimes during the 1971 war.

The most persecuted politician of Bangladesh

Khaleda Zia's principled and determined leadership against the Ershad-type autocracy (1983-1990), Moeenuddin-Masududdin-Fakhruddin dictatorship (2007-2008) and finally against Sheikh Hasina's anti-democratic despotic rule (2009-to date) together with the life-long struggles, sufferings and sacrifices she made for the country and her people brought her love, respect and recognition from the patriotic people of Bangladesh but that also made her a target for hateful propaganda, revenge and retribution by her detractors and enemies. She is the only political leader in Bangladesh who was subjected to false propaganda, arrested on trumped up charges and arbitrarily imprisoned by three authoritarian regimes on five different occasions. During the anti-Ershad mass movement, she was arrested three times: on 28th November 1983; 3rd May 1984; and 11th November 1987; but, fortunately, she did not have to stay in prison for long periods of time. The alleged offence for which Begum Zia had to suffer imprisonment was leading mass movements against dictatorship and for the restoration of the democratic system with proper accountability and rule of law. Sheikh Hasina was a junior partner in the anti-Ershad movement but she had always shown double standards in her politics. This delayed the downfall of Ershad but, ultimately, he had to step down in December 1990.

Begum Zia was arrested again by the Moeenuddin-Fakhruddin interim regime on 3rd September 2007. Police picked her up from her residence at Shahid Mainul Hussain Road in Dhaka Cantonment and took her straight to the CMM court. Khaleda's lawyers applied for her bail but the application was summarily rejected and she was sent to a specially prepared sub-jail in the parliament building area. On the 18th January 2008, Begum Zia's mother breathed her last in Dinajpur in north Bangladesh and the next day her dead body was flown from there to the Zia family house in Dhaka cantonment. On the same day, Begum Zia was released on parole for only six hours to attend the funeral of her mother and share the grief with other members of the family and friends. In extreme distress and grief, and also for the cruel way the Moeenuddin-Masududdin regime treated this former prime minister of the country, she broke down in tears. She was produced in court for the first time on 1st June 2008, nine months after her illegal arrest. She was finally released on bail on 11th September 2008 after passing 372 days in the special sub-jail.

The Moeenuddin-Fakhruddin regime also jailed Sheikh Hasina and put her in a sub-jail close to the one where Khaleda Zia was incarcerated. After some "negotiations" she agreed to cooperate with the regime and their foreign mentors and she was released. She gave a public undertaking that if she was allowed to form the government, she would "legalise" the activities of the Caretaker government (CtG) of Moeenuddin, Fakhruddin and Masududdin and would not pursue any charges against General Moeen or other members of the regime. Mr Pranab Mukherjee, then India's Minister for External Affairs, played the most dubious role in the secret negotiations in concluding a deal between General Moeen and Sheikh Hasina. According to this deal General Moeen was to help Hasina in the elections scheduled for December 2008, and in return Hasina would ensure his 'safe exit' without any charges being pursued against him or any member of his regime.

Begum Zia did not agree to any such proposals from the CtG regime for compromise, capitulation, and surrender. So she remained a "deadly villain" in the eyes of Sheikh Hasina, General Moeen and their foreign sponsors, including India. Khaleda Zia's sufferings did not end even after the army-led CtG regime fell and Sheikh Hasina assumed power through a manipulated and controversial "democratic" election in late 2008.[12] Hasina was declared winner with a convenient two-thirds parliamentary majority, which was legally required for constitutional amendments as intended by the Awami League Chief and her advisers.

Khaleda Zia was made the leader of the opposition in the parliament, but her sufferings, instead of being reduced, in fact, increased many times during the new regime. This came as a surprise to many people but not to those familiar with the personality and diabolical politics of Sheikh Hasina. To her, Khaleda Zia is not simply a "political" opponent but a "dangerous enemy" to be subdued and overwhelmed by any cost or means, legal or illegal, moral or immoral, decent or ugly.

Immediately after coming to power in 2009, Sheikh Hasina withdrew all the sixteen cases of bribery and corruption filed against her by the CtG regime of 2007-2008 and also hundreds of cases against many members of the top echelons of her party. But she resurrected similar cases against Khaleda Zia in order, clearly, to harass, punish and exclude the latter from the political process of Bangladesh. Hasina and her henchmen officials manipulated the investigation process and the court proceedings, and, finally, on the 8th February 2018, a kangaroo court sentenced her to a five-year prison sentence.[13] Despite having serious medical conditions, she was taken to prison on the same day and kept in a kind of solitary confinement in a dilapidated and unhealthy abandoned prison. She was released on the 24th March 2020 on a conditional bail for six months. Begum Zia is thus not yet a free person. She is still trapped in a political "spider's web" weaved by Sheikh Hasina's fascist regime with help from the Indian rulers! Begum Zia has not engaged in any anti-government campaign for the last 2/3 years, but she still remains the main target for personal ridicule, lies, vilification, abuse, revenge and punishment by dictator Sheikh Hasina and her acquiescent loyalists.

Begum Zia made tremendous personal and family sacrifices in her fight for democracy, and at the end of 1990 she became victorious in her mission to restore the democratic system of governance in Bangladesh. In the very first election (after the fall of Ershad) held in 1991, her party the BNP won by an overwhelming majority and formed the government.[14] Khaleda Zia took oath on 20 March 1991 as the first woman prime minister of Bangladesh, second in the Muslim world after Benazir Bhutto of Pakistan. A simple housewife thus rose to the Himalayan height of popularity and emerged as a great democratic political leader of Bangladesh.

Notable Achievements 1991-1996, 2001-2006

It is a general rule that the leaders and governments (whether elected or unelected) of all modern countries assume and exercise state power on the basis of certain plans for economic development of the country and welfare of its people. This is true also in the case of Bangladesh. All political parties announce their plans and campaign for public support. The success or failure of a political party depends on the public support it can gather behind its programs.

The main reason behind the massive support for a separate, sovereign country in the erstwhile East Pakistan was the economic disparity between the two wings of Pakistan. The people of this region suffered the worst forms of marginalization, exploitation and humiliation during the British rule (1757-1947) at the hands of the colonial authorities and their loyal, mostly Hindu upper caste, landlord and money lending classes. And they no longer wanted to suffer the same fate in Pakistan. It is, therefore, no coincidence that the proclamation of independence by the Tajuddin-led provisional government on 10 April 1971 included the words "equality, human dignity and social justice" as the basic guiding principles of the new state. Begum Zia has remained loyal to these basic principles throughout her political life. But the Constitution framed by the Awami League government in 1972 incorporated the four principles, "nationalism, secularism, democracy, and socialism," which would come to be known as "Mujibism." This opened the door for creating a personality cult for Sheikh Mujib -- a culture not conducive to a democratic order but favourable to the growth of repressive fascism. The Awami League leader Sheikh Hasina and her supporters still do not see any harm in this anti-democratic culture.

Begum Khaleda Zia has never believed in the so-called Mujibism or one-party dictatorship. She has never used any fake theoretical ladder to reach a high moral ground over her opponents or to introduce any form of "Zia-ism." To our knowledge, Khaleda Zia, like her husband Ziaur Rahman, has never used any foul language or derogatory remarks about Sheikh Mujib or even Sheikh Hasina personally. Even when she criticizes various policies pursued by Sheikh Hasina, she does so firmly and strongly but in a decent, polite, diplomatic and sophisticated way, maintaining her dignity as a person and as a model of responsible leadership.

Khaleda Zia's leadership of the BNP in general and also while running the government and in the opposition has never been authoritarian. I have learned from some of my friends and acquaintances, who have worked very closely with Begum Zia for nearly four decades, that she took most important decisions in consultation with other top leaders of the party. Begum Zia took a decision only after giving an issue sufficient time and thought and did never acted in a hurry and on a sudden impulse.

Begum Zia was never comfortable with the so-called four principles of Mujibism included in the 1972 Constitution of Bangladesh, but has remained loyal to the three basic principles of "equality, human dignity and social justice" as included and highlighted in the original proclamation of independence.[15] She upheld these principles equally for all citizens of the state irrespective of their ethnicity, religious faith or economic status.

The other aspect of her political career has been to stand firm on the questions of independence, sovereignty and national interests of Bangladesh. And for this and also for other reasons, she had to pay a terrible price in terms of personal and political vendetta by Sheikh Hasina and her sponsor India in collusion with the Anglo-US imperial order.

Nation building efforts

Khaleda Zia served the government of Bangladesh as prime minister for slightly more than ten years (1991-1996, February-June 1996, 2001-2006) in one very brief and two full five-year terms. During this period, she took/advanced several nation building initiatives that require mention for properly evaluating her role in the history of Bangladesh. Most of these initiatives for nation building have been described in somewhat greater details by other authors.[16] In the current essay we mention only a few such initiatives to record, recognize and appreciate her contributions to the cause of democracy and development in Bangladesh.

1. Return to Parliamentary democracy

The first Constitution of Bangladesh (1972) was based on the Westminster-style parliamentary system of government. But this was discarded by Sheikh Mujibur Rahman himself in 1975 to introduce a dictatorial one-party Presidential system with all powers concentrated in the office of the president. All forms of political dissent and media freedoms were banned and the judiciary was brought under executive control. The presidential system continued until the fall of H M Ershad and it was only after Begum Zia came to power in 1991 that the constitution was amended (12th Amendment) and a multi-party parliamentary system of government with all attendant freedoms were restored.[17] That was one act through which Begum Zia showed respect to public demand and proved her commitment to the democratic will of the people. During the 1991-96 term, the parliamentary standing committees were reconstituted to include and ensure the participation of the opposition party members. She introduced the Caretaker System (CtG) of interim government in 1996 in order to fulfill the demands of the opposition parties including the Awami League and Jamat-e-Islami. This was in sharp contrast with the rule of Sheikh Hasina, who treated some provisions in the constitution as legal obstacles to implementing her agenda.

2. Hasina's march towards autocracy

Ironically, it was the Awami League leader Sheikh Hasina, who was once the main proponent and militant agitator (1991-96) for the CtG system. She captured power through a fraudulent election and amended the constitution to remove the CtG system in 2011. This she did quite unilaterally and arrogantly, in total disregard of all objections from the opposition parties and also from a section of her own party. She gave lip service to "democracy" and a parliament composed of people's elected representations, but in reality she loved autocracy with absolute power concentrated in her hands. So she started using different state organs and carry on a barrage of false propaganda by loyal journalists and fake intellectuals to demonize the BNP and its founder Ziaur Rahman, Jamat-e-Islami, and their allied forces. Hasina's special target for revenge and brutality has been Khaleda Zia and her son and political successor Tarique Rahman.

In gradual steps, she was able to suppress all opposition forces, hang the so-called killers of her father, hang some top leaders of Jamat-e-Islami and the BNP who were found guilty in questionable legal processes conducted by highly partisan judges. Implementation of all these agenda would take time and also legal cover. So she had to abandon the CtG system and hold "elections under her care" so that absolute "victory" could be ensured for herself and her party by rigging and manipulation. So she effected several drastic amendments to the constitution with the help of her rubber-stamp parliament without any popular consent or participation of the opposition. Thus, Hasina succeeded in doing what her father had started with but could not finish, i.e., in turning a democratic country into a one-party dictatorial and corrupt enterprise. All institutions, including the civil bureaucracy, judiciary, media world, justice system, academic world, democratic dissent, freedom of expression, armed forces, police and diplomatic services have been highly politicized, with appointments and promotions to top jobs being based on party loyalty and/or bribery rather than qualifications, experience and competence. The situation in Bangladesh is quite grim and if the state of affairs with rampant corruption and stripping of state assets by the ruling elites are allowed to continue under Hasina's watch, the country would soon achieve the status of a "failed state."

3. Khaleda's contributions to education sector

From the very beginning of her administration in 1991, Begum Zia gave priority to the development of education in the country, to women's education in particular. She believed quite rightly that the country could progress and emerge as a modern welfare state only if the women were sufficiently educated and took part in the developmental activities. In 1992, she started a country-wide adult education programme for eradication of illiteracy from the society. In 1993, she started compulsory primary education, and the food scheme for education. These programs were aimed at providing some basic education to both men and women and was a great success. In the same year, the government launched an "open university" offering opportunities for adults and factory workers to receive an education within their own flexible schedule. On 18th June 1994, her government declared "free" education for all women with further incentives for attendance, including stipend up to class 10. This encouraged and enabled the low-income families to send their girls to school regularly. Begum Zia reiterated her total support to women education by signing the "education for all" declaration of Delhi in 1995.

Education for women was also a top priority for Begum Zia's government during 2001-2006. Her government declared free education for women up to class 12. Begum Zia helped the initiative for the establishment of the Asian University for Women (AUW) with a view to widening opportunities for modern education. In 2004 her government made grants of more than 100 acres of land in Chittagong for the proposed campus, and in 2006 the Bangladesh Parliament ratified the *Charter of AUW guaranteeing its* status as "an international, non-sectarian, and fully independent university with complete institutional autonomy, academic freedom, and exemption from taxes."

Other notable achievements in the education sector included reducing the "session jam" at the universities, removing the practice of copying or cheating during the public examination, increasing the salaries of school teachers with 80% being paid by the government funds, building/renovating thousands of educational institutions with greater emphasis on technical and vocational education.

4. Economic breakthrough

During the first term of Begum Zia's government, Bangladesh succeeded in recording significant economic progress (GDP growth rate at 5% for 1991-2000) and removed the stigma of being branded as a "bottomless basket." The country achieved self-sufficiency in food production, with low-interest loans for small peasants and writing off their previous loans up to Tk 5,000. Land taxes for small peasants owning up to 25 bighas of agricultural lands were waived off. Facilities for irrigation and fertilizers at low cost were provided and these measures made positive impact on the production of rice, pulses, vegetables, onions, and fruits. Production of poultry and dairy products increased manifold. Building of small-scale industries and cottage industries were encouraged to reduce rural unemployment. All these measures helped revolutionize the agricultural sector and improve the rural sector of the economy. The expansion of the road and telephone networks and increasing the production and distribution of the gas and electricity, together with pro-business fiscal policies, made Bangladesh an attractive destination for foreign investments.

Emphasis was laid for rapid industrialization and increasing manufacturing capacities of the country. Special economic zones were established at different locations in the country and significant financial stimulus including a five-year tax holiday were offered to encourage investments by foreign companies. But in negotiating all deals with foreign companies and international bodies, priority was always given to protect the national interests of Bangladesh. The interests of local industries, especially of those in the clothing, sugar, drug, ceramic and animal hide/leather sectors that earned foreign exchange, were given full government support.

The BNP government adopted a liberal policy towards the establishment of new banks, insurance and service companies in the private sectors. Doors were also opened for the establishment of schools, colleges, universities, medical colleges, hospitals, health centres, training institutes for nurses and technicians for specialized jobs, etc., in the private sectors, subject to certain conditions and guidelines imposed by the government. All these initiatives helped to speed up the governmental efforts for development.

Due to economic liberalization and other business and trade policies, and also by attracting foreign investments, an expanding RMG sector and increasing remittances from expatriate workers, the economy improved continuously and significantly to achieve a remarkable GDP growth of 7.06% since 2006-2007. The country saw a dramatic fall in the overall poverty level. Based on several important themes -- energy, infrastructure, urbanization, human capital and technology -- Bangladesh was included in 2005 for the first time in the Goldman Sach's list of the so-called "N-11" group of countries that could potentially rival the G7 countries. The N-11 included Bangladesh, Egypt, Indonesia, Iran, Korea, Mexico, Nigeria, Pakistan, Philippines, Turkey and Vietnam.[18]

5. Foreign Relations

The foreign policy of Bangladesh has always been "friendship to all, malice to none." Khaleda Zia tried to follow this policy throughout her administrations. She improved bilateral relations with all development partners and with the Middle Eastern countries for increasing employment opportunities for Bangladeshi workers and destination of Bangladeshi exports. Relations with the USA and EU countries were excellent making them friendly destinations for Bangladeshi RMG exports. Special attention was given to the countries in the East and Southeast Asia under the "Look East Policy"[19] and attempts were made to strengthen the bonds of economic, diplomatic and strategic relations with China. Relations with India were good, but not to the full satisfaction of the Indian establishment, whose main purpose was, and still is, to keep Bangladesh under pressure and extract only one-sided benefits from a weak and subservient Bangladesh. India's hostile policies to Bangladesh and especially to Khaleda-led BNP had far reaching consequences, including the execution, in 2007, of a new type of "Regime Change" in Dhaka.

6. National defence and security

It has been a priority for all BNP governments to strengthen the national defence forces -- the army, the navy, the air force, the border guards, the police, and the auxiliary ansar force. Khaleda Zia governments tried to tighten the security system of the state against all attempts at destabilization, sabotage and subversion by the internal and external enemies. However, there were some serious lapses in preventing infiltration and subversion by foreign agencies, especially RAW and MOSSAD during 2001-2006 and these failures led to serious consequences for the security of Bangladesh and existential crisis for the BNP. The defence forces are much better off today with greater budget and resources but they are also target of infiltration and indoctrination by foreign agencies. Despite some shortcomings, the armed forces are still considered as the last frontier of national defence and security.

Before the Awami League leader Sheikh Hasina could come to power and establish her partisan grip on the armed forces, many local pro-Indian media personalities carried out anti-army propaganda campaign. They suggested that Bangladesh did not need "powerful" standing army as "India will never attack or occupy Bangladesh." They were also brainwashed into thinking that "India is so powerful and Bangladesh so weak that if India wanted to occupy Bangladesh, it could do it in 3/4 days; so why maintain an expensive army?" Before Sheikh Hasina was able to consolidate her autocratic power in 2009, she also passed derogatory remarks about the armed forces, not once but on several occasions.[20] She thought that the armed forces had killed her father and they supported Khaleda Zia's rise to popularity and power.

In contrast, Khaleda Zia has always believed in and supported a self-reliant defence force with necessary personnel, training and equipment. She was not ready to outsource the defence and security of the country to any not-so-friendly foreign power. Begum Zia's government also established the "Coast Guard" force for the first time to carry out surveillance and anti-smuggling operations and also to prevent piracy and illegal fishing by foreign vessels in Bangladesh's coastal waters in the Bay of Bengal.

Khaleda Zia: rare Example of honesty, dedication and patriotism

The personal life and political career of Khaleda Zia has been full of many challenges (cyclones, floods, tidal waves, etc.) and powerful rivals/enemies (like H M Ershad, Sheikh Hasina, Moeen U Ahmed, India, etc). She faced all these challenges with calm, cool, foresight and dignity, always keeping in mind, and giving priority to, the interests of her nation and people. Along with two kids and in absence of her husband, the young lady had to spend a prisoner's life in Pakistani army detention in 1971, but she did not deviate from her belief in the righteousness and final victory of the Bangladesh cause. Years later, under a different set of adverse circumstances, when some powerful enemies of Bangladesh wanted her to send into exile, she refused to surrender and said, "I do not have any address outside Bangladesh; this is my home and I am not going anywhere else under threat or duress." Begum Zia is the only Bangladeshi political leader since her entry into politics in 1982 who could not be coerced into submission by offering money, evicting her from her family home, isolating her from other family members or sending her behind bars. This is in sharp contrast with her main personal and political rivals, H M Ershad and Sheikh Hasina, both of whom are known to have "fatal attraction" to money and underhand deals.

The Bengali-speaking inhabitants of the Ganges delta are often "accused" of speaking "too much or exaggeration," "too loud" and "out of context," loving rumors and fantasies rather than facts, and wrestling in the mud rather than engage in a clean fight. Such wholesale categorization is, of course, wrong and exaggerated for a people who were once one of the richest peoples on earth. They lost independence to a foreign power but fought for 190 years to defeat colonialism and then waged an armed resistance to establish an independent country of their own. These are the same people who have also been waging relentless battles for the last five decades against local fascism and foreign hegemonism. Like all other peoples, the Bengali people also have their "bads" and the "goods" among them, and those who know Khaleda Zia would say without any reservation that she represents the "best" in Bengali society.

Khaleda Zia has an impressive personality, always at the center of all events, social or political. She speaks at a normal speed, with clarity, confidence and grace, and with consideration and respect to her audience. These characteristics and the style of delivery are in sharp contrast with those of most other Bangladeshi politicians. My interactions with Begum Zia are limited to only three/four of her meetings/gatherings in London. I was also invited in one such meeting, in 2015, to deliver a speech which was closely followed by Begum Zia, Tarique Rahman and other leaders present in the gathering. I also have the experience of watching her speaking to several gatherings and public forums. Her distractors and political opponents would often try to downgrade her educational achievements but I saw her once speaking to a group of British MPs in the House of Commons. She spoke in fluent English, a little bit slowly but very smoothly; she made her points one by one like a teacher in the classroom. And she made all the points in a systematic way without any help from a written script. It was an excellent presentation in correct English with British accent.

The political life and career of Khaleda Zia is so vast and so full of personal and national challenges that one cannot describe and analyze all topics in one single or two volumes. During the last two years, one book by journalist Mahfuz Ullah and another by Professor Emajuddin Ahmed and Abdul Hye Sikder (ed) have dealt with the subject in elaborate ways. But these are basically descriptive narratives of the apparently disconnected, day-to-day events, without exploring their inter-connections and long-term implications for the future of the country and her inhabitants. These studies are quite important for Bangladesh and its neighbourhood, especially in the context of the rising geo-strategic rivalry among the big powers (India, China, USA and their respective allies) for control of the land, river and sea-based trade routes across the Himalayan mountain range and in the Indian Ocean region. Securing concessionary rights for investments in the infrastructure, and production and distribution of gas and electricity to influence the political, economic, cultural, security and defence policies, and also to control the old and new trade routes and communication networks -- remain the core areas of "big power" rivalry in the region.

Khaleda Zia - A Victim of Regime Change

The arrest of Begum Zia and her eldest son and political successor Tarique Rahman in 2007 by the military backed CtG was highly significant and a turning point in Bangladesh politics. It is true that the Awami League chief Sheikh Hasina was also arrested at the time, but that was for eye wash only. The talk of "minus-two" formula was a deception; the real agenda of India backed by the Anglo-American power bloc was to remove Khaleda Zia and the BNP from the political arena of Bangladesh and install their stooge Sheikh Hasina and her Awami League to power. The Moeenuddin-Masududdin-led CtG was used to "soften up" the political leaders, especially to initiate and execute some harsh punitive measures against Khaleda and the BNP leaders. With Khaleda's BNP discredited and severely wounded, the path was made more or less clear for Hasina's journey to power through an "engineered" election on 29th

December 2008. The Awami League won 263 seats out 300, whilst the BNP got only 32 seats! The whole exercise was a part of a deeper conspiracy to eliminate the Khaleda Zia's patriotic politics and redraw the political order of Bangladesh to suit New Delhi's strategic interests. Thus, Begum Zia became a victim of "Regime Change."

The real nature and significance of the event escaped attention by most people, because *the "regime change" in Dhaka was implemented not as a military campaign of "fireworks" (as in Iraq and Libya) but by the so-called "soft power" techniques planned and executed, in several steps, over several years. It is not immediately evident, but there are plenty of evidences to suggest that the anti-Khaleda, anti-BNP, anti-Islam, anti-Bangladesh campaign was launched by the Indian hegemonists sometime in early 2002 and this continued unabated until the 11th January 2007 (so-called 1/11).* As Khaleda Zia could not be persuaded, coerced, threatened or blackmailed into submission to foreign pressure to act as a vassal to the India-US axis, she was targeted for political elimination and a more compliant, power hungry and unscrupulous Sheikh Hasina was picked up for support. India's support to Sheikh Hasina was quite open, direct and indecent (money, propaganda and diplomatic support). The US-led bloc of countries showed some reservations regarding the rigged elections, human rights violations, extra-judicial killings, enforced disappearances, rampant corruption, etc., but they did not find any problem in carrying on with the autocratic regime since 2009. Hasina came to power in 2009 by a fraudulent election in late 2008, helped by the military and civil authorities, retained her power in 2014 by a Nazi-style manipulation, violence and thuggery, and again in 2019 by a night-time stuffing of the ballot boxes with the help of the police, army and civil authorities.

All the charges brought against Khaleda Zia for alleged bribery, corruption, arson and other unlawful acts were fabricated and politically motivated. The only case, in which she was "convicted" for corruption and stealing money from a charitable fund, was also wrongly framed, "investigated" by a handpicked officer and the verdict delivered by a kangaroo court. Whatever might have been the outer camouflage as reported by the highly compliant media, the whole "legal" drama of the trial of Khaleda Zia was played according to the script written by Sheikh Hasina herself. To Hasina, Khaleda was "guilty" even before she was arrested. The reason: Hasina would be surely defeated by Khaleda in any free and fair election. And the only way she could hold on to power was to keep her nemesis (Khaleda) in jail and hold a "fake election," by force or by fraudulent means, with the help of Bangladesh "deep state" (civil and military bureaucracy) and police administration. India was expected to provide the necessary shield against all foreign criticisms, which it did in a shameless way, in 2008, 2014 and 2018, in exchange for many one-sided benefits India extracted from Bangladesh!

Conclusion

At the time of writing this essay, Begum Zia is living at her residence in Dhaka with her family, except her only surviving son and political successor Tarique Rahman and his family, who have been compelled to live as exiles in London for about twelve years now. Some media reports say that she has been released on "a conditional bail" for six months, but the exact conditions are not known to the public. Nothing is straight or transparent in Hasina's Bangladesh! It is most probable that she is still in "jail" with her residence being treated as an unofficial jail and she is forbidden to speak to the media or others. Whatever may be the truth or game behind it, we wish all the best for Begum Zia and her family.

Begum Zia is undoubtedly one of the greatest leaders and she has earned a glorified place in Bangladesh history. She achieved this great height not because she was born into it or somebody else has thrust it upon her. She earned it by her four decades-long struggles and services to democracy, justice and sovereign interests of Bangladesh and her people.

---

[1] The militant political force known as *Jatiya Shamajtantrik Dal* (JSD) appeared as a 'meteorite' in the political sky of Bangladesh during a highly difficult, painful and controversial period early in 1972-75. The birth of this party and its emergence as a challenge to Sheikh Mujib's Awami League rule, its role in the 1975 November uprising and subsequent demise as an important political force have remained shrouded in many mysteries. An excellent account of the rise and

decline of this party is given by Mohiuddin Ahmed in a book, *Jashoder Utthan Poton: Osthir Shomoyer* Rajniti, Prothoma Prokashan, 2014.

[2] M B I Munshi, *The India Doctrine (1947-2007): A Contemporary Study on Indian Hegemony and Geo-Strategic Perspectives on South Asia,* LAP LAMBERT Academic Publishing, August 7, 2012. This is an important work on the foreign policy and geo-strategic objectives of India that considers itself as the legitimate successor of the British Raj in South Asia and strives to establish a so-called 'Akhand Bharat' or 'Greater Hindustan' from Myanmar to Afghanistan. Despite diplomatically decent talks and pronouncements, the Indian policy makers from Jawaharlal Nehru to Narendra Modi have all tried to bring the smaller states in the region like Pakistan, Nepal, Bhutan, Bangladesh, Myanmar, Sri Lanka, Afghanistan and Maldives under its so-called sphere of influence and hegemony.

Also, Zoglul Husain, "A Brief Outline of Indian Hegemony in Bangladesh*", in Bangladesh: A suffering People Under State Terrorism*, Sabria Chowdhury Balland (ed), Peter Lang, 2020, pp. 29-42.

[3] NAM is the abbreviated form of Non-Aligned Movement, a forum of 120 developing states, not aligned with any of the power blocs led by the US or Russia. Drawing on the principles agreed at the Bandung Conference in 1955, the NAM was established in 1961 in Belgrade, former Yugoslavia, through the initiative of Jawaharlal Nehru (India), Kwame Nkrumah (Ghana), Ahmed Sukarno (Indonesia), Gamal Abdel Nasser (Egypt) and Josip Broz Tito (Yugoslavia). The purpose of the organization was to ensure "the national independence, sovereignty, territorial integrity and security" of the member countries "against imperialism, colonialism, neo-colonialism, racism, and all forms of foreign aggression, occupation, domination, interference or hegemony as well as against great power and bloc politics." The abbreviation OIC stands for the Organization of Islamic Cooperation (OIC), formerly the Organization of the Islamic Conference. Founded in 1969, OIC is an international organization of 57 member states, 53 with Muslim majority populations, with a collective population of over 1.8 billion. (Wikipedia)

[4] The seven-point agreement described in the article "The Sugar-Coated Poison: India's Offer of Help to Restructure BDR" by K M A Malik, *Weekly Bangla Mirror,* London, 17th April, 2009, reads as follows:

(i) A para-military armed force for Bangladesh will be raised under the supervision of the Indian military experts; this force shall be stronger and more active than the regular armed forces of Bangladesh.

(ii) Bangladesh shall procure all military equipment from India and under the planned supervision of the Indian military experts.

(iii) Bangladesh shall direct her foreign trade under the supervision and control of the Indian government.

(iv) Yearly and five-yearly development plans for Bangladesh shall conform to Indian development plans.

(v) The foreign policy of Bangladesh must be compatible with and conform to that of India.

(vi) Bangladesh shall not unilaterally rescind any of the treaties without prior approval of the Indian government.

(vii) In accordance with the treaties signed before December (1971) war of Pakistan and India, Indian force shall enter into Bangladesh at any time and shall crush any resistance that may erupt there."

[Original source in Bengali: Oli Ahad, *Jatio Rajniti (1945 to 1975)*, 2nd Ed., Bangladesh Cooperative Book Society, Dhaka, p. 450.]

Mr Tajuddin Ahmad, the prime minister of the Bangladesh government-in-exile in India in 1971, was coerced into signing the seven-point document as a precondition for India's military intervention to accelerate the defeat and surrender of the Pakistani occupation forces and to install a 'pro-Indian puppet' government in Dhaka. The 25-yr Treaty of Friendship, Cooperation and Peace between India and Bangladesh, signed on 19th March 1972 is quoted in full by Mahmudur Rahman in his book, "*The Political History of Muslim Bengal - An Unfinished Battle of Faith*", Cambridge Scholars Publishing, 2019, pp. 380-384.

[5] https:// www.nytimes.com / 1974 / 06 /29 /archives/bhutto-regrets-crimes-in-bangladesh.html.

[6] In addition to Note#1 above, also see: Amanullah Kabir and Sayid-ur-Rahman (ed), *7 November: Etihaser Moarh,* Jhinuk Prokash, Dhaka, 2002.

[7] https:// www.thedailystar.net / frontpage / zia-makes-radio-announcement-independence-1554046

[8] A K Khandaker, *1971: Bhetore Baire,* Prothoma Prokashan, Dhaka, 2014; Major Rafikul Islam, *Ekatturer Muktijuddha : Protirodher Prothom Prohor*, Nalonda, Dhaka, 2011.

[9] www.nytimes.com/1989/ 06/11 / world / bangladeshi-insurgents-say-india-is-supporting- them.html; www.thehindubusinessline.com/news/Chittagong-Hill-Tract-tribals-may-have-mainland-India-links/article20675915.ece; Abu Rushd, *RAW in Bangladesh: Portrait of an Aggressive Intelligence*, English Edition, 2005.

[10] The debate regarding the "Nationality" of the people of Bangladesh, Bungalee (Awami League narrative) or Bangladeshi (BNP narrative), has been going on for a long time, but the question has not yet been resolved. A detailed discussion of the topic is presented by Q M Jalal Khan in a chapter titled, "Bangladesh Nationalism: A Cause and Concept Right and Just", in his book *Bangladesh: Political and Literary Reflections on a Divided Country*, Peter Lang, 2018, pp. 367-391, and references therein. Another excellent discussion dealing with the question of Bengali Nationalism vs Bangladeshi Nationalism and the Role of Islam is presented by Mahmudur Rahman in his book, T*he Political History of*

Muslim Bengal - An Unfinished Battle of Faith, Cambridge Scholars Publishing, 2019, pp. 102-138; pp. 213-247.

[11] *Amar Fashi Chai* by Matiur Rahman Rentu (1999). The writer was a freedom fighter and the personal aide of the Awami League President, Sheikh Hasina, during 1981 to 1997. Mr Rentu and his wife worked for the Hasina family at her Dhanmondi residence and witnessed many events and deeds that were carefully hidden away from the public eye. The book is a store of 'secret' information exposing the hypocrisy of Hasina's politics regarding democracy, her relations with H M Ershad and Khaleda Zia as well as her secret dealings with India and other Western powers. She started anti-Zia, anti-Khaleda disinformation campaigns from the very beginning and succeeded in building up a 'personality cult' around her father and herself. After Hasina came to power, she banned the book and forced Mr Rentu and his family into exile. Mr Rentu died in Paris in 2007. [https: // mazams.weebly.com/uploads / 4/ 8 / 2 / 6 /48260335/amar_fashi_chai_bangla.pdf]

[12] K M A Malik, "Bangladesh General Elections 2008: A transparent process or machination of the 'Evil Axis'?", The Weekly Bangla Mirror, 9th and 16th January 2009.

[13] Oliullah Noman, *Andhokar O Nipironer Karajibon*, Matribhasha Prokash, Dhaka, 2011. Mahmudur Rahman, *Jel Theke Jele*, Ananya, Dhaka, 2012. Justice Surendra Kumar Sinha: (a) *A Broken Dream: Rule of Law, Human Rights and Democracy*, Amazon Kindle Edition, September 26, 2018; (b) "The Supreme Court as the Guardian of Independence, With Reflections on the State of Rule of Law, Minority Situation, Quality of Education and Rampant Corruption", Sabria Chowdhury Balland (Ed), *Bangladesh: A Suffering People Under State Terrorism*, Peter Lang, 2019, pp. 11-27.

[14] After the fall of the Ershad regime, General Elections were held on 27th February 1991 under a neutral Caretaker Government (CtG) system with all large and small parties taking part. Out of a total 300 directly elected seats, BNP won 140, Awami League 88, Jamat-e-Islami 18, and Jatio Party 35 seats. BNP achieved the parliamentary majority and formed the government with support from Jamat-e-Islami.

[15] https://en.wikisource.org/wiki/Proclamation_of_Independence_(Bangladesh)

[16] Mahfuz Ullah, *Begum Khaleda Zia: Her Life, Her Story,* The Universal Academy, Dhaka, 2018; Emajuddin Ahmed and Abdul Hye Sikder (ed), *Khaleda Zia: Tritiyo Biswer Konthaswar*, Book Avenue, 2019.

[17] Some Constitutional Amendments under Khaleda and Hasina governments:

The Twelfth Amendment Act was passed on 6 August 1991, following a constitutional referendum. It amended several articles and restored the executive powers to the Prime Minister's Office, as per the original 1972 constitution, but which had been held by the President's Office since 1974. In the new arrangement, the President became the constitutional head of the state; the Prime Minister became the executive head; the cabinet headed by the Prime Minister became responsible to the Jatiya Sangsad. Moreover, through Article 59 of the Constitution this Act ensured the participation of the people's representatives in local government bodies.

The Thirteenth Amendment Act, 1996, introduced a non-party Caretaker Government (CtG) system which, acting as an interim government, would give all possible aid and assistance to the Election Commission for holding the general election.

The Fifteenth Amendment was passed on 30 June 2011 to make some significant changes to the constitution. It scrapped the CtG system and also made following changes to the constitution: (i) increased number of women reserve seats to 50 from existing 45; (ii) after the article 7 it inserted articles 7(a) and 7(b) in a bid to end take over of power through extra-constitutional means; (iii) restored secularism and freedom of religion; (iv) incorporated nationalism, socialism, democracy and secularism as the fundamental principles of the state policy; (v) acknowledged Sheikh Mujibur Rahman as the Father of the Nation.

The Sixteenth amendment of the constitution was passed by the parliament on September 17, 2014 which gave power to the Jatiyo Shangshad to remove judges if allegations of incapability or misconduct against them are proved. On 5 May 2016, the Supreme Court of Bangladesh declared the 16th Amendment illegal and contradictory to the Constitution. This was not to the liking of Sheikh Hasina, who harassed and forced the Chief Justice Surendra Kumar Sinha to resign and go into exile. [https://en.wikipedia.org/wiki/Amendments_to_the_Constitution_of_Bangladesh]

[18] https:// www.goldmansachs.com / insights / archive / archive-pdfs / brics-book/brics-chap-13.pdf].

[19] K M A Malik, "Welcome initiatives in Bangladesh foreign policy", The Weekly Holiday, Dhaka, 10 January, 2003; also K M A Malik, *Challenges in Bangladesh Politics: A Londoner's View*, Adorn Publication, Dhaka, 2005, pp. 31-35.

[20] K M A Malik, "Sheikh Hasina's tirade against the armed forces", The Weekly Bangla Mirror, London, 1 October, 2004; also in *Challenges in Bangladesh Politics: A Londoner's View*, Adorn Publication, Dhaka, 2005, pp. 153-157.

Chapter 2

Begum Khaleda Zia: Her Patriotic Politics and Its Historical Context

Zoglul Husain

Introduction:

In this article we will have a glimpse on the patriotic politics pursued by Khaleda Zia of Bangladesh, but this article does not deal with her biographical details or administrative successes or failures. We will look at her patriotic politics, in its four distinct aspects: (1) the emergence of the patriotic or nationalist politics in Bangladesh, (2) the root and political heritage of Khaleda Zia's patriotic politics from the anti-colonial nationalism in British India, (3) her stunning success in politics from 1982 to 2006, and (4) the eclipse of her politics since 1/11 of 2007 to date, by political forces beyond her control. We will then draw a brief conclusion.

(1) The emergence of the patriotic or nationalist politics in Bangladesh

In this section we will look at the emergence of the patriotic politics, which Khaleda Zia stood for, or for that matter the patriotic politics, which her party, the Bangladesh Nationalist Party (BNP), founded by her husband Ziaur Rahman in 1978, stood for.

When on the night of 25 March 1971, the Pakistan Army launched a most barbaric and genocidal crackdown on the unarmed people of East Bengal (also called East Pakistan and, from the crackdown, called Bangladesh) to quell the movement for autonomy, the Awami League leader, Sheikh Mujibur Rahman, surrendered to the Pakistan army in collaboration with Yahya Khan of Pakistan. The rest of the Awami League leadership mostly fled to India. In this dark and dreary situation, when the people were desperate for leadership, they heard over radio the firm and powerful voice of Ziaur Rahman, who declared independence of Bangladesh, and who started and organised the independence war. The people were electrified by the call of Ziaur Rahman and they joined the independence war most resolutely. This was the beginning of the patriotic politics, or the nationalist politics, in Bangladesh, although it did not come to the surface as much until Ziaur Rahman came to power in 1977. At the time, it was a patriotic freedom war, also called liberation war, for the right to self-determination, as a consequence of, and in resistance to, regional disparity and national suppression within a multinational Pakistan, which culminated in a genocidal military crackdown in East Bengal from the night of 25 March 1971.

Bangladesh won the independence war on 16 December 1971 with help from India. India gave shelter to the large number of people who fled the genocidal Pakistani military crackdown in Bangladesh, it organized and equipped the freedom fighters of Bangladesh in their freedom war, and when the Pakistan army in Bangladesh was nearly defeated by the freedom fighters of Bangladesh, the Indian army joined the war on 3 December 1971 to complete the victory on 16 December 1971. Bangladesh thus achieved independence with Indian help.

During the independence war, the political forces of Bangladesh were in the main divided into 3 camps: (i) Pakistan-America, who wanted to quell the rebellion in Bangladesh; (ii) India-Soviet Russia, who wanted to divide Pakistan and turn Bangladesh into a subservient state or vassal state under India-Soviet Russia; and (iii) the overwhelming majority of the people and the patriotic army of Bangladesh, who wanted Bangladesh to be fully independent and sovereign, without bowing to any of the above two axes of forces.

During the war, the small number of Bangladeshis, who supported Pakistan, belonged to the first camp above. The leadership of the Awami League and their supporters, who surrendered to India, belonged to the second camp. Their leader in exile in India, Tajuddin Ahmad, formed a government of Bangladesh in exile in India, and signed a 7-point agreement with India, in which Tajuddin Ahmad sold out the national interest of Bangladesh and surrendered its sovereignty to India. From then on until the present, the Awami League has become a party of national traitors. And so, it remained for the third camp above, i.e. the overwhelming majority of the people and the patriotic army, to belong to the patriotic politics of Bangladesh.

As Bangladesh became independent with help from India, the India-Soviet axis as above, dominated Bangladesh, militarily, politically and economically, after its independence. Sheikh Mujibur Rahman, who never wanted independence of Bangladesh and, on the night of 25 March 1971, collaborated with Yahya Khan of Pakistan and surrendered to Pakistan, was freed by Pakistan after the independence of Bangladesh. For his political power in the independent Bangladesh, he now collaborated with the hegemonist India, but he only gained the power of a puppet. The Mujib regime of 1972-75 was as good as a puppet regime to the India-Soviet axis. Mujibur Rahman was in office, but not in real power. His fascist regime killed 30 thousand patriots, and through its terror, tyranny, oppression, repression and plunder, it caused the man-made famine of 1974-75, in which 500,000 people died as a direct consequence of the famine, and a further one million people died in its after effects. Mujibur Rahman discarded all vestiges of democracy and founded a totally fascist party called BAKSAL as the only legal party in the country on 25 February 1975. All other parties were banned, all newspapers, except for four compliant ones, were banned. All organizations not approved by the government were banned. During the tenure of the regime, India plundered Bangladesh as much as it could, and dominated it as much as it could. However, wherever there is oppression, there is resistance.

An undeclared army-people alliance was built up to rescue Bangladesh from this dark and dreary situation, created by Mujibur Rahman's fascism and India's fascist hegemonism. Of course, at the people's level, the people of Bangladesh remained grateful and friendly to the general people of India, who stood by the people of Bangladesh in 1971. To reciprocate their support and solidarity, the people of Bangladesh extend their support and solidarity to the Indian people in their struggle against the Indian internal and/or external oppressors. The Mujib regime was toppled by the patriotic army-people uprising of 15 August 1975, and Mujibur Rahman was assassinated, along with 19 others of the members of his family and relatives. Sheikh Hasina and Sheikh Rehana, daughters of Sheikh Mujib, were saved as they were abroad at the time.

India hit back with a counter coup on 3 November 1975 led by Khaled Mosharraf. But this was short-lived, and 4 days later, on 7 November 1975, there was a further patriotic and glorious army-people uprising, which brought Ziaur Rahman to power. 7 November 1975 has since been called the National Revolution and Solidarity Day by its supporters. In retaliation to the patriotic army-people uprising, which was anti-fascist and anti-hegemonist, India prepared for a military intervention in Bangladesh, and moved its army to the Bangladesh border, and readied its airports nearby. The army-people alliance now led by Ziaur Rahman in Bangladesh also prepared for guerrilla war in defense. However, India's ally the Soviet Union dissuaded India from intervention, for fear that the US 7th fleet nearby might get involved in such a war, as to some extent it did in December 1971. From 10 December 1971, 6 days before the Pakistani army surrendered in Bangladesh, the US 7th Fleet moved towards Bangladesh, basically to save West Pakistan (called Pakistan from 16 December 1971), and it was trailed by Soviet nuclear submarines, as the Soviet Pacific Fleet moved towards Bangladesh. Also, the British fleet moved towards the Arabian sea, if need be to attack the West coast of India, in support of the US 7th fleet. After independence of Bangladesh on 16 December 1971, the war ended, and the 7th fleet returned to its base at Yokosuka, Japan, and the other fleets also returned to their bases. The US 7th Fleet manoeuvre was later interpreted as PsyWar to save West Pakistan (later known as Pakistan).

The glorious and patriotic army-people uprisings of 15 August 1975 and 7 November 1975 brought Ziaur Rahman to power officially in 1977. With Ziaur Rahman in power the country smiled again. Ziaur Rahman now openly declared his patriotic politics, or the nationalist politics as he called it. It was the politics of freedom and sovereignty. The emergence of Ziaur Rahman as the leader of the country at this crucial juncture of history of Bangladesh was a momentous event. Ziaur Rahman disciplined the army and established the chain of command and immediately introduced multiparty democracy. He lifted the ban on all parties, which were imposed by Mujibur Rahman. He lifted the ban of all newspapers and the other media. He gave freedom to the judiciary. And, so, democracy was restored in full under Ziaur Rahman's patriotic politics. Ziaur Rahman founded the Bangladesh Nationalist Party (BNP) on 1 September 1978 on a 19-point program.

The basic principles of the party were: to expand democracy, achieving economic development, uniting the country on the basis of nationalism and achieving self-reliance among the people, protecting Bangladesh from colonialism, etc. The founding manifesto of the BNP claimed that the people of Bangladesh want to "see that all-out faith and confidence in the almighty Allah, democracy, nationalism and socialism of social and economic justice are reflected in all spheres of national life." (Wikipedia article, Bangladesh Nationalist Party). Ziaur Rahman united and disciplined the country and made rapid development on the basis of a free-market economy.

Ziaur Rahman forged alliance with the US and China, the countries at the time existed as allies in an axis. He avoided antagonizing the India-Soviet axis as much as he could. However, Zia was assassinated in 1981 in an Indian plot within a section of the Bangladesh army, with alleged cooperation from Gen. H. M. Ershad and Sheikh Hasina.

The dictatorial regime of H. M. Ershad was in power from 1983 until 1990. His government was toppled by a mass uprising, led by all opposition parties, particularly by the BNP led by Khaleda Zia.

Khaleda Zia joined the BNP politics in 1982, on request from the BNP leaders, after the death of her husband Ziaur Rahman. She was elected Chairperson of the BNP in 1984 uncontested. She is still the Chairperson of the BNP after 36 years. She is still the most popular leader in Bangladesh, since Ziaur Rahman's death. Through the fascist conspiracy of the Hasina regime, Khaleda Zia was sent to prison on 8 February 2018 for 17 years, on totally trumped up charges. But, because of the pandemic situation as prevailing now, the government did not want to take a risk of her infection under prison conditions, which could whip up a consequent political uproar, and so, from 25 March 2020, the government released Khaleda Zia for six months by suspending her sentence on humanitarian grounds, on the condition that she stays at her residence and does not go abroad, the conditions tantamount to house arrest for six months. "The government made the decision on Khaleda's release as per section 401 (1) of the Criminal Code of Procedure (CrPC), which allows such suspension of sentence," according to the Law Minister. (The Daily Star, 25 March 2020). Further decisions are to be made after the expiry of six months.

Khaleda Zia became Prime Minister 3 times. She followed the patriotic or the nationalist politics as established by her husband Ziaur Rahman. Her politics remained patriotic all through, although her administration and the BNP had various lapses besides their achievements. We will come to this later.

(2) The root and political heritage of Khaleda Zia's patriotic politics from anti-colonial nationalism in British India

Since the independence of Bangladesh, main stream politics of Bangladesh has been divided into two strands: (i) the Awami League politics of BAKSAL fascism and national-treachery by selling out national interest and surrendering sovereignty to hegemonist India, and (ii) the BNP's patriotic or nationalist politics for freedom and democracy.

In this section, we will discuss the root and political heritage of Khaleda Zia's nationalist politics from anti-colonial nationalism in British India.

The politics that Ziaur Rahman and later Khaleda Zia pursued, had a very rich heritage from the days of the Pakistan Movement in British India, when the Muslims of India, in addition to their movements for national liberation and economic emancipation, had to fight for the right to self-determination i.e. fight for the creation of Pakistan, in which the Muslims from Bengal took a prominent role. Pakistan was created because of communal disparity within British India and Bangladesh was created because of regional disparity within Pakistan.

The politics of the present has its heritage or legacy from the past. The political heritage may be considered from the perspectives of world history, regional history or local history, depending on the context. For example, Western political heritage consists of the body of political thoughts and actions from the Greek antiquity to the present. Similarly, in the world context, the political heritage begins from the earliest recorded history in ancient Mesopotamia and ancient Egypt, unless one wants to consider pre-history. The political heritage can be both positive and negative, for example, a genocide is a negative political heritage, on the contrary, if the political heritage is beneficial to the human society or humanity, it is positive.

Political heritage can be considered from a relevant node of timeline in history depending on the contextual objective. In discussing Khaleda Zia's political heritage briefly, we will consider it for the period spanning from the anti-colonial independence struggle in British India to the creation of Bangladesh, as we have already discussed the emergence of patriotic or nationalist politics in Bangladesh. We will divide the period in the following phases: (i) Anti-colonial independence movement in British India, (ii) Creation of Pakistan, and (iii) Creation of Bangladesh.

(A) Khaleda Zia's political heritage from the anti-colonial independence movement in British India

It is of utmost importance to understand our political heritage from the anti-colonial independence movement in British India, as the present politics in Bangladesh is a latter-day development of the same strands of politics at a different juncture and stage of history. Ziaur Rahman and later his wife Khaleda Zia followed the positive heritage, staying on the positive side of history, while Sheikh Mujibur Rahman and later his daughter Sheikh Hasina followed the negative heritage, staying on the negative side of history.

So, what is the positive political heritage that we observe in the anti-colonial independence movement? The European colonial system existed for more than five hundred years, from 1402 to 1945, and it ended within a couple of decades after the end of WWII in 1945. Colonialism is full or partial military control over another country, occupying it by settlers, and plundering and exploiting it economically. Thus, colonialism consists of national subjugation on the one hand and economic exploitation on the other. The anti-colonial independence movement conversely consists, in the main, of national liberation movement on the one hand, and the movement for economic emancipation on the other.

The anti-colonial independence movement in British India had those two elements, the national liberation and the economic emancipation, but, in addition, there was another hugely important element, which was the movement for the right to self-determination of the Muslims. The movement for the right to self-determination of the Muslims in British India created Pakistan from British India, while the movement for the right to self-determination of the Bangladeshis within Pakistan created Bangladesh from Pakistan. I usually say, Pakistan was created because of communal disparity in British India, and that Bangladesh was created because of regional disparity in Pakistan. In order to understand the politics of Bangladesh, we need to elaborate on the movement for right to self-determination of the Muslims in British India.

The communal disparity between Hindus and Muslims in British India was the creation of the British as a consequence of their divide and rule policy.

When the British came to India, the Mughal empire was the richest in the world, and Bengal was its richest province. Bengal was thus the richest, or one of the richest, countries in the world. The British plundered it most brutally and reduced Bengal to one of the poorest countries with occurrence of famines, which it never had in the past.

The British applied a divide and rule policy in India, they drove away the Muslims from power, property, jobs, business, education, etc., while they created a high caste Hindu elite class as the second tier of administration under the British rule. With the help of the British rulers this class thrived. Later, as the British were preparing to leave India, Hindu-Muslim unity was tried. The Lucknow pact was arrived at in 1916, Muhammad Ali Jinnah was hailed as an apostle of Hindu-Muslim unity by Sarojini Naidu, but the Congress later repudiated the pact, and partition then became inevitable.

Historian William Hunter expressed the conditions of Muslims in British India, especially in Bengal, quite aptly. "In his search for the causes of the increasing Muslim discontents in Bengal, William Hunter found in

1871 that a hundred and seventy years ago it was almost impossible for a well-born Musalman in Bengal to become poor; at present it is almost impossible for him to continue rich" "(Iftekhar Iqbal, Paper prepared for XIV World Congress of Economic History, Helsinki August 2006, The Sundarbans forest systems in Bangladesh: indigenous response to capitalist enterprises and the patterns of colonial control, c.1830-1905). The situation was similar throughout India. So, for the Muslims in British India, the demand for Pakistan was a case for "Right to Self-Determination" ("In drafting the Declaration of Independence (of America) in June 1776, Jefferson stated his fundamental philosophy of government, upon which the modern concept of self-determination rests," from the article, Self-Determination - The American revolution, American Foreign Relations). Also, nationalism can be intertwined with religion, race, ethnicity, etc. The two-nation theory was thus based on a valid ground in the above historical context. So, the creation of Pakistan was an historical necessity, as later was the creation of Bangladesh from Pakistan.

The Muslims had to achieve (i) national liberation from British colonialism and (ii) the right to self-determination from the upper caste Hindu ruling elites, who formed the second tier of the British administration in India. The movement for economic emancipation was not that great at the time and so the movements for national liberation and right to self-determination were given the priority over the movement for economic emancipation, which was relegated to a secondary position. This was the main and basic weakness of these movements.

This basic weakness is still there today in the politics of the BNP and its leader, Khaleda Zia. The weakness was that the movement for economic emancipation was relegated to the background, at most to a secondary position. The Muslim League leadership was controlled by the rich people, although there were many leaders, who were committed to alleviation of poverty. Because the party was controlled by the rich people, who wanted to be richer after independence, they formed an oligarchy of the rich, and that was the main problem of Pakistan, and later in Bangladesh. The patriotism and benevolence of Ziaur Rahman and Khaleda Zia, in Bangladesh, could not stop these get rich quick leaders, though Ziaur Rahman could manage them to some extent, and Khaleda

Zia in her first term as Prime Minister could also manage them to some extent.

(B) The Creation of Pakistan

After the fall of Bengal in the battle of Palashi (Plassey) in 1757, there were rebellions and resistance struggles against the British for about 100 years, of which the following are well known: Fakir-Sannyasi rebellion (1770-1820, Titumir (d. 1831), Hyder Ali (d. 1782), Tipu Sultan (d. 1799), Paika rebellion (1817), etc., and the Indian Rebellion of 1857 (also known as the Sepoy rebellion), which has been called the First Indian War of Independence. The next phase of the resistance was the political movement for Indian independence.

"The Indian Independence Movement was a series of activities with the ultimate aim of ending the British rule in India. The movement spanned a total of 90 years (1857–1947). The first nationalistic revolutionary movement for Indian independence emerged from Bengal." (Wikipedia article, Indian independence movement).

Another development during the independence movement was the awakening of the Muslims of India. It was mentioned before, how the Muslims in India were driven away from power, property, business, professions, jobs and education, because of the British policy of divide and rule, which also created a second tier of British administration from the high caste Hindus. Now the Muslims started to wake up.

One of the pioneers of the awakening was the Aligarh Movement, led by Sir Syed Ahmed Khan, who founded the Muhammadan College in 1875. This movement gradually led to Muslim awakening, which in turn led to the Pakistan Movement.

The Bengal Muslims played a significant role in Pakistan Movement. To save the Muslims, there was Muslim awakening in Bengal too. In 1863, Nawab Abdul Latif of Faridpur founded the 'Muhammedan Literary Society' in Kolkata (formerly, Calcutta). In 1877, Syed Ameer Ali founded the 'Central National Muhammedan Association.' Munshi Meherullah (1861-1907) of Jessore played a very important role in the campaign and organization. Many writers, campaigners and organizers joined this movement for the awakening of Muslims in Bengal. This awakening of Muslims in Bengal since 1860s is called the second renaissance of Bengal, the first being from the first decade of the nineteenth century, which was pioneered by Raja Ram Mohan Roy and Iswar Chandra Vidyasagar, and in which the Muslims were virtually excluded.

This awakening of Muslims led to the founding of the All India Muslim League in 1906 in Dhaka (the present capital of Bangladesh), under the patronage of the Nawab of Dhaka, Sir Khwaja Salimullah. In 1940, the Lahore Resolution was moved by the sitting Chief Minister of Bengal A. K. Fazlul Huq, it was adopted on 23 March 1940, and its principles formed the foundation for Pakistan's first constitution. Just 7 years after this, Pakistan was created in 1947.

(C) The creation of Bangladesh

Bangladesh became independent from Pakistan because of regional disparity within Pakistan.

We discussed that, in British India, there developed two types nationalism: firstly, the anti-colonial nationalism and, secondly, the Pakistani nationalism as a right to self-determination of the Muslims from the subjugation of upper caste Hindu administration, forming the second tier of the British administration, which ruthlessly dominated and exploited the Muslims. The movement for economic emancipation was embedded in those two nationalisms. Relegation of the movement for economic emancipation to the background or to a secondary position was a basic weakness of the movement, as mentioned before. This is a general weakness in most developing countries, though there are notable exceptions such as China, which however was a semi-colony, not a colony.

When Pakistan started its journey as a new state, initially it had a short spell of democracy. But soon the feudal big landowners, rising industrialists, leaders of military and bureaucracy together formed an oligarchy. They grabbed power, and their policies gave rise to regional disparity within Pakistan as well as economic disparity within the people. East Bengal (or East Pakistan, or after independence, Bangladesh) bore the brunt of the disparity, both regionally and at the people's level.

There were many factors such as geographical distance, socio-economic conditions and cultural issues. Bangladeshis were the majority in Pakistan, but the ruling oligarchy exploited Bangladesh, and deprived the Bangladeshis in business, civil service and military service, etc. Thus, alienation and grievances created a volcano of Bangladeshi nationalism, which finally erupted in the freedom war of 1971 after the Pakistan government's barbaric and genocidal military crackdown in East Bengal on the night of 25 March 1971.

The language movement of 1952, although victorious within 4 years, showed the arrogance and antipathy of the ruling elites in Pakistan towards Bangladesh and its people. It gave rise to Bangladeshi nationalism. I will not, in this article, go into the controversy between Bengali nationalism, as expressed by the Awami League, and Bangladeshi nationalism, as expressed by the BNP, but I describe it as Bangladeshi nationalism. The effect of the language movement in Bangladesh was telling. The language movement along with the disenchantment of the people with the Muslim League government brought about a landslide victory for the United Front against the Muslim League in the election of 1954 in East Bengal.

The United Front won the election with slogans of 'Huq-Bhashani Zindabad (long live),' Huq in the slogan referred to A. K. Fazlul Huq, Prime Minister of Bengal (1937-43), who presented the Pakistan resolution in 1940, and Bhashani referred to Maulana Abdul Hamid Khan Bhashani, the leader of the then Awami league, both being veteran leaders of the Pakistan movement.

But the Pakistan central government intervened and the Fazlul Huq ministry was removed from power within a few months of winning the election in 1954, through the exercise of section 92A of the Government of India Act 1935, and emergency rule was imposed. The allegation against Fazlul Huq was that he wanted secession of Bangladesh. "The New York Times published an article claiming Huq wanted independence for East Bengal" (Wikipedia article, East Bengal). This emergency rule was resented throughout East Bengal.

In 1957, in his famous speech, Maulana Bhashani, the dreamer of independent Bangladesh, delivered his famous "As-salamu alaykum" speech, to warn the Pakistan government that unless the demands of East Bengal are met, East Bengal would be compelled to bid farewell to Pakistan. Maulana Bhashani was still the leader of the Awami League. But after this speech, Shaheed Suhrawardi and his follower Mujibur Rahman opposed Maulana Bhashani's political stand, and shortly afterwards, Maulana Bhashani and his supporters were compelled to leave the Awami League and found a new Party, the National Awami Party (NAP), which upheld Bangladeshi nationalism with pro-people programs.

The Pakistan administration was already in shambles. Martial Law was imposed by Ayub Khan in 1958.

After the death of Shaheed Suhrawardi, Mujibur Rahman upheld the demand for provincial autonomy through his declaration of 6-point programmes in 1966. This created a huge wave of support for Mujibur Rahman. The Ayub regime of Pakistan filed a sedition case against Mujibur Rahman and 34 others in early 1968, implicating that the accused were conspiring with India against the integrity of Pakistan. This was the famous Agartala Case.

Starting from a student unrest in November 1968, a huge movement in 1969 developed throughout the country. This historically very significant movement in Bangladesh, known as the 1969 Mass uprising in East Pakistan, was led by Maulana Bhashani, it also spread to West Pakistan and caused the downfall of the Ayub regime. During the course of the movement, the Agartala conspiracy case was withdrawn on 21 February 1969, and Ayub Khan handed over power to Yahya Khan on 25 March 1969. This led to Yahya Khan being in power in Pakistan. He called election in 1970.

In the election of December 1970, Mujibur Rahman and the Awami League achieved a landslide victory, which Bhashani NAP did not contest. The Awami League won an absolute majority of 160 seats and Zulfikar Ali Bhutto's Pakistan People's Party won 81 seats in the National Assembly of the 300 seats. In the Provincial Assembly of East Pakistan in the provincial elections held ten days later, the Awami League won 288 of the 300 seats.

This was an unexpected shock to the Yahya regime. They hatched a most heinous conspiracy. In the name of negotiations with Mujib, they bought time and brought arms and troops to East Bengal, and on the night of 25 March 1971, they launched a most barbaric and genocidal military crackdown on the unarmed people. Shortly afterwards, the independence war started with the help of India, and Bangladesh became independent on 16 December 1971 after achieving a glorious victory.

Mujibur Rahman never wanted independence of Bangladesh, he wanted to be the Prime Minister of Pakistan and he used the movement for autonomy as a pressure lever for his bid to be the Prime Minister. This is why he arranged with Yahya Khan his own security and the security of his family, as well as a monthly allowance of 1,500 Rupees (about 5 lakh Taka now) during the war, for his family, and then surrendered, with the understanding that, after the rebellion is quelled, he would be made the Prime Minister. So, Mujib was the first collaborator with the Yahya regime and he was the first national traitor in the freedom war of Bangladesh.

(3) Khaleda Zia's stunning success in politics from 1982 to 2006

The rise of Ziaur Rahman as a star in the political firmament of Bangladesh was stunning. It was stunning because Ziaur Rahman had no political experience when political power was bestowed upon him by the patriotic army-people uprising of 7 November 1975, which he did not lead. But, by this time he became widely respected as a military leader as, in 1971, when Mujibur Rahman surrendered to Pakistan army, the Awami League leadership fled to India, and the people were in a desperate situation without leadership, it was Ziaur Rahman, who declared independence of Bangladesh. He organised the freedom war, which electrified the people, who resolutely joined the freedom war. Then after being in power in 1977, Ziaur Rahman, through his patriotic, honest, bold, determined and efficient short rule, lifted the country from an abyss, which it had been thrown into by the fascist Mujibur Rahman regime, to a respectable high ground, which won the admiration of the whole world, except for the ones who wanted to subjugate Bangladesh.

When Ziaur Rahman was assassinated in an Indian plot, allegedly with cooperation from Sheikh Hasina and Gen H. M. Ershad, and shortly afterwards, pro-India Gen. Ershad took over power, the BNP felt like they were leaderless, although there were many office bearers in the party. Also, many BNP leaders joined Gen. Ershad. The leaders of the BNP requested Ziaur Rahman's wife, Khaleda Zia, to join the BNP. Khaleda Zia had no political experience at all. Although she was the first lady, when her husband Ziaur Rahman was the President, she was not involved in politics at all. Thus, Khaleda Zia's rise in the political firmament was as stunning as her husband's rise in the recent past. Also, in spite of the heavy obstacles, both of them achieved a great deal.

The implementation of the patriotic politics by the BNP was an arduous task, both due to the weakness of the internal set up of the BNP, as members of various orientations joined together to form the party so that the organization lacked coherence, and the external conditions of its intense and severe conflict with the Awami League fascism and the Indian fascist hegemonism acting together. In the prevailing world geopolitical situation of a deadly rivalry between the US and the Soviet Union, the BNP sided with the US and China, while the Awami League and India sided on the Soviet side. But after the dissolution of the Soviet Union in 1991, India forged alliance with the US, which eclipsed the BNP since 1/11 of 2007, and brought Bangladesh under Indian dominance with Sheikh Hasina in power.

When Ziaur Rahman came to power, he defined his politics of Bangladeshi Nationalism. He stood for freedom and sovereignty on the one hand and, on the other, through restoration of multi-party democracy, he stood for democracy. On the contrary, as we have seen before, the Awami League stood for fascism and subservience to Indian hegemonism. The divide is still there today: the BNP stands for freedom and democracy and the Awami League stands for fascism and subservience to Indian hegemonism. Thus, the BNP is a party for patriotism and nationalism, though it has many shortcomings and lapses, but the Awami League is a party of fascism and national treachery, which in course of time, will be consigned to the negative heap of history.

Khaleda Zia boldly and firmly held up the banner of freedom and democracy, as she was entrusted by the BNP. As mentioned before, she joined the BNP politics in 1982, on request from the BNP leaders. She was elected Chairperson of BNP in 1984, uncontested.

As soon as Khaleda Zia joined the BNP in 1982, she embarked on a nine yearlong arduous struggle for restoration of democracy, and she fought valiantly until the fall of Gen Ershad's dictatorship in the mass uprising in 1990. She led the movement for restoration of democracy with alliance of other parties, and the support of the significant movement of the students, including the student wing of the BNP. She was detained under house arrest in 1983, 1984 and 1987. In 1987, the police detained her during a meeting at the Hotel Purbani in Dhaka. Her spirited, undaunted and inspiring leadership earned her top popularity next to Zaiur Rahman, and she was popularly called "the uncompromising leader" and "the mother of democracy." On 24 May 2011, the New Jersey State Senate of the US honoured Khaleda Zia as a "Fighter for Democracy" (Wikipedia article, Khaleda Zia).

In 1983, a 7-party alliance was formed under the leadership of Khaleda Zia, and she started the movement against the military rule of Gen Ershad. At around the same time, the Awami League formed a 15-party alliance and they also joined the movement for restoration of democracy together with the Khaleda Zia led alliance. But as the pro-India Gen Ershad called an election in 1986, pro-India Sheikh Hasina betrayed the united movement and joined the election. The Sheikh Hasina led 15-party alliance broke up to form two alliances, an 8-party alliance and a 5-party alliance. Sheikh Hasina led the 8-party alliance and joined the election. But the Khaleda Zia led 7-party alliance boycotted the election, and from 1987, started a 1-point movement of ouster of Gen. Ershad from power. Gen. Ershad was compelled to dissolve the parliament, and then the Awami League led by Sheikh Hasina was back again to the street to join the movement for democracy.

The general discontent of the people with Gen. Ershad's dictatorship and the movement by all party opposition, strengthened by the student movements, raised a tumultuous political storm, which swept Gen. Ershad from power. His government fell in 1990.

In the election of 1991, Khaleda Zia won the absolute majority and formed the government. She won all the 5 seats she had contested. Indeed, she won all 5 seats contested in the elections of 1991, 1996 and 2001. She is almost as popular as her husband Ziaur Rahman still today.

Politically, she followed the line of Ziaur Rahman, which is based on Bangladeshi nationalism and democracy, i.e., freedom and democracy, as opposed to the Awami League's policy of subservience to India and fascism since 25 March 1971. She took steps for development of children, the empowerment of women, and general economic development, and was successful in these. Unfortunately, power corrupts, and the BNP during 1991-96 became somewhat corrupt. The main obstacle to Khaleda Zia during this time was the opposition from India and its puppet Sheikh Hasina, who was the leader of the opposition. The BNP mishandled a by-election at Magura in 1994, which stirred up a huge opposition movement jointly by the pro-India Awami League and also pro-India Gen Ershad's Jatiyo (National) Party. Sheikh Hasina held hartal (general strike) 173 times during this government. Instead of uniting, organizing and mobilizing the people and taking a strong stand against Indian hegemonism, the BNP was in a resigned situation, and in the name of respecting democracy, it showed weakness to the Awami-India conspiracy.

Most of the opposition boycotted the 15 February 1996 election, and Khaleda Zia was elected Prime Minister again with all seats in the parliament, but in a difficult situation. She amended the constitution to allow for a non-party caretaker government to oversee the election, and to show respect for democracy, as she always did, called for election in June 1996. In the election Sheikh Hasina won and formed the Government during 1996-2001. Khaleda Zia became Prime Minister again in the election of 2001. The elections of 1991, 1996 and 2001 were free and fair and were acceptable.

During Khaleda Zia's term of 2001-2006, although the general political line of freedom and democracy was adhered to, and economic development programmes went on alright, there developed in the main two problems. Firstly, the party noticeably got involved in corruption, which weakened the party, and secondly, the BNP faced dreadful conspiracy by India, this time supported by the US as a result of geopolitical changes since the fall of the Soviet Union in 1991. When India moved from the Soviet camp to the US camp during this time, the US wanted alliance with India as a counterweight to China.

India with support from the US and its allies, including the UN, engineered a military takeover in Bangladesh on 1/11 of 2007 to reduce it to a subservient country.

India prepared for it for a long time. It perpetrated many false flag terrorist attacks in Bangladesh, and took full advantage of the Islamophobic political environment in the world since 9/11 of 2001. During this government the Jamaat-e-Islami (JI) party became an ally of the BNP. In the previous Sheikh Hasina government, the JI was an ally of the Awami League. Now, because the JI became an ally of the BNP, India and the Awami League launched vicious campaign, national and international, of "Islamic terrorism" and "Islamic fundamentalism" against the JI and the BNP as its ally. The second pretext of military takeover was corruption, which was present, but nowhere near the reckless plunder and lawlessness of the Mujibur Rahman regime or even the Sheikh Hasina regime of 1996-2001. Indeed, the reckless corruption and lawlessness of the Sheikh Hasina regime since 2009 till to date, knows no limits. However, on those two pretexts, "Islamic fundamentalism" and corruption, the military takeover of 1/11 of 2007 was engineered.

(4) Khaleda Zia's politics eclipsed since 1/11 of 2007 to date by political forces beyond her control

A new phase of politics in Bangladesh started from 1/11 of 2007, when the geopolitics of India and the US took over the national politics of Bangladesh, and Bangladesh was brought under the influence of India with help from the US. 1/11 of 2007 was a huge conspiracy by India, which was supported by the US and its allies, including even the UN representative in Bangladesh. Its objective was to snatch the independence of Bangladesh, plunder its natural and other resources, and trample its democratic and human rights. Without US help, India would not be able to implement the conspiracy. The whole thing was beyond the control of Khaleda Zia, and her patriotic politics was eclipsed, and this eclipse has continued till today in 2020.

The Indian conspiracy, supported by the US, brought the army into power for two years, which with the pretext of eradicating corruption, repressed in the main the BNP, to weaken its influence and render it powerless, although token punitive actions were also meted out to other parties to make a show of neutrality. Khaleda Zia was interned on 3 September 2007 on trumped up charges of corruption and was released by court verdict on 11 September 2008. To make a show of neutrality, Sheikh Hasina was also interned on 16 July 2007 and released by court verdict on 11 June 2008. The BNP was subjected to the steam roller of repression.

These were all done by the ruthless military regime of Gen. Moeen in order to transfer the power from the BNP to the Awami League.

A general election was called in December 2008. The election, mainly contested by the BNP and the Awami League alliances, was rigged with ballot box stuffing to give Sheikh Hasina a landslide victory, so that she could amend the constitution at will.

After military takeover of 1/11 of 2007 by Gen Moeen U Ahmed, a caretaker government was formed under Fakhruddin Ahmed with the aim of holding an election in December 2008. It was done because, in the election scheduled on 22 January 2007, the BNP alliance was expected to win again. So, the Moeen-Fakhruddin caretaker government cancelled the election of 22 January 2007. They prepared the ground for two years to remove the BNP alliance from power.

First, they tried to exile both Khaleda Zia and Sheikh Hasina, the policy became known as the minus-2 plan. The idea was to give the power to someone chosen by India and supported by the US. But the plan failed miserably, because Khaleda Zia, known as an uncompromising, courageous and determined leader, refused to leave the country, even after her two sons were tortured barbarously. As a result of the torture her elder son Tarique Rahman's back was severely injured, for which he had to go to London for treatment and he is still there in 2020 leading an exiled life, and the younger son Arafat Rahman had injuries in the chest, for which he died in 2015.

Following these heinous actions, they installed Sheikh Hasina in power through a rigged election by ballot box stuffing the night before the election scheduled on 29 December 2008 and declaring a predetermined result by giving the Awami League a "landslide victory," so that it could amend the constitution with two-thirds majority. Before the election the

BNP alliance was bulldozed, a huge number were put into prison, and the rest driven away from their homes, only allowing a small number to return home before the election. Also, the conspirators divided the BNP by creating a faction called the 'reformists,' who opposed Khaleda Zia leadership within the party and collaborated with the conspirators. The 'reformists' however, later came back to the party through a process of unification. Thus, after the rigged election, the conspiracy was completed, and Bangladesh had an Indian puppet government supported by the US and its allies.

Since then, Sheikh Hasina has remained in power after two more rigged elections in 2014 and 2018. Thus, Hasina has remained un-elected Prime Minister since the rigged election of 2008. The BNP launched two huge movements in 2013 and 2015, but the first was sabotaged by government agents and there was severe repression, and in the second the BNP was dissuaded from the movement by the US and its allies. The US and its allies kept supporting the Indian conspiracy, although they showed duplicitous support for democracy in Bangladesh. And that is still the situation as of 2020.

The Sheikh Hasina regime since the election of 2008 (it formed the government on 6 January 2009) has been a totally fascist regime subservient to Indian hegemonism, like the regime of her father, the Mujibur Rahman regime of 1972-75. The present Sheikh Hasina regime, since 2009, perpetrated three massacres (on BDR, Jamaat and Hefazat), indiscriminate killings, terror, tyranny, abductions, reckless plunder, oppression, repression, in many cases in connivance with India and Indian commandos, and above all, it has sold out national interest and surrendered sovereignty to hegemonist India.

Khaleda Zia's and the BNP's policies and power have been completely eclipsed since the India-Awami League conspiracy of 1/11 of 2007, supported by the US and its allies, including the UN. It is not known if and when the eclipse would be over. With about 90% of the people opposed to the Awami League and the Indian hegemonism, the situation can become volatile and it can brew a political storm, which can bring about new developments in the political arena of Bangladesh anytime.

The eclipse of Khaleda Zia's patriotic politics is beyond her control, as the eclipse has been imposed by India and supported by the US and its allies. We discussed before that one of the basic weaknesses of the anti-colonial independence movement in British India, and the right to self-determination movement to create Pakistan, was that although the movement for national liberation and the movement for right to self-determination was in the forefront, the movement for economic emancipation was relegated to the background, at most to a secondary position. This was because the anti-colonial independence movement and the movement for creation of Pakistan was led, in the main, by rich people who wanted to be richer after independence at the cost of the general people, although there were many leaders who were committed to alleviation of poverty.

The leadership of the BNP, with the best of intentions to be patriotic, was not immune from the above weakness. The get rich quick group within the BNP was visible during Khaleda Zia's government of 2001-2006, although they were nowhere near the reckless plunderers of the lawless Awami League counterparts. This Khaleda Zia Government achieved remarkable economic development so that one of the largest investment banks in the world, Goldman Sachs, listed Bangladesh in 2005, as one of the next 11 emerging countries after the Asian Tigers.

The BNP is a constitutional party, pro-US in outlook, following the free market economy of the US. It did not and could not unite, organize and mobilize the people to develop a formidable and invincible resistance to the Awami League fascism and the Indian hegemonism. It lobbied the US in vain, as the US, in its policy of using India as a counterweight to China, supported Indian hegemony, while being duplicitous in maintaining a friendly approach to the BNP and equally deceitfully supporting the democratic process.

The BNP even tried to appease India, before the 2018 election. They sent a 3-leader delegation to India in June 2018, but it was in vain. In the election of 30 December 2018, rigged by ballot box stuffing, a predetermined result was announced, in which the BNP was given a meagre 6 seats out of 300. So, the BNP's policy of appeasement failed miserably. The BNP is now in a state of virtual surrender, but it is still very popular as it gets the benefit of the huge anti-fascist and anti-hegemonist sentiment in the country. The BNP has now been quietly waiting for what the future unfolds.

Conclusion:

Khaleda Zia's politics has always been patriotic, supporting freedom and democracy, as her husband Ziaur Rahman's politics had been. Both Ziaur Rahman's and Khaleda Zia's rise as stars in the political firmament of Bangladesh have been stunning and glorious. Both are the most popular leaders in Bangladesh. While since 25 March 1971, the Awami League followed the politics of fascism and subservience to India, the BNP followed the politics of freedom and democracy. While the Awami League, since 25 March 1971, followed the politics of national treachery, the BNP followed the politics of patriotism.

But the BNP's politics has a basic weakness, which it inherited from the anti-colonial independence movement and the historically necessary movement for the creation of Pakistan. The weakness is, as discussed above, relegation of the movement for economic emancipation to the background, and thereby letting the rich and the get rich quick groups control the politics of the BNP. Because of this the BNP has failed to unite, organize and mobilize the people to build a formidable and invincible resistance to the Awami League fascists and Indian hegemonists, both during the Ziaur Rahman government and the Khaleda Zia government. Ziaur Rahman was assassinated in an Indian plot allegedly supported by Sheikh Hasina and Gen. Ershad, and Khaleda Zia has been sent to prison since 8 February 2018 for 17 years by the same conspiracy. But it has been mentioned before that 90% of the people are opposed to fascism and hegemonism. This may brew a storm.

Wherever there is oppression there is resistance. The people of Bangladesh are suffering under the two mountains of fascism and hegemonism. But imbued by the patriotic politics of Ziaur Rahman, Khaleda Zia and the other leaders who fought for the country and the people, the people will unite and fight until victory is achieved. They will fight to recover their freedom from the hegemonists, and democracy from the fascists. They will win and establish freedom, democracy, justice, human rights and harmonious development. The movement for national liberation and economic emancipation will certainly be victorious.

Chapter 3

Begum Khaleda Zia: A Tale of Courage, Patriotism, Betrayal and Tragedy

Mahmudur Rahman

[Author of *The Political History of Muslim Bengal: An unfinished battle of faith*, Mahmudur Rahman, the most famous political dissident of Bangladesh, now in forced exile, describes Sheikh Hasina as a fascist devil Lucifer, Hitler Pinochet, Shah of Iran, Saddam, Kim of North Korea, perhaps even worse, describing Bangladesh under her as an utterly horrifying 'autocracy', an 'Orwellian state', a 'ruthless police state' and 'an extremely polarized and wounded nation [...], no better than a personal fiefdom,' suffering from 'the oppression of the fascist regime' and 'the terror of authoritarian secularism.'][1]

Introduction

I was in a dilemma when the editors of the book requested me to write an article on the life of Begum Khaleda Zia. They wanted to publish a book on her politics and democratic struggle. Already a number of books have been written about her life and legacy, including the ones, authored or edited, by Shafik Rehman, Prof Emajuddin Ahmed, Abduk Hye Sikder and the late Mahfuz Ullah, all eminent in their vocation as well as profession, from journalism to teaching, creative or critical writing, media-savvy personality to intellectual occupations. So, there were three points of my concern: (i) how the new initiative would add value, (ii) whether I was the right person to evaluate a great democratic leader, and (iii) has the time arrived to say the final word about an icon of democratic struggle suffering in the fascist prison?

As an academic and presently a student of history, I naturally wish to remain honest and objective in my evaluation of political events and characters. But any writer would inevitably experience in life that it is an extremely difficult task to dissociate oneself completely from emotion while writing about someone he or she personally knows and respects. Furthermore, Khaleda Zia is not only the most popular living political leader in Bangladesh and a former prime minister, she is also a tragic victim of current fascist regime and Indian hegemony. She is a woman who lost her husband at 36, she is a mother who lost her younger son in exile, she was a former prime minister and opposition leader who was evicted from her house by a brutal dictatorial regime, and she is an elderly politician who was sent to prison, at the age of 73, in the most ridiculously fabricated case by a shameless, dysfunctional and biased judiciary under the brutal dictator Sheikh Hasina. I have no intention to write an autobiographical article here, but in order to remain honest to my readers, it is necessary to provide some basic information about my association with Khaleda Zia. Only then I would be able to write about her with total intellectual honesty and freedom. Knowing from the beginning about my affiliation with the Zia family, the readers would also be in a better position to judge her as a person and politician. I now travel back 19 years to start the story.

It was a sunny and warm mid-October afternoon at Dhaka in 2001. In the general election held on the first day of the month, Bangladesh Nationalist Party (BNP)-led four party alliance had trounced the incumbent Awami League by securing 226 out of the total 300 directly contested parliamentary seats. Khaleda Zia, the charismatic Chairperson of BNP, became the Prime Minister for the third time since the Westminster style parliamentary system was introduced in the country in 1991. I was then working as managing director of a globally reputed ceramic tableware company in Bangladesh. On that fateful moment, I was in deep conversation with the Chairman of the company in my office. My cellphone buzzed. A serious and unknown male voice from the other side curtly told me that the honorable Prime Minister wished to see me immediately at her office. The meeting with the Chairman was cut short and I rushed to the Prime Minister's office with the same nervousness that

I felt facing the first job interview of my life 24 years earlier as a young engineer. After all, an ordinary citizen rarely gets a call from the Prime Minister of a country. Previously I just met her once as a senior member of the country's engineering community. There was, however, no reason for her to remember the occasion. Presently, I had no idea about the agenda of the meeting with the head of the government. A huge surprise was waiting for me.

I was ushered into the waiting room by a smart, young ADC of the Prime Minister. He politely offered me a cup of tea. The wait was not long. I entered into the PM's room and found Amir Khashru Mahmud Chowdhury, the newly appointed commerce minister in conversation with Khaleda Zia. We were old acquaintance. He smiled at me with a subtle wink as if he already knew something. The Prime Minister asked me to take a seat. Without wasting time in small talks, she offered me, a person with no political background to join her government, as the Executive Chairman, Board of Investment. It was a shock, to say the least! I was reluctant to accept the offer for a very selfish reason. Government salary for the offered position was less than one tenth of the salary and perks that I was receiving from the private company as its CEO.

The graceful Prime Minister overruled my objection in a very dignified manner by quoting her late husband, President Ziaur Rahman, a great patriot and the only visionary statesman that the independent Bangladesh has ever seen. She told me that it was the ideal of President Zia that all citizens have responsibility towards their country and national interest must always take precedence over personal interest. The Prime Minister further added that it is the responsibility of a true patriot to answer to the call of duty from the state. Although I never had the opportunity to meet General Zia, he was my hero from the day, as a teenager, I heard him declare the independence of Bangladesh in late March 1971. I was checkmated with that reference of Shaheed Zia, a true patriotic leader with proverbial integrity. I later came to know that Tarek Rahman, the eldest son of the Prime Minister had contributed to a great extent in influencing her mother to include me in the government. I had the opportunity to meet him earlier only once like her mother when he was managing the party newspaper, Daily *Dinkal*. Tarek Rahman apparently remembered our interaction.

From the moment of accepting the offer to join the government, my association with Begum Zia lasted for nearly two decades until the day before she was sent to prison by the fascist regime on 8 February 2018. On her last night of freedom, I went to meet her at the party Chairperson's Gulshan office. She was calm and resolute knowing fully well that the next day, the dysfunctional and biased judiciary in Bangladesh would sent her to jail at the instruction of the tyrannical Prime Minister Sheikh Hasina, one of the most ruthless dictators of the present era.

I left the country on August 25 the same year following the daylight attack on my life inside the court premise in a district town of Kushtia by the death squad of Sheikh Hasina. I went there in response to a summon of the Chief Metropolitan Magistrate in a defamation case lodged by the President of the local unit of Chatra League, the student front of the Awami League. My crime was to criticize Sheikh Hasina in a speech given few months back at Dhaka Press Club in regards to her wild and wanton abuse of human rights and enactment of draconian laws in the effort to take away the freedom of press and expression. The attackers belonging to the ruling party were given security by a large contingent of police led by the Officer-in Charge of the Kushtia Sadar Police station at the instruction of the Prime Minister's office. I survived the attack with serious injury in the head and face requiring multiple stitches. Anecdote is told and for rest of the article, the author fades into the background.

Let's now start to follow the long, eventful and heroic journey of a remarkable woman, unique leader and a great patriot.

Early life of Khaleda Zia in the shadow of a great national hero

Khaleda Zia was not born in a political family. Her father, Iskandar Majumdar was a tea planter in Jalpaiguri, although their ancestors hailed from Noakhali. He later settled in Dinajpur and became a successful businessman there. Khaleda Khanam Putul, the third of five children of Iskandar Majumdar and Taiyaba Majumdar, got married to Ziaur Rahman, then a young captain in the Pakistan army in 1960. She was only fifteen at the time of her marriage. After marriage, she continued her study at Surendranath College in Dinajpur for some time and then moved to West Pakistan with her military officer husband. There is no record of her being involved in the student politics during study in the school and college. She became mother of two sons: Tarek and Arafat were born in 1965 and 1969 respectively. Bangladesh was liberated in 1971, General Ziaur Rahman became the Chief of Bangladesh Army in 1975 and then the President of Bangladesh in 1977. Exposure of Khaleda Zia in the national and international politics practically started as the First Lady of the country in the late 1970s.

However, she was by no means insulated from politics during the early 1970s. In fact, her personal struggle began from the moment her husband revolted against the Pakistan army and declared independence on the midnight of 25 March, 1971 at Chittagong cantonment. Major Siddiq Salik, PRO of the then East Pakistan Command of the Pakistan army writes, about Zia's revolt,

> Major Ziaur Rahman, the second in command of 8 East Bengal, assumed command of the rebels in the absence of Brigadier Mazumdar (who had been tactfully taken to Dacca a few days earlier). While the government troops clung to the radio station, in order to guard the building, Major Zia took control of the transmitters separately located on Kaptai Road and used the available equipment to broadcast the 'declaration of independence' of Bangladesh".[2]

Lieutenant General Jacob, Chief of Staff of India's Eastern Army during the liberation war of Bangladesh, writes the following account of Zia's heroic resistance against Pakistan army in Chittagong in 1971:

> Maj Zia resisted the Pakistani Army in Chittagong with all available Bengali regular and paramilitary forces. Heavy fighting erupted in the Headquarters of the East Pakistan Rifles, where the Pakistani Army used tanks, aircraft, artillery and fire from naval gunboats. The position was captured on 31 March. The next assault was on the Reserve Police lines, which fell without much resistance. Zia then fell back towards Belonia, blowing up the

strategic Feni road bridge which connected Dacca with the part of Chittagong.³

While Major Zia was fighting during the long nine months of the liberation war against the Pakistani forces, Begum Zia was kept under house arrest with two minor sons at Dhaka cantonment by the Pakistani regime.

Begum Zia experienced the second period of army captivity in November 1975 in the same Dhaka cantonment. However, this time her husband was also with the family. Brigadier General Khaled Musharraf led a military coup against the government headed by President Khandaker Moshtaque Ahmed on 3 November 1975. The then Army Chief Major General Ziaur Rahman was held captive with the family in his official residence at Dhaka cantonment for three days by the rebel army. He was also forced at gunpoint to resign. However, the highly unpopular and controversial coup collapsed within 72 hours. The glorious Sipahi-Janata revolution defeated the India-sponsored army coup and General Ziaur Rahman was reinstated as the Chief of Staff. Brigadier Khaled Musharraf and other rebel officers were killed in the nationalist revolution. Anthony Mascarenhas gives a vivid description of the people and army jubilation at the defeat of the rebels in his book, *A Legacy of Blood*:

> The jawans took over the radio station at 1:30 am, announcing to the night staff on duty that 'Sepahi Biplob' (Sepoy Revolution) has begun and will continue under Ziaur Rahman. The astonished didn't quite know how to take it. When they realized that the jawans were not threatening them and that Khalid Musharraf had been defeated, they all joined with the wildly celebrating troops .... As the radio continued proclaiming 'Sipahi Biplob' and that General Zia had taken over, thousands of people who had at first alarmed by the firing in the cantonment, poured into the streets to celebrate. For three days' they had believed that India through Khalid Musharraf was threatening their hard-won independence. Everywhere jawans and civilians exchanged salutations, embraced one another, danced in the streets. The night was filled with cries of Allahu Akbar, Bangladesh Zindabad, Sepahi Biplob Zindabad and General Ziaur Rahman Zindabad.⁴

Ziaur Rahman, already a national hero because of his declaration of independence in 1971, became an adorable household name after the Khaled Musharraf coup fiasco. Being a practicing Muslim, strong nationalist and exemplary honest person, Zia realized that without a strong revival of Islamic faith among the majority population, Bangladesh would not be able to maintain its sovereignty in the face of sustained and ferocious cultural aggression from India. He could not have missed the importance of the ideology of Islam as a counterbalance to the Bengali Hindu ideology propagated by the pro-Indian, Islamophobic elements in the name of Bengali nationalism. As the elected President of the country, Zia gave the nation the distinct Bengali Muslim identity by incorporating 'Bismillah-ar-Rahman-ar-Rahim' and 'absolute trust and faith in the Almighty Allah' in the constitution of Bangladesh.

Peace and happiness in the life of Khaleda Zia were, however, short-lived. As the popularity of her husband among the common masses of Bangladesh soared to a level that nearly even eclipsed the peak popularity of Sheikh Mujib after his return to Bangladesh from Pakistani prison in 1972, the conspirators within the Bangladesh army became increasingly active. There were as many as nineteen coup attempts during only six years of Zia's rule and he was killed in the last one led by Chittagong GOC, General Manzur in 1981. Khaleda Zia became a widow at the age of only thirty-six. President Zia was so extraordinarily honest that he never even owned a house of his own in Dhaka. Begum Zia had no place to shift from the official residence of the President with her two sons, one teen-age and the other minor. The bereaved nation gratefully gifted the official cantonment residence of the slain president to his widow on a perpetual lease, to be her residence for life, by unanimously passing the transaction in the parliament followed by execution of necessary legal deeds. Neither Khaleda Zia nor the people of Bangladesh could foresee that 29 years later a fascist regime led by Sheikh Hasina would rescind the transaction and evict the widow of General Zia from the only house that she knew as her own. That sad story will come later.

Although General Manzur succeeded in killing the most popular serving president in the history of Bangladesh on a rainy night in Chittagong, he himself was killed within the next 48 hours in his own cantonment by the angry and grieving soldiers under his command. They refused to wait for the court martial of the general. The associates of Manzur were later court martialed and hanged. Writing on the assassination of Ziaur Rahman, Mascarenhas bitterly criticizes the Bangladesh army officers for their unpatriotic rebellion and cowardice in the murder of a hugely popular president. He writes,

> The refusal of the common soldier to get involved in the mutiny and Zia'a assassination was the outstanding feature of the Chittagong events. The uprising failed principally because the soldiers refused to join in and the rebel officers were left without an Army. In doing so the jawans to a great extent retrieved the reputation of the Bangladesh armed forces which was disgraced by the cowardly acquiescence of some officers in Chittagong to the dictates of the mutineers or the equally disgraceful tacit acceptance by others of the fait accompli.[5]

By killing President Zia, General Manzur in fact opened the gate of the President House, Bangabhaban, for his sworn enemy, the then Chief of Army Staff, General Hossain Mohammed Ershad. A cunning and corrupt general, Ershad bought his time by initially endorsing the then Vice-President Justice Abdus Sattar to become the President after Zia's assassination, according to the constitution. Justice Sattar also won in the subsequent presidential election held on 15 November, 1981 contesting as a BNP nominee by defeating Awami League nominee, Dr. Kamal Hossain by a huge margin. However, Ershad had been eyeing Bangabhaban from the day Zia was killed. Finally, on 24 March 1982, General Ershad staged a bloodless coup and forced the physically fragile and mentally weak Justice Sattar to hand over power to him.

General Ershad, a repatriated officer from Pakistan, was actually a mole of Delhi. First the elimination of President Zia and then removal of the BNP government nicely suited the Indian agenda to control the domestic politics in Bangladesh. Ershad immediately targeted the decimation of the BNP, the flag-bearer of nationalist politics in the country. A group of opportunist BNP leaders jumped onto the Ershad bandwagon causing great anguish among the patriotic political forces in

Bangladesh. The stage was set for a new face to carry forward the political vision of President Zia. The young leadership in the BNP, especially the students, were completely disillusioned by the meek surrender of Justice Sattar and failure of senior leaders to wage any people's movement against the coup d'etat of Ershad. These young guns took the initiative to bring Begum Zia, a housewife still mourning her husband's death, to national political arena for the sake of the survival of the party. The story of the gradual transformation of a politically inexperienced housewife into the most popular democratic leader of Bangladesh would remain a source of permanent inspiration for the vast majority of the population who believe in the sovereignty of the country and their separate and distinct Bengali Muslim identity.

Arrival of the 'Uncompromising Leader'

Begum Khaleda Zia always had a hunch that General Ershad had a role in the assassination of her husband. I remember once she asked my personal opinion about him. It was probably just before the completion of her term in 2006 when Ershad was having a negotiation with the BNP to join the alliance. I honestly told her that I believed General Ershad had strong Indian connection and, therefore, cannot be trusted. She apparently endorsed my view. The role of the former President in the build-up of 1/11 military coup in 2007 proved my earlier assessment.

In October 1982, Ershad and his wife went on a two-day official tour to India at the invitation of Indira Gandhi. She never extended such invitation to President Zia and the relation between the two leaders always remained frosty. During Zia's rule, the Ministry of External Affairs of India used to forward the logic that Indira Gandhi, being a democratic leader, could not be seen to endorse military government in a neighboring country. Interestingly, in the case of Ershad, no such tall talk of idealistic consideration prevented the same Indira Gandhi from befriending the army strongman Ershad. The Indian prime minister told in her speech given at the banquet in honor of Ershad, "May this visit be the starting point of a new chapter of trust and cooperation between our two countries which share a past and must live in peace and close cooperation in the future."[6]

Ironically, while Zia became a democratically elected president in 1978, Ershad in 1982 was the Chief Martial Law Administrator.

Begum Zia commenced her active political life in 1982 as the chairperson of the party established by her late husband but considerably weakened in his absence by factionalism and opportunism. A rookie politician had to face three formidable enemies at the same time right from the day she joined politics. Ershad was continuously trying to split and crush the BNP as a political force. Sheikh Hasina had a personal grudge against Ziaur Rahman and, therefore, Begum Zia was by default her mortal enemy. Above all, India, the undeclared guardian of both Ershad and Hasina, considered the very concept of Bangladeshi nationalism a threat to India's hegemonic aspiration. As a result, Begum Zia, the torch bearer of Zia's idealism, was unwelcome to the political establishment in New Delhi. On joining politics, Begum Zia spearheaded the historic democratic movement against the autocratic regime of Ershad until his ultimate fall in 1990.

Political acumen of Khaleda Zia was tested with the announcement of parliamentary election by Ershad in 1986. There was initial understanding among all the opposition political parties to boycott the election to block Ershad's move to gain legitimacy. However, Sheikh Hasina, in a dramatic volte-face, decided to participate just a few hours before the scheduled beginning of the submission of nomination papers. It is widely believed that the sudden change of heart of the Awami League president was the result of secret negotiation with Ershad in which India had played an important role. Even, Jamat-e-Islami, the traditional ally of BNP, followed the Awami League and announced their decision to participate in the election in a show of abject opportunism. Begum Zia took a great political risk, within only four years of joining politics, by steadfastly refusing to participate in the stage-managed election. All political analysts thought at that time that Begum Zia would forever be marginalized in the national politics by boycotting alone the parliamentary election. It was risky but a very courageous decision that would pay her rich dividend 5 years later in the first truly participatory election under the caretaker government.

As expected, the 1986 parliamentary election was marred by widespread violence and wholesale rigging, thereby vindicating Khaleda Zia's political stand. Ershad manipulated the election result to win an absolute majority in the parliament. The decision of Khaleda Zia to boycott the election under Ershad made her immensely popular among the general masses and she was hailed as the 'Uncompromising Leader' against autocracy. The Awami League and the other parties who participated in the election were branded as traitors. Sheikh Hasina found herself in an embarrassing situation as the Leader of Opposition in a parliament despised by the electorates. Within less than next two years, political compulsion forced Hasina to acknowledge her mistake and in order to redeem herself in the eyes of the public, she decided to resign from the parliament along with all the party members. Other smaller parties also followed her. Ershad had no option other than dissolving the parliament. The dissolution of the parliament was a huge political victory for the BNP that greatly enhanced the stature of Khaleda Zia as the true flag bearer of nationalist politics and undisputed leader of democratic movement in Bangladesh. Transformation of a housewife to a patriotic mass leader was completed within less than 6 years. An incredible achievement indeed! Eminent BBC journalist, Sirajur Rahman gives the following assessment:

> Although during Ershad's nine years of military autocracy, the Awami League and Sheikh Hasina made some superficial criticism, the stand of the Awami League had been inconsistent, shifting. Sheikh Hasina often opposed Ershad, other times she remained neutral. On the other hand, BNP Chairperson Khaleda Zia took an uncompromising stand against military government from the very beginning, it never changed. By the end of the nineties, people were giving total support to Khaleda's position.[7]

Ershad's days in power were numbered. Even India began to consider its onetime client nothing more than an irritant. Delhi establishment was by then receiving the intelligence feedback that Awami League would return to power in a free and fair election. After all, Awami League has been the historic ally of India since Pakistan days. Democratic movement against

Ershad regime gathered huge momentum in 1990 when All Students United Front was formed under the then DUCSU leadership affiliated to the student wing of the BNP. With Indian support gone, Ershad's power structure began to crumble. He declared state of emergency in the country. But, the army refused to rescue him and sided with the popular uprising. On 6 December 1990 Ershad finally succumbed to the peoples' revolution and resigned as President of Bangladesh. Incumbent Chief Justice Shahabuddin Ahmed was sworn in as the Chief of Caretaker government. Fall of Ershad paved the way for the first absolutely free and fair election in the history of Bangladesh. Even her political opponents had to grudgingly admit that Khaleda Zia was indeed the true 'Uncompromising Leader' of the country.

The first woman Prime Minister in Bangladesh

Election was scheduled on 27 February 1991. In the run-up to the election all the political pundits were forecasting a landslide victory for Awami League. Bangladesh media is generally known for its clear Awami bias and allegiance to India. Infiltration of anti-Islamic elements in the Bangladeshi media has been going on since the days of Pakistan. Most of the media were fed with the information from the Indian High Commission that Awami League was going to sweep in the election. It was like a crescendo in support of Sheikh Hasina. Bolstered by the positive coverage, she gave a boastful interview a few days before the election to an India media arrogantly claiming that the BNP would not get more than 10 seats in the parliament. She further predicted that fallen dictator Ershad's Jatiyo Party would emerge as the main opposition party. Indian intelligence was predicting that Awami League would at least approach two-third majority, if not absolute majority. Let us hear about the premature Indian mood of nervous jubilation from the proverbial Horse's mouth, i.e. the diary of the then Indian High Commissioner, Krishnan Srinivasan:

> Our present guess is that with its allies, the Awami League will approach but not secure 200 seats…..If the Awami League do not get at least a majority, we shall have egg on our combined faces, not only here but also in India, since it had always been India's presumed wisdom that the Awami League represented the silent

majority in Bangladesh…..We keep making electoral assessment – as does everyone else. Our latest is that the Awami League and its allies could win 150 seats or thereabouts.[8]

Alas, how wrong were the Indian intelligence and the pro-Awami Bangladesh media! Just prior to the election, Khaleda Zia presented herself in the last television speech as fresh, sincere, accommodating and patriotic. Sheikh Hasina, on the other hand, appeared shrill and vituperative. Furthermore, Khaleda's uncompromising stand against the military dictator Ershad during the democratic struggle of the 1980s made her immensely popular among the young voters. The combination of Zia's legacy and Khaleda Zia's personal charisma tilted the balance decisively in favor of the BNP in the ballot. The party won 140 seats against only 88 of Awami League. Begum Zia personally won from all the five constituencies that she had contested in the election. To rub salt into the wound, Sheikh Hasina lost in two constituencies out of the three that she participated. Begum Khaleda Zia was sworn in as the first female Prime Minister of Bangladesh on 20 March 1991. She was also the second female Prime Minister in a Muslim country after Benazir Bhutto who earlier became the Prime Minister of Pakistan in 1988. A bitter and inconsolable Sheikh Hasina refused to accept the result of the most free and fair election in the history of Bangladesh. In her first address in the parliament, she ominously declared, "I will not allow this government to function even for a single day in peace." She kept her promise in letter and spirit.

Indian antipathy towards Khaleda Zia increased manifold when she raised the issue of unilateral withdrawal of Ganges water by India in the upstream in defiance of all international laws and agreement in her maiden speech in the UN general assembly on 1 October 1993. Her late husband was the first Bangladeshi leader to do so in 1977 that compelled India to sign Ganges water sharing agreement with Bangladesh. Sheikh Mujib sacrificed national interest in 1975 by agreeing to India's unilateral commissioning of Farakka barrage, a terrible symbol of water aggression of India against her downstream smaller neighbor. Ershad also succumbed to the Indian pressure and remained silent on the issue during his entire eight and half years' rule. Begum Zia proved in her speech in the UN General Assembly that she was no less a patriot than her husband President

Ziaur Rahman. However, in the next general election held in 1996, the BNP lost with 116 seats against 146 won by the Awami League, although Khaleda Zia repeated her 1991 performance by winning from all the five seats that she contested. Sheikh Hasina became the Prime Minister for the first time and Khaleda Zia, the leader of the opposition.

Return to power in an Islamophobic world: beginning of an end

The global geopolitical situation underwent dramatic changes in the aftermath of the 9/11 attack on America. Prior to that, the US policy toward Bangladesh was generally to accept nationalist and pro-Islamic parties in the democratic governance so long it did not threaten the US interest in South Asia. But, post 9/11, the Washington administration and Western media were clearly hostile to anything related to Islam. Both India and Israel were enthusiastic supporters of the new jingoistic policy in Washington. They also worked closely to fuel Islamophobia around the world. Khaleda Zia returned to state power with Islamic parties in alliance in a dangerously hostile global geopolitical environment.

In the 2001 general election in Bangladesh, held only three weeks after the demolition of Twin Towers in New York, Indian intelligence again failed to gauge the mood of the electorates. This time the defeat of Awami League was much worse than 1991. They were reduced to 59 seats only making the party the smallest opposition in Bangladesh parliament since 1991. Anti-Bangladesh propaganda commenced almost immediately after Khaleda's return to power. Islamophobic writer and journalist Bertil Lintner wrote a clearly motivated article in Far Eastern Economic Review in April 2002 with the incendiary title, "Cocoon of terror." The piece was a vicious attack against Islam, the people of Bangladesh and its government. He wrote,

> A revolution is taking place in Bangladesh that threatens trouble for the region and beyond if left unchallenged. Islamic fundamentalism, religious intolerance, militant Muslim groups with links to international terrorist groups, a powerful military with ties to the militants, the mushrooming of Islamic schools

churning out radical students, middle class apathy, poverty and lawlessness all are combining to transform the nation.[9]

Lintner was not alone in the nasty campaign. B. Raman, Jaideep Saikia, Subash Kapila, Anand Kumar, Sudha Ramachandran, Balbir Punj and possibly hundreds of other Indian journalists started a deliberate campaign for a regime change in Dhaka. The Indian journalists were joined by the likes of Alex Perry, Eliza Griswold, Chris Blackburn, and Christopher Walmoor in Washington and other western capitals with the common objective to convince their government of the need to topple the BNP-led four party alliance. In the domestic front, the so-called secular, anti-Islamic and pro-Indian media also started concerted campaign to discredit the government. In spite of all provocations, Khaleda Zia remained calm and resolute. She took hard decisions, some of which being controversial like the Operation Clean Heart and the formation of the RAB, to tackle the terrible law and order situation that she had inherited from the immediate past Hasina government. Khaleda also emphasized on the need to revive the moribund economy. Indeed, the turn-around of the economy within a very short time was exemplary that elicited praise from all multilateral agencies even though there was allegation of corruption against some of the ministers. By the year 2005, GDP was growing at nearly 7 percent, food production increased substantially, export grew by 20 percent and Bangladesh was able to overtake India in nearly all the social sector indicators. It was difficult to justify the change of a relatively successful, democratically elected government although the powerful Indo-Jewish lobby in Washington never stopped in their campaign to portray Bangladesh as a failed state. Unfortunately, the apparent success in economic governance could not deter the conspirators within the men in uniform whom Begum Zia considered as her family. A perfect storm was slowly but surely brewing inside the cantonment since 2005.

Betrayal

Ziaur Rahman was an extremely modest person in his personal life. He was given an official residence as Deputy Chief of Staff inside Dhaka cantonment in 1972. Eventually he became Chief of Army Staff and then President of the Republic. But he never changed that residence.

The same house was given to his widow on lifelong lease arrangement after the assassination of Zia. That widow became democratically elected Prime Minister of the country, not once, but three times, including a very short tenure of the 6th parliament. But Khaleda Zia also never felt the necessity to shift to the luxurious official residence of the Prime Minister. Many of the senior leaders of the BNP suggested to her to leave the cantonment as it was not convenient for them to regularly go to the restricted area for consultation. But how could she leave that house?

Since liberation of Bangladesh, that was the only place she knew as her home. She raised her family there. This was the place where the bullet-ridden, lifeless body of her loving husband was brought in a coffin in 1981, her two minor sons grew up to become adult in front of her in that house, she received her two daughters-in law there, her granddaughters were placed into her lap for the first time in the same house. Shaheed Mainul Road house could never be a simple lifeless structure of cement and iron rod to her, it was a living entity and part of her soul. How can a person just leave behind so much memories, both happy and sad? Even the 19 coup attempts against Ziaur Rahman and the assassination of her husband by a section of the army could not free Khaleda Zia from that deep sense of family connection to the institution. Unfortunately, it was a one-sided feeling. The army, especially the officers apparently never shared the same feeling. On the contrary, the English saying that 'familiarity breeds contempt' was borne out in the relationship between Zia family and the Bangladesh Army.

Senior army officers at the Dhaka cantonment started discussing about a military takeover from 2005. The appointment of General Masud, a relative of Khaleda Zia and former Rakkhi Bahini officer as GOC of the 9th division provided additional support to the conspirators. Khaleda Zia probably posted General Masud in the most strategic division with the expectation that he would come to her rescue at a time of need. After all, Masud was brother-in-law of Khaleda's younger brother Major (Retd) Sayeed Iskander. Their wives are siblings. Khaleda Zia promoted General Moeen, a friend and batch mate of Sayeed Iskander as Army Chief expecting him to treat her with loyalty that 'an elder sister' could always and naturally expect. The then Chief of DGFI was also a course mate of

Sayeed. The Chief of SSF, General Mehedi Rumi, came from a veteran BNP family. His late father was a member of the parliament and his elder brother, a sitting member of the parliament from the BNP in 2006. Looking at these people, Khaleda Zia must have thought that all around her were family members. She felt secured. The reality was completely different. They were waiting to stab her on the back. So many Brutus*es* were there in the army!

The personal relationship between Tarek Rahman (the elder son and declared political heir of the Prime Minister) and General Masud reportedly got strained over some family issue. Masud actually hated Tarek intensely. To him and his friends, Tarek was a mere ambitious upstart meddling into state affairs. They saw Tarek grow from a boy into a very influential political leader before their very eyes. How can they suddenly accept him as the future Prime Minister? A vicious character assassination campaign was planned and executed with the aim to sway public opinion inside the cantonment against Tarek Rahman. General Masud was maintaining close contact with Indian, UK and US embassy officials. As a former Rakkhi-Bahini officer, he was a trusted accomplice of Indian intelligence. He was constantly feeding anti-Tarek propaganda to the foreign diplomatic circle in Dhaka. General Moeen as the Army Chief kept himself in the background as part of the grand strategy. However, he acknowledges the conspiracy in the army in his memoir written while he was still serving in the army. He writes:

> I used to regularly brief the division commanders about the situation of the country and listened to their opinion. Some of them pressed me to take immediate action. Particularly, GOC of Savar division, Major General Masud always used to express his concern in severest of terms at the dismal condition of the state and political situation.[10]

The gang of betrayers was just waiting for the green signal from their foreign mentors. The signal was finally given on 7 January 2007. The next three days were spent in the preparation of a new version of coup de'tat. On 11 January, General Moeen went to the President House accompanied by General Masud to force President Iajuddin Ahmed at gunpoint to resign from the position of Chief Adviser and accept the new formula of so-called army supported Caretaker government. Only a few mid-ranking officers raised objection and were quickly neutralized without shedding any blood.

Both Khaleda Zia and Sheikh Hasina were given the option of exile which the latter accepted promptly. Begum Zia boldly rejected the insulting offer and dared the junta to arrest her. First Tarek was arrested and few weeks later the younger son of Ziaur Rahman, Arafat, was also arrested. Both of them were severely tortured in the DGFI torture chamber at Dhaka cantonment, only a few blocks away from where the hapless mother was living under heavy army guard. Under unofficial house arrest since 11 January, she herself was formally arrested on 3 September by the junta. She was released from prison after one year on 11 September 2008.

Before the release of the former Prime Minister, both her sons were sent to exile by the military government. Tarek and Arafat became semi-crippled as a result of inhuman torture by the army. Arafat would later die at the age of only 46 in exile in 2015 from the complication originated from torture in custody. Khaleda Zia also lost her octogenarian mother in 2008 while she was still in prison.

By the early 2008, the military junta became extremely unpopular and was looking for a safe exit. After the mindless and sadistic torture of Tarek and Arafat in the DGFI interrogation cell at the personal instruction of General Masud, Sheikh Hasina was the obvious choice for the army to ensure their safe exit. An election drama was staged on 28 December in which the intelligence wing of the army under the instruction of their Chief General Moeen manipulated the election process to award a landslide victory to the Awami League. Indian intelligence wing, RAW, duly assisted the then army-backed government of Bangladesh in ensuring the victory of the Awami League. In the process, the Bangladesh Army not only had betrayed Khaleda Zia, they also surrendered the nation's sovereignty to India.

Hasina's triumphant return to power is possibly the greatest victory for India's geo-political strategists in relation to Bangladesh since break-up of Pakistan in 1971. Ironically, Washington was also elated at the electoral victory of the principal Indian client in Bangladesh as part of their post-9/11 regional strategy in South Asia. Indian role in the whole episode was later acknowledged by none other than Pranab Mukherjee, the former Indian President in his memoir published in 2017. He writes about the Indian intervention during 2007-2008 with the arrogance of a master,

> Sheikh Hasina had been a close family friend, and when I was the External Affairs Minister, India tried to help her cause by building adequate international pressure for free and fair elections after the caretaker government. In fact, when some Awami League leaders deserted her at the time she was in jail, I rebuked them for their stand and told them that to leave someone when they are down is unethical. The general election was held in December 2008, and Sheikh Hasina won a thumping victory.[11]

India and her client in Bangladesh emerged as the ultimate victor at the conclusion of 1/11 coup. As a country, Bangladesh has lost its sovereignty. As people, we have lost our freedom and cultural identity. The Bangladesh Army has lost its patriotism, courage and respect. Interestingly, the USA is also a loser. By assisting Bangladesh to become an undeclared colony of India, Washington has lost all its influence in a country of 170 million people.

Tragedy

The personal life of Khaleda Zia is full of tragedy. She lost her husband when she was only 36. Her mother died when she was in prison during 1/11 army government. Her two sons were dragged away by the DGFI personnel from cantonment residence in front of her. She protested but could not save them. Both the sons were also tortured in custody by the men in uniform who acted like agents of India. Her hand-picked generals betrayed her by repeating the 1757 Plassey treachery of Mir Zafar, the Commander-in-Chief of the army of Nawab Siraj-al-Doulah, the last independent ruler of Bengal. (One can find a lot of similarities between the betrayal of Mir Zafar, a relative of Seraj, and the Moeen-Masud gong). Many believe that even Khaleda Zia's ambitious younger brother, Sayeed Iskandar, gave tacit support in the 1/11 army takeover as he hoped to elbow out Tarek Rahman in the process and inherit the political legacy of her. Some of her political colleagues in the party also repeatedly betrayed her during the Ershad regime and again during Moeen-Fakhruddin rule. In spite of unbearable agony, Begum Zia never compromised on the issue of the sovereignty of Bangladesh. Even after the 2008 election debacle, Khaleda Zia gathered all her inner strength and tried to reorganize BNP.

In the meantime, Sheikh Hasina was planning to use the biased and dysfunctional judiciary in Bangladesh to evict Khaleda Zia from cantonment residence, her home since 1972. Nazmun Ara Sultana led the High Court bench and most surprisingly declared the 1981 lease of the house illegal in November 2010, twenty-nine years after the then parliament, the supreme law enacting body in the country, approved the transaction. Sheikh Hasina rewarded her by appointing her as the first female Justice in the Supreme Court of Bangladesh.

Begum Khaleda Zia, the widow of the former Army Chief and President, was forcibly evicted from her residence on 13 November 2010. The army not only remained silent at this gross injustice, an enthusiastic section of it even participated in the most inhuman eviction. First 1/11, and then the eviction of Khaleda Zia, both represented a definitive U-turn by the army, turning its back on its pro-nationalist past. The sad episode also exposed the organizational weakness of the BNP as a major political party. The party leadership and activists hopelessly failed to organize even a small protest at the most insulting and unjust treatment to their party chief. A crest fallen, shocked, weeping Khaleda Zia was seen on national television that evening.

Loss of home was nothing in comparison to the next tragedy in the life of Khaleda Zia. In 2015, she was waging her last meaningful political battle against the ruthless fascist regime of Sheikh Hasina. The BNP and its allies were in the midst of a nation-wide movement to restore democracy in Bangladesh. Sheikh Hasina responded with all the brutal force of the state. The notorious RAB and police besieged the Gulshan office of Khaleda Zia cutting power and water connection. There were about a couple of dozen leaders and workers, mostly women with her inside the building. On 24 January 2015, information reached at the besieged office of the Chairperson of the BNP that the exiled youngest son of her died in Malaysia. The body of Arafat Rahman arrived a few days later. She saw the lifeless face of her beloved son for the last time in that office building under siege. No political leader in the history of Bangladesh suffered more than Khaleda Zia in the struggle to establish the democratic right of the people and to safeguard the sovereignty of the country. Searching for parallel in the world history, I have only found Nelson Mandela receiving the news of the death of his eldest son while he was imprisoned in the notorious Robben island.

Tale of tragedy of Khaleda is not over yet. Sheikh Hasina once again used shameful judiciary of Bangladesh to send her arch political rival to prison at the age of seventy-three. Despotic government in Bangladesh has initiated nearly fifty politically motivated and fictitious cases against Khaleda Zia. In one such case, she was awarded a jail sentence of 5 years on 8 February 2018. According to the law of the country, if the accused is a woman, elderly and physically infirm, she should get bail immediately from the High Court unless sentenced to death by the lower court. Furthermore, in all cases where the punishment is up to 5 years, the accused, male or female, should get bail from the higher court on appeal. On both counts, the former Prime Minister was entitled to get bail. But in the 21st century Orwellian state called Bangladesh the wish of Sheikh Hasina is the only law that matters. Following Hasina's instruction, Khaleda Zia was denied bail in High Court and Supreme Court in total disregard of the constitution and human rights. However, I would rather not call this episode of political persecution as the personal tragedy of Khaleda Zia. It is expected in today's Bangladesh under the fascist Hasina regime. Tragedy is elsewhere.

The BNP is supposed to be one of the two largest political parties in the country, the other being Awami League. The party was in state power for more than fifteen years and probably has few million documented general members. It is also perceived as a formidable political party with grass-root organization. Tragedy of Khaleda Zia is that her party and its leadership have repeatedly failed her. Also, on the last occasion, the party failed to organize any meaningful democratic movement in protest of the most shameful miscarriage of justice. She is not only a victim of persecution of Sheikh Hasina's fascist regime but also a victim of indifference and selfishness of the BNP leadership groomed during the last forty years by herself. This is her tragedy.

Personal Memory

Unfortunately, I never had any opportunity to meet President Zia, my only political hero in Bangladesh. Although Begum Zia was my reporting boss for five years from 2001-2006, I became close to her only after the military junta released her from prison in late 2008. At that time, most of the BNP leadership were either in jail or in hiding. Tarique and Arafat were in exile. She rather compelled me to help setting up her office in Gulshan. Incidentally, it was Begum Zia, the then Prime Minister, who presented the IEB highest award to me. Glorious and nostalgic memories. It was a professional relationship during the period I served her in her government. She was an honest, outstanding and patriotic Prime Minister, who never interfered in the discharge of my duty, first as Executive Chairman Board of Investment and later as Energy Adviser. From 2008, the relationship became more personal. She was so compassionate that she came to my residence to see my ailing mother. After Arafat died in Malaysia, my wife was the first person outside her family to get the opportunity to meet her at Gulshan office (then under siege by police) to personally express condolence. I was in jail in 2015.

Epilogue

A frail, wheel chair bound Khaleda Zia was conditionally and temporarily released on 25 March 2020 by the executive order of Sheikh Hasina, the person who herself has manipulated and twisted the judiciary and law to send the former prime minister to prison. This executive order will be reviewed every six months to determine the fate of Khaleda Zia. Nobody should be misled into believing that the BNP Chairperson has obtained any freedom. Her location has only changed from prison to a rented house. She is very much in the clutch of the most ruthless fascist ruler that the people of Bangladesh or East Bengal or East Pakistan has seen since 1947. Under the circumstances, the political future of the last truly charismatic leader of the country is uncertain. She is our "Last of the Mohicans." Only time will tell whether Khaleda Zia can emerge like the proverbial Greek Phoenix from ashes for one last time. Bangladesh needs the "Uncompromising Leader" for its own survival.

[1] *The Political History of Muslim Bengal: An unfinished battle of faith* (2018). www.cambridgescholars.com/ download/sample/65022. See the Prologue; Ch 6, "Independent Bangladesh: Mujib's Dilemma and Autocracy"; and Ch 11, "The Terror of Authoritarian Secularism").

[2] Salik, S, *Witness to Surrender*, University Press limited, First Edition, Dhaka, Bangladesh, 1997, p. 106. General Subid Ali Bhuiyan, Shamsher Mubin Chowdhury and others have clearly written that Zia declared independence at around 12:00 midnight, 25 March 1971. He did so immediately after the crackdown started by the Pakistani army at Dhaka at 11:00 in the night of the 25th.

[3] Jacob, J.F.R., *Surrender at Dhaka: Birth of a Nation*, The University Press limited, Third Impression, 2004, p. 35

[4] Mascarenhas, A., *A Legacy of Blood*, Hodder and Stoughton, London, 1986, p. 110.

[5] Mascarenhas, A., *A Legacy of Blood*, pp. 163-164

[6] Bhasin, A. S., *India-Bangladesh Relations Documents, 1971-2002*, Volume-1, Geetika Publishers, New Delhi, 2003.

[7] Rahman, S., *Etihas Kotha Koy*, Shikor, Dhaka, First edition, 2002, p. 124

[8] Srinivasan, K., *The Jamdani Revolution*, Academic Press and Publishers Library, Dhaka, 2009, pp. 287-300

[9] Lintner, L., "Bangladesh – a Cocoon of Terror," Far Eastern Economic Review, 4 April 2002.

[10] Ahmed, M. U., *Shantir Shopney*, Asia Publications, First impression, 2009, p. 323

[11] Mukherjee, P., *The Coalition Years*, Rupa Publications, New Delhi, 2017, p. 114

Chapter 4

Begum Khaleda Zia: The Pragmatic and Patriotic Leader That She Is

Jasim Uddin Ahmad

Begum Khaleda Zia was the first woman Prime Minister of Bangladesh. She became the Prime Minister twice in the country's history from 1991 to 1996, and again from 2001 to 2006. Khaleda Zia is also the second Prime Minister in the Muslim majority countries, after Benazir Bhutto of Pakistan, to head a democratic government. In the global ranking of PMs, *Forbes* magazine, in its list of 100 Most Powerful Women in the World, ranked Khaleda Zia at #14 in 2004, # 29 in 2005, and # 33 in 2006.

I had the honor and privilege to meet Begum Khaleda Zia on several occasions during her tenure as the Leader of the Opposition in the Parliament (1996-2001) and later as the Prime Minister during 2001-2006. I am going to mention a few of those occasions in the following short write-up.

Going a few years back, we had an exclusive meeting with Begum Zia in 1987. At that crucial time, she was the Chairperson of Bangladesh Nationalist Party (BNP). An 11-member Delegation of Teachers from Jahangirnagar University headed by Prof. Syed Safiullah met her at the Dhanmondi residence of Mirza Golam Hafiz, a BNP Standing Committee member. We had an elaborate discussion on the prevailing political situation of the country, Zia Foundation and Zia Parishad. She urged us to form an organization with the nationalist intellectuals of the country. Although we suggested that the news of the meeting should not come to the media, to our surprise, that was a lead news in a few Dhaka dailies. But this initiative could not be continued due to some reasons.

After the defeat of the BNP in the 1996 national election, Abdul Mannan Bhuiyan was given the responsibility of the Secretary General of the party. He, with the directives of Begum Zia, formed a 13- member Think Tank of the party headed by Prof. Moniruzzaman Miah of Dhaka University. I was also included in the committee. After the formation of the Committee, she invited us to her Sena Nibash (cantonment) residence. She said she was very happy to see many leading intellectuals of the country in the think tank and urged us to make dedicated contributions for the nation. We were provided with an office space at 88, Kakrail with logistical support. We used to meet there frequently, discuss issues and submit our recommendations to Secretary General Mannan Bhuiyan and Party Chair Begum Zia, who was then the Leader of the Opposition.

In the end of December, 1999, the BNP organized a discussion meeting in front of the Party Office at Naya Paltan to discuss different issues related to the upcoming new millennium. Begum Zia sat in the front row of the audience and listened to the discussions. I spoke on the role of Computer Technology and E-commerce in the coming 21st Century. Many important points of deliberations in that meeting were included in the 2001 Election Manifesto.

In 1999, I was elected as the President of the Federation of Bangladesh Universities Teachers Association (FBUTA), the apex organization of the Teachers' Associations (TA) of all the Public Universities of Bangladesh. During that period, I also served as the President of Jahangirnagar University Teachers' Association (JUTA). After a long period of time, a Teachers' Association Leader from the anti-Awami League bloc was able to win this coveted post in a highly contested election. Begum Zia was very impressed and happy on my victory in the FUBTA election.

The FBUTA leaders were invited to the Office of the Leader of the Opposition. The group consisted of myself, Prof. M. Faruque (who was Secretary General of the FBUTA), Prof. Khalilur Rahman and others. Abdul Mannan Bhuiyan, the party Secretary General, was also present and moderated the discussion. Begum Zia congratulated us on our success in the election. She discussed the misdeeds of Awami rule and said there was an urgent need for greater unity of all the professionals, including teachers and other forces in the country for the coming general election in 2001 to defeat Bangladesh Awami League headed by Sheikh Hasina Wazed. She requested us to unite and form an organization of like-minded university teachers.

We visited many of the Public Universities and could come to a consensus to form an organization named "Ganotantric Shikkhak Parishad" (Democratic Teachers Association). I was the President and Prof. Khalilur Rahman was the Secretary General of the Ad-hoc Committee. (We requested another appointment with Begum Zia to discuss our progress and future plans. We requested her to be the Chief Guest at the 1st Convention of Ganotantric Shikkhak Parishad. She gladly accepted our invitation.

The 1st Convention of Ganotantrik Shikkhak Parishad was held at the Auditorium of National Press Club, Dhaka in January 2001. Teachers' representatives from various public universities of Bangladesh attended. Begum Khaleda Zia graced the Convention as the Chief Guest. Prof. Maniruzzan Miah, former Vice Chancellor of Dhaka University, was present as a Special Guest. Leaders of many of the Pro-BNP professional organizations also attended the convention. Begum Zia inaugurated the convention and gave a historical speech outlining her vision about higher education and academic research in Bangladesh, emphasizing the continuation of widely accepted education policy and visions initiated by late President Ziaur Rahman. Her speech was given lead coverage in the national dailies. The news of the convention was also covered with due importance in all electronic media.

In the convention, I was elected the President and Prof. Khalilur Rahman, Secretary General of Gonotrantric Shikhak Parishad unanimously. Gonotrantric Shikhak Parishad played a significant role with Shoto Nagorik Committee (Group of Hundreds of Distinguished Citizens) in mobilizing public opinion against misdeeds of Sheikh Hasina regime. As expressed by many national and international neutral election evaluators, the large participation of teachers, professionals and intellectuals took BNP to a new height, which was one of the important factors for achieving BNP's landslide victory with two-third majority in the 2001 national election. The important role of these teachers and professionals led to formulating a number of pro-people policy and programs for reformation and reorientation and for instilling and rebuilding the patriotic Bangladeshi national feelings.

For quite a long time, we were mobilizing national and international opinion against the unilateral upstream water withdrawal and diversion of rivers by India. We organized many International and National Conferences, Seminars and Workshops under the banner of International Farakka Committee. Atiqur Rahman Eusufzai Salu is the Chairman of International Farakka Committee (IFC) and I am the President of Bangladesh Farakka Committee. In August 2002, IFC Chairman, Atiqur Rahman Salu and myself met the Honorable Prime Minister in her office and apprised her about the forthcoming publication of a national documentation (Ifcinfor.org). We published a very important documentation, entitled "National Documents on Arsenic and Farakka," in 2003. I was the Editor for this publication.[1]

In the first page of this document, we expressed our profound gratitude to Shaheed President Ziaur Rahman, who in 1976, raised the Farakka issues at the United Nations for the first time. We also expressed our great appreciation to Prime Minister Begum Khaleda Zia for expressing the legitimate concern of Bangladeshi people due to Farakka Barrage in her speech at the United Nations General Assembly on Oct 1, 1993.

After the publication, we sought an appointment with PM Office, to present the publication to the Prime Minister. She was glad to give us an audience on August 4, 2003. We presented the published document to the Prime Minister at her office. Atiqur Rahman Salu, Chairman of IFC, Syed Tipu Sultan, Secretary General IFC, Prof. Syed Safiullah, Eng. S I Khan, Mustafa Kamal Majumder, Dr. Nazma Ahmad, myself and others were present. Begum Zia was very happy on the publication and congratulated us for our historic works. She unveiled the cover of the Document before a crowded media, the news of which came out in the national dailies the following day (August 5, 2003).

We informed the Prime Minister that we were planning to organize a program on the bank of Brahmaputra river near Chilmari Bandar, Kurigram. The program will be a "Long March and Grand Rally"

and sought the support of her Government. She gladly agreed to our request and asked the Minister for LGRD—Local Government and Rural Development-- to extend all required support.

We also requested her to give necessary directives to the Ministry of Foreign Affairs so that the Document could be distributed to the United Nations, other relevant UN agencies, International Donor Agencies and Foreign Missions. She accepted our request and instructed the Political Secretary to follow up the matter.

On March 4, 2005 the Long March and Grand Rally was held at Chilmari Bandar on the bank of Brahmaputra in protest and demand for the cancellation of the River Interlink project of India. The news was reported in the national dailies the next day, March 5, 2005. It was a huge rally of protesters, where more than half a million people participated from all walks of life, from Bangladesh, the USA, the UK, Germany, and other parts of the world. Prof. K M A Malik was the coordinator of the Chilmari Long March Committee in the UK. It was a grand success. People raised their voices against the unjust water withdrawal of common rivers by India. Loud slogans like *Hamak Pani Hamak Deo* (give us our share of water) were heard everywhere all the time. Speakers recalled and remembered the great leader of the peasants and masses, Maulana Abdul Hamid Khan Bhasani, who first led the Farakka Long March in 1983 and Shaheed President Ziaur Rahman, who first raised the Farakka issues in the United Nations in 1976. This event was only possible with the dedications of our leaders, hard work and mobilization of masses. It needs special mention, that without the support from Khaleda Zia's Government, it would have been really hard to successfully organize the event. This is the largest rally ever held in Bangladesh for protesting the diversion of upstream waters by India.

After the conclusion of the Long March and Grand Rally, we went to PM Office and offered our thanks and gratitude to Begum Khaleda Zia for helping and supporting our programs. "Rather we should greet you with the flower bouquet," remarked the Prime Minister when we presented her one, along with a book. "You have performed a great job for the country. We are proud of you." She was visibly pleased.

I was appointed the Vice Chancellor of Jahangirnagar University on 21 November 2001. It was a great honor for me with the news widely appearing in the media. During my tenure I could start many development projects at the University. The foundation stone of a residential hall for female students named "Begum Khaleda Zia Hall" was laid and construction work started. Begum Zia always gave utmost importance to the University Education.

As I was also the President of Association of Universities of Bangladesh, an organization of the Vice Chancellors of Public Universities of Bangladesh, I was able to arrange meetings with the Prime Minister to discuss the situation prevailing in different universities. She always gave patient hearing for more than two hours and gave directives to concerned authorities for solving the problems raised.

The BNP and its front and allied organizations used to invite me as a Distinguished Speaker in most of their Discussion Meetings, Seminars, Conventions, etc., especially during the period of 1998-2006. In special discussion meetings on the Martyr Anniversary of the late President Zia, she sat in the front row of the audience to listen to the speeches by the intellectuals who were seated on the stage. During these meetings, Begum Zia would be in the audience among other political leaders. But the scenario has now changed. Now the politicians, even the leaders of different front organizations take their seats on the dais, while the intellectuals, if invited, sit among the general audiences.

In 2003, there was some disturbance in many universities of Bangladesh and Begum Khaleda Zia invited me to the PM Office for an exclusive meeting. We discussed many issues and I proposed some suggestions, she listened carefully and implemented them gradually.

I was awarded the Ekushey Gold Medal (Ekushey Padak)—an honor, along with the other great recognition, Shwadhinota Padak-- both first introduced by her husband, the great president Ziaur Rahman in 1976/77--for my significant contribution in Education in 2006. After that, I had the opportunity to see her during the Independence Day Reception of the President of Bangladesh at Bangabhaban. I told her, "Madam, I would like to thank you for awarding me the Ekushey Padak this year." She smiled and replied, "You deserve it." She was always very modest.

From my close interactions with her, I have no hesitation to state that Begum Khaleda Zia is a unique nationalist leader with a wide vision to take Bangladesh forward with progress and success in all sectors. Our earnest prayer to God/Allah the Almighty, *"May Allah give her a long life with good health, so that she can serve and save our nation in coming days. – Ameen."*

---

[1] Ahmad, J U (Ed), National Documentation on the Problems of Arsenic and the Farakka, International Farakka Committee Inc., New York, 2003

Chapter 5

Begum Khaleda Zia: The Shining Light of Political, Economic, and Educational Reforms in Bangladesh

A N M Ehsanul Hoque Milan

Introduction:

Begum Khaleda Zia is a politician, a leader and the first woman to be the head of a democratic government of Bangladesh.

Bangladesh was on the move of rapid prosperity and growth through economic liberalization under the leadership of President Ziaur Rahman (1936-1981) that did not have a chance to last long. Unfortunately, on the 30th of May 1981, he was assassinated by conspirators, who thought that by killing him they would be able to thwart the nation's march towards democracy and economic emancipation. Their mission was not successful. Begum Zia, widow of President Ziaur Rahman, has surprised them and the rest of the nation by responding to the wishes of the people for her to come forward and fill the void left by her immortal husband. She joined politics that was uplifted and idealized by him, compared with the terrible and murky situation he inherited from the previous one-party Awami-BAKSAli regime of Sheikh Mujibur Rahman. With dedication to the service of the nation, Khaleda Zia took the helm of Bangladesh Nationalist Party (BNP), set up by her husband, and transformed it into an embodiment of the expectations of the people of this country.

To start with, it was a tough nine-year long period for Begum Zia. She had to campaign hard and fight for democracy against the autocratic government of General Hussain Muhammad Ershad, which followed

Ziaur Rahman's government. Her movement succeeded and the dictator was toppled in December 1990. With her extraordinary abilities, courageous leadership and relentless hard work spanning over a decade, she became a formidable leader with millions of loyal followers. Her undaunting struggle and determined leadership in the protracted movement against the autocratic forces providedimmense inspiration to the nation.

People's Choice:

In recognition of her unwavering and uncompromising role in the struggle for the restoration of democracy, the people of Bangladesh gave their mandate to her party, the BNP, in the first ever free, fair and democratic election held in1991 to run the country. Khaleda Zia became the first Woman Prime Minister of Bangladesh. Under her effective leadership the country was able to achieve enviable success in establishing multi-party democracy and good governance, the ideals that her husband President Zia had already pursued and established during his about five years of short rule in the second half of the 1970s and that were trampled by the military dictator H M Ershad in the 1980s.

During her first term, Prime Minister Begum Zia showed unparalleled resilience and political forbearance in the face of the opposition party Awami League's nonstop agitation and long-term hartal (work stoppage) programs.

On 6th December 1993, the Awami League leader Sheikh Hasina demanded that the elections should be held under a Caretaker Government (CTG). In 1994, major opposition political parties, including the Awami League, Jatiyo Party and Jamat-e-Islami, led a movement in support of the CTG. The opposition protest was vicious and brutal. It created destructive obstacles with continuous hartals (strikes), which at times stretched for long unbroken 96 hours at a time. But Begum Zia's government handled the crisis very smoothly and efficiently.

Also, during that time, Begum Khaleda Zia allowed complete freedom to media to broadcast the opposition's sequencer, although it was causing serious unrest. The door was made wide open for anyone interested in entering the media world in Bangladesh. For the first time, the country saw the new editions of satellite TV channels, including the CNN and the BBC.

Withdrawal of the river water at the upper riparian by India during the dry seasons created desert like situation in Bangladesh. On the other hand, release of excessive flood water by India during the rainy seasons inundated vast areas in Bangladesh. Begum Khaleda Zia raised this issue in the United Nations, as her husband Ziaur Rahman did in 1976. She raised it, clearly and forcefully, on the 23rd October 1995, at its 50th anniversary in New York. "Over 40 million people in my country," said Begum Zia, "are facing poverty and destruction owing to deprivation of our rightful share of the waters of the Ganges River by India through unilateral withdrawal at Farakka. [...] The Farakka Barrage has become an issue of life and death for us. Owing to obstruction of the natural flow of water upstream, Bangladesh is being pushed over to the threshold of poverty and destruction. This is a gross violation of human rights and justice."

As per constitutional provision, the 6th Parliament Election was held in February 1996. The Awami League and a few other opposition parties did not participate on the question of the CTG. Khaleda Zia became Prime Minister for the second consecutive term. At the same time, demand for the CTG became intense. Heeding to public demand, Begum Zia enacted the 13th Amendment to the Constitution for a free, fair and participatory election to be conducted by a neutral caretaker government. This was a historical turning point in that she, as the head of the government, undertook with a view to institutionalizing the democracy in its primary task of establishing fair and neutral elections in the country. The Prime Minister immediately handed over the power to the newly constituted Caretaker Government on 30th March 1996. In the election held on 12 June 1996, the Awami League formed the government.

In the October of 2001, general elections under Justice Latifur Rahman-led Caretaker Government, the BNP-led four-party alliance won two-third majority and Begum Zia became Prime Minister for the third time.

Economic Reforms:

This time round, the Prime Minister gave special attention to financial sectors. She undertook a series of economic reforms aimed at liberalizing the economy and enhancing foreign investment. Market was made free and private sector expanded with further incentives. With the grant of 100 percent foreign ownership and unlimited joint venture projects, foreign investment grew manifold. Value added tax (VAT) made the economy strong. The foreign exchange reserve reached an all-time high and the rate of inflation was all-time low.

In addition, the following are some of Begum Zia's far reaching administrative initiatives:

1. Re-introduction of the canal digging program that was suspended during the previous non-BNP administrations. The canal digging program was aimed at enhancing agriculture products and reducing floods;
2. Distribution of voter ID cards among the voters;
3. Establishment of Coast Guard for containing piracy and smuggling in the Bay of Bengal;
4. Creation of Securities and Exchange Commission (SEC) for the efficient functioning of the country's stock market;
5. Lifelong family pension for widows;
6. Entry level in Government service increased from 27 to 30 years;
7. A new Export Processing Zone (EPZ) was set up in the Adamjee Jute Mills compound, Narayanganj;
8. For the environmental conservation in the country, CNG-driven 4-stroke Baby Taxis were introduced on the roads in place of two stroke diesel driven. Also, harmful polythene bags were withdrawn from the country (Banglapedia, op. cit).

Thus, discussing her tremendous contributions to various spheres of the country's development in a single paper is almost impossible. As such, I may confine myself to the education sector during her three terms as Prime Minister. I was honored to be part of the sector as a state minister under her wise guidance.

Primary Education System:

The key component of a country's socio-economic development is education. To focus on the desired vision of a life, education is an indispensable element. For mental growth of children, as well as to build them as good citizens, every developed nation gives due importance to the education sector. Constitution of Bangladesh ensures it. Article 17 narrates the importance of the citizens' access to education.

And in education, Primary Education is the foundation. To enhance the development of human resources in a densely populated country like Bangladesh, the primary education is essential. To address primary education as a fundamental right of citizens, to make it valuable, useful as well as to expand literacy campaign, a separate division called Primary Mass Education Division (PMED) was established in 1992. It was elevated to a full ministry in 2003, known as Ministry of Primary and Mass Education (MoPME).

Begum Khaleda Zia's Government made Primary Education compulsory for everyone. To facilitate education for the poor children, she inaugurated a new concept in 1993, known as "Food for Education" program. The program was aimed at increasing primary enrollment and attendance and, at the same time, reducing dropouts.

International Food Policy Research Institute (IFPRI) revealed that within a one-year period of the introduction of the project, enrollment in Primary Education increased by 20.4%, attendance increased by 14.7% and the drop-out rate decreased by 7.6%. One-fourth of the country was covered and about two million children belonging to poor families (40%) benefited from the program (Ref: World Data on Education, 6th Edition, 2006/07).

Later this program (Food for Education) was changed to a "Stipend for Primary Education." Under this program, a poor family received Taka 100/- per month if there was one school-going child and a family having more than one school-going child got 125/- Taka. This program was financed from Begum Zia's own government resources, and it became the largest single project in the history of Bangladesh. There was a time when poor students never dreamt of enjoying or having the opportunity to go to school. Usually, such children spent their time in helping their parents for their livelihoods. With this program, children from poor and neglected families had the benefit of the light of education.

Between 2001 to 2006, Begum Zia personally looked over the primary Education Ministry. According to the 2005 Poverty Reduction Strategy Paper (PRSP), the goal was to create an opportunity for unified and common primary education for all children. The paper also set a target of 100 percent enrollments in the primary level. Gross enrollment rates increased by 97.90 percent in the year 2005, and the dropout rate was drastically reduced from 47.20 percent to 20.90 percent. Gender parity was achieved. Also, the pass rate of grade five completion examinations was significantly raised to 92.30 percent (World Bank, 2014). This initiative marked as a stepping-stone for the present and recent past history. It was also appreciated domestically and internationally. Her government took all the necessary steps like infrastructure, teaching privilege, necessary education materials and, above all, development of education to reach the desired goal.

In the context of Bangladesh, "Non formal education policy 2006" led by Begum Zia's Ministry of Primary and Mass Education, her favorite, was designed to meet the learning needs of educationally disadvantaged families. It was made flexible in terms of organization, time and place, and covered the basic literacy such as life skills, lifelong learning facilities, and the enhancement of earning capabilities for poverty reduction. As such, the program that took place in the country during President Zia's administration with the slogan of "Each One Teach One" got back its momentum in Begum Zia's administration, while each Secondary School Certificate (SSC) candidate had to take part in teaching one illiterate adult how to sign his or her name.

Prime Minister Khaleda Zia attended the International Children's Conference in May 2002, during the 27th special session of the UN General Assembly. At the conference, the Prime Minister announced that "You will find Bangladesh in the forefront of efforts to give our children the best possible first start in life."

Secondary and Higher Education:

During Begum Zia's tenure, a double shift started in many schools and many new teaching posts were created. A new assessment system for SSC examinations was also introduced in 1992. The secondary school curriculum was revised, a new teacher training institute was built, ten teachers training colleges were upgraded, and five new higher teacher training institutes were established. Under the Secondary Education Sector Improvement Project (SESIP), a School Performance-Based Management System (SPBMS) was developed. Currently SSC and HSC examinations are administered and monitored by 11 boards, out of which four -- Barisal, Chattogram, Dinajpur, Sylhet--were established during 2001-2006, that was Begum Zia's third term.

Female secondary scholarship program (FESP) started in 1992 with the support of Norwegian Agency for Development (NORAD). This stipend program continued from July 1992 to December 1996, and the project has been described as highly successful. Based on the success, the Government launched, in January 1994, a nationwide stipend program for the girls in secondary schools (Grade 6 to 10) in 460 Upazillas (Sub-Districts) with the support of the World Bank, Asian Development Bank, and NORAD. This program was called "Female Stipend Program," which extended up to Grade 12 during Begum Zia's third term (FSSP 2003). She made a commitment to the nation that she would raise this program up to degree level in her next term if she came to power again. Furthermore, to continue her extended support to the girls, Feni Girls Cadet College in Chittagong Division and Joypurhat Girls Cadet College in Rajshahi Division were built in her third term of the government. Other records of her government are what as follows:

> 1. Copying in SSC and HSC examinations was a very common but serious practice in the country after independence. Numerous policies had been taken by the previous administrations to stop this detrimental cheating virus, but without much success. During Khaleda Zia's time, this copying menace in examinations was completely rooted out with a view to strengthening the quality of education.

2. "Leakage of Question Paper" was another serious issue in the country. Khaleda Zia set up a record in that there was not a single instance of leakage during her tenures.

3. She established another unique record in the history of Bangladesh by distributing free books to the children on every New Year Day.

Public institutions have played a key role in facilitating higher education in Bangladesh. Currently, there exist several types of higher education institutions, such as, General and Specialized Universities, Medical Colleges, Bangladesh Institute of Technologies (BITs), Institute of Postgraduate Medicine and Research (IPGMR), Institute of Postgraduate Studies in Agriculture (IPSA). In addition, colleges offer degrees under an affiliating national university.

Private Universities:

Earlier in 1991-96, the BNP government approved a total of 16 private universities. During her third tenure (2001-2006), Begum Zia established a total of 38 private universities:six in 2001, thirteen in 2002, fourteen in 2003, two in 2004 and three in 2006.

From the 1990s, higher education in private sector proliferated concurrently. In order to meet the challenge in this private sector, Private University Act 1992 was enacted. Its broad-based objectives were:

1. To extend a penetrating higher education in the society.
2. To facilitate the access of the general public to higher education.
3. To create a class of skilled workforce.
4. To Specify administrative responsibilities relating to colleges.
5. To modernize and improve the syllabi and curricula for graduate and the post graduate levels,
6. To raise the qualitative standard of education and training.
7. To improve the efficiency of teachers.

Education in the Engineering & Technology Sector

During her third term as Prime Minister (2001-2006), Begum Zia created another important milestone in the higher technical education.

Under a new Act, she ordered transformation of all the BITs into Engineering Universities. These were:

1. Rajshahi Engineering University.
2 Khulna Engineering University.
3. Chittagong Engineering University.
4. Dhaka Engineering University (The first public university).

In addition, she renamed the Islamic University (IU) to Islamic University of Technology (IUT) and inaugurated it in November 2001. Earlier, the IU was set up by President Ziaur Rahman in 1979.

The BNP government under Begum Zia, established the Khulna University (KU) in 1991 and two special universities in 1992. The other is Bangladesh Open University (BOU) for continuing education along with job, business and domestic responsibilities. In total, Begum Zia's administration in 2001-2006 established ten universities that included four engineering universities, three general universities, and three specialized universities for veterinary, agriculture, and science and technology. Moreover, Begum Zia's government played a key role in establishing the Asian University for Women (AUW) in Chittagong.

Reforms in the Education Sector:

In the beginning of her third term, Prime Minister Begum Zia formed an Expert Education Committee to identify immediate implementable reforms in the education sectors of the country. It was headed by Dr M Abdul Bari. Several recommendations of the Bari Committee were reconsidered in the Education Commission of 2003 headed by Mohammad Moniruzzaman Mia. While the Bari Committee was of limited objective, the Mia Commission had a much wider TOR. The initiative got momentum when the BNP government passed the Private University Act in 1992. North South University (NSU) got the permission to offer degree level courses in November 1992 and was inaugurated by Prime Minister Begum Zia in February 1993.

Reforms in Madrasah Education:

The word "Madrasah" literally means 'a place of learning,' it refers to a specific type of religious school or college. The number of teachers in these madrasahs is 1,14,033 of which only 12.67 percent were female teachers, Begum Zia's government tried to increase the quota for female teachers to 30% in the Madrasah system (Khandker, Pitt and Fuwa, 2003). Of late, her government had been working to modernize Madrasah education in order to improve the quality of education in the Alia madrasahs. Also, a project was undertaken to establish 100 Madrasahs in the country, which are known as Technical Madrasahs. As a result of this recognition from the government, the graduates from madrasahs enjoy the same opportunity to continue schooling at mainstream higher educational institutions (Asadullah, Chakrabarti, and Chaudhury, 2010). Later, in 2006, the government recognized Fazil and Kamil as equivalent to a graduate degree and a postgraduate degree respectively under Ismalic University, Kushtia (BEI, 2011). Due to this equivalent status, the graduates of Alia madrasahs can continue their education in colleges and universities and join in the mainstream job market.

In contrast, Qawmi madrasas are mostly privately run. Many non-governmental institutions are involved in the promotion of the Qawmi madrasahs affiliated with the *Deobandi* faith. Her government led by the BNP decided to acknowledge the Qawmi madrasah education in 2006.

Technical and Vocational Education and Training (TVET):

Begum Khaleda Zia's Government, immediately after assumption of office gave due importance to technical & vocational education and training. Bangladesh is the country that has a comparative advantage in the production of labor-intensive goods and services. Populations in the most developed nations are declining; on the other hand, Bangladesh has now become the most densely populated country in the world. In the recent decades, foreign remittance has become one of the main sources of economic growth and development. The remittance would be higher with the same number of expatriates if the work force were provided with quality TVET. Basically, TVET is the mirror of the double role of education and training for social and economic development. Therefore, developing human resources can be a viable proposition to meet industrial demands. Also, for comparative advantage, skilled manpower needs to be developed through TVET. Semi-skilled and unskilled workers constitute around 70 percent (Asian Development Bank 2015) of the Bangladeshi workers working overseas, who sent $15.31 billion as remittance (Bangladesh Business News 2015). The World Bank ranked Bangladesh as the 8th on the list of the world's top ten remittance recipients (The Financial Express 2014).

In 2001-2006 the number of public TVET institutions increased from 143 to 186. In terms of encouraging private initiatives, the number of private TVET institutions increased from 994 to 2987 (around 200 percent). (Source: Bangladesh Education Statistics 2015). Effective steps were taken for promoting vocational education. Existing vocational institutions were upgraded into colleges, and a project was taken to build 64 polytechnic institutes in 64 districts including old 18 districts. Also, for gender parity in technical education, Chittagong Mohila Polytechnic Institute and Khulna Mohila Polytechnic institute also were established in 2005.

Towards the Benefit of Teachers:

The secondary school system in Bangladesh is a combination of public and private partnerships. The monthly payment order (MPO) for the teachers started in 1979 with 50 percent of their salary during the time of President Ziaur Rahman. From 1981 to 2001, it increased up to 80 percent. During Begum Khaleda Zia's third term, it increased up to 95 percent as a salary from the government to the non-government schools and colleges. Rest of the 5 percent was given during the caretaker government of 2007-08. Recruitment of teachers and employees of non-Government schools, colleges and madrasas used to be handled by the management committee and was also influenced by the local politicians. As a result, quality and talented candidates are deprived. According to the statistics from the boards, certain clusters (divisions) are over saturated with regards to establishing new academic institutions. But to create employment, new institutions were built and finally the government had to take the burden of paying their salary (MPO).

Aiming the problem, Begum Khaleda Zia's Government took a distinctive decision to form an organization, named NTRCA (Non-Government Teachers Recruitment Certificate Authority) established in 2005, under the Ministry of Education. The mandate of registering and certifying quality and competent people who can be appointed as teachers in non-government educational institutions and to impact pedagogical skill and training to them in order to improve the quality of education. Though the registration examination is a transparent way, the promising talented candidates shall enter into the quality teaching pool. This in the public and private sector, the academic institution becomes homogeneous in the teacher recruitment. So during her time establishment of the Non-Government Teacher Recruitment Certificate Authority has grown hope and high aspirations in the society that the quality teachers would now be required in the non-government educational institute.

Non-Government Teacher Welfare Retirement Benefit:

Education is considered as the backbone of a nation. Begum Khaleda Zia's Government always valued the teachers. But the non-government teacher did not have the provision for any type of retirement allowance. To extend her gratitude to the non-government teachers, she introduced on 1st December 2002, Non-Government Teacher Welfare Retirement Benefit program. There was no provision for the non-government teachers to have any allowance for the festivals. During her 3rd term she introduced the festival allowance for non-government teachers allocating initially by 25% of their salary to the teachers and 50% for the government employees. It was supposed to be raised later, but till today it has remained the same.

Women's Empowerment:

Bangladesh is the only country in the world today where women hold all these three top positions: Leader of the Parliament, Leader of the

Opposition, and the Speaker of the Parliament. A holistic or comprehensive approach to sustainability is one of the most important ways to support and maintain gender justice and equality. Begum Khaleda Zia believes that rights and opportunities are mandatory themes that should be equally extended to all, further reminding us that true gender equality is still a long way off. Because of her serious initiatives, Bangladeshi women in recent decades have advanced considerably in terms of education, equality, employment and empowerment. More girls now attend primary and secondary schools and public examinations, and the girls often outperform boys academically.

Under the Female Stipend Program, an increasing number of adolescent girls attend Secondary Schools in the rural areas, resulting in a significant drop in the child marriage. President Ziaur Rahman established the Ministry for Women's affairs in 1978. He encouraged both the NGOs and the government agencies to undertake programs for empowerment of women, raised the number of parliamentary seats reserved for women from 15 to 30 (from 5% to 10%), and reserved 10% of all public sector jobs for women. Following her husband's lead, Begum Zia enacted the 14th amendment to the constitution in May 2004 to increase the number of reserve seats for women in the parliament from 30 to 45 (from 10% to 15%).

On the whole, Begum Zia was committed to strengthening gender equality and gender parity in Bangladesh. This is the foundation upon which woman's advancement must rest. Acid attacks on women in Bangladesh have been growing at an alarming rate. Her Government introduced the Acid Offence Prevention Act 2002 to control acid crimes. Laws, namely, the Acid Crime Control Act and the Acid Control Act aimed to control acid use and prevent acid violence. Through these acts, the government wanted to ensure legal justice for the victims. The acts showed that the government was also committed to eradicating the acid violence. In addition, Repression of Women and Children Act 2003 prohibited the trafficking of women and children for the purpose of commercial and sexual exploitation. Penalties under this sex trafficking statute ranged from ten-year imprisonment to death penalty.

Bangladesh's Penal Code prohibits forced labor. Begum Zia reinforced the law. The legendary and Nobel prize winner Mother Teresa praised Begum Khaleda Zia for her social works. She further apprised the Bangladesh Prime Minister of her own social works being done by her own organization, the Calcutta-based Missionaries of Charity, to serve the poor in various countries (Vaccine Weekly; United States, Atlanta-May 8, 1995). The report further said that Begum Zia assured all possible help when Mother Teresa requested for land and other facilities to build a rehabilitation center for leprosy and AIDS in Bangladesh. (NewsRx, Atlanta-May 8, 1995).

Conclusion:

Begum Khaleda Zia was the first in Bangladesh and the second in the Muslim world as a woman Prime Minister. She was the first Muslim woman to address in the United Nations General Assembly as an elected head of the government (Crossette, 1993). Like Shahid President Ziaur Rahman, Begum Zia has a most resolute and deepest affection for the country. She holds the banner of ideas of President Zia and is very committed to completing the unfinished works of her husband.

Her devotion and sacrifice for the nation is and was unparalleled. She received the reciprocal response from the noble aspirations of the people of the country. She believes in and worked for democracy, freedom of expression, freedom of religion, free press, guarantees of justice, human rights and economic development. She bonded herself with her motherland since 1971 from the liberation war. Now she is 75 and she was elected three times as the Prime Minister of Bangladesh, through free, fair and impartial elections.

She is perhaps the only woman leader in Bangladesh who never lost in national elections. Until recently, she was in jail. It was not her first time; she was in jail on 2nd July, 1971; 28th November, 1983; 3rd May, 1984; 10th November, 1987; 2nd September, 2007; and this is the 6th time on 8th February, 2018; now she has been released conditionally for six months through executive order of the government. Her struggle for democracy continues for the nation and it creates an immense aspiration for the future generation of Bangladesh. She is ready to sacrifice her life for the best interest of the country. She never dreams to be in power politics by collateralizing the country and making the undue beneficiaries happy, contrary to the wills of the citizens of the country. For her, the country comes first. She is a charismatic politician of Bangladesh who can draw the biggest crowd wherever she goes like a pied piper. Her leadership can be taken as a model in many countries in the world to follow.

As a State Minister for Education in her cabinet, I had the privilege to work under her. With utmost patriotism, she would remain a model for nationalism, and above everything else, she would remain an icon of democracy for the People's Republic of Bangladesh. Despite human limitations, because of her determination and fearlessness against all odds, Begum Zia remains a lighthouse for the Bangladeshis in fighting for their sovereignty, independence, dignity, humanity, democracy rights, and social justice. And the nation extended to her its unwavering support in these endeavors. The conspirators are still thinking to minus Begum Zia from Bangladesh politics. If they become successful, they would be able to thwart the nation's march towards democracy and economic emancipation. Every concerned citizen should collectively halt this minus formula for the nation's bright future.

References:

Asadullah, M. N., Chakrabarti, R., & Chaudhury, N. (2015). "What determines religious school choice? Theory and evidence from rural Bangladesh." *Bulletin of Economic Research, 67* (2), 186-207.

Barbara Crossette (1993). *Conversations: Khaleda Zia; A Woman Leader for a Land That Defies Islamic Stereotypes*, New York Times. *Retrieved from* https://www.nytimes.com/

Khandker, S., Pitt, M., & Fuwa, N. (2003). Subsidy to promote girls' secondary education: the female stipend program in Bangladesh. https://www.banglapedia.org/

Vaccine Weekly; United States, Atlanta-May 8, 1995. NewsRx, Atlanta.

Asian Development Bank (2015).

Bangladesh Business News (2015).

The Financial Express (2014).

https://asian-university.org/who-we-are/history/

Chapter 6

Begum Khaleda Zia: Her Eviction from Home and Imprisonment -- Hasina's Ugly Exposure of Zia-Phobia!

R Chowdhury

Begum Khaleda Zia, Chairperson of the Bangladesh Nationalist Party (BNP) and Leader of the Opposition in the Parliament, was thrown out her cantonment residence on November 13, 2010 in full media glare. Watching the drama in the television, her ouster did not seem a peaceful one, nor was it a voluntary action, as claimed by the Inter Service Public Relations (ISPR). Dozens were wounded in the police-public clash on the issue. Distressed but undaunted Begum Zia told the reporters that security forces had broken her front door and dragged her out of her home. "They entered my bedroom and ransacked all the furniture," she added. "They even beat my personal staff."[1] She was a three-term Prime Minister.

The ISPR press release on the issue left much to be desired and many questions remained unanswered. As the concurrent Defense Minister, Prime Minister Sheikh Hasina Wazed controls the ISPR. No wonder she was seen enjoying a Nero's grin when her archenemy was being publicly humiliated.

The way the judiciary, administration and Awami cadres played with the issue, it appeared that this was a crisis of the highest order that must be resolved immediately if the nation were to survive! Yet, some top Ministers and Awami stalwarts shrugged at the final episode to feign that it was a judicial matter and the government had nothing to do in its process. Borrowing a line from Abraham Lincoln, I may say the Hasina administration might fool all the people some of the time and some of the people all the time, but it could fool all the people all the time. Members of the public knew on whose direction those actions were taken. They were also not unaware of the partisan credentials of the learned judges who gave the verdict on the issue. They had no ambiguity about the loyalty of the Law Minister and the Attorney General, as well as the enthusiasm of the Home Minister.

Then Brigadier-General Ziaur Rahman was allocated House No. 6 on Shaheed Moinul Road in the Dhaka Cantonment after he took over as the Deputy Chief of the Army Staff in June 1972. He continued to stay in that house when he became the army chief in 1975, and when he retired as Lieutenant General to become the President in 1977. Ziaur Rahman was killed in 1981, and his bereaved family was allowed to stay in the house under a government order. Later, President Hussain Muhammad Ershad granted the ownership of the house to Begum Khaleda Zia, as a token of the nation's love, respect and gratitude to the assassinated president. Begum Zia and her family had been living in the house for nearly four decades. Nobody ever raised any question about its validity or legality.

However, things changed when Sheikh Hasina Wazed started her second inning in the helm of Bangladeshi affairs in January 2009. It looked as if her singular mission this time was to destroy Zia's image and Zia's family. (Also read Hasina's Zia Phobia[2])

Mystery still shrouds the assassination of President Ziaur Rahman on May 31, 1981. Zia was leading Bangladesh to a self-assertive road, much to the discomfort of India, which invested so heavily in its materialization before, during and after 1971. India always desired that Bangladesh would be integrated with its northeastern region for political, economic and strategic advantages. Zia posed a big challenge in that design. Most analysts, therefore, believed that the RAW (Research and Analysis Wing---the CIA of India) had a hand in Zia's killing. They also suspected the connivance of India-trained then Army Chief Lieutenant General H M Ershad. Major General M A Manzur, then Chittagong Area Commander, was made a scapegoat in the conspiracy and gunned down before he could talk. Days earlier, Zia had allowed Sheikh Hasina to return from her self-exile in India. Intriguingly, Hasina was caught trying to flee to Agartala in India following Zia's assassination![3]

The Awami League and its sponsors/supporters tried to eliminate Ziaur Rahman. But over two million people gathered at his funeral, an unprecedented event in Bangladesh! That spoke of the love and respect Zia the man and leader commanded from the people of Bangladesh.

Circumstances forced Begum Khaleda Zia to join politics and carry her the late husband's mission forward. However, Ershad and Hasina jointly connived to thwart that. In his book *Democracy and the Challenge of Development*, Maudud Ahmed tells of the 'box of crores' from Ershad to Hasina as stated by Sheikh Selim, Hasina's cousin.[4] That made Khaleda an "Uncompromising Leader" in the face of all odds, repeated humiliations and harassments by the Ershad regime. During the elections in 1991, following the ouster of Ershad, Ziaur Rahman, the former leader, became the issue. Everywhere people sang: জিয়া তুমি আছো মিশে, সারা বাংলার ধানের শীষে ! (You are embodied in every sheaf of paddy, Zia!). Sheaf of Paddy was the election symbol of Zia's BNP, presently led by his able wife Khaleda. The emotional slogan created magic in peoples' hearts and they overwhelmingly voted the BNP. Hasina's anti-Zia slogans and activities boomeranged.

In 1996, Sheikh Hasina managed to win a majority and formed the government, thanks to helping hands from the Election Commission (CEC Abu Hena being an Awami supporter), a section of bureaucracy and media. An ever-active RAW was behind them all. Sheikh Hasina spent much of her energy during her first administration fulfilling her two oft-quoted promises: rehabilitating the image of her father Sheikh Mujibur Rahman and hanging his killers. She largely succeeded in her dual missions. At the same time, she tried to demean, defame and obliterate everything Zia, Khaleda or the BNP did or stood for. The public response was shown in the rejection of Sheikh Hasina in the next election in 2001.

In the elections to be held in January 2007, Sheikh Hasina saw that the BNP-led alliance was heading for another victory. She could not allow it. She started an all-out destructive activity, at a huge loss of men and materials, to foil the election, on one pretext or the other. That gave the pretext to Army Chief, General Moeen U Ahmad, to betray the nation. In a palace coup, he replaced the existing neutral Caretaker Government (CTG)--charged to hold elections-- with one of his choosing, declared emergency and ran a martial law-type administration for the next two years. According to most analysts, it was a pre-arranged conspiracy by India to subjugate Bangladesh, as the subsequent developments testify. New Delhi tagged along the US, the UN and other major players on the false premise of preventing Dhaka from going the Islamic fundamentalist way, a Western phobia. Bangladesh lost its sovereignty to India from that time.

A stooge of India, General Moeen did not make any secret of his admiration for Sheikh Mujibur Rahman and preference for Awami League, destructive dictatorship of Mujib and the oppressive fascism of his daughter Hasina notwithstanding. Nor did he hide his dislike of the BNP, which installed him as the Army Chief in the first place, superseding a few seniors on the recommendation of his old pal Major Sayeed Eskandar, brother of Khaleda. Royal-style treatment and a cavalry gift to Moeen in New Delhi point to an underhanded horse trade. It was widely believed that the Moeen-backed caretaker administration had worked to see Hasina's Awami League win the election they masterminded in December 2008, a fact later publicly admitted by Hasina's newfound "brother" and Jote partner, Ershad. Former Indian President Pronob Mukherjee also revealed it in his book *The Coalition Years, 1996-2012* (2017, Kolkata) of an Indian collusion with the Moeen-led CTG to ensure a Hasina victory in the next election.[5]

Securely settled in power and backed by her sponsors, Hasina started a crusade to demolish Zia, his family and the BNP. While she nullified over 7,000 cases, ranging from corruption to murder, against her and her own party members, she not only strengthened those cases against the BNP and opposition leaders filed by Moeen's CTG, but also continued to add, almost on a daily basis, new cases against them. Flimsy and unsubstantiated cases kept adding against Khaleda and her two sons, Tarek Zia and Arafat Zia. All of them were finally taken to custody. The younger Zias received inhuman torture in the hands of Moeen's goons. They had to be sent abroad for treatment. The administration of Hasina has been issuing daily warnings to the effect that these two Zia-sons would be sent to the torture cells again if they dared to return home, surely serving punishing mental doses to the mother. Arafat had already succumbed to the aftereffects of torture in Bangkok in January 2015. Tarek is still recuperating in London.

Zia's name has been removed from the Dhaka International Airport after 30 years, his murals destroyed wherever they appeared, nameplates bearing his name taken off every public place. Even there was a muted conspiracy to dismantle his Mazaar near the Sangsad Bhaban. Zia's successful presidency---which stood in stark contrast to Mujib's repressive and failed administration in 1972-1975---has been wiped off the history books of Bangladesh by re-writing the constitution, thanks to a compliant judiciary. That was not all. Awami leaders "discovered" Zia to be an agent of Pakistan during the liberation war of Bangladesh in 1971![6]

Yet Hasina could not feel safe with a free Khaleda, who drew huge loyal crowds whenever she was open in the public. Partisan and loyal investigators and prosecutors, and a compliant judiciary connived to sentence the elderly and ailing Opposition Leader to a 17-year solitary confinement on a flimsy and unsubstantiated charge. She faces about three dozen more similar made-to-order cases that may fetch a few hundred years for Khaleda with Hasina's wrath-filled going rate.

Meanwhile, Covid-19 brought a temporary relief to the jailed former Prime Minister. Hasina feared if her nemesis became a victim of the Pandemic in custody, she would not be able to handle it. In end March (2020), Khaleda was sent from jail confinement to "house arrest." The release order said, the Executive Order was "temporary" and "restricted." She could not seek better treatment outside the country. Nor could she involve in politicking.

Evicting Khaleda Zia from her residence of four decades and sending her to suffer jail terms for no fault of her own are a few examples of Hasina's Zia-phobia. Lately, she and her Awami sycophants are engaged in a futile attempt to divert the public attention from mounting crises the nation faces by implicating President Ziaur Rahman in the coup of August 15, 1975 and Jail Killing on November 3, 1975. Their claim is based on an interview given by Captain Abdul Majed on death row. It was said to have been obtained on a promise of "pardon" or commuting the "death" to "life." Once done, Majed was led to the gallows for involvement in the coup, in which Hasina's father Sheikh Mujib died.

Political observers and analysts, who researched on the August coup, dismissed the claim outright. Zia was under house arrest when the jail killing took place. However, living in Hasina's Bangladesh, few can open their mouths under strict censorship, more so, for fear of their lives. But online sources are galore to tell the truth.

Science teaches us, "Every action has an equal and opposite reaction." That theory has been found working in politics too. In the case of Zia, to defame or demonize him and his family had always seen the overwhelmingly opposite effect among the people.

Sohrab Hassan, an editor of Prothom Alo says: "The opposition can be silenced with the threat of cases. The media's voice can be curbed with the Digital Security Act. But not law, no case and no threat can silence the voices of the common people."[7]

---

[1] https://www.bbc.com/news/world-south-asia-11751417

[2] http://newsfrombangladesh.net/view.php?hidRecord=305937, or https://defence.pk/pdf/threads/hasinas-zia-phobia.47771/)

[3] "*Amar Phasi Chai*" by Motiur Rahman Rentu, 1996, Dhaka. Motiur Rahman, one-time close aide of Sheikh Hasina, gave some insight into the conspiracy theory in the Zia-assassination.

[4] *Democracy and the Challenge of Development* by Maudud Ahmad, University Press, Dhaka 1995.

[5] https://countercurrents.org/2017/11/pranab-mukherjee-tells-it-all/

[6] Read "Ziaur Rahman: A Pakistani Spy!" *Facts, Not Fiction* by Rashed Chowdhury, 2017 Amazon.

[7] http://aequitasreview.org/bangladesh-the-awami-league-doesnt-seem-to-have-any-answers-by-sohrab-hassan/.

Chapter 7

Begum Khaleda Zia: Her State-Building Strategies and Policies

Syed Serajul Islam

Introduction

In 1990, after the overthrow of the military regime of General H M Ershad, the Bangladesh Nationalist Party (BNP) got a landslide victory in a general election held in 1991. The party leader Begum Khaleda Zia was sworn in as the first woman prime minister of Bangladesh. She was only the second female Prime Minister, after Pakistan's Benazir Bhutto, in the Muslim majority countries of the world. The second time Khaleda Zia became Prime Minister was in 1996. However, it was only a two-month long short-lived government because, as a great democratic leader believing in the process and institutionalization of democracy, she gave up power to promote democracy and achieve peace, national unity, tolerance and understanding. With those noble and lofty goals in mind, she introduced the historic measure of interim Care-Taker Government (CTG) for the sake of participatory elections and peaceful transition of power—a measure that was later fascistically cancelled by the Hasina regime in 2011. The third term she became Prime Minister was in 2001 and continued until 2006. During her tenures her government made immense contribution to the society, economy and politics of Bangladesh. This chapter is primarily designed to discuss her contributions during her three terms as Prime Minister of Bangladesh.

Prime Minister Khaleda Zia's First Term in Office (1991-1996)

Until 1991 the existing system of Bangladesh was a Presidential system of Government. There was a demand to replace the presidential system with a parliamentary system. Immediately after the election in 1991 in the *Jatiya Sangsad* (parliament) Khaleda Zia initiated the historic 12th constitutional amendment bill on 6 August 1991 to introduce the parliamentary form of government replacing the presidential system. The bill was passed unanimously and consequently, on September 19, 1991, she took oath as the Prime Minister of Bangladesh under the new parliamentary system.

Khaleda Zia's government achieved massive success in many areas during her first term (1991-1996). It was only thirty-nine days after she became the prime minister that many areas of southern Bangladesh were hit by one of the worst cyclones and tidal waves of the 20th century. Despite acute shortage of relief and rehabilitation materials, she handled the calamities quite efficiently.

During her first term, a major contribution was in the education sector. Primary education was not free and compulsory in the country. She is the one who introduced free and compulsory primary education in Bangladesh. She also made education for girls' tuition free up to Grade 10, the end of High School system in Bangladesh. Also, she introduced stipend for the secondary level female students throughout the country. She initiated a "Food for Education" program in 1993 to promote education among the poor people of Bangladesh. Her government made the highest allocation for the education sector during the Fourth Five Year Plan (1990-95) period. Under the auspices of the Office of the Prime Minister, the government created a separate Primary and Mass Education Division in order to accelerate the literacy rate among the masses. To enhance the country's higher education the Khaleda government set up a National University and an Open University and also allowed the establishment of private universities and medical colleges in the country.

Another major contribution of the Khaleda government was in the industrial sector. In 1991she declared a new industrial policy paving the way for private foreign investments. Her government also introduced a rapid expansion of the private sector, particularly, in the subsector of small and medium enterprises. Without any restrictions, hundred percent foreign ownership and joint ventures were allowed in Bangladesh. Simultaneously, there were massive cutbacks on custom duties at the import level as part of the free-market trade liberalization policy of the government.

For the first time in Bangladesh the local currency was made partially convertible. Consequently, foreign exchange reserve reached an all-time high level in the country. Many measures were taken to reduce dependence on foreign aid for the country's development. The Government increased the share of local resources in its budget from 21 percent to over 40 percent in five years.[1] During 1993-94 fiscal year value added tax (VAT) was introduced for the first time in the country at production and import level. That created a way to generate new revenue for the government.

To boost up the agricultural production and reduce floods, her government reintroduced the canal digging program that was initially introduced by her husband President Zia. Farmers were not having water due to Farakka and Teesta barrages built by India. In her address to the United Nations General Assembly in 1993, she highlighted the problem thus:

> While we are assembled here to celebrate the founding of this august body, over 40 million people in my country are facing poverty and destruction owing to deprivation of our rightful share of the waters of the Ganges River by India through unilateral withdrawal at Farakka. While withdrawal of water during the dry season causes serious drought, the release of excess water during the rainy season creates severe floods in a vast area of Bangladesh. Besides the colossal loss in economic terms, this is causing serious degradation to the environment and to the ecology. The Farakka Barrage has become an issue of life and death for us. Owing to obstruction of the natural flow of water upstream, a process of desertification is evident throughout the northern and western parts of Bangladesh. Vegetation is dwindling, salinity is spreading in the south, threatening industry and agriculture with ruin. Fish

and animal resources are facing extinction. Innumerable people of various occupations who depended on the River Padma for their living are becoming unemployed. Many are being uprooted from their homes and hearths. As the whole world voices concern for the protection of the environment and human rights, at that very moment a big part of the population of Bangladesh is being pushed over to the threshold of poverty and destruction. This is a gross violation of human rights and justice.[2]

(It is to be mentioned here that during her tenures, Khaleda Zia visited the United Nations five times to address the General Assembly sessions. Those speeches were very significant that highlighted her immense contribution to the various sectors of her country. She did not attend the 49th session of General Assembly held in 1994 but she attended the 50th session of 1995. Her second term lasted only for two months and therefore she had no address to the UN in 1996. She returned to power again in 2001 and then in 2002 she addressed the General Assembly.)

Also throughout Bangladesh, trees were becoming or growing less and less due to unfavorable weather and the people cutting them indiscriminately for residential and fuel purposes with no concern for the clean and green environment. Khaleda Zia during her tenure introduced a nationwide social movement for tree plantation. She also actively initiated a policy for the development of livestock sector. That led to the swift establishment of various poultry and dairy farms throughout Bangladesh. This not only contributed to the growth of chicken meats for the public but also contributed to the GDP and per capita income of the people in the country. In Bangladesh's history, initial work on Barapukuria Coal Mine and Madhyapara Hard Rock projects were completed for the first time. Agreements were signed with Chinese and Korean companies for full implementation of these projects. During Khaleda's time new gas fields were also discovered at Bhola and in the Bay of Bengal.

During the Khaleda government, some administrative measures were taken which made a significant contribution to the functioning of the government. Her government established the national pay commission for increasing the salaries and allowances of government employees. The Government implemented the recommendations of the commission by 1) increasing the age limit for entry in government service from 27 years to 30 years; 2) simplifying the pension-sanctioning procedure; 3) introducing life-long family pension for widows and children's in case of deaths of government employees; 4) fixing minimum wage for workers in several sectors; 5) establishing the Coast Guard for stopping piracy and smuggling in the Bay of Bengal; 6) creating a Security and Exchange Commission for looking after the country's stock market; and 7) also for the first time enacting a bill in parliament for distributing voter identity cards among the eligible citizens and launching a project for that. Another very important contribution of the Khaleda government was that she established a permanent Law Commission for continuous updating of laws in the country.

The Khaleda government made a significant progress in the communication sector as well. The road connection with the northern part of Bangladesh was blocked by long river, Jamuna. She started during her tenure the physical construction of the Jamuna Multipurpose Bridge in 1994. Her government started the construction of the Meghna-Gumati Bridge on the Dhaka-Chittagong Highway for uninterrupted road connection between Dhaka and Chittagong. The Government also started the construction of a modern railway station in Chittagong and undertook a project to upgrade Chittagong Airport into the second international airport of the country.

The Khaleda government opened up the free press. Consequently, this made the number of newspapers and periodicals nearly double. For the first time in the history of Bangladesh, satellite TV channels like CNN and BBC were allowed to broadcast their programs in the country and very soon other international channels followed. During her time also the cellular mobile telephone started its journey.

To strengthen regional cooperation among the South Asian countries, Khaleda Zia refreshed the South Asian Association for Regional Cooperation (SAARC) by hosting a summit in Dhaka in 1993. Earlier, President Zia, her husband, was the one who took the original initiative for establishing the SAARC. Prime Minister Khaleda Zia was elected chairperson of the regional forum of the SAARC. This greatly enhanced Bangladesh's international image.

The Khaleda government also showed exceptional political tolerance towards the political opposition parties. However, in 1994, the major opposition political parties---the Awami League (AL), the Jatiya Party, and the Jamaat-e- Islami--led a movement for a caretaker government for holding parliamentary elections and that disrupted the work of her Government during her first term. The pace of development could have been much higher had there not been the destructive stoppages and blockades staged by the opposition Awami League during her administration. Sheikh Hasina, the chief of AL, publicly declared that she would not allow Khaleda to govern in peace. The 173 days of Hartal (stoppage) with colossal damage to men and material were conducted only for the demand of Caretaker Government to oversee national elections. Ironically, once in power, the same AL quashed the Caretaker system to ensure its perpetuity in authority by managing the elections so that it can amass autocratic power and prolong its hanging on to authoritarian control.

There were hardly any complaints against the Khaleda government regarding politicization of administration. Although there were many countrywide strikes, blockades and other forms of disruptive activities by the opposition the Government maintained the law and order in smooth way.

Prime Minister Khaleda Zia's Second Term in Office (February 1996-March 1996)

On February 15, 1996 Khaleda Zia gave the election in which her party BNP emerged victorious and she became the prime minister for a second consecutive term. The major opposition parties, however, did not participate in the elections. They demanded the introduction a neutral caretaker government for conducting parliamentary elections.

To meet those demands, Khaleda Zia made a considerable contribution. In the parliament she introduced the 13th Amendment bill to the Constitution for adding a caretaker government. The bill was unanimously passed and the parliament was dissolved. Immediately after that, on March 30, 1996, Khaleda Zia handed over power to a caretaker government. Under the caretaker government headed by Justice Muhammad Habibur Rahman on June 12, 1996, the BNP was defeated by the Awami League and became the Opposition in the parliament under the leadership of Khaleda Zia.

Prime Minister Khaleda Zia's Third Term in Office (2001-2006)

A neutral caretaker government headed by Justice Latifur Rahman conducted the next parliamentary elections in 2001 in which the BNP-led four-party alliance won more than two-thirds of the seats in the parliament. Khaleda Zia was sworn-in as Bangladesh's Prime Minister for the third time on October 10, 2001. During the third term of Khaleda Zia as Prime Minister, Bangladesh achieved a high growth in socio-economic sectors and a gradual rise in foreign direct investments. In the country's history, average GDP growth rate during her whole period remained above 5 percent for the first time. Also, there was an increase in per capita national income which rose from $374 US dollar in 2000-01 to $482 US dollar in 2005-06.[3] There was a steep rise in remittances sent by expatriate workers from foreign countries. The foreign exchange reserve went up from a mere $1 billion dollar in 2001 to more than $ 5 billion dollar by 2006.[4]

In the industrial sector, there was a healthy growth. Although the Multi Fibre Arrangement quota system was abolished in 2005, the garments industries continued to progress due to the government's handling of the sector efficiently. Due to investment-friendly economic policies and strategies pursued by the government many foreign companies were attracted for investment in Bangladesh. Until March 2006 several thousand industrial projects were registered with the Board of Investment. In fact, this was more than double compared to the previous five years of Hasina regime. Consequently during 2005-2006, the contribution of the industrial sector to GDP exceeded 17 percent and the growth rate in the sector was more than 10 percent.[5] In 2004-2005, after paying all outstanding dues of officers and employees of this loss-incurring state-owned enterprise of Adamjee Jute Mills, the government established a new Export Processing Zone (EPZ) on that compound.

In the education sector the Khaleda government achieved a great success. In primary schools the enrolment rate went up to nearly hundred percent. Tuition fee for girl students was made free up to Grade 12 in order to obtain a gender parity among boys and girls in higher secondary education system. To increase further women education at higher levels two new girls' cadet colleges and three new polytechnic institutes for women were established. With the assistance from the USA a plan was also taken for establishing an Asian University for Women in Chittagong town. The Government opened a number of new public universities. Simultaneously, even the Government provided licenses to many new private universities. To expand higher education in the areas of science and technology, the Government took necessary steps for promoting vocational education, and thus, upgraded the existing vocational institutions into colleges. To modernize the Madrasa (religious) education system, the Khaleda government announced the Fazil-Kamil (Madrasa) degrees as equivalent to national bachelor's and master's degrees respectively. It also planned for recognizing the Dawra certificate of Qaumi madrasas (traditional religious institutions) in the near future.

In the healthcare services, the Khaleda government adopted various programs for creating infrastructural facilities to the doorsteps of the masses. The Government increased "the number of beds from 31 to 50 in *upazila* (sub-district) hospitals, from 50 to 100 in hospitals of new district towns, and from 100 to 250 in hospitals of greater district towns."[6] Side by side the Government established some new medical colleges and hospitals. Due to measures taken by the Government, infant and maternal mortality rates came down in the country. Due to strengthening of the family planning program the rate of population growth decreased to less than one and a half percent.[7]

Furthermore, the Khaleda government took some administrative measures. It established an Anti-Corruption Commission replacing the old Bureau of Anti-Corruption for strengthening the organization to make the country free from corruption. A new position, called the Tax Ombudsman, was created by her government. To improve the law and order situation her government established a new force, called Rapid Action Battalion (RAB) and initiated Operation Clean Heart. (Ironically, RAB/police are used by the authoritarian Hasina regime to oppress Khaleda Zia and her party BNP). The Government introduced a new national pay scale for government servants in 2005. To decentralize the administration further, her Government created some new Upazilas.

The Khaleda Zia government enhanced the communication sector significantly during her third term. The railway service via the Jamuna bridge was not initiated earlier. During this term, the railway service between the eastern and north-western part of the country via the Jamuna Bridge started. Additionally, many important road-bridges were constructed, such as, Fakir Lalon Shah (Pakshi) Bridge on the Padma, Shikarpur and Dwarika Bridges on Dhaka-Barisal highway, Haji Shariatullah Bridge over the river Arial Khan on Dhaka-Khulna highway, Khan Jahan Ali Bridge over the river Rupsha on Khulna-Mongla highway, Mollarhat Bridge over the river Madhumati, Dhaleshwari Bridge on Hemayetpur-Singair road, the second Buriganga Bridge at Babubazar, the Chandpur Bridge over the river Dakatia, the Fenchuganj Bridge over the Kushiara, and the Dharla Bridge on the Kurigram-Bhurungamari road. Another notable project was the construction of the Third Karnaphuli (Shah Amanat) Bridge in Chittagong which was undertaken with assistance from the Kuwait government. To improve communication between India and Bangladesh, direct bus service between Dhaka and Agartala started and a proposal for the direct railway link between Dhaka and Kolkata was processed during her term.

The Khaleda government also attached significant importance to the development of the telecommunication sector. The Government doubled the number of fixed telephones in the country. The Government set up digital telephone exchanges in all districts of Bangladesh and attempted to bring all sub-districts gradually under digital telephone network. During the third term of Khaleda the total number of fixed and mobile telephone connections in Bangladesh went to more than the one and a half crore. The Government gave licenses to several private companies to provide and make more accessible fixed-phone services to the people. At the same time, Tele-talk Bangladesh owned by the Government was also providing mobile phone services to the people. During her time the mobile phone services started its operation in Bangladesh. Through linking up with a submarine cable also the Government attempted to connect Bangladesh with the information superhighway. All this resulted in speeding up overseas communication and internet connections easier.

The Khaleda Zia government formulated a Poverty Reduction Strategy Paper as a medium-term plan document in correspondence with the Millennium Development Goals declared by the United Nations. Every year the budgetary allocation for poverty alleviation programs was gradually increased. A social safety net programs for direct poverty alleviation of hardcore and underprivileged people in the rural areas was initiated by the Khaleda government. A number of measures were adopted for the welfare of neglected areas and peoples of the country, such as in *Monga-infested* (famine-like state) northern region of Bangladesh, and in Char areas. It raised the monthly allowances of the widows, old age persons, and distressed women. The Government also made a plan for providing them with training and micro-credit in order to make them gradually self-reliant. As a result of all these policies, the population below poverty level in Bangladesh came down to a massive level during the Khaleda administration.

At the beginning of Khaleda's term the power generation capacity in the country was very low. Her Government set up a network of 89 thousand kilometers of new transmission lines for supplying electricity. Thus, system loss in the power sector was reduced from 28 per cent to 22 percent. Also, nearly 50 thousand villages came under the reach of rural electrification program.[8] The Khaleda government also took some important measures for environmental conservation in the country by withdrawing 20-year old buses and trucks, introducing CNG-driven 4-stroke baby taxis on the roads in place of 2-stroke diesel-driven ones, and banning the production and marketing of harmful polythene bags in Bangladesh.

During the third term, Prime Minister Khaleda Zia pursued a progressive and decisive foreign policy enhancing good neighborly relation with South Asian countries and promoting look–east policy. Khaleda Zia also carried the responsibility of South Asian Association of Regional Cooperation (SAARC) Chairperson after hosting the 2005 summit. Furthermore, Bangladesh became a member of the Association of Southeast Asian Nations Regional Forum (ASEAN-ARF). This was when

Bangladesh showed strict adherence to the United Nations Charter and got elected to a number of United Nations' bodies, such as, the United Nations Human Rights Council, Peace Building Commission and Economic and Social Council, etc. During her term Bangladesh began to involve more and more to the peaceful and negotiated settlement of international disputes and foreign peacekeeping forces by sending the highest number of troops to the United Nations Peacekeeping Missions. In her address to the UN General Assembly session in 2005, she said:

> We, in Bangladesh, are particularly proud of our contribution to peacekeeping on many simultaneous fronts across the globe. In all, we have contributed more than 39,000 troops to 24 missions and are currently among the largest contributors. Sixty-seven of our blue-helmeted soldiers have died in that cause. Our commitment to peacekeeping remains unflinching. We also fully support the establishment of the Peace building Commission. A priority concern for us is our close identity with Africa. Through our peacekeeping efforts, we have established special bonds of friendship.[9]

Conclusion

The above analysis indicates that Prime Minister Khaleda Zia achieved a lot of success in social, economic and political lives of Bangladesh. In an article in New York times, Barbara Crossette wrote on October 17, 1993, "at the World Bank, nobody calls Bangladesh a basket case any more. Although it still ranks among the least developed nations -- and is vulnerable to horrifying natural disasters -- the country outpaces much of Africa and a few Asian nations in certain measures of improved quality of life."[10] In 2006, American Business magazine *Forbes* commented that she had managed to promote strong GDP growth in her poverty stricken country.

As a prime minister, Khaleda Zia had immense contribution to the national development of the country. In her speeches to the UN, she expressed her concern for the establishment of democracy and promotion of human rights throughout the world. She pursued good neighborly relations with South Asian countries. However, she also expressed concern about India's attitude on sharing water with Bangladesh as the country has been severely affected by India's unilateral withdrawal of water from the Ganges river. During her terms, Bangladesh contributed to international peace force under the UN continuously and consistently. This was when Bangladesh showed strict adherence to the United Nations Charter and got elected to a number of United Nations bodies. The international media reported the tremendous progress achieved by Bangladesh during the Khaleda administrations.

---

[1] Helaluddin Ahmed, "Zia, Begum Khaleda," *Banglapedia,* December 21, 2015.

[2] Dag Hammarskjöld Library, UN, New York, Khaleda's Address to the *48th session of the General Assembly of the United Nations*, October 1, 1993

[3] Dag Hammarskjöld Library, UN, New York, Khaleda's Address to the *60th session of the General Assembly of the United Nations,* September 14, 2005. See also, *Banglapedia,* op.cit.

[4] *Ibid.*

[5] *Ibid.*

[6] *Ibid.*

[7] Ibid.

[8] *Banglapedia, op.cit.*

[9] Dag Hammarskjöld Library, UN, New York, Khaleda's Address to the *60th session of the General Assembly of the United Nations,* September 14, 2005.

[10] Barbara Crossette, "Khaleda Zia; A Woman Leader for a Land That Defies Islamic Stereotypes," *New York Times,* October 17, 1993.

Chapter 8

Begum Khaleda Zia: The Greatest Political Phenomenon of Bangladesh and the Hasina Regime's Smallest-Minded Semi-Release of Her from Long and Unjust Imprisonment

Q M Jalal Khan

1. Mixed Joy at the Conditional Freedom of the Most Popular and Patriotic Leader of Bangladesh Diabolically Victimized in a Corrupt Police and Prison State Under Sheikh Hasina

It was a cynical and sinister-minded, less than a "quarter" release for the greatest and most admired "Daughter" and also "Mother" of Bangladesh, Begum Khaleda Zia.[1] Quite senior in age, Begum Zia was lacerating in confinement most unjustly imposed upon her by the torturer tyrant Sheikh Hasina and her partisan court in the corrupt, cruel and cancerous police state that Bangladesh has been reduced to as a consequence of the she-dictator-cum-she-dracula's dark and dreary, and foolish and fascist occupation of power for about an age—more than twelve years now. By no means, the most hated Hasina regime should have taken to jail today's most highly regarded political personality Khaleda Zia, who, by virtue of her being most popular and admirable politician, is indeed a people's leader and people's prime minister of Bangladesh. As the former First Lady of the USA, Michelle Obama said, in 2016, referring to the Trumpism-infected Republicans, "The lower they go, the higher we rise."

As also the New York-based millionaire Dr Mina Farah (once a Hasina supporter, now rightly turned into a deep anti-Hasina mine fighting against her fascist mis/rule with the force and power of a warplane like an F-16 fighter jet, which is her (Mina Farah's) verbal assaults and rebuttals hurled over the social media and YouTube videos), argues that unless it was a criminal act, for no administrative lapses whatsoever, if there were any (perhaps hardly none), Begum Zia should have been sentenced by the lame and loony Hasina*ized* corrupt cronies and lackeys in judges and justices, who, including the passive and incompetent military, have made themselves a burdensome liability and a laughing stock of the nation, instead of being its proud assets.[2]

Still the mother of democracy দেশমাতা Begum Zia was sent to jail in what millions of people think was a politically motivated and personally manipulated miscarriage of justice under the awfully authoritarian and corrupt regime of Hasina. For the endless list of the latter's (Hasina's) nefarious notorieties, she is 'lovingly' and 'respectfully' called মাতারাণী 'Mother of Mafia' -- a specially awarded and 'privileged' nomenclature -- by the brave and brilliant UK-exiled Col (Ret) Shahid Uddin Khan and many others.[3] In the eyes of the nation, the vindictive conviction of Begum Zia, far from being carefully crafted with truth, reason, sense and sanity, was foolishly and frivolously maneuvered and premeditated, to the exposure of the evil conspiracies of the horribly fascist Hasina regime and its *gopali* and gestapo police.

Proverbially composed, polite, popular and patriotic with an inviolable seat in the hearts and minds of the people of Bangladesh, Khaleda Zia (like Shakespeare's tragic heroines--Lavinia, Ophelia, Desdemona and Cordelia) remains as innocent as she ever was, without any blotting blemishes that the regime would like to paint her with. It wanted to do so in a pretty loose and lousy manner, quite laboriously, lunatically, senselessly and frantically.

Just as "black will take no other hue," no Awami venom and vitriol would ever touch the iconic image and status of Khaleda, who remains as popular and prominent as she is (and as her husband President Zia was). Undisputedly, in many ways, such as in her suffering, sacrifice, struggle and achievement, she is unique, elevated even to the height of the greatest political figure of Bangladesh in her own way. (Let me hasten to add that her husband President Ziaur Rahman, in his mythically spectacular rise and role with the masses and the military by his side, remains the other unique and greatest political figure in Bangladesh). She is too stellar, phenomenal and stately to be torn and tarnished by the devilish designs of the fascist Hasina regime. With the interest of the nation as the first and last in her consideration, under the banner of Bangladeshi Nationalism, Khaleda stands uniquely tall and vindicated as she deserves. Naturally, the people of Bangladesh were beside themselves with joy at the news of her release, no matter how small-minded it was. The Hasina police, particularly Covid-19, were in control of the public outpouring of that joy, pushing the overflow to take the soft and virtual route in this age of social media, which is also, unfortunately, under the tight control of Hasina's digital acts allowing no freedom of expression.

2. Expression of Joy and the Context of Poetry and History

Yet many were swift to express their joy either in the sweet "heard melodies" of Rabindranath Tagore or by humming "those unheard" and "ditties of no tone," which are even sweeter. Those immortal phrases are from Keats's *Ode on a Grecian Urn*, which concludes with "Beauty is truth; truth beauty." Converted both to her person and politics, Begum Zia is a perfect representation of the aesthetic and spiritual philosophy captured in those captivating words.

On his part, Tagore composed a 22-line lyric "আজি বাংলাদেশের হৃদয় হতে কখন আপনি" in 1905 in the context of the Partition of Bengal that he strongly opposed in favor of a united Bengal. Despite, his "আমার সোনার বাংলা," also composed about the same time in the same context, has been made, nearly 66 years later, the national anthem of the separate East Bengal that emerged as an independent country, Bangladesh, in 1971. Tagore never wanted Bengal to split, just as Sheikh Mujibur Rahman, one of the leading political leaders of Bangladesh, never wanted the united Pakistan to break up into Pakistan (currently, former West Pakistan only) and Bangladesh (former East Pakistan). As the evidence of what he is reported to have said in early 1972 suggests, Mujib also did not like "আমার সোনার বাংলা" to be the national anthem of Bangladesh because, apart from other reasons, the song has had nothing to do with the struggle for the newly independent country.[4]

Anyway, turning to the specific subject in question, the first and the last stanzas of the first-mentioned song are as follows:

আজি বাংলাদেশের হৃদয় হতে কখন আপনি

তুমি এই অপরূপ রূপে বাহির হলে জননী!

ওগো মা, তোমায় দেখে দেখে আঁখি না ফিরে!

তোমার দুয়ার আজি খুলে গেছে সোনার মন্দিরে॥ ....

(When did you come out of the heart of Bangladesh,
O, Mother dear, with such inexplicable splendor!
It's impossible to take away eyes from you!
The doors of your golden temple have unlocked.) ....

আজি দুখের রাতে সুখের স্রোতে ভাসাও ধরণী—

তোমার অভয় বাজে হৃদয়মাঝে হৃদয়হরণী!

ওগো মা, তোমায় দেখে দেখে আঁখি না ফিরে!

তোমার দুয়ার আজি খুলে গেছে সোনার মন্দিরে॥

(You flood the world with the flow of happiness on the distressed nights
O the mindblower, your word of fearlessness drum the heart
It's impossible to take away eyes from you!
The doors of your golden temple have unlocked.)[5]

That is how, especially in the tune of the last four lines, millions of supporters of *DeshNetri* (Leader of the Country) and *DeshMata* (Mother of the Country) Begum Khaleda Zia and her party, Bangladesh Nationalist Party (BNP), have expressed their feelings with tears of joy at the news of her release, albeit less than half release, from the meanest and most mischievous imprisonment she was suffering from for more than two years.[6] Though communally charged, the poem may be contextualized with "Ma" (mother/motherland) and "Bangladesh" taken as standing for the released prisoner Begum Zia. Her loving attachment to the land has always been so deep that, at her release, regardless of how temporary it was, the people of Bangladesh started singing the following popular patriotic song with a greater dimension and deeper emotional feeling expressing the lasting patriotic bond between her and her country Bangladesh:

হায় রে আমার মন মাতানো দেশ,

হায় রে আমার সোনা ফলা মাটি।

রূপ দেখে তোর কেন আমার নয়ন ভরে না

তোরে এতো ভালোবাসি তবু পরান ভরে না।।

All patriotc songs of Bangladesh become more beautiful and meaningful by virtue of the ripple, resonance and reverberation they create in relation to the chord established by Khaleda Zia and her husband President Zia between them and the land and soil of Bangladesh.

The ruthless Hasina regime whose members freely fly around and abroad for their treatment did not allow the suffering Khaleda to seek medical care in the hospital of her choice even at home—United. The regime found yet another mean opportunity to cause mental and psychological agony to Khaleda by taking her, against her wishes, to a hospital that bore the name of Hasina's father Sheikh Mujib. Like the brewing controversy over the selective racism of M K Gandhi whose status as the father of the nation in India is being seriously questioned nowadays, Mujib also remains a highly controversial figure to the people of Bangladesh, who is not recognized by millions of people and many political parties the way Hasina and her regime would like them to recognize.[7]

Qaid-e-Azam Mohammad Ali Jinnah never ever addressed Gandhi, even at the risk of physical assault, by his questionable title "Mahatma"/ "Great Soul" because he, Jinnah, thought the latter was only a great communal leader of the Hindus, not of the Muslims and Hindus together as a united people of India.[8] Similarly, millions of people of Bangladesh and dozens of political parties and their leaders should have the freedom what or how to call Sheikh Mujib. Instead, they are being forced, most unfortunately, by the fascistically ruling Hasina and her police to call her father by the names or titles which he did not live up to due to his authoritarian BAKSAL, bloody RakkhiBahini, corruption-caused famine, carefully staying away from the liberation war and living in Pakistan through a safe and negotiated surrender, while leaving the Bangladeshi people exposed to genocide, etcetera. Due to her jealous and vindictive nature (like the violent men and women in life, especially in her Bangladesh today, as well as in the ancient folklore and the Renaissance English revenge plays), Sheikh Hasina is cynically inclined to, even immersed in the politics of division and destruction, as subversive of the state as it could unbelievably be.

Comparable to the vengeful Queen Tamora in *Titus Andronicus*, Shakespeare's first and bloodiest tragedy, Sheikh Hasina failed to adopt any constructive measure of peace, unity and harmony following Khaleda Zia's stateswoman-like speech in the parliament in 2013.[9] She (Hasina) could take the lead from the noble opposition leader Khaleda's momentous amd memorable speech in which she paid tribute to all the founding fathers of Bangladesh, not just one or two, as they deserved. Khaleda's epoch-making and state building speech could be seized upon by Hasina for the beginning of mending the wall with India, bridging the gap within the people of Bangladesh, changing the name of Bangladesh Awami League (BAL) to something more native, and uniting the nation under the banner of the patriotic Bangladeshi Nationalism, not Joy Bangla, which is saturated with foreign Hindutva spirit. Hasina missed out on those great goals and aspirations of the people, lamentably and miserably, for the sole and silly purpose of pursuing her tyrannical, totalitarian, anti-state, and Indian backed mean and myopic oppression, repression and persecution. Hasina does so in a proto-Nazi-and-proto-BJP-and-proto-RSS style of fantastically narcissistic fascism.

In a way, Khaleda Zia's confinement, nefariously imposed upon her by the rogue regime, reminds one of the young English poet and essayist Leigh Hunt. After two years of imprisonment for what the royal authorities unjustly considered a libel (due to a lack of flattery and sycophancy) to the young extravagant Prince Regent (later King George IV), Hunt was released on 2 February 1815. He was a man of liberal politics and wrote his masque *The Descent of Liberty* in prison. His friend John Keats, a major English Romantic poet, eleven years younger than Hunt, celebrated the latter's release by writing a sonnet, "Written on the Day that Mr. Leigh Hunt Left Prison." In the poem, Keats describes his subject as: "Kind Hunt was shut in prison, yet has he/In his immortal spirit, been as free/As the sky-searching lark, and as elate./ Minion of grandeur!" He describes Hunt as one who became more famous, "far happier, nobler was his fate!" due to his "fortunate incarceration," to use a borrowed oxymoron, during which he was reading the greatest epic or narrative poets of England, Spenser and Milton, and thereby took "happy flights" with them to the imaginative region of his own.

The politically engineered jail sentence passed on Bangladesh's political legend Khaleda Zia bears historical significance when many other great minds—poets, writers, thinkers, philosophers, politicians—faced the wrath of tyrants and met with the similar fate of imprisonment throughout the ages and centuries. Mention may be made of a few politicians and statesmen only, such as the early 6th century Boethius of Rome, Mary Queen of Scots, Sir Thomas Malory and Sir Walter Raleigh (both of England), Nelson Mandela of South Africa, Anwar Ibrahim of Malaysia and Mahmudur Rahman of Bangladesh.[10] Similarly, (would-be) Desh Nayok Tarique Rahman in exile is a 53-year old dynamic leader who embodies the spirit of Bangladeshi Nationalism and patriotism. He is the torch bearer of the Zia family and Acting Chairman of the BNP, next only to his mother in popularity, way above any Awami leader. He has been suffering and sacrificing for more than twelve years now, facing the fate of the historic exiles, such as the ancient Trojan hero Aeneas, 5th century (BCE) Greek historian Thucydides, 17th century English political philosopher Thomas Hobbes, King Charles II, English philosophical historian Edward Gibbon, French philosopher Voltaire, French emperor Napoleon and Russian writer Dostoyevsky.

As mentioned at the outset, Bangladesh's three-time former Prime Minister, Khaleda Zia is of singularly stellar prominence in the politics of Bangladesh. She was released from prison on Wednesday, 25 March 2020, after about twenty-six months in jail. It was since February 8, 2018 that Khaleda Zia—a Voice of the Third World/ 'খালেদা জিয়া : তৃতীয় বিশ্বের কণ্ঠস্বর,' as a book by that title (April 2019), by Professor Emajuddin Ahmad and poet Abdul Hye Sikder, describes her—was languishing in jail, confined to a damp corner in a deserted and dilapidated dungeon and then for less than adequate treatment in the jail-cell of a hospital which was not the hospital of her choice.

3. Khaleda Shouldering the Burden of Police Brutalities and Battling Hasina's Kangaroo Courts

Horrendously subjected to a number of fishy and flimsy lawsuits cynically harped upon her by the fascist Hasina regime, the 75-year old leader, Begum Zia, was released at the point of her near death with the predicament of a number of stringent strings attached. That also came in the midst of the dangerous corona pandemic that, as if a blessing in disguise, added to the আপোসহীন (uncompromising) DeshNetri and DeshMata's legendary popularity while making the regime's plan of lavish 400-crore taka cult-worshipping *Mujib-and-Modi-and-Tagore-Borso* extravaganza (some say, Awami-BAKSALi Banga-Virus) dull and dreary, vapid and vacuous, almost conspicuous by its absence, as are the press freedom and the freedom of speech.[11]

That is why there are dozens of court cases against Khaleda Zia. That all are fictitious and fabricated is borne out by the fact that there is no criminal evidence whatsoever to implicate her at all.[12] Elsewhere I argued:

> When hundreds of millions and billions of dollars have been and are being looted from the banks and businesses every now and then under this regime, Khaleda has been savagely silenced and sentenced for slightly mismanaging a peanut worth (only 2 crore and a half, which, still intact and, in fact, grown into triple the amount, is nothing compared with Hasina's old and octogenarian finance minister Maal Muhith's dismissal of 4000 crores blatantly stolen by others under Hasina's watch as simply nothing and with the countless of other crores brazenly embezzled under the carefully careless connivance of the Awami regime).[13]

God/Allah the Almighty does not like the excesses committed in any form, be it torture, tyranny, repression, persecution, abduction, rape, murder, abuse of power, vote rigging, looting, stealing, smuggling, widespread corruption and spendthrift expenditures, especially in a poor country like Bangladesh. It is particularly under Sheikh Mujib and his daughter Sheikh Hasina that those excesses have been and continue to be committed in Bangladesh where millions are unemployed and living below the poverty line, forcing many to look for crumbs from dustbins and waste disposal landfills. However, deprived of the loving company of her immediate family for decades, Khaleda Zia's plight as a political prisoner was further exacerbated by her jail-cell loneliness (cut off from her long political and public career) and her old age complications that allegedly went without adequate medical care in the hospital where she was forced to stay for her treatment.

Khaleda's release followed the temporary suspension of her seventeen-year sentence in a framed and formulated draconian case. It was by an executive order from the horrendously ruling Hasina, whose corrupt regime is widely thought to be maliciously interfering with the biased and dysfunctional judiciary as it does with all the rest of the state machinery, including the spineless and lame-duck Election Commissions since 2009. Under the power and control that the Hasina regime wields in an absolute authoritarian way as the German Nazis did, the obliging judiciary, far from being free and independent, is willingly (or sometimes maybe unwillingly) dependent on the regime's regressive and retrograde whims and caprices--an allegation that, as tons of evidences suggest, is an open secret in the popular perception of the people of Bangladesh.

In her critical condition for which the regime's inhuman neglect and illegal imprisonment of her is responsible, the ailing opposition leader, already in her advanced age, cannot move or stand or even sit up on her own; she cannot even use her hand to eat. One can only speculate about the regime's reasons to release the great leader. There could be a combination of factors: infectious spread of corona; Khaleda's deteriorating health throughout the period of her incarceration in jail; repeated political and family requests for her release; her inability to engage in any political action program anyway at this stage; Hasina showing her power through her so-called executive order; international pressure and pressure from human rights groups, if any, and so on.

By virtue of being the most popular leader and Chairperson of the largest political party of the country and more as a result of a series of massively rigged elections and after elections, Khaleda Zia still actually holds the same laurel of premiership in the people's hearts and minds. Though out of power, she remains the People's Leader and People's Prime Minister, as opposed to the "midnight vote dacoit" regime's prime minister in power. Accused of illegally occupying the office by force and through the wholesale rigging and mugging of votes, Sheikh Hasina is completely afraid of facing the voters and believes in voter-less "s/election" farce on the empty stage. Imprisoned by her repressive regime, to the extent of being fantastically fascistic, Khaleda was put in jail out of the "unelected," autocratically "auto-elected," and vote dacoit Hasina's vindictive venom and vitriol.

Also popularly called "Mother of Democracy and Humanity," Khaleda is opposite to Hasina, who is "Mother of Loot and Tyranny and Dictatorship and Enforced Disappearances." In 1917, when the poor and helpless Rohingya refugees started to enter Bangladesh, they were shot at and repulsed by Hasina's forces. Many were killed or drowned in the river. Appeals came from Khaleda and the BNP and other countries, especially Turkey, and many humanitarian organizations, including the UN, to allow them in. Hasina had to give in to pressure. Khaleda is Hasina's only and unbeatable political rival unbeatably excelling the latter in every aspect of life and leadership: honesty, dignity, decorum, morality, popularity, fairness, firmness, openness, tolerance, truthfulness, democratic principles, nationalist spirit, and patriotic impulse.

4. Khaleda in the View of Others Patriotically Imbued and Nationalistically Concerned

In an email post, former Bangladesh Ambassador to Japan Serajul Islam says: "The Prime Minister and her ministers had all along maintained that there was nothing that the Prime Minister could do about Khaleda Zia's release because her release was in the hands of the judiciary that was independent of the executive branch. Now the Law Minister says

Khaleda's conditional release was the decision of the Prime Minister." Similarly, Professor Syed Serajul Islam of Lakehead University Canada says: "What is there to thank PM Hasina for? All along we heard that her government had nothing to do with Khaleda Zia's release or her bail and the court was independent. Now, suddenly, for whatever reason, she is granted conditional release and the Law Minister says Hasina has granted the release. This indicates that Madam Zia has been in jail for personal grudge of Hasina against her formidable rival. I do not see any reason for the BNP to thank Hasina." One cannot agree more with what the two distinguished people said. The statements made in the present tense above by them are an ever continuous and customary reality with the administration of the Hasina-brand fascists while the past tense statements are the ever continuous and customary falsehoods and fabrications by the same regime of unprecedented corruption, repression, terror and tyranny.

There are conspiracy theories behind Khaleda's release as suggested by R Chowdhury of the USA, a former army officer, decorated freedom fighter, diplomat and currently a political analyst and essayist on Bangladesh affairs. Mentioning the case of the Palestinian leader Yasser Arafat, Chowdhury claims he got the clue to those theories from two sources. "Surely, Khaleda Zia was a 'bomb' to Hasina, the reason to put her in jail in the first place. As the bomb continued to tick even in confinement, the regime wanted it to be deactivated sooner than later. So, a slow poisoning was administered. Short of six months lifetime, the regime decided to send Khaleda Zia to her family to die. So was the release condition not to go abroad for treatment, which could detect the 'poisoning,' if any. To my query why Khaleda Zia's personal physicians could not detect it, the response was that their চৌদ্দ গোষ্ঠী (they along with their whole families going back through fourteen generations) would be eliminated if they opened their mouth. The second source did not mention the poisoning theory. According to him, the authorities discovered that KZ had six months to live. They did not want it to happen in their custody."

One cannot but concur with what R Chowdhury says: "Additionally, during the short press briefing, the Law Minister said that the Prime Minister's action was in response to the request made by Begum Zia's family members--he even read out the names--who met the PM.

What a demeaning act! Before the journalists asked too many questions, the Minister ran away from the venue. My question: Is it the first time such a request was made? Why such charity!! Why should there be any reason for the BNP to thank Hasina?"

It is in the same manner that Engineer Rashed Anam of the USA writes: "আওয়ামী দখলদার স্বৈরাচার এখন আর বলে না এটা আদালতের বেপার! বিচার বিভাগ থেকে শুরু করে সমস্ত রাষ্ট্রীয় প্রতিষ্ঠানগুলোই যে একক ভোটহীন অবৈধ স্বৈরাচারীর পায়ের নিচে সেটা আবারো জাতির কাছে নগ্নভাবে প্রদর্শিত হলো ! ৭১ এর চেতনা বটে ! বাকশাল-২ তে স্বাগতম ! খা কাপুরুষ-মিসকিন বিএনপি খা ! স্বৈরাচারীর দয়ার ও করুনার ভিক্ষা খা ! খেয়ে মর ! নিজেরা কিছুই করতে পারে না, রাজনৈতিক মূল্যবোধটা, রাজনৈতিক অবস্থান ও আদর্শের গলাবাজি করার জায়গাটাও রাখলো না ! দেওলিয়া টোটালি ! স্বৈরাচারীর পা ধরে দয়ার ও করুনার উপর ছুড়ে দেয়া উচ্ছিষ্ট খেয়েই অস্তিসর্বশ্ব নিয়েই বেঁচে থাক বিএনপি! Kick out all these imbecile "gone case" "waste case" leaders and reform and revive a true professional nationalist democratic political party."

Highly active in political commentary and campaigning, Zoglul Husain of the UK observes in the same vein as if he were speaking the mind of the entire Bangladesh nation: "The government has committed a grave crime by sending Khaleda Zia to prison on trumped up charges. If it has suspended the sentence for 6 months for its own tactical reasons, there is nothing to thank the government for it. We demand withdrawal of all false charges against her and punishment of all those involved in planning them and the deliberate imprisonment of her. We demand compensation."

One of the finest political and intellectual minds of Bangladesh, Dr Asif Nazrul once asked the BNP leaders how they were sleeping at night with Begum Zia in prison. Well, I'm none of the BNP hierarchy, but I had my share of sleepless nights due to her plight as seen on the media or felt about her misery in confinement. On a further personal note, I dreamt about her for two consecutive nights, Sunday and Monday, to wake up on Tuesday morning (March 24) to hear the breaking news of her release. During the first night, I saw her kind of half-walking in her prison room in the PG hospital from a field outside. In the second dream, I was visiting her there in prison along with somebody else; I don't exactly recollect who he was. Beginning her jail sentence more than two years ago, I had a number of sleepless nights, as I am sure many others also had, feeling quite perturbed.

Khaleda suffered too much for too little to nothing--without her family beside her and without her political as well as personal freedom, with her husband and former President Ziaur Rahman assassinated in 1981 when she was still at the prime of her life—an assassination in which, as alleged by Matiur Rahman Rentu, her archrival Sheikh Hasina (along with Gen Ershad) might have had a hissing and hatching hand.[14] It is beyond doubt what Ambassador Serajul Islam and senior journalist Zainal Abedin of New York observed about the political standing of Khaleda Zia. In their view she surpassed all subcontinental leaders, not just those of Bangladesh, in her long-standing sacrifice and struggle for freedom and democracy since the early 1980s.[15]

Ambassador Islam would also say, "You know my view on Begum Zia; that I would unhesitatingly place her ahead of all leaders in South Asian history for contributions to the cause of democracy and people's rights. All leaders of South Asia who suffered in the hands of colonial/dictatorial/fascist rulers had given some cause for which they were incarcerated. Begum Zia went to jail in 2018 on a 100% cooked up case but she accepted her jail sentence because she knew that was the best way to expose and prove to the people of Bangladesh and outside who were watching the unadulterated fascist nature of the present rulers of the country. It is a matter of great regret that the BNP failed miserably to stand up to her sacrifices and do anything for her release" (May 1, 2020).

5. Gotten Squarely Squatted by Sheikh Hasina's Hinduized and Indianized THAADs (Terminal High Altitude Area Defense) and Carnivorus Hyenas, the BNP, However, Is Not Without Its Own Faults and Follies

Khaleda's party—the BNP--has been rendered as weak and frightened as the toothless and spineless EC (Election Commission) by the frightening torture, tyranny and intimidation inflicted on it by Sheikh Hasina and her diabolical state apparatus of all kinds. All the repression and persecution are being metedced out to the BNP through police brutalities and shamelessly yielding and obliging law courts. The BNP felt so helpless that, at the release of its top leader, regardless of how dubious her detention and release were, it rushed to thank the regime: "তারা এ জন্য প্রধানমন্ত্রীকে ধন্যবাদ জানানা।"

Although all credit goes to the extended Zia family and none whatsoever to the party's useless highest body (which utterly failed to secure her release either through the legal battle in the regime's already jejune and jaundiced courts or open movement in the streets), the party's unimpressive and uncharismatic Secretary General Mirza Fakhrul Islam Alamgir thanked the regime as though there was an indirect admission of guilt on the part of its freed leader. Simple, senile and docile BNP Standing Committee leadership under the frightened Mirza Fakhrul is only good in swiftly thanking the fascist Hasina and the members of her rogue regime for anything and everything they are deceived into thinking to be good. They hope (against hope) for some sympathy from what is one of the dullest and dreariest and most oppressive regimes in modern history. The BNP was quick to do so after Hasina's so-called "sea-conquest" against Myanmar; it did so with regards to the initially Hasina-supported *Shahbugee shontrashi* (শাহবাগী সন্ত্রাসী) terrorists, only to regret and withdraw its hastily made "thank you" in no time. Now it has done so again — extending a "quick rental" thank you, however cold or lukewarm it must have been.

People pity the hopelessly poor BNP trying to catch at a straw and swim with its hands and feet tied, brought to its knees by the fact that hundreds of its supporters were killed, injured, abducted, tens of thousands sent to prison and hundreds of thousands of lawsuits were filed by the regime against its thousands of both local and national leaders and its rank and file members. Most of them have been busy running back and forth between home and the corridors of courts. Even then, the party, as large as it is, should have been strong and organized enough to hold its ground by standing up to Hasina with a show of people's power.

Unfortunately, its Standing Committee members (some of them being too weary and worn-out) are never on the street and can never make it to the street, always remaining seated, as cold and cowardly and homebound as they ever have been. They find themselves in that position of stasis, stagnation and sterility, particularly in the absence of the party's two top leaders--Khaleda and Tarique, both of whom are formidably impressive in their own (exemplary) ways, suffering under the yoke of the Hasina steamroller. It is the fascistically foolish Hasina, a Mir Jafar-Lhendup Dorji-type stooge-and-puppet-and-lacky of India, who should say sorry hundred times for the injustice done to the most majestic and most popular leader of Bangladesh, Begum Khaleda Zia.

Khaleda Zia, unofficially the supreme leader of Bangladesh, should not have ever been in prison. Nelson Mandela never thanked the white minority government for his release after 27 years of imprisonment because he said he had no reason to thank them for releasing him and that he should not have been put in prison in the first place. One may ask, "Where have the dozens of mega corruption cases against Hasina gone? Where are the hundreds of millions and billions of dollars stolen and smuggled by the goons and gangs, allied with or connived at by the ruling axis? How come the regime is able to get away with its countless lies, blunders, scams, scandals, mischiefs and massacres?"

The weak and poor BNP with their older septuagenarian and octogenarian men, disabled from within and without (minus the two top ailing or exiled leaders) in its upper echelon—the Standing Committee--should have some courage, dignity and integrity; they should not prostrate and kneel down before the autocratic Hasina regime surrounded by and infested with countless crooked elements in looters, smugglers, sycophants, rapists, abductors, murderers, সন্ত্রাসী terrorists and intimidators in its different branches and beyond countrywide. To achieve the lowest common denominator with the BNP, the Bangladesh Awami League (BAL), the least popular, should and must have weeded out all those culprits and criminals, be they in uniform or white clothes and must have held itself accountable in the conspiracy of the BDR massacre and thousands of other misdeeds and mischiefs committed all across the country, especially in the capital Dhaka.

DeshNetri and *DeshMata* Khaleda Zia is Bangladesh's only and unique leader in terms of her nobility, popularity, and magnanimity, all of which match her lofty looks, noble stature, and leader-like garb and gait.

Just as her husband President Zia rose and set like a luminary in the political sky of Bangladesh, throughout her life, Khaleda also was in the state of rising in uncommon majesty ascending through the political clouds around her. Now she is seriously, perhaps even critically ill at the hands of the crappy, cacophonous and cantankerous Hasina-orchestrated legal game: a decadent show of depraved and dependent courts – both higher and lower. It is the mean and monstrous Hasina, accused of vampire vote dacoity, who is responsible for Khaleda's near death deterioration. Nearly twenty-six months of her lonely detention and the regime's denial of proper treatment contributed to the worsening of Khaleda's physical and psychosomatic illness. There must have been millions who suffered feeling psychologically and intellectually shocked and shaken at the imprisonment of a person who is also regarded, as mentioned above, as "Mother of Democracy and Humanity."

6. A People's Party That Is Zia's and Khaleda's BNP:

The fact remains that the BNP is the party of the lordly, magnificent and magisterial President Ziaur Rahman (1936-1981), a great statesman, who proclaimed the independence of Bangladesh in March 1971 and then founded this popular and patriotic party later in the decade.[16] He was at the forefront of both the emergence and existence of Bangladesh—first as a decorated freedom fighter in 1971 and then at the head of an army-people uprising in November 1975. It was the following year that President Zia, who may be regarded as হাজার বছরের শ্রেষ্ঠ বাংলাদেশী (the greatest Bangladeshi ever, of a thousand years!) introduced the highest state award স্বাধীনতা পদক/Swadhinata Padak (Independence Day Award) and the next highest Ekushey Padak/একুশে পদক, thus making history as he did in every step he took during his short administration. It was he who allowed Sheikh Hasina to return home from India in 1981 and enter politics for which she should have remained ever grateful to him. Unfortunately, as the events unfolded, starting with his internationally (Indian?) conspired assassination by a number of misguided and deviant soldiers the same year, it seems, by allowing her to return and enter politics, Zia invited his own end: শেখ হাসিনাকে দেশে আসতে দিয়ে, জিয়াউর রহমান "খাল কেটে কুমির এনেছেন" (he brought a calamity by his own imprudence and made way for his own calamity and that of his family as well as that of his party).

President Zia's achievement in terms of his numerous contributions and milestone reforms during his only five years of rule (or less) was outstanding. His remarkable feats lie in his introduction of multi-party democracy, revolutionary economic, industrial (especially garments) and agricultural liberalization, and the export of manpower by virtue of which the country is reaping a great harvest today. However, Zia's most major and far-reaching contribution was perhaps his ideal of Bangladeshi Nationalism[17]—an all-inclusive comprehensive identity for the Muslim-majority, yet multi-ethnic and multi-religious geographical territory called Bangladesh.

Politically, Bangladeshi Nationalism (বাংলাদেশী জাতীয়তাবাদ) separates Bangladesh from the neighbouring fanatical and communally strife-ridden Hindu-majority India and Indian West Bengal. As one political science scholar puts it, Zia "conceptualized Bangladesh Nationalism as a confluence of all religious, linguistic, and ethnic identities in the country." In his book, জ্যোতির্ময় জিয়া এবং কালো মেঘের দল/Luminous Zia and the Black Clouds (2011), poet Abdul Hye Sikder describes President Zia's manifold measures and singles out the highly resonant historic ideal of Bangladesh nationalism, which he thinks embodies Zia's political philosophy about the definition of Bangladesh as a nation and its specific vision and mission, goals and aspirations, and dreams and destinations. Poet Sikder says: "আমার কাছে এ সবকিছুর চাইতেও যে অবদানকে আরও বেশি ব্যঞ্জনাময় বলে মনে হয়, তা হলো তাঁর 'বাংলাদেশী জাতীয়তাবাদ'। আমাদের জাতীয় জীবনে যে আত্মপরিচয়ের সংকট কৃত্রিম ও অকৃত্রিম দু'ভাবেই ছিল, দেশটা কেন, কাদের জন্য, এই দেশের লক্ষ্য ও উদ্দেশ্য কী, গন্তব্য কী, স্বপ্ন কী --এর সবকিছুর সমাধান তিনি তাঁর এই রাজনৈতিক দর্শনের মধ্যে সংস্থাপন করেন।" In light of his incandescent collective vision and his vigorous pursuit of lofty national goals, President Zia remains হাজার বছরের শ্রেষ্ঠ বাংলাদেশী (the greatest Bangladeshi ever, of a thousand years).

It is true there was no political entity called Bangladesh before 1971 but the geographical land was there from time immemorial. As just mentioned, Zia's most lasting legacy was to introduce and establish the idea of the independent Bangladesh through the concept of Bangladeshi Nationalism. This is in contradistinction with Hindutva-dominated Indian West Bengal-centric Bengali Nationalism (বাঙালী জাতীয়তাবাদ), which is mirrored in Sheikh Mujib being called হাজার বছরের শ্রেষ্ঠ বাঙালী। (If the BBC survey was conducted in 1973-1975, the result would have been very different). Similar contradistinction is conveyed by West Bengal-centric Joy Bangla (parallel to Joy Hind) and Bangladesh-centric Joy Bangladesh. By the same logic, the conceptualization and consolidation of Bangladeshi Nationalism are reflected, enshrined and embodied in Zia being হাজার বছরের শ্রেষ্ঠ বাংলাদেশী। It was him whose incalculable state building measures and tremendous success provided forward looking lighthouse directions to the nation and made Dr Morshed Hasan Khan describe Zia as being incomparably luminous (জ্যোতির্ময় জিয়া) in a Naya Diganta column of 26 March 2018, for which, by the order of the fascist regime, he lost his job as a professor of Marketing at Dhaka University on 9 September 2020.

To repeat, President Zia saved Bangladesh twice, first in 1971 and then in 1975. He did not run away from the battlefield the way Sheikh Mujib did to find himself in the safe custody of Pakistan (which he wanted to lead and keep united). It is ironic that Mujib surrendered to seek refuge in Pakistan leaving his own people in East Pakistan (would-be Bangladesh) to be massacred by the Pakistani soldiers. As part of a prearranged deal, he made sure his family and then his pregnant daughter Hasina were also secure, carefully left under the protection and financial support of the Pakistani military government in Dhaka. Like him and his family, many people, however, took or sought the help of the Pakistanis and cooperated with them in those days for different reasons! Many of them are now close relatives of Hasina and other Awami leaders and many belong to her party Awami League. Given the complexity of connections and relationships—political or otherwise--it is hard to define who was a

Rajakar and who was not. A conveniently selective pick-and-choose strategy is legally, politically, morally, and ethically reprehensible.

Depending on the context of time, all fiery speeches are not the same. Wanting to remain with the united and unbroken Pakistan and wishing to be its Prime Minister, Mujib's 7 March speech was only a wishy-washy and half-hearted oration about the independence of Bangladesh; it fell short of the clear and complete declaration of independence which remained for the bold and valiant (and would-be President) Ziaur Rahman to proclaim about twenty days later. In late December 1971, Mujib lamented the fact that Pakistan was finally, regrettably, broken up and that its Eastern wing went independent against the wishes deep down in his heart. According to Stanley Wolpert's book *Zulfi Bhutto of Pakistan*, "I told you (Z A Bhutto), it will be a confederation. This is also between you and me ... You leave it to me ... Absolutely leave it to me. Trust me ... My idea was we will live together and we will rule this country. You know the occupation (Indian) army is there."

Then there is the three-time former Prime Minister and BNP Chair Khaleda Zia, who, of stunningly majestic stature and outlook and stately leadership style, has been living a politically fighting but personally lonely life since the prime of her life following the assassination of her husband Zia in 1981. There are many highlights of her political career that have established her as a leader of bold stands and supreme sacrifices, remarkable for her honesty and dignity with moral and political supremacy far outweighing her awfully authoritarian opponent Hasina and Hasina's corruption-ridden rogue regime. Some of Khaleda's accomplishments as an opposition leader as well as Prime Minister are:

- her uncompromising movement to tear down the military dictator H M Ershad in the 1980s—a movement that she and her BNP led with success, far ahead of any other parties, that caused even the army under General Nuruddin to blink;
- her clean government for more than two terms (corruption-free compared with insane and endless Awami sea-loots and massive and monstrous Awami vote-rigging since 2009);
- her patriotic and nationalist fervour in view of her party's most lasting legacy of Bangladeshi Nationalism that was

wisely introduced by the party's founding president Ziaur Rahman in the late 1970s -- a nationalism which, while attentive to national interest and integrity, also embraces internationalism in the sense of regional and global engagement, influence and reliability;
- her numerous state-building measures and policies;
- her historic introduction of the interim Caretaker Government system to ensure the peaceful transition of power through credible elections;
- her quest for freedom, democratic tolerance, national unity and integrity (compared with the fiendish Awami fascism of oppression and repression at home and its mew-mew kitten surrender of national interests to India);
- her patriotically-tinged and nationalistically-driven decision to cancel her meeting with the anti-Bangladeshi Hasina-backer Indian President Pranab Mukherjee during his early March 2013 visit to Dhaka;[18]
- her absolutely brilliant performance during the telephone conversation with Hasina, in October 2013, about the valid and legitimate reasons for her to boycott the would-be totally unfair and one-sided election under Hasina in January the following year;
- her resilience in the face of her forced ouster from her decades-old Shaheed Mainul Road residence at the cantonment area; and,
- her repeated confinement to her Gulshan office and also her Gulshan home that remained surrounded, time and again, by Hasina's sand-and-cement trucks for days and weeks and her illegal imprisonment for a long period of time (about twenty six months).

The uncompromising mother of land and democracy (দেশমাতা গণতন্ত্রের মাতা আপোষহীন নেত্রী) Khaleda Zia deserves a deluge of attention with the nation's immense debt of gratitude to her, to be generously highlighted and celebrated, especially in view of Hasina trying to obliterate her with a horribly and devilishly ritualistic commitment. DeshMata Khaleda's historic role and status, her suffering and sacrifice for the cause of peace and freedom, and the injustice done to her by the Hasina regime since 2009 (not to speak of her anti-Ershad movement in the 1980s) need to be noted and observed equally firmly and faithfully. Dr Emajuddin Ahmed, Shafik Rehman, and (late) Mahfuz Ullah did a great job in bringing out her distinctive achievement and contribution and those of her husband President Zia to national and international attention by writing excellent books on them (see the Preface and Appendix A). Others also can play a similar role by writing about her and his selfless and patriotic struggle and bringing their historic and exemplary achievements and accomplishments to the attention of the reading public and the political scene of the world. That will go a long way in countering and dispelling the horrific and harrowing picture that the illegal and illegitimate Hasina regime has been laboriously trying to give them with the help of her (Hasina's) loonies and lackies in the state machinery, including the police, the judiciary, and the EC. Elsewhere I said:

> On a lighter note, like the comic scenes that at the same time intensify and accentuate the serious themes in a tragedy, the two parties (B/AL and BNP) are as divided as their present leaders. One is only Sheikh Hasina of the AL, with her late husband's name hardly used at the end of her good name. Even when he was alive, his wife Hasina hardly wanted to be known by him. (Critics have their own versions about the couple's allegedly cold relationship). The other is Khaleda Zia of the BNP, with her late husband's name always fondly attached to her already beautiful name. Khaleda is older but, even after the age has taken its toll on her, she remains more beautiful, graceful, stylish, glamorous, ladylike, fashionable, fair complexioned, reserved and serious-looking, speaking both Bangla and English with an impressive and impeccable accent and nice pronunciation.[19] One (Hasina) starts her day early and the other (Khaleda) late. They also differ in their traditional wear to make a personal statement about Bangladesh. While one (Hasina) wears printed cotton saree, the other (Khaleda) prefers lace and chiffon saree with matching satin veil.
>
> These may seem to be small details but no less significant, like the small plants and flowers and ferns and creepers that add to the beauty of the vegetation under the trees of a forest. Women's

outfit, more than men, especially the first ladies,' is always a news item, a source of their charm, attraction, and gracefulness, all over the world. Hasina wears what goes well with her. Khaleda does the same. Their clothing style and body wear makes a statement about their demeanor and conduct. Apart from major political and ideological differences, those in style and personality also come into play everywhere.

Could there also be, then, a psychological warfare of personal jealousy and personality clash between Hasina and Khaleda? One came to power as the daughter of one of the great political leaders of the country; the other as the wife of a military general, who was also a great liberation hero after having declared the independence of Bangladesh (albeit in the name of Sheikh Mujib) and who later became a great war hero and a great president of the country. Both women are grooming their sons to take charge of their respective parties and eventually the country. Could this family orientation further contribute to their rivalries?[20]

Unlike many couples of disrepute and tense and torn relationships with no love lost between husband and wife (one does not have to name any too familiar a couple here), the bond of love between Zia and Khaleda is/was as fabulous as a fairy tale turned to human reality. According to the reliable sources, the unbelievably beautiful Khaleda. perhaps in her mid-teens, and the equally smart and brilliant Ziaur Rahman fell in love with each other the first time they saw each other. As a young army officer, he used to visit Bogra, Rangpur, and Dinajpur on his holidays. He used to come from Karachi and other places. A very smart young man who fell in love with the irresistibly beautiful Khaleda, Zia frequently took her out on a speedy motorbike ride. As the backseat passenger she naturally had to hold him tight. Her family did not want this public sight to continue.

Also considering the distance between the two wings of Pakistan and the short holidays available, guardians of both families decided that they should get married without delay. That is what must have happened. This story has also been confirmed, according to yet another source, by Zia's cousin brother Mahbubur Rahman. Did Khaleda know then the man she was going to be wedded with was the would-be President Zia, who evolved to be one of the greatest sons of the soil and came to the rescue of the nation again and again? Did she know then she would become the most successful Prime Minster of the country? Did she have any idea then of the sad conspiratorial calamities that would befall her one after another?

Well, while she could not finish her college education because of love and marriage in the context of those days in Bangladesh culture, Begum Zia was and is still an avid reader of books and newspapers, gifted with her excellent command of both Bangla and English. She is just one of those dozens of great leaders of the world who did not have a chance to finish their college education.[21] Formal higher education does not always matter or is not always a factor in climbing up the political ladder. How many Presidents, PMs, MPs, ministers, millionaires, business tycoons and real estate magnates of Bangladesh and elsewhere are college graduates? As the list under Note#20 above shows, there are many great people of the world who were not highly educated. Moreover, it is better **not** to be able to continue with higher education upon valid grounds than being rough and rude, evil and obnoxious, expelled, and resorting to cheating in exams: হাসিনা নকলে ধরা খাওয়া থার্ড ক্লাস স্টুডেন্ট ছিলা টিচারদের কাছে শুনেছি আব্দুল হাই শিকদারের লেখাতেও পড়েছি, পলিটিক্যাল সাইন্সে ৩ পাওয়া ছাত্রী [...] মুই কার খালুরে? বদুকাকা? বখাটে স্বভাবেরা।

Khaleda's and Zia's son Tarique Rahman is a dynamic leader of mission and vision. A great nationalist patriot, an honest, sincere, polite and clean man, much maligned by the vicious Awami circle, he is no comparison with the corrupt Awami scoundrels, mountebanks, hoodlums and hooligans, who turned all Bangladesh into a hellish and hermaphrodite place of corruption -- কাউয়া ভবন খাওয়া ভবন মুরগি ভবন and ঘাদানি ভবন (*kaowa, khaowa, murgi* and *ghadani* bhaban).[22] Terrific Tarique, suffering from terrible Awami wrath, does not need any advice from those talking big and voicing bombast from their comfort zones at home and abroad. There is no point quarreling over the BNP leadership despite its shortcomings. No one is infallible. In these hard times inflicted by Hasina, who is an embodiment of an evil force, to the power of infinity, all nationalist patriots need to get united to thwart and topple the recklessly repressive and regressive Awami regime and its cliques and cronies and coteries.

However, it is true Mirza Fakhrul and the majority sitting on the BNP standing committee are weak and cowardly. They have to go. But let the time decide when and how (see Appendix H).

Tarique may have made some mistakes early in his life, but those may be seen with forgiving eyes, especially in view of the innumerable Awami-BAKSALi macabre monstrosities during 1972-1975 and then, since 2009, until today. Orphaned early, the strong and impressive man of great parentage has suffered immensely and is still suffering in exile, away from home and mother, both the son and the mother suffering most unjustly and living their lonely lives for fear of the wolves and hyenas out there in and beyond the horribly Indianized and Hinduized regime and its police/RAB/judiciary. As mentioned earlier in this article, (yet-to-be) দেশনায়ক/*DeshNayok* Tarique must have gone through a maturing process and has transformed himself into a bold and brilliant leader, far superior to those devils and dragons who oppose him for no good reason. He may be compared to Prince Hal, who after some initial youthful pitfalls, grew to become King Henry V (1413-1422), one of the greatest kings of England.

7. The BNP as a Political Party Cannot, However, Be Expected to Be Free of Whatever Share of Blunders and Blemishes It Must Own

The mistakes and missteps the party of President Ziaur Rahman, Prime Minister Khaleda Zia and her likely successor Tarique Rahman—the BNP—may have made in the past are nothing compared with the carelessly countless and numerous crimes and blunders made by the party of Sheikh Mujib and Sheikh Hasina—the Awami League. A political party is not a party of angels and prophets. Being a platform of people of all kinds of beliefs and backgrounds, a political party would make mistakes, more or less, compared with other parties. The Awami mistakes are incomparably endless and still counting on a daily basis. While one may hold the BNP accountable for a few mistakes it may have made, one cannot indict it in these fascist times under the pretty devilish rule of Sheikh Hasina.

Like any other popular, democratic, patriotic and nationalist party of the widest following possible, the BNP is far from being perfect and far from perfectly stepping forward like the routine mechanical tick-tick of the hands of a clock. No party, no person ever can. However, the BNP's failures, whatever they were, are due more to the fascist and ferocious excesses of the Hasina regime than its own internal weaknesses and shortcomings. Still Begum Zia remains the most oppressed political legend of Bangladesh, the greatest political phenomenon of Bangladesh and the most popular leader of Bangladesh with the nation as the first and last consideration for her as it was for her husband President Zia, the greatest son of the soil, our Abraham Lincoln, (to repeat) our হাজার বছরের শ্রেষ্ঠ বাংলাদেশী (the greatest Bangladeshi ever, of a thousand years!). In her sacrifice, suffering and struggles, Khaleda, as mentioned above, surpassed all the subcontinental leaders in the region. One must not forget her uncompromising forceful fight and successes during the 1980s and 1990s through 2006.

Yet, in the face of the mighty backing from India, China, America and the rest of the world for the Hasina regime, which opted to sell out to them at the expense of Bangladesh's national interest, Khaleda's men and might failed to protect many leaders from being hanged (although they did as much as they could throughout the late 70s, 80s, 90s through 2006). They also failed to protect her from being ousted from her home and protest against the BDR and other massacres and the farces staged in the name of "election." The combined networks and circumstances of all-engulfing and all-swallowing police, useless and passive military in their "mind-forged manacles" (a phrase taken from William Blake's short lyric "London"), conniving and obliging judiciary, negatively and nefariously loyal administration, corrupt business conglomerates, partisan goons and gangs and gangsters, and hissing hoodlums and hooligans have completely subjugated the opposition BNP-led political alliance. In other words, the entire state machinery, tainted, twisted and manipulated into various Icarus-type Awami wings, no matter how temporarily waxen they may be, has for now been able to bring it to its knees since 2009. However, the weak and hopeless BNP under Mirza Fakhrul and others is no less responsible for its broken hip dead river কোমর ভাঙ্গা মরা গাং stage dire and dreary fate.

In a way, politics is an art of compromise, to the extent of making strange bed fellows, sometimes taking into consideration political expediency only, not the high-minded ethics and morality. Khaleda sent the alleged Zia-killing suspect Ershad to jail but then she also wanted to make friends with him, just as she made friends with the Jamaat too. Hasina also had previously made friends with the Jamaat, as she always did with dictator Ershad, many Razakars and many betrayers of her own father, starting with Inu, Imam, Matia, Tofael, Razzak, Humayun Rashid Chowdhury, and so on. But it is Hasina whose art of compromise is mostly rusty, nasty, dirty, and dusty. It is all for her sole and single purpose of accumulating and exercising fascist power and control over the decades with the help of Hindutva India and her RAW and RAB police unleashing widespread oppression and repression in every field of life and society and community. May the Bangladeshi nation be saved from the crooked clutches and conspiracies and may there be a way out through a miracle--divine, political or military!

One only wishes Bangladesh's ailing leader Khaleda Zia, gracious and glorious (মহান ও মহৎ) as she is, may recover fully and completely and be blessed with a second life to be able to provide, once again, a lighthouse leadership that the people of Bangladesh have been deprived of for the last 12 years. Let Bangladesh be free, as soon as possible, from all kinds of viruses—corona, corruption, cruelty, terror, tyranny, discrimination, double standards, rigging, mugging, lying, stealing, rape, abduction, disappearance, murder, immorality, immodesty, lack of the rule of law, absence of social justice, partisan politicization, flattery, sycophancy, nepotism, favoritism, increasing Hinduization and anti-Islamism, and so on. It is only the democratic BNP-led opposition, now under tyrannical suppression, that, through a free and fair electoral process, can bring back the country to its right track from its present institutional destruction, corruption, demoralization and stagnation.

8. Teachings From COVID-19

In a way of small diversion or digression, the world is immersed in its pride and arrogance about its material wealth, military might, cruise missiles, lavish luxuries, extravagant spectacles, tall towers, sky scrapers, sprawling cityscapes, royal pomp and splendor, political power and control, large corporations, atheistic/secularist arts and culture, nudities, night clubs, perversions and sexual orientations that it is shamelessly and vaingloriously promoting in the name of (unlimited) individual freedom and animalistic, unsocial and uncivilized free-mixing and free-love. The only lesson the world should learn from its being hopelessly under the grip of the small and invisible, yet unconquerably and overwhelmingly powerful coronavirus is intellectual humility, simplicity and integrity of character, spiritual awareness, religious faith and piety and submission to the Creator God/Allah the Almighty.

PPE (personal protection equipment, like a graduation gown, a raincoat or a fully-covering Muslim burqa), masks (like face covering Muslim scarf), gloves, social distancing, washing hands, avoiding shaking hands, maintaining cleanliness and staying, as best as possible, in the privacy of home and family (as opposed to outdoors indulgence in free-mixing, drinking and eating all kinds of nasty food made out of nonedible insects and animals)—all these suggest the validity of the religiously/Islamically recommended life style. All the corona induced precautions prove the fact that the all-powerful, all-knowing and all-seeing God cannot be wrong in His instructions and injunctions and that He is right in His infinite knowledge as revealed in His holy books and passed on to the humankind through His chosen people and prophets, especially Prophet Muhammad (peace be upon him).

It is as if, as some religious communities around the world would assume, the coronavirus was a divine blessing in the guise of a penalty inflicted upon humanity, but ultimately intended for the good of humanity with lessons to be learnt from—lessons taking us closer to earth, nature, and simplicities of (rural and rustic) life as depicted in Shakespeare's romantic comedies, Alexander Pope's "Happy the Man," pre-Romantic and Romantic poetry (especially Wordsworth's, Cowper's, Thomson's, Goldsmith's), Thomas Hardy's Wessex novels, Robert Frost's poems,

Henry David Thoreau's *Walden, or Life in the Woods* and the vast amount of environmental writings. It is as if God sent down His wrath in the form of this civilization-collapsing and world order changing corona calamity due to excessive violations of His edicts and injunctions by certain classes, circles, societies, parades and carnivals, who may thus be awakened to rise to a higher level of moral and ethical reform and regeneration. As a politically aspiring writer and thinker from the USA puts it, "This crisis is taking a heavy toll on everything that makes us human, defying logic."

The above is not to question or undermine human progress, human achievement, and freedom of speech and expression but to reflect, review, reassess and re-examine human advancement in all the fields of human endeavor in the context of the vastness, endlessness and immensity of God's power, God's creation, and His mercy and compassion. Certainly, we depend on God-gifted scientific knowledge and medical studies for treatment of COVID-19 and, hopefully, for a coronavirus vaccine. But everything has a limit, including the freedom of religion and all other freedoms, regardless of how basic or fundamental they may be. In their own interest, God-created humans cannot just do or believe as they wish. All religions recommend limit and restraint as much as they allow for freedom. So is the case with human society, civilization and culture that has grown by taking into account both restriction and openness in a positive and constructive way, not in a senseless, anarchical and beastly manner. Similarly, gender should not be understood as an wide array of identities (as the LGBT community wrongly tends to do), but, simply and conclusively, as only the male-female binary.

9. Conclusion

Returning to the main subject, it is the boastful and belligerent braggarts and upstarts belonging to the unholy axis of garrulously pompous Donald Trump, Benjamin Netanyahu, Narendra Modi and Sheikh Hasina in particular who should learn the values of honesty, morality, decency, dignity, political fairness, tolerance, transparency, openness and accountability from this awfully awesome pandemic plague. It is especially the dictatorial Hasina, acting like a hungry hyena towards the democratic political opposition of Bangladesh, who should be humbled by this crippling COVID-19 catastrophe so that she can stop and move away from her horribly dictatorial rule and rise above her government's unlimited corruption, massive vote-rigging, and indescribable oppression meted out to the BNP-and-Khaleda-led political opposition of the country.

What the former Awami speaker Humayun Rasheed Choudhury said about Sheikh Mujib--that even as many as one hundred hangings would not cleanse Mujib of his sins--also applies to the horribly ruling Hasina odiously oppressive with baseless opprobrium, vilification and vituperation against Khaleda Zia and the opposition led by her. What another former Awami speaker Abdul Malek Ukil (describing Mujib as a Feraoun) and other political leaders such as the initially anti-Awami-then-turned-Awami Matia Chowdhury, quarter Awami Hasanul Haq Inu, Col Abu Taher, semi-Awami Rashed Khan Menon, Mujahidul Islam Selim, and now pro-BNP ASM Abdur Rob said about Mujib in those days (1972-1975) would also apply to Hasina for her fascist rule thriving on corruption, oppression, subversion, fake and fictitious claims and outrageously committed crimes. Many of her present Awami to pro-Awami cronies wanted to throw Mujib's body into the Bay of Bengal in August 1975 (for example, Col. Taher, whose brother Anwar Hussein is now an Awami flatterer), called Mujib a "beiman" (liar/untrustworthy), wanted to peel off Mujib to make a dugdugi/ডুগডুগি drum with his skin, celebrated Mujib's assassination by dancing on army tank, and withdrew/took away his "BangaBandhu" title (for example, Hasanul Hoque Inu, Matia Chowdhury and Mujahidul Islam Selim).

To reiterate, the BNP is the largest and most popular party of Bangladesh. It is vastly popular and enormously superior to Bangladesh Awami League (BAL). But, let the people decide. Time is overdue, as it was in 2014 and then in 2018, for the foolishly but ferociously repressive, vote-rigging and illegal Hasina regime, cut off from the people, to take a 180 degree turn for the sake of 180 million people of Bangladesh. They hardly support the threatening and throttling, and choking and suffocating Hasina regime but they can hardly say anything in her police and prison state. As the plethora of evidence suggests, Hasina is an anathema and a parasite to the people of Bangladesh; she is another "Banga-Virus" as her father Mujib was a "Banga-Shatru," "Banga-Beiman" and "Feraoun" (as termed by Indian writer-journalist Kuswant Singh and many of her past and present Awami cronies). As such, she should immediately go, regardless of whose lap she tilts towards and finds herself on--China or India

Since the people of Bangladesh know for certain Sheikh Hasina is to India what Mir Jafar was to East India Company (and its Robert Clive) and what Lendhup Dorji of Sikkim was to India, she would always remain a vassal, a lackey, a stooge and a servant permanently chained and fettered in bondage to India. However, regardless of India or China, people want her out. They demand that she goes in no time through a peaceful transition and that those who are chosen by voters in a free, fair, clean and competitive general election held under a neutral caretaker administration come to power.

The first seven points for such a democratically elected and people mandated patriotic government should be: (1) to trumpet, "Down with Fascist Hasina," or, to say, with Dr Hashmi, "Hell with Hasina's Fascism;" (2) to ditch and ban pro-Hindu and pro-India "Joy Bangla" and "Bungalee nationalism," both soaked in the Hindutva; (3) to throw out the existing stale, rotten, torn, tattered, loosely adhered to, conveniently tailored and re-tailored, and expediently and expeditiously made and re-made constitutional clauses and patchworks; (4) to remove the misused, misleading, and Hindutva-promoting and Islam-bashing term "secularism" from the constitution; (5) to draft a new and fresh and pro-people constitution, infused with the spirit of the inclusive Bangladeshi Nationalism, with the aim of establishing the rule of law and social justice on the land of Bangladesh; (6) to solemnly declare the fascist Hasina regime of 2009 onwards totally illegal and invalid; and (7) to hold all the culprits of the regime and their accomplices in the police, RAB, judiciary, and administration accountable and try them all on ICT for the fascist, black, brutal and brutish misdeeds they have committed since 2009 to suit the dark, dreary, and dull Awami BAKSALi-Hindutva-saturated Indian agenda.

---

[1] For a few glimpses of Begum Khaleda Zia:
- https://youtu.be/voXPd0p1IFw Khaleda in prison, behind bars

- www.youtube.com/watch?v=0aP7wuBCxRA (Khaleda giving a momentous and memorable speech in the parliament as opposition leader)
- https://youtu.be/10IiwKp4jdA (Zia and Khaleda visiting an African country)
- www.youtube.com/watch?v=WaEWS9QCgy8 (Khaleda casting her vote)
- www.youtube.com/watch?v=dm4FS_ZopqM (Khaleda exchanging Eid greetings)
- www.facebook.com/photo.php?fbid=10216294378863741&set=gm.767645134067549&type=3&theater Begum Zia's fantastic address on the occasion of the founding anniversary of the BNP in 2015.
- www.youtube.com/watch?v=uXdEO1BrX54 (President Zia along with Mrs Zia visiting Malaysia);
- www.youtube.com/watch?v=iBdzm31zba4&list=PLExHoCI_4SUvTdjqejJA50HC-ilJQb-n7&index=80&app=desktop (watch Khaleda addressing a crowd);
- www.youtube.com/watch?v=iBdzm31zba4&list=PLExHoCI_4SUvTdjqejJA50HC-ilJQb-n7&index=80&app=desktop (watch Khaleda resigning and addressing a crowd);
- https://youtu.be/HVgx5w0RKvM "কোথাও আমার হারিয়ে যেতে নেই বাধা || ১৯৯৪ সালের স্কুল বিতর্ক || তৎকালীন প্রধানমন্ত্রী খালেদা জিয়া" Great debate to watch with great comments from Prof Emajuddin Ahmed in presence of the great leader Begum Zia;
- President Zia arriving in Egypt www.youtube.com/watch?v=AVDDLSFxP-4;
- President Zia arriving in his treacherous mortal enemy India: www.youtube.com/watch?v=U-B46TaUOz8
- https://youtu.be/x_a8WW7KKF0"টকশোতে শহীদ জিয়াউর রহমানের জীবনী নিয়ে ঝড় তুলল"
- www.youtube.com/watch?v=MhqJK4pit24 Honest, smart and brilliant President Zia
- ঢাকার শাহীন স্কুলে তারেক জিয়া গেছিলো ভর্তি পরীক্ষা দিতে https://www.facebook.com/photo.php?fbid=1495707290631195&set=a.100794310122507&type=3&theater
- http://everything.explained.today/Khaleda_Zia/

[2] https://youtu.be/4jIZeJXTOjY
www.facebook.com/Minafarahofficial/videos/409438473420889/?sfnsn=wa
www.facebook.com/pg/Minafarahofficial/videos/
https://youtu.be/VtKtAGiLE1U জেনারেলরাই যখন বিশ্বাষঘাতক

[3] Col Shahid Uddin Khan with Dr Kanak Sarwar:
https://youtu.be/V4z3F5hHXb4; https://youtu.be/Ol0vMwGOFSE;
https://youtu.be/Y8ih5GW3FJs

⁴ See my *Bangladesh: Political and Literary Reflections on a Divided Country* (New York: Peter Lang, 2018), Chapter 14: When Bangladesh Is Divided Over Its National Anthem: A Politico-Literary Perspective, pp. 465-492.

⁵ http://lyricsbengalisong.blogspot.com/2014/03/aaji-bangladesher-hridoy.html

⁶ Here, it needs to be quickly pointed out that Tagore's poem, being a worship of the Hindu deity Durga, is considered to be highly communal and has, therefore, been dropped from the Class VII Bangla textbook in the Muslim majority Bangladesh. www.dhakatimes24.com/2017/01/07/15334/ পাঠ্যবই-থেকে-বাংলাদেশের-হৃদয়-বাদ

⁷ www.youtube.com/watch?v=fgCeEsQT_mc by Dr Kanak Sarwar, Dr Pinaki Bhattacharya and AKM Wahiduzzaman;
nazmamustafa.wordpress.com/2015/08/24/একুশে-আগস্ট-২০০৪-সচেতনের/ বিএনপি সরকার পতনের লক্ষ্যে চালানো হয় ২১ আগস্ট গ্রেনেড হামলা! ; amardesh.co.uk/1078-2/ মুজিবের রাষ্ট্রবিনাসী বাকশাল; WWW.YOUTUBE.COM/WATCH?V=RGFKQJ2BT_Q&FEATURE=YOUTU.BE "ইনসাফ শো-তে পিনাকী ভট্টাচার্য"

Dr Abid Bahar of Canada would say, "This is my understanding of Mujib: He was a thuggish politician and was a 100% trickster; it is his same nature that is all over there in his political life from Faridpur to Calcutta to Dhaka. He surrendered to the authority several times when he sensed trouble. On the 25th March. The other important event that he stayed away from trouble was during the language movement. Unfortunately, such an unworthy person was elevated to the position of "father of the nation." S K Sinha rightly says in his book "Broken Dream" that for all the troubles today, Mujib's belief in authoritarian politics is responsible. Unfortunately, we judge him from the 7th March speech only, which is as if the nation is only scratching the surface to know the real Mujib.

⁸ See ভারতবর্ষ তথা বাঙ্গালা বিভক্তির প্রসঙ্গে 'দেশ' পত্রিকায় প্রকাশিত কৃষ্ণা বসুর লেখা "কায়েদ-ই-আজম জিন্না ও ভারত বিভাগ" প্রবন্ধ www.facebook.com/photo.php?fbid=3642978982380855&set=a.223935527618568&type=3

⁹ www.youtube.com/watch?v=0aP7wuBCxRA

¹⁰ Although Adolf Hitler wrote his 1925 two-volume autobiographical manifesto Mein Kampf (My Struggle or My Fight) when he was in prison, he is being omitted from this list for obvious reasons. His book describes the process by which he became antisemitic and outlines his right wing white supremacist political ideology for Germany.

¹¹ http://southasiajournal.net / bangladesh-mujib-borso – coronavirus - and-real-mujib/

¹² newsbdtoday.com/Editor-Choice/details/360/আবেগ-নয়-মেধা-দিয়ে-বুঝুন-খালেদা-জিয়ার-বিরুদ্ধে-কিসের-রায়-এবং-কেনো

¹³ See my *Bangladesh Divided: Political and Literary Reflections on a Corrupt Police and Prison State* (New York: Peter Lang, 2019), p. 252.

¹⁴ Matiur Rahman Rentu ("I Want/Wish to be Hanged/Executed," 1999), http://amarfashichai.blogspot.co.uk (in English), p. 9; http://amarfashichai.blogspot.co.uk/2013/07/amar-fashi-chai-by-motiur-rahmanrentu.html (in

English); https://mazams.weebly.com/uploads/4/8/2/6/48260335/amar_fashi_chai_bangla.pdf (in Bangla). Rentu is referenced in this context and other issues in my *Bangladesh*, pp. 249, 254, 314, 338, 376; and also my *Bangladesh Divided*, pp. 64, 129, 130, 146, 147, 148.

[15] Mohammad Zainal Abedin, "Begum Khaleda Zia: The Most Oppressed Political Legend in the 21st Century," in Sabria Chowdhury Balland (ed), *Bangladesh: A Suffering People Under State Terrorism*, pp. 137-144.

[16] See Chapter 9, "The Quagmire of Partisan Politics Over the Dead: Controversies Over the Image and Status of Mujib and Zia," in my *Bangladesh*, pp. 309-346.

- Also, an amazing article, প্রসঙ্গ স্বাধীনতার ঘোষণা :মিথ্যা এবং শত মিথ্যা যোগফল শুধু যে মিথ্যার বেসাতি www.eurovisionbd.com/শহীদ-জিয়ামিথ্যা-এবং-শত-মি/ by H Shahadat Suhrawardy;

- "কায়েদে আজাদী" শাহাদাত সুহরাওয়ার্দী (a poem), www.eurovisionbd.com/কায়েদে-আজাদী-শাহাদাত-সুহ/

- www.dailynayadiganta.com / sub-editorial/505751 / জিয়াউর-রহমান-ক্ষণিকের-স্মৃতি;

- Dr Asif Nazrul on President Zia, https://youtu.be/x_a8WW7KKF0; https://www.facebook.com/Dr.Asifnazrul/?hc_ref

- Barrister Mainul Hussein on President Zia, www.youtube.com/watch?v=KkeFVJEFTbQ;

- জিয়াউর রহমান কখনোই বিলাসিতা পছন্দ করতেন না www.facebook.com/bangladeshipirates/videos/447643742593233/UzpfSTEwMDAyNjc3NTgxNjg3Mjo3MDY3OTY5MDY3NTkxODU/?tn-str=*F;

- www.facebook.com/bangladeshipirates/videos/447643742593233/UzpfSTEwMDAyNjc3NTgxNjg3Mjo3MDY3OTY5MDY3NTkxODU/?tn-str=*F

- www.facebook.com/photo.php?fbid=1316421415363897 Dr Ahmad Sharif denying Mujib and extollong Ziaur Rahman

[17] See Chapters 11 & 12, "Bangladeshi Nationalism: A Cause and Concept Right and Just" and "Secularism in Bangladesh: Questions of Politicocultural and Religious Conflict" in my *Bangladesh*, pp. 367-392 & pp. 393-444, respectively.

[18] Dr Taj Hashmi writes: "India's former President Pranab Mukherjee just died today (31st August 2020 at 84). I wish I could mourn his death! I can't, because he was a little monster, a vicious and evil imperialist for Bangladesh. He was as anti-Bangladeshi as many of his colleagues in the Indian Administration. While he was India's External Affairs Minister, once he misbehaved with Bangladeshi Prime Minister Khaleda Zia -- violating all codes of conduct and diplomatic norms -- while she was on an official visit to India. He was instrumental in promoting the notorious and evil Moinuddin-Fakhruddin Regime in 2007-2008. Pranab Mukherjee and Manmohan Singh and the Indian Administration as a whole was anti-Bangladesh, and the Hindu-Fascist Modi Regime is not different

from its predecessors. Pranab Mukherjee was so crude and indecent, imperialist and intrusive with regard to Bangladesh that while the rustic Chetonabazi Vulgar Crowd at Shahbagh was promoting anarchy in the name of "trial of War Criminals" in early 2013, Pranab he was visiting Bangladesh as the President of India. He was so crude and undiplomatic that he also went to Shahbagh in support of the Hasina's Biryani-fed Crowd, and spoke in favour of the rally. It was a naked intrusion into a sovereign country's internal affairs. However, the crude and pro-Indian Hasina Regime thought it was a positive thing for Bangladesh and the Fascist Hasina Regime. Shame on Parnab and Shame on Hasina! I share an old article by me (written in 2017) "Pranab Mukherjee Tells it All", which is about his inadvertent confession about his nasty role in promoting the Fakhruddin-Moinuddin Regime, which was a precursor to the present fascist Regime under Hasina, which was installed in 2008 through doctored, pro-Indian (pro-American/pro-British) elections in 2008. Please read it. Thanks! The link to my Article: https:// countercurrents.org / 2017 / 11/ pranab-mukherjee-tells-it-all/ ; https:// amardesh.co.uk / ভারতের-প্রাক্তন-রাষ্ট্রপ/ ; amardesh.co.uk / হাসিনার-মুখে-প্রণবের-গুণ/

[19] https:// www.youtube.com / watch?v=hFQttBV3yNQ; www.youtube.com/ watch?v=ccwH2hGt-Ps; https://www.youtube.com/watch?v=hFQttBV3yNQ

[20] See my *Bangladesh*, p. 186.

[21] Here is a short list (collected from internet sources) of those who did not even finish their school education, or were college dropouts:
1. George Washington, President of the United States
2. Abraham Lincoln, President of the United States
3. Harry Truman, President of the United States
4. Grover Cleveland, President of the United States
5. Zachary Taylor, President of the United States
6. Andrew Johnson, President of the United States
7. John Glenn, Astronaut, U.S. Senator
8. Barry Goldwater, U.S. Senator
9. Benjamin Franklin, U.S. Ambassador
10. Winston Churchill, Prime Minister of England
11. John Major, Prime Minister of England
12. Robert Frost, Poet
13. Florence Nightingale, Nurse
14. George Eastman, Founder of Eastman Kodak
15. Ray Kroc, Founder of McDonald's
16. Dave Thomas, Founder of Wendy's
17. Ralph Lauren, Fashion designer and Entrepreneur
18. Doris Lessing, Nobel Prize recipient in Literature
19. George Bernard Shaw, Playwright
20. Peter Jennings, News anchor for ABC
21. John D. Rockefeller, Founder of Standard Oil
22. Ted Turner, Founder of CNN

23. Quentin Tarantino, Movie director
24. Mark Twain, Author
25. Carly Fiorina, CEO of Hewlett Packard
26. Charles Dickens, Author
27. Andrew Carnegie, Industrialist
28. William Faulkner, Nobel and Pulitzer Prize winner
29. Li Ka Shing, Wealthiest man in Asia
30. Richard Branson, Founder of Virgin Atlantic Airways and Virgin Records
31. Enzo Ferrari, Founder of Ferrari
32. Henry Ford, Founder of Ford Motor Company
33. J. Paul Getty, Founder of Getty Oil
34. Larry Ellison, Founder of Oracle
35. Tom Anderson, Founder of MySpace
36. Mark Zuckerberg, Founder of Facebook
37. Steve Jobs, Founder of Apple
38. Steve Wozniak, Founder of Apple
39. Bill Gates, Founder of Microsoft
40. Paul Allen, Founder of Microsoft

For more references, one could visit: mashable.com/2016/09/22/12-entrepreneurs-who-dropped-out-of-college/ and www.cnbc.com/2017/05/10/10-ultra-successful-millionaire-and-billionaire-college-dropouts.html

[22] K*aowa* means the black bird crow; *murgi* means chicken; *ghora* means horse; and *ghadani* means *Ghatak Dalal Nirmul* Committee—the so-called pro-BAL and pro-India committee which calls for the elimination and execution of the so-called 1971 collaborators for supporting the Mslim majority Pakistan remaining united and not breaking up only to cause East Pakistan/Bangladesh to fall under the hegemonist Hindutva Indian occupation and domination. All terms are used in derogatory sense to describe some Awami elements, who either said there were some *kaowas* in the BAL, or supplied chicken to the Pakistani soldiers in 1971 or received horses from India as a questionable gift that may be an euphemism for bribe (Moeen U Ahmad) or have been demanding the hanging of Bangladeshi citizens who once supported Pakistan as their just and lawful political right.

Chapter 9

Begum Khaleda Zia—Her Life, Her Story by Mahfuz Ullah: My Speech at the Launch of the Book, November 18, 2018

Asif Nazrul
(Translated by Ahmad U Shihab)

The Famous Poster

Thank you, friends. Thank you all. At the outset, let me also thank Dr. Mahfuz Ullah, a very close and dear person of mine, for organizing this occasion.

In the late nineteen eighties, when I was a student of Dhaka University, I would be awestruck watching a famous poster. You all know which poster I am talking about. It was the famous picture depicting an arrested Begum Khaleda Zia from a political meeting at Dhaka's Purbani Hotel. The camera caught a moment when she stood by the side of the police van and addressed the crowd, with the raised fist of challenge. I was thrilled that such a great leader was born in Bangladesh. And, today, I am proud to be talking about that great leader: Begum Khaleda Zia. Thank you, Mahfuz Ullah Bhai, for giving me the opportunity to speak on this occasion.

Let me admit at the outset that I am not much qualified to talk on the life or biography of a great person. I was earlier talking to (Nurul) Kabir Bhai (Editor of the New Age) that I had read only a few biographies. You may have read the Mein Kampf or its translation, the life of Nelson Mandela and a few others. So did I. I also read the incomplete biography or Diary of Bangabandhu (Sheikh Mujibur Rahman). But I never made any academic discussion on them or any other biographical works. As you know, I work at Dhaka University, so I will relate my personal experiences only.

My father was an ordinary government officer, but he was a man of fine judgement. He called Sheikh Mujib "Sheikh Saheb." In 1975, I was a boy of nine years. One day, I noticed that my father suddenly became very upset. He kept pacing up and down holding the small red radio set we had, and kept repeating to himself: "Sheikh Saheb has been killed...Sheikh Saheb has been killed." I did not understand why such an incident made him so distressful. Later, in 1981, when President Ziaur Rahman was killed, I saw my father weeping profusely. By then, I understood why he was crying. Because, I was also crying. Just a year earlier, the President invited some brilliant students--those who took top places in various board exams-- to Bangabhaban and talked to them. I was fortunate to be one such student.

Nation Sunk in Sorrow at the Loss of President Zia

Later, during my short spell in journalism, I interacted with many people and personalities, heard and learned many facts and stories. People talked many things about Ziaur Rahman. Mahfuz Ullah Bhai will bear it out that all of them were unanimous on a few things about the man (Zia).

First, his extreme, spotless and unquestionable honesty. In Bangladesh, whenever somebody assumes any position of authority, everybody comes to know his family members and his relatives, even distant ones. President Ziaur Rahman was an exception. Hardly anybody knew who his brothers or sisters were, much less his relatives. Shahadat Chowdhury (former Editor of the Weekly Bichitra) told us that the President had a standing order that none of his family members would ever enter the BangaBhaban or Secretariat. Second, Ziaur Rahman had tremendous capacity to work hard. Few could match his pace. Third, the Declaration of Independence. (On March 27, 1971), Ziaur Rahman made the first declaration of independence, first in his own name. It was immediately modified to have been made on behalf of Bangabandhu Sheikh Mujibur Rahman. Everybody agrees that his declaration provided a tremendous inspiration to the people, who instantly took up arms to fight for the independence of Bangladesh. When such a leader was lost (in 1981), the whole country was sunk in deep sorrow and despair. Never in the history of Bangladesh so many people (more than 2 million) gathered to mourn the death of a person as did for Ziaur Rahman. That demonstrated what a great leader Zia was and how popular he was.

As the wife of President Ziaur Rahman, Begum Khaleda Zia entered the political arena carrying that sympathy. But I was astonished to note how quickly she transformed herself from that status of sympathy to a position of dignity, honor and respect on her own right. We no more see her as the wife of Ziaur Rahman; we know her as Khaleda Zia. In addition, she developed a unique personality of her own, an unparalleled image of herself, greatly manifested during the anti-Ershad movement in the late eighties. She became known as "The Uncompromising Leader." She did not deviate from what she said. She did not move even a hairbreadth from her stand if it was a matter of national or public interest, or if it was for the establishment of democracy, human rights or environmental concerns.

Ever Charming Khaleda Even When Wronged

While fighting for those issues, she had undergone insurmountable hardships. I doubt if any other leader in Bangladesh ever suffered as much for the sake of the country as Begum Zia did. Yet, she was never broken. She remained as resolute and strong-minded as ever. When I saw her being taken to the courts, to the jails, to the hospitals, I did not notice any regret or remorse in her demeanor. She took it all in stride for the sake of the country and its people.

Nonetheless, we saw her making a few compromises at times when the issues were in the interest of the people. Let me give a few examples. Her party the BNP initially did not believe in Parliamentary Democracy. But when the people demanded it, she accepted and made it into law. When the majority demanded a Caretaker Government to oversee national elections, she immediately accepted and instituted it in the constitution. In 1996, when there was a growing demand for a more credible and participatory elections, she did not hesitate to dissolve the Parliament and hold a fresh and fine election within a few months. When there was something in public or national interest, she did not vacillate to compromise. But if there was something against the nation or its people, she never bowed to pressure.

I have noted another aspect of Begum Zia's characteristic political conduct. She knew exactly what to say on what occasion. She also knew what words carried what meaning. When she spoke at the United Nations General Assembly for the first time, she openly challenged how Bangladeshi people suffered because of Indian hegemony. She was aware of the presence of India in audience, yet she did not waver to tell the truth and facts, loud and clear, before the world body.

Begum Khaleda Zia and Bangladesh are Synonymous with Each Other

Begum Zia became a synonym of a Bangladesh of honor, dignity, self-respect and sovereignty; she became a symbol of Bangladesh. She has millions (crores) of followers and supporters across the country. It was not easy to write a book on such a person. It definitely was a challenging task for the author, particularly when the person is still alive.

When we go abroad and visit bookstores, we see huge collection of biographies and autobiographies of important people. Usually, there exist separate sections or shelves to display them. There are about 50 books on the US President Donald Trump. There are even books on various characters he had relationship with. Most top sportsmen have their life stories told. Unfortunately, Bangladesh lacks in that area, virtually none. There are some limited memoirs, compilations of tidbits on leaders, but not much in the form of complete biographical works.

At the same time, we have no dearth of readers. While going in cars, often book sellers stop us in the city streets and offer books. They give us books on Nelson Mandela, Abul Kalam Azad, even on General Pervez Mosharraf. That suggests people buy them and we have readers. Then why our writers are shy of writing on our leaders? Question arises, why we don't have biographical books? Why people do not write biographies of great men and women and leaders? Reasons are not far to seek.

Many countries and institutions offer fellowships for writing on great people. Unfortunately, Bangladesh doesn't have such provisions, a big hurdle or handicap indeed to write in this field. Another setback is the absence of reference materials. The Awami League and the BNP have large websites but contain little reference materials. Whatever reference they give cannot be found; some websites cannot even be opened.

Pervasive Political Animosity

The most important reason is our political sensitivity and mutual hostility. It is so strong amongst us that if one writes something on Begum Zia, one is automatically branded as a BNP person. If one loves Ziaur Rahman, one cannot be a Mujib follower. Ridiculous. Is it not ridiculous? When we look at the sky, can't we admire both the cloud and the sky? If we can say good things about Bangabandhu Mujib's struggles, why can't we appreciate the sacrifices of those who risked their lives and fought for the independence of the country, like Ziaur Rahman and other war heroes? If one can praise Sheikh Hasina, why can't one do so for Khaleda Zia, for what she rightly deserves? What's the contradiction? Why they have to be immediately stamped with a partisan seal? Our political mindset became so poor that we cannot undertake the risk of writing on political leaders and their issues. I fail to understand it. I cannot accept this mentality of ours. It is very difficult for me to accept this mentality of ours.

Despite all these difficulties, bottlenecks and handicaps, Dr. Mahfuz Ullah undertook a huge trouble to write and produce two great books. The first one was on Ziaur Rahman. I read it. It was a great accomplishment. He now came up with his second. It is *Begum Khaleda Zia: Her Life, Her Story*. I read parts of it. Hope to read the rest the soonest.

Before I start reading a book, I usually see the footnotes and bibliography. If satisfied, I go to read the chapters in the book. Looking at those footnotes and references, I noted how painstakingly Dr. Mahfuz Ullah had worked while drafting and producing these works. In most cases, he had to depend on primary sources, i.e., his own professional notes. There are not much secondary sources and references. He took few materials from books and journals published earlier. My reiteration: he worked very hard in completing these two great books.

Yet, it does not give complete life of Begum Zia. The author covered up to 2006, with a mention of a few events of 2008. To me, it is an outstanding achievement. Congratulation, Dr. Mahfuz Ullah! Following his example, hopefully more such biographies would be written. Once these books are in the market, there could be critiques, evaluations, even further research. The amount of labor Dr. Mahfuz Ullah had put into it, the commitment he made, and, above all, the risk he had taken are enormous. He should be commended and respected not by the BNP men and women alone but by independent observers also. He has positioned himself in an unparalleled status by presenting these two great books on Ziaur Rahman and Begum Khaleda Zia.

To me, after reading a part, or a chapter, if the reader doesn't get a jolt, it is no book. I read the first book and a few other chapters of this second book. There is jolt in every page, every chapter. The book has many things about Begum Zia, which I did not know or they did not come to my attention before. I am glad I read them and know them now.

Controversy Over Her Birthday

The book also mentions of a few controversies surrounding Begum Khaleda Zia, willfully generated by hostile quarters. The author deals with them and answers the questions, if any. One of them is her birth date. When Begum Khaleda Zia became Prime Minister the first time (in 1991), her bio-data was written and circulated to all and it went to the media. There, her date of birth was shown as August 15, 1945. Everybody read it, knew it. Nobody challenged it, neither then nor in the next many years. When she fell out of grace, it became a big issue, big question. A flood of protests flowed from the vested coteries, even court cases filed. Why? The author dealt with the issue very effectively with fine and proper justifications.

If one reads the book, one will find some very interesting stories about Begum Zia's childhood. Little known is one that she used to take singing and dancing lessons. She would go to the teacher daily very early in the morning. In those days, she participated in a number of cultural functions. Another interesting fact was about her father. He was an elected leader of Tea Planters Association, a respectable position.

And, this book is not for the BNP alone or for people who love Begum Zia. This is a book for those who want to know the political history of Bangladesh, the Anti-Ershad Movement in Bangladesh. Today, we hear of attacks at political rallies. Let me remind you, Begum Zia was the first person in Bangladesh to face such attacks and experience them. Her political meetings and gatherings had routinely grenade and bomb attacks, indiscriminate firings. I urge all to read this book to know all these and many more assaults that were made on her person during her long political career. For obvious reasons, most media outlets are shy of mentioning all such attacks and the suffering meted out to Begum Zia by hostile quarters. Read the book to know more, if not all.

Fate of Bangladesh and Khaleda Intertwined

I want to conclude by saying one important thing. It is a comment from Begum Khaleda Zia herself. An outstanding comment! She said that the welfare and future of Bangladesh were entangled with her personal life. When Bangladesh looked good, she felt good. When the country went through troubles, she was troubled too. It is a feeling in her, a realization. We know Bangladesh is not good today. As such, we can also assume how Begum Zia could be. In fact, her heath is no good. We hope Bangladesh turns sound and good so that she can also be good in mind and body. Her definition of sound health of the country is a Bangladesh with self-respect, dignity and honor with its sovereignty uncompromised, not feeling oneself safe by sending and keeping the family members abroad.

Thank you all very much.

Chapter 10

Begum Khaleda Zia:
A Beloved Icon of Patriotism, Fighter for Democracy, and Victim of Fascist Injustice

Nazma Mustafa

Three-Time Popularly Elected Prime Minister

A forerunner of the struggle for peace, harmony and democracy in Bangladesh, Begum Khaleda Zia is her own example. She is an uncompromising leader for which she is widely respected in her country and beyond. She was the first woman to become Prime Minister three times in a Muslim country through free and fair and credible elections. Her husband, Ziaur Rahman, was the declarer of the independence of Bangladesh, a leader in the liberation war, a General and Chief of the army and finally a highly popular President. When her husband was assassinated in 1981, she was forced into politics. The nation saw how a mother and housewife quickly turned to be successful politician on her own right. Her strong point was, she never compromised on national interest. She was the first female leader to be democratically elected the Chief Executive of a Muslim majority country, two years after Benazir Bhutto accomplished that feat in Pakistan. In a unique political achievement, Khaleda Zia never lost in any elections. In the national elections in 1991, 1996 and 2001, she won in all five constituencies she contested. It speaks volumes about her vast popularity.

A Symbol of Patience and Humility

Begum Zia possesses a sober but an impressive and imposing personality. From day one of her political life, she came under tremendous pressure and had undergone insurmountable sufferings from hostile quarters. I may serialize a few: (1) During the liberation war in 1971 she was arrested with her two infant sons and remained under military custody; (2) She was devastated at the killing of her husband Ziaur Rahma at the peak of his popularity as a highly (nationally and internationally) successful President. Following his untimely and gruesome assassination, she was catapulted into politics launching a democratic movement to topple the autocratic military ruler H M Ershad; (3) She took charge as Prime Minister to guide a politically devastated nation; (4) She faced continuous conspiracies and obstacles orchestrated by Awami opponents to unseat her from power, including a planning stage incident to sink a ferry boat by which she might take a journey along a river in northern Bangladesh (see below for more under Hasina's conspiracy to kill Khaleda); (5) The arrest and inhuman torture of her two sons on political grudge in 2007-2008 (the younger one already succumbed to the physical defilement and the older is still recuperating from the critical physical damage he received); (6) Her forced eviction from her official residence. She was virtually dragged out of her house by police under the order of Sheikh Hasina; (7) Her facing a series of false and fabricated cases, including a ridiculous one for throwing petrol bombs in a bus. It was reported that the terror attack was in fact committed by the ruling thugs but was thrust on Begum Zia; (8) Her new home and office were attacked by Sheikh Hasina's sand-and-cement trucks accompanied by the police; and, finally (9) She was sent to rot in solitary confinement in jail on absolutely false and unsubstantiated charges. It was the last attempt to break the former Prime Minister mentally and physically. The attack continues. Even in jail, she continues to count the charges, now totaling 34, all flimsy, false and fabricated.

Caretaker Government (CTG)

In 1996, Begum Zia enacted the neutral CTG to conduct national elections. All the elections held under the CTG were generally fair and acceptable. Once back in power in 2009, through behind the scene conspiracies, Sheikh Hasina realized her Awami League had no chance of winning any future election under a neutral CTG because of her various undemocratic and anti-national misdeeds. Banking on her absolute control of the Parliament, Hasina quickly abolished the CTG through the 15th Amendment, and reverted to the elections under the ruling authority. The BNP Chairperson Begum Khaleda Zia had repeatedly warned that the 15th Amendment was aimed to manage election and continue in power. Her message was clear on the "Democracy Killing Day" in February 2013. In February 2018, Begum Zia was sent to a solitary jail confinement to serve a politically engineered sentence of 17 years.

Mass Movement for Democracy

In the mid-eighties, opposition to the dictatorial rule of General Ershad took differing patterns. The Awami League and a few minor parties formed a 15-Party Alliance. Nationalist and Islamic parties flocked around the BNP to form a 7-Party Coalition. Leftists and Communists formed a 5-Party Coalition. These groups remained separated on ideological issues, at times even fighting with each other. Consequently, Ershad reigned supreme. After Hasina and her Awami League joined the farcical elections in 1986, its supporting elements shrunk to 7. Khaleda's 7-Party alliance and Jamaat e Islam boycotted the elections. During this time Begum Zia was harassed and put under house arrest a number of times. But she never gave up and continued the anti-Ershad movement. In 1987, she took the initiative to start a united movement. Hasina's alliance joined in. The left group also cooperated. Ershad tried various attempts to avert the trouble and survive. By the end of 1990, he had to finally step down handing over the power to a Caretaker Administration under the newly appointed Vice-President Justice Shahabuddin Ahmed.

In the election in 1991, the BNP won majority and formed the government with Khaleda Zia becoming the Prime Minister. She quickly established a parliamentary democracy in the country. Her achievements in mass education, women's empowerment and dealing with natural disasters were unique. She brightened the face of Bangladesh in international forums, including the SAARC and the OIC. The name of "Zia" has been associated with the life of the Bangladeshis since the birth of the country. It was a heartburn for Sheikh Hasina. She could not tolerate that people were praising Ziaur Rahman in place of her father

Sheikh Mujibur Rahman. Back to power in 2009, she charted a blueprint to remove Zia from history and rehabilitate the image of Mujib. India has always been by her side, as she was promise bound to take care of Indian interests in Bangladesh, even if that went against the national interests of Bangladesh.

Awami *Logi Boitha* and 1/11 Conspiracies

Sheikh Hasina's seizure of power came through conspiracies and terror tactics designed by India with the connivance of then Army Chief General Moeen U Ahmed. The US went along on its own logic. In the elections to be held in January 2007, the Awami League (AL) saw it had no chance of winning a majority. It needed to create a chaos in the law and order situation to stop the elections. It used *logi-boitha* –poles and oars of country boats, Awami League's election symbol--for terror acts. The *logi-boitha* terror and *tandob* on October 28, 2006 killed dozens of innocent people and wounded hundreds. As per pre-planned arrangement, General Moeen took the pretext of political unrest to intervene and impose Emergency on January 11, 2007. Democratic rule ended. Islamic values were abandoned. Indian hegemony took roots. Hasina was quick to claim that the military takeover (in civilian form) was the fruit of her so called bloody *andolon* (movement).

In the beginning, the Moeen-backed CTG tried to show neutrality. To justify its takeover and existence, it went after the known and unknown corrupt leaders of the past. Leaders of the immediate past BNP administration became the most victims. The CTG went for big fish too. Sheikh Hasina received 15 charges, including one of murder, and was arrested. Soon, Begum Khaled Zia got four and was lodged in the makeshift jail in a house next to Hasina's. Thousands from both parties were detained and filled the jails. Meanwhile, a "showcase" of behind the scene computation and permutation took place. Begum Khaleda Zia remained as uncompromising as before. She would not cooperate with the national betrayers. Hasina thus won the bet. She was upstaged as the darling of the military-backed administration. According to analysts, the game was played to reach the desired result.

Next was a calculated campaign to defame and malign the BNP, which was the immediate past of government of Begum Khaleda Zia. In addition, the Zia family was also targeted. When the military had done with beating and managed enough ransom money from the victims in the process, the hitherto "unbailable" leaders kept stepping out of jail as puritans.

At India's instance, the military helped Sheikh Hasina's Awami League to win the elections in December 2008. Once in power with solid majority in the Parliament, Prime Minister Hasina quashed all her 15 cases plus more than ten thousand against her party members. At the same time, she not only kept those against the BNP men, they were further strengthened. In addition, fresh cases kept adding up against the BNP leaders and activists. Begum Zia ended up with 35, and still counting. On a flimsy and unsubstantiated Zia Charitable Trust case, she was clamped with a 17-year jail term. It is a clear inhuman assault on the three-time former Prime Minister aimed at breaking her physically and mentally.

With the advent of the deadly Coronavirus and her failing health, Hasina released Khaleda on March 25, 2020. Earlier, the regime kept saying that they could not do anything about her bail as it was a "court decision."

The Zia Orphanage Trust Case

In the Zia Orphanage Trust case against BNP chairperson Begum Zia, filed by the CTG in 2008, it has already been proved that the funds remained unused, hence no misuse took place. Full amount of the fund is still in the bank, in fact, increasing four to five times by now. None of the prosecution witnesses testified that the money had been seized or embezzled. The Anti-Corruption Commission (ACC) could not prove the charges, yet she was convicted. Before and during the court proceedings, Sheikh Hasina and her cohorts kept giving the verdicts themselves. The blindly obedient court issued the formal order, in compliance with the desire of the ruling Awami party leaders. This was totally a farce and miscarriage of justice.

Khaleda's has been sent to the old and abandoned jailhouse at Nazimuddin Road. The 73-year-old ailing former Prime Minister was the only prisoner in this empty fort. During the anti-Ershad movement, she faced imprisonment in 1983, 1984 and 1987, and was kept confined at her residence following those arrests. This was the first time she was lodged in a jailhouse.

Below are some of the relevant facts that came in the media to show how meanly and maliciously the case was framed against Begum Khaleda Zia.

Points of Discrepancy and Dishonesty in the Case

1. The prosecution submitted rough photocopies without original documents to support. Unauthenticated photocopies are not admissible in the courts of law.

2. There was no signature of Begum Khaleda Zia on the submitted photocopies. The prosecution could not present such evidence, nor could the court accept it. Yet it did. A great travesty of justice!

3. The cashbook presented looked manufactured. Even the grocery stores have better quality cashbooks. No checks or its stubs were presented to substantiate the transactions.

4. Corruption was alleged in the Zia Orphanage Trust. However, no allegation was found in its sister charitable institution, the Zia Memorial Trust, established in Bagerhat. It was unusual that one part of the trust was corrupt while the other was not.

5. Projects run on the allocation of money from the Zia Trust Fund were not taken into account. It was strange why those projects were not brought in the charges.

6. On November 2006, Zia Orphanage Trust paid money to Mr. Sharafuddin Ahmed to purchase a piece of land to set up an orphanage. Sharafuddin Ahmed could not or did not buy the land. He deposited the full amount of Taka 2.5 crore (25 million taka) back to the Trust. As such, the Trust did not incur any financial loss in this transaction. So, where is the corruption?

7. Why wasn't the corruption charge made over the entire fund? Supposing corruption took place, as the ACC alleged, it was in November 2006, when Begum Khaleda Zia was no longer the Prime Minister. After she relinquished charge of the office of Prime Minister, Dr. Kamal Siddiqui, former Chief Secretary at the PM's office, was signatory to matters relating to the Zia

Orphanage Trust Account at the Sonali Bank. It is also a pertinent question if signatures belonged to him because he was no more the Chief Secretary in November 2006 (Kind of contradictory. If Kamal Siddiqui was not the Chief Secretary in November 2006, how could he be signatory to the Zia OT Account either?) Question was also raised if a Prime Minister could be a public official in accordance with Article 66 (3) of the Constitution, and the relevant Section of the Criminal Penal Code.

8. If this alleged corruption case did not occur in 1993, it occurred in 2006. Then it had to be adjudicated under relevant Sections of the Trust Law or The Penal Code of the time. And the case did not have to come under the jurisdiction of the ACC.

9. Begum Khaleda Zia's government took oath of office on September 19, 1991. Zia Orphanage Trust did not exist in June 1991 How could a non-existent account be brought for charging a Prime Minister who took office three months later? It there was an account in June 1991, it must have been a fraud one, forged. Why was it not investigated and the forgers were not found out?

10. Government's witness number 19 has stated that he resigned from the post of Accountant from the PM's Office on January 31, 1993. How could he make entries in April, July and October, 1993 when he was not in service? The witness subsequently admitted that he was summoned by the PM's Office later and made those entries (in April, July and October 1993). Question arises if such back dated entries were possible and acceptable by the court when the person concerned was not in employment. Obviously, questions arise if those entries were made in 1993 (when "misuse" was alleged) or in 2008 (when the case was filed). The court was informed that the account holder did not see any account related to 'Prime Minister's Orphan Fund' in 1993. If entry was required in April, July and October 1993, it ought to have been done by the Acting Accountant, witness number 21. All these issues remain vague or made up and not answered yet.

At one point, the court termed Prime Minister Sheikh Hasina "arrogant," "hot-headed" (on August 7, 2017)! In his ruling, Chief Justice Surendra Kumar Sinha recorded on the issue, "The inviolable unity we built in 1971 has been thwarted by the enemies. Today we live in a free, independent and sovereign country. But still today we are indulging in arrogance and ignorance."

While all these arguments are valid and legal, it is a shame that Begum Zia's two dozen lawyers fighting for her on the case for many years failed to highlight them. Even if they did, these points must have been ignored or dismissed by the partisan and loyal court which wanted to punish Begum Zia at any cost.

Case on the Number of War Martyrs

Begum Khaleda Zia faced a new charge for questioning the number of martyrs in the liberation war of Bangladesh in 1971. As the Chief Guest at a political rally organized by the freedom fighters, Begum Zia pointed at the doubt harbored by the general public about the actual number of martyrs of the 1971 war. She demanded to ascertain the correct number. Immediately, an Awami affiliated lawyer of the Supreme Court issued her a legal notice challenging her statement. The ruling elements maliciously insinuated various conspiracies behind Khaleda's demand, such as pressure from the Jamaat-e- Islam (which was a political ally of the BNP), Pakistani trap or it had something to do with her recent trip to London.

Upon release from Pakistan, Sheikh Mujibur Rahman arrived in London and declared that Pakistan military killed 3 million (thirty lakhs) Bengalis in 1971. Serajur Rahman of BBC claimed to have told Mujib upon arrival in London that some 300,000 people might have died in the war. It could be a mistake or a slip of tongue, the 3 lakhs became 3 million. The wrong statement of three million martyrs by Mujib was firmly established in the Awami administration. It could not be challenged. My father was an Awami League leader in those days and we had to remain quiet even knowing it to be widely unrealistic.

In fact, Mujib did assign a Commission to ascertain the number. After working for almost a year, it came up with a staggeringly low number of 60,000. Feeling embarrassed, Mujib cancelled the Commission's work, but Mujib's mistakenly ordained figure of three million remained stuck in the Awami psyche and further deviation or discussion on the issue were forbidden. Surprisingly, no subsequent governments felt it necessary to find the truth. Various authorities kept assuming numbers quoting their own sources.

Sharmila Bose, an Indian origin journalist, researcher and intellectual, made extensive research on the people killed during the war in 1971. She recorded her findings in the book *Dead Reckoning: Memories of the 1971 Bangladesh war*. Pro-Awami coterie challenged her work saying that it was a Pakistan sponsored propaganda. Ridiculous! First, she rightly depicted the picture of the torture and atrocities committed by Pakistani forces. Second, coming from a respectable and famous family (she was a grandniece of Subhas Chandra Bose, the nationalist leader of India, and daughter of Trinamul Congress leader Krishna Bose), Sharmila's integrity could hardly be doubted. If her research involved logic, her findings must be taken into account in history.

Bose emphatically claimed that her work was the first of its kind in gathering information at the grassroots level and interviews from both sides giving their respective accounts and comments on the war. Some 20 years earlier, two US historians, Richard Sessions and Leo Rose wrote a book titled *War and Secession: Pakistan, India and the Creation of Bangladesh*, which gave some accounts of death in 1971 but it did not reach the general public. Bose's research was indeed the first of its kind.

Sharmila Bose's arguments should have cleared the doubts. Her book *Dead Reckoning* pointed out the facts why Pakistan broke, giving birth to Bangladesh. It is important to have an open discussion about the actual cause and roles of the participant involved. One-sided history will not establish the truth.

Let us give the 3-million theory a closer look. The war ran for eight and a half months, in other words, roughly 261 days. By dividing 3 million (3,000,000) with 261, it comes to 11,494, meaning that many people must have been killed a day on average. If this looked doubtful, questions will definitely arise. People can easily find out how many of their friends, relatives and neighbors were lost in 1971. Truth and transparency are important. The fact is, Khaleda Zia did not make any slip of tongue by raising doubt about the number of martyrs; it was Sheikh Mujib who made the slip; he mistakenly converted 3 lakhs to 3 million. Anyway, all these arguments are futile to the Sheikh Hasina. Like Aesop's Tales, Khaleda committed a crime by questioning her father's given number and so she must be punished. This is Hasina's justice. This is Hasina's democratic rule.

Other Cases

Khaleda Zia remained immensely popular. Her personality and dignity were incomparable to those of Sheikh Hasina. In a fair election, Khaleda's BNP could not be defeated. At the same time, Hasina would not abandon her throne. Hasina is both scared of her nemesis and elections. Taking advantage of the massively engineered Parliamentary majority, her administration quickly quashed the neutral Caretaker system that was enacted to ensure fair elections. Hasina's next hurdle is Begum Zia. Through evil orchestrations, the three-time Prime Minister was sent to jail even though the charges against her were fictitious and could not be proved. Dr. Asif Nazrul, a renowned professor of Law at Dhaka University called it a "highly controversial verdict." General public also knows it was a politically motivated verdict to keep Khaleda away from politics so that Hasina could sail easily through her election mechanizations and manipulations. Begum Zia was refused bail over and over again. She could not receive required health care. Her personal physicians were not allowed to visit her or treat her.

The BNP Chairperson has 17 cases going in the court, including Niko (Dec 9, 2007), Gatco (Sep 2, 2007) and Barapukuria Coalmine Graft (February 26, 2008). She faced a total of 37 cases but Charge Sheet could be framed only for 17. The Niko took an interesting turn. It involved a contract with the Canadian Gas Company, Niko. The International Centre for Settlement of Investment Disputes (ICSID) on February 25, 2019 ruled on the Niko case that "the evidence does not establish the agreement procured through corruption." The regime deliberately kept the ICSID ruling out of the public knowledge. Interestingly, the Niko case was filed during the military-backed Caretaker government in 2007 and Sheikh Hasina was also implicated in it. When Hasina became Prime Minister, her name was removed from the case by the compliant High Court (according to David Bergman, a journalist based in Britain, Editor, English Netra News).

Conspiracy to Rebuild One Party BAKSAL

The points discussed above make it clear that the Hasina government has engaged in a plot to destroy democracy in the country and its main political opposition led by Khaleda Zia. Sheikh Hasina recently renewed her stay in power for another term in a style reminiscent of her father's notorious establishment of one-party rule, BAKSAL, in which no opposition parties would be allowed to contest the incumbent in the national elections. Similarly, she returned to power after a fake, completely rigged election that has had no credibility.

To divert public attention away from her misdeeds, Hasina had her party leaders file a litany of vile and baseless legal cases against Khaleda Zia (while having her kangaroo courts quash dozens of serious cases against herself), which in any fair judicial investigation would turn out to be false and made up. The reasons they gave in support of those cases were fake and funny. For example, they blamed Khaleda Zia for not appearing before the judge on February 20, 2019, but the facts are different. In the hearing of the Niko case on March 3, 2019, Khaleda Zia stated that she was ready to come to the court on February 20, but they did not bring her there. Keep in mind, she was in jail, not free to move (*Nayadiganta*, March 3, 2019).

Hasina's Misrule and Continuous Attack on the Opposition

Under Hasina's mismanagement in the last ten years, about six lakh crore takas (BDT 6,000,000,000,000) have been smuggled out of the country. The recent reports by three reputed organizations highlighted the news of this humongous money laundering out of Bangladesh under Hasina's misrule. They included the Swiss Bank, the Global Financial Integrity (GFI), and the US-based investigative journalists' organization ICIJ (*Jugantor*, June 30, 2018). The amount of money the directly or indirectly Awami-supported looters and culprits smuggled out of the country is equal to one and a half times the national budget. With that money, one could build 16 Padma bridges for which the government is raising money from multiple sources at home and abroad. The Hasina regime presided over this colossal smuggle of cash out of the country.

According to a story published in the *Manabjamin* (January 11, 2018), Sheikh Hasina accused the Zia family of smuggling $ 12 billion out of the country and presented the details of her accusation to the parliament. The BBC Bangla also carried this story. But two BNP advisors protested to the BBC news that this story was false. They argued that, unlike in the case of the current government's colossal money smuggling out of Bangladesh, no international organizations published reports of money smuggling by the Khaleda Zia government. Nor were there any news of such money laundering out of Bangladesh during the tenure of Khaleda Zia as prime minister. Earlier, Khaleda Zia demanded an apology from the prime minister for falsely accusing her government of smuggling money (December 20, 2017, BBC Bangla).

The BAL (Bangladesh Awami League) leaders accused the Zia family of looting Tk 5 crore (BDT 50,000,000) from the treasury of Bangladesh (*Kalerkantho*, December 18, 2017). They accused Khaleda Zia and her son, Tarique Rahman, of using the money for terrorist purposes (*Janakantha*, December 9, 2017). Some international media also carried the story of this accusation. However, the Anti-Corruption Committee didn't give any details of the charge. Instead, a member of the committee stated that officials would investigate the issue. Three years have since passed. They have issued no investigation results until the time of this writing (mid-2020). In other words, Hasina and her colleagues fabricated the story of money laundering by Khaleda Zia and Tarique Rahman as part of their propaganda campaign to ruin their reputation.

Academics and journalists rejected the lies and deceits of the Hasina government. We read about how Hasina herself expressed her frustration over the fact that only few media outlets published about what she was promoting as the 'corruption' of the previous Khaleda Zia administration (bdnews24.com, December 8, 2017). Adding to her frustration, the University Teachers' Association of Bangladesh (UTAB) said they found those allegations false and fabricated. A joint statement of a thousand journalists made media headlines that the stories circulated by the Hasina government against Khaleda Zia were fake. No doubt, dedicated journalists are the mirror of the society.

Sheikh Hasina never misses a chance to falsely attack or accuse the Zia family. She directly blamed the BNP Chairperson Khaleda Zia for the killings of two foreigners in Bangladesh (Amar Desh desk report, October 10, 2015). She said Khaleda Zia was spreading panic by killing foreign nationals in Bangladesh while she (Khaleda) was sitting abroad in London. Sheikh Hasina announced this blame at her Ganobhaban meeting with the newly elected officials of the district bar associations allied with her party. She tried to blame every misfortune on Khaleda Zia and her son Tarique Rahman. She would have her party cadres commit criminal acts and shift the blame on to Khaleda Zia and her party BNP. We learned that her party cadres detonated petrol bombs on a bus, killing and maiming innocent people during a protest, but she blamed Khaleda and the BNP for setting the bus on fire.

Hasina's Conspiracy to Kill Khaleda Zia

In the great book *Amar Fanshi Chai* ("I want my execution," published 1999 and widely available online), Matiur Rahman Rentu, an eminent freedom-fighter who served as Hasina's private secretary for 16 years (from May, 17, 1981 to January to 15, 1997), presents a first-hand account of her cruelties and intrigues. The book was published when Hasina was in power. Within a short time, it was banned in Bangladesh. The book shows how "As a person, Sheikh Hasina is dishonest, unethical, hypocrite and without any scruples or conviction." As a close aide to Hasina, Rentu came to know most of her plots against the Zia family and others but failed to expose them promptly for fear of reprisal. That is why, in the book, he asked for his execution in the first place.

In a chapter titled, "The advance of taka fifty thousand" in the book, Rentu describes how, on October 2, 1994, Hasina bribed a boatman, who used to ferry traffic across the Dharla river in Kurigram, to drown the then Prime Minister Khaleda Zia by secretly sinking his boat. During her first ride across the Dharla en route to Nageswari and Fulbari, Hasina noticed that the river had very sharp currents and waves. She also learned from the boatman that he could drown even his powerful riders by secretly opening holes into the bed of his boat. So, on the way back, she sent her entourage in another boat and took her ride with the same boatman. Rentu was her only companion during the trip. She then offered to give the boatman Tk. 500,000 if they would drown Khaleda Zia and handed him Tk. 50,000 as an advance. Even as the poor boatman was extremely reluctant to take the bait, she forcefully gave him the money. When Rentu suggested she had just wasted the money, she replied:

> No, I haven't dropped money into water; just made an investment. Since I had traveled in this route, I am sure Khaleda Zia will follow suit and come this way. Then this investment will be of use. This is why I held out the temptation of Four and a half lakh taka. You can get even the tiger's eye with money. If Khaleda Zia travels this way, then the job will be done. The greed of four and half lakh taka will prompt the boatmen to finish the job. Have the boatmen ever seen taka fifty thousand? I gave fifty thousand taka just to create greed for money in them.[1]

Rentu integrates the voice of his wife Nazma Akhter in the book. She also served the honorary house secretary of Sheikh Hasina for almost nine years (1988-1997). The book is available on the internet. Reading the book will open your eyes to how the country is moving politically backward and losing its independence today.

Ironically, so far, Hasina has made some 19 fake news headlines by dramatically announcing that some people were planning to kill her. She has been part of the conspiracies to assassinate President Zia, and she planned to kill her political opponent Khaleda Zia. Hasina came from India with an Indian plan to kill President Ziaur Rahman, Khaleda Zia, and the top soldiers of our country to turn Bangladesh into a vassal state for India. All her complaints of the threats to her life is a game she plays in the national stage.

One Freedom Fighter's Demand

To clarify my points, I need to provide a few details. The history of Bangladesh is a great thriller. Some specific truth from historical viewpoint include the following. In 1988, after 17 years of independence,

Brigadier Amin Ahmed Chowdhury collected a list of 'freedom fighters' from the Indian government. In that list, the rank of Matiur Rahman Rentu, whose book I discussed above, was 462. Rentu's publisher noted that reading this book would save the upcoming generations from political deceit. Inside the book, Rentu himself complained that the independent Bangladesh did not compile a complete list of the freedom fighters.

The nation's beloved leader Khaleda Zia is a concrete image of patience. She overcame all the uphill battles in her life with dignity and grace. Because of this, future historians would rank her with the likes of Nelson Mandela. On the contrary, I believe Hasina will go down in history as the villain of the nation.

Khaleda Zia Fought Against an Axis of Two Tyrants

Since the assassination of President Zia, Khaleda Zia has fought an axis of two major evil forces in her life. One is H. M. Ershad and the other, Sheikh Hasina. This axis of evil continues to bite at the heart of the nation even today. Ershad is dead, but his legacy of evil collaboration with Hasina continues. Both conspired to assassinate President Ziaur Rahman. Ershad was directly involved, while Hasina knew about it and was probably involved in the planning of it.

Lt. Colonel Mahtab Uddin, who served as President Zia's physician, cleared all the facts. He was with Ziaur Rahman on that day. In an article published in Naya Diganta (May 29, 2015), Colonel Oli Ahmed Birbikram, Chairman of Liberal Democratic Party (LDP), described in detail that Ershad had visited Chittagong two days before the assassination. Ershad cleared his highway to power by hanging 11 innocent freedom fighters whom he blamed to be the killers of President Zia. Ershad ordered their execution because he thought if they were alive even with life sentences, they could expose his role in the plot to kill President Zia. Their death by hanging was thus for the security of Ershad, the real culprit.

Hasina has always been allied with Ershad from day one while pretending to play the role of an opposition leader just to keep the BNP out of power.

As Rentu states in *Amar Fashi Chai*, a week before the assassination of President Ziaur Rahman, Hasina informed her top lieutenants of the impending murder and instructed them what to do in the lead up to and after that horrible event. Rentu also recounts how secretly and repeatedly Hasina cajoled General Ershad to seize power from President Justice Abdus Sattar, who succeeded President Zia. So, all her postures as an opposition leader during the reign of Ershad were part of a drama to deceive the nation (*Amar Fashi Chai*, pp. 83-100). For the rest of their lives, both of them covered up their treasonous misdeeds. Khaleda Zia alone has fought them with grace and is still fighting for the restoration of true democracy in Bangladesh. The movement against autocrat Ershad continued in five phases till 1986. On the night of March 21,1986, the BAL Leader Hasina shook hands with dictator Ershad and agreed to participate in the upcoming national election in which he ran for president. Her collaboration with Ershad to support his game plan was a complete betrayal to the opposition political movement led by Khaleda Zia. But Khaleda Zia did not give up the anti-Ershad movement.

Orphan Drama in Talk Shows

Actor Shahriar Nazim Joy hosted a television talk show to malign Khaleda Zia. The newspapers carried a story that a boy held a water pipe on a building that caught fire. The picture of the bravery of the boy became viral, and the boy received rewards. Shahriar Nazim Joy brought the boy to the talk show. Before the show began, Joy had told the boy what to say when he would be asked, "What would you do with the prize money?" When asked the question in the show, the boy said he would give the prize money to an orphanage and would not be like "Khaleda Zia, who misappropriated money from an orphanage fund." The reference here was to the false and fabricated case in which Khaleda Zia received cooked-up prison terms without mentioning that it was all baseless and fictitious. People later came to know about this trickery and condemned Joy for his unethical action. Joy did it to curry favor with the Hasina government. So, what was the message the nation received from this sort of drama?

Sheikh Hasina's ministers assure her that the coronavirus would not reach her and that she is more robust than Covid-19. On the other hand, it is difficult to see that Khaleda Zia would be freed unconditionally. The government wants Khaleda Zia to apply for parole, but she is opposed to doing that. As long as Sheikh Hasina is in power, it is difficult to see Khaleda Zia really freed. Khaleda Zia was in prison on entirely false and fabricated cases. It may be that the real orphans' prayers would make her truly free at some point.

Khaleda's Release Amid the Corona Crisis Mystery

As the deadly coronavirus kept spreading in Bangladesh, the Hasina administration quietly released Begum Zia on March 25, 2020 on executive order, which was earlier denied citing legal issues. Observers believe that the regime feared that ailing Khaleda's death in jail would bring nationwide political protests shaking Hasina's hold. Hasina released Khaleda Zia from prison for six months on condition that she remained in her Dhaka residence to receive treatment and did not go abroad. So, this release was hypocritical, only as good as house arrest. The BNP leader, Fakhrul Islam Alamgir, quickly thanked the government for it. Many people criticized him for unduly thanking the government, which freed Khaleda Zia for a short time only in a politically strategic move. On the other hand, the government did not care for the honor and dignity of the opposition leaders, given that it has always falsely smeared and maliciously attacked the members of the Ziaur Rahman family and their party BNP.

In observance of the birth centenary of Sheikh Mujib, his daughter Sheikh Hasina, took elaborate programs and called the year, Mujib *Borso* (Mujib Year). One such program was that 15 million children from 65,620 primary schools across the country would read in unison an open letter from Sheikh Hasina eulogizing her father. The program, however, got suspended indefinitely because of the Coronavirus outbreak as the schools were closed. Sheikh Hasina wanted to impose on children that Sheikh Mujib was 'the father of the nation,' who, according to her, was the epitome of sacrifice and noble character, while in fact he was completely far from it. He was assassinated by a group of people who were near to him. His lack of honesty is comparable to his daughter Sheikh Hasina, whose election rigging by stuffing the ballot boxes the night before the election on December 31, 2018 bore her outright villainy. Had Coronavirus pandemic been delayed by one year, then she would have been able to celebrate the Mujib *Borso* programs as she desired, but it seems that Allah was not willing that she did.

As a leader, Khaleda Zia never compromised on principles. She did not bow to anyone but Allah. They would not let Khaleda Zia out of the prison in the absence of the pandemic caused by the coronavirus. The virus went to Italy from Wuhan, and then it came to Bangladesh from Italy. The government did not prepare to confront it. Still, when it began to spread in Bangladesh, the government panicked as if they were afraid of ghosts as if they imagined Khaleda Zia might trigger the fall of the government in such a critical situation. Many people used to say that Khaleda Zia would be released when Sheikh Hasina would think that Khaleda's death was near. History shows people like Pharaoh do whatever they like. But they eventually fall into the unseen strategy of Allah. As we read in the Qur'an, they plot and plan, and Allah also plans; but Allah is the best of planners.

The People of Bangladesh Have Been Fighting Two Viruses

One is the coronavirus and the other, Sheikh Hasina virus. Some people say that Khaleda Zia was released because of her old age, but when she was put in prison two years ago, she was not very young either. The government was trying to give the impression that Khaleda Zia's siblings appealed for her release for receiving better treatment for her health problems, hiding the trickery of the government. When the Pharaoh of Egypt saw death before his eyes, he welcomed Prophet Musa (Moses) and he said, "I believe in the God of Musa" (Verses 10: 90-92 in the holy Quran). That was the belief of trickery, so his faith was not accepted. Like the miraculous crossing of Moses and his community through the sea, which drowned the Firaoun (Pharaoh), it was probably a miracle that Allah changed the Mujib *Borso* (Mujib Year) to Corona *Borso* (Corona Year).

Convicting an innocent person in a court of justice is a crime, but the Hasina government took a lot of pleasure just doing so. The chorus of

Hasina's ministers in support of this crime was like upholding banners of corruption. They claimed that the suspension of Khaleda Zia's jail term by six months was for humanitarian reasons, and they praised Sheikh Hasina's wisdom and vision to be unimaginable. They were Hasina's official agents who shamelessly described the government's corruption as greatness and farsightedness. Apart from the flattery of these ministers, the too-narrow conditions imposed on Khaleda Zia's release for six months was a testimony of the government's narrower deception. Sheikh Hasina is an evil politician, who stole the elections, got all her corruption cases in court dropped, and is now heavily leaning on the shoulder of Khaleda Zia like a demon.

Coronavirus has also infected prisoners in jail, but the government is stubborn about it. It has abandoned all laws. Many countries have been releasing prisoners because of coronavirus. Still, the government has not released Maulana Delwar Hussain Sayedee, a renowned religious personality, who was arrested and detained on false charges. This government's rule is like the oppressive regimes of Qarun, Namrud (Nimrod), Firaoun and Shaddad, who wanted to survive but could not succeed.

Suddenly this treacherous government changed its policy on the release of Khaleda Zia. There was a saying in the past that Khaleda Zia's conviction and imprisonment were matters of court verdicts and had nothing to do with the government. They were pressing Khaleda Zia to appeal for parole, but Khaleda Zia firmly refused the government proposition. But now, with the coronavirus, the government did not want to take any risk. Let us examine the devil in detail. According to Law Minister Anisul Haq, the government decided to release her for 6 months after staying her sentences in "accordance with Section 401(1) of the Code of the Criminal Procedure showing generosity because of her age and on humanitarian grounds." His words sounded like rain without any clouds. Previously the government was deaf to all appeals, including those from Khaleda Zia's siblings and relatives. But now suddenly the government discovered the "age" and "humanitarian grounds!"

Despite the best efforts of the BNP, the government previously denied the bail appeals. It did not want to face the election with Khaleda Zia free. The government ordered the court to carry out its plan.

The recent drama in Firozpur court shows how the government trampled the court when any verdict went against any government goons. Another case of irregularity in court through government intervention was the secret bail of the casino owner G. K. Shamim, which a social media storm forced them to cancel. The Hasina government, the judiciary of Bangladesh, and the Indian government are collaborators in a huge conspiracy. Together, they have supervised the abductions and murders of hundreds of innocent Bangladeshi citizens to ensure the political survival of the Hasina regime. We are horrified to recall what happened to the BNP leader Elias Ali, the garments industry leader Aminul Islam, and citizens/journalists like Chowdhury Alam, Sagar, Runi, Tonu, Rifat, Abrar and Felani. Such sordid abductions and murders have been going on since Sheikh Hasina took power in 2008/2009. We should remember that public memory may be short, but God knows all.

Hasina has transformed the government into a machine of repression. Another of its drama was accusing Khaleda Zia's son Tarique Rahman of being behind the grenade attack on her party gathering on August 21, 2004, which her propaganda machines later framed as an attack intending to kill her. In the talk shows by the Awami Subhash Singh Roy and others like him, the concocted government stories are discussed and supported. They take their cues from their leader Sheikh Hasina. Another glaring example was the BDR massacre, which they narrated as a mutiny within the ranks, but which was actually internationally conspired involving secret government plans. Tarique Rahman has been accused many years after the event; it was a judicial conspiracy. The government wants to repress Khaleda Zia's family with all sorts of intrigues and trumped-up charges. It maliciously accuses the BNP of 19 attempts on Sheikh Hasina's life and metes out jail sentences and other repressions to all the persons they target. In my Blog (www.nazmamustafa.com), I have a Bangla column, in which I clarified the issue.

The government keeps its talk shows heated-up with its evil designs. There is no scope for its claim to any credit for the release of

Khaleda Zia as it was due to a natural phenomenon. In America, 9/11 happened with lots of controversies being talked about there, but the truth is that it happened and it killed people and someone did cause it. People may not judge it, but God will. Many people have been dying in Bangladesh. In the bombing of August 21, 2004, many people died, including Zillur Rahman's wife Ivy Rahman. But Sheikh Hasina has always remained safe. In these dramas, she mysteriously triumphed.

Simple Personal Life of Khaleda Zia

She has lived a humble life as a housewife and as a mother. She managed her household within the budget that her husband's salary could afford. Her husband also lived a frugal life. In the early 1980s, one popular TV show by Fazle Lohani documented how frugally they lived. All his life as a military official, Zia did not have more than one or two items as curry for a meal. They had a lifestyle of the ordinary people living in the villages of Bangladesh. As an ideal country-style couple, they had two children whose usual clothes were the altered versions of their father's old dresses. So Khaleda Zia did a great job as a housewife. It is almost impossible for most people to organize a family as economically as she did. Her humility as a human being, as a wife and as a mother did not vanish when she joined politics and held the reins of the statecraft.

Memories

I remember a story from the 1980s. We were in Dhaka. An electric mechanic came to our house. In the context of our conversation with him, he talked about the Zia family. The man knew the Zia family well and had personal acquaintance with one of President Zia's brothers. He spoke very highly of Zia's honesty and truthfulness. He said throughout his entire professional life, Zia did not allow anyone, not even his close relatives, to take any advantage of his privileged position of authority. He particularly mentioned that President Zia expressed his inability to give his brother a job, telling him to manage his life with his own skills. He said to his brother, "If you face any problem, rather go to your Bhabi (sister-in-law) because I'm not just your brother only, I'm for all the people of the country. My head is busy with the well-being of the entire country." I felt awed when I heard those words for the first time in my early life, and they have much inspired me and shaped my thinking.

Last comment

We have all heard how the media pundits use some random words like "Batting Begums," "two Begums," or "two women" about their discussion of the political roles of Khaleda Zia and Sheikh Hasina in Bangladesh. In my view, there is no resemblance between the two, except for womanhood. None of Sheikh Hasina's evil qualities like cruelty, betrayal, and ruthlessness is present in Khaleda Zia. If I had the opportunity, I would like to write a biography of Khaleda Zia, who went way beyond all others as a leader in her statecraft. Her legacy will continue. Future historians will celebrate her achievements.

I hope the youth of Bangladesh come to know the great sacrifices of President Zia and Khaleda Zia in the building of the nation. Understanding the legacy of the Zias will inspire the younger generations. The youth will be proud to follow them and walk in their trails of honor and glory. That way, they will be able to liberate the nation from the clutches of today's BAL terrorists and their acts of mischievous murders, disappearances and jail sentences.

---

[1] http://amarfashichai.blogspot.co.uk (in English);

http://docshare01.docshare.tips/files/2977/29771574.pdf (in English);

https://mazams.weebly.com/uploads/4/8/2/6/48260335/amar_fashi_chai_bangla.pdf (in Bangla);

http://amarfashichai.blogspot.co.uk/2013/07/amar-fashi-chai-by-motiur-rahmanrentu.html (in Bangla)

Chapter 11

Begum Khaleda Zia: Mother of Democracy, Bangladesh's Most Popular, Yet Most Tormented Political Leader

Mohammad Zainal Abedin

Part I: Begum Khaleda Zia: The Most Oppressed Political Legend of the 21st Century

Begum Zia, the former Prime Minister (PM) of Bangladesh, is the most tormented leader in the political history of the contemporary world. No woman politician from the Algerian revolutionary Jamila Bouhired to Nobel Peace laureate Aung San Suu Kyi of Myanmar faced such political and psychological torture let loose on Begum Zia by Sheikh Hasina. She has been a prey to Sheikh Hasina's vindictive politics that prompted her to imprison Begum Zia using a deliberate and politically motivated corruption charges. It was done to humiliate Begum Zia and oust her from politics, crush the Zia family, and the BNP (Bangladesh Nationalist Party) that she leads.

Suu Kyi was never in jail. She was under house arrest. She neither directly led any mass movement against a military ruler what Begum Zia did, nor did Suu Kyi hold any dignified official position like PM that Begum Zia had. Still the world recognized Suu Kyi as one of the most prominent political prisoners of the world. Global media ran after her and the West roared to end her house arrest and subsequently crowned her with the Nobel Peace Prize. But neither the global media nor the Western world is vocal about Begum Zia, who faces hardship since Sheikh Hasina was installed as the Prime Minister of Bangladesh in 2009.

Begum Zia is a predetermined victim of Sheikh Hasina and her alien ally — India. During her terms as Prime Minister of Bangladesh Begum Zia did not concede to Indian pressure. India failed to get such privileges from her government as it succeeded to get from the Hasina government that subsequently transmuted Bangladesh as its satellite state.

Begum Zia did not depend on the blessings on any individual country or block to remain in power. "We don't have masters, but friends abroad." This is, perhaps, her prime fault why none among the international community stood for her. To deter Begum Zia from coming to power in 2006, the Indian government invested millions of dollars and its intelligence agency RAW paralyzed Bangladesh by disrupting electricity, blockading roads and highways and seaports, even killing the political activists that paved the way to declare emergency led by a so-called caretaker government-backed by the Armed Forces. RAW managed to hold a predetermined election that installed Sheikh Hasina as Prime Minister, a person of Indian choice.

Begum Zia was the common target of India and Sheikh Hasina. India's design was to crush the patriotic forces of Bangladesh using the Sheikh Hasina-led government to turn Bangladesh as its satellite, while Sheikh Hasina did it to remain in power through transforming Bangladesh into virtually a one-party dictatorial country.

In face to face discussions two out of the four architects of 1/11 informed me Begum Zia was not ready to drift from her principle and declined to accept their offer that compelled them to hold a staged election to bring Sheikh Hasina to power. Begum Zia, being a true patriot, remained uncompromised and adamant to protect the interest of her country and her ideology — democracy and human rights. She like a true patriot did not bend down under the pressure of her internal or external adversaries nor surrendered the interest of her country to the hegemonic power to come to and remain in power burying the democratic process.

Begum Zia depends on Allah, Who blesses her to attain the support and love of her countrymen. She is a role model of the patriotic uncompromising leader whose countrymen accurately entitled her as "The Mother of Democracy."

Another fault (?) of Begum Zia is that she, as well as the BNP that she leads and enjoys sky-high popularity among the cross-sections of the Bangladeshi people. This causes tremendous mental agony to Hasina and the neighboring India. Sheikh Hasina needed power and India needed unlimited strategic and economic advantages from Bangladesh to transmute it to a satellite state. Begum Zia's patriotic and uncompromising character, above all, her sky-high popularity, appeared as an insurmountable bar to Hasina and her ally India to reach their respective goals.

Sheikh Hasina did not and still does not consider anyone in Bangladesh as her contender other than Begum Zia. Any free and fair election will surely elect her (Begum Zia). Sheikh Hasina will never get power through such an election. India's apprehension is that if the patriotic forces are not crushed, India's dream will remain unfulfilled. So, they used Gen Moeen gang to install Sheikh Hasina in 2008 via a rigged and predetermined election on condition of exempting them from punishment.

After assuming power in 2009, India using Sheikh Hasina desperately started to crush the patriotic forces. They know Zia family is the lifeline and vanguard of BNP. BNP could be crushed if this family is crushed. Subsequently, Sheikh Hasina and her guardian India have been relentlessly plotting and intriguing to keep away the living members of the Zia family — Begum Zia and her son Tarique Rahman — from politics. Tarique Rahman who went under inhuman torture to London in 2008 for treatment was/is not allowed to return to Bangladesh. To deter him from entering Bangladesh, Sheikh Hasina arranged lifelong imprisonment for him. So, he leads an exiled life in London. If he dares to return to Bangladesh, he would surely be arrested.

Begum Zia's youngest son Arafat Rahman who also survived identical sort of torture in 2008 died in Singapore hospital in 2015 in the effect of torture. The two brothers were prey to deliberate political vindictiveness. To minus her from politics, Begum Zia was imprisoned in fake and fabricated charges.

International community astoundingly observed the deliberate imprisonment of Begum Zia, as same type of corruption charges were also filed against Sheikh Hasina by the Moeen gang. But Sheikh Hasina withdrew all the charges against her, in one she was sued of murdering a pro-Jamaat activist, as the victim was beaten to death by her cadres whom she ordered to throng Dhaka along with oars and sticks that followed the State of emergency on January 11, 2007. Begum Zia was never accused of murder. Internationally recognized jurists and law experts opine that Begum Zia cannot be imprisoned, while keeping Sheikh Hasina outside the jail. So, the imprisonment of Begum Zia was not fair.

Political observers and analysts are of identical opinion that there is no other transparent, democratic, uncompromising, patriotic and uncommonly polite political personality in Bangladesh other than Begum Zia. She accepted all the demands of the opposition parties while she was in power. She did not misuse state power to squeeze and isolate her political foes. She neither ever drifted from the democratic process and values nor ever indulged herself in totalitarian ideas in words and deeds. She never stood against the hopes and aspirations of the people. Her government never thought of one-party or one-man rule. She did not use state power for self-interest. Despite relentless propaganda, Bangladeshis, for all those reasons, strongly believe that she cannot commit corruption of any type. The more slanderous propagation and harsh oppression against her increase, the more her volume of popularity and her acceptability expands among the common people of the country.

All these qualities fetched mass-popularity, acceptability, electability, exceptionality and substantiality for Begum Zia. Her arch-rival Sheikh Hasina feels envious and worried seeing her sky-high popularity and acceptability. Hasina publicly mourned saying despite she did so many developmental works, people neither liked her, nor wanted to vote for her party. Sheikh Hasina's such self-realization did not rectify her, rather prompted her to eliminate and annihilate the Zia family. Hasina succeeded in this respect to a great extent, but Begum Zia's pure, selfless and greedless character frustrated all the evil designs of Sheikh Hasina to erase Begum Zia from the minds of the Bangladeshis.

Begum Zia neither leased the interest and existence of Bangladesh to another country nor she bowed down under the pressure of the neighboring hegemonic country. If she would have betrayed with the country fulfilling the demands of India, neither she nor her family members nor her party, the BNP, would have faced such a disastrous situation. And she would not have suffered; she could rather lead a luxurious life if she, betraying with the country and denouncing the transparent democratic process, agreed with India via Sheikh Hasina to mutually share the ministerial portfolios and parliamentary constituencies that Ershad and others did since 2014. Sheikh Hasina offered Begum Zia any positions for her party men on condition of participating in the fake and planted election of 2014 under Sheikh Hasina. Begum Zia rejected this offer and boycotted the election demanding that the election be held under a non-party caretaker government.

It is worth mentioning that the Moeen gang arrested Begum Zia and Sheikh Hasina under the so-called 'minus two formula.' Corruption charges were framed against both of them and the process was initiated to expel them from Bangladesh. Sheikh Hasina responding to that initiative left Bangladesh under the cover of treatment of her ears. A plane was ready at Zia International Airport to exile Begum Zia. But defying the pressure of the Moeen gang, she bluntly said, "I will die in my homeland, if need be, but I will not go abroad."

I would like to recollect another uncompromising aspect of Begum Zia that was narrated by one of the four generals of the emergency period. In brief, what he said was as follows: After the collapse of the minus two formula, they (the Moeen gang) proposed to Begum Zia that they would pave the way for her party to win in the election on condition of impunity (of their misdeeds and mistakes). Rejecting their offer, Begum Zia pointedly said, the law of the land will take its own course.

Failing to convince Begum Zia, the same proposal was placed before Sheikh Hasina who instantly and gladly grabbed the offer and assured them their impunity.

This was the inner reason of how Sheikh Hasina came to power in 2008 with an overwhelming majority enjoying the planted election and fabricated results through the orchestration and instrumentation of the Army-backed India-influenced government.

Noticeable that Sheikh Hasina honored her commitment and allowed all of the Uddin-axis to leave the country and acquitted them of any punishment. At least three of them now live in America. One was awarded ambassadorial position in Australia who is now engaged in big bucks hotel/restaurant businesses in Dhaka. The General who narrated the above story of the inner reason of Sheikh Hasina's returning to power, most probably, now lives in Dubai. According to the critics, this was arranged by Sheikh Hasina and her foreign mentors.

Observers added that since Sheikh Hasina came to power enjoying Indian RAW and local army support, she keeps Begum Zia in constant tension and harassment so that she (Begum Zia) suffers from mental and psychological anxieties and that she cannot give total attention to Hasina's atrocities and pro-Indian activities or wage any movement against her. The more Begum Zia suffers, the more Sheikh Hasina gets relief and sadistic pleasure.

Earlier, using the court, Hasina evicted Begum Zia from the house donated to the Zia family by the late President Justice Abdus Sattar after the assassination of President Ziaur Rahman who left nothing behind for his family.

Hasina always suffers from Begum Zia phobia and did everything to keep her away even when she was free. Hasina did not allow her to move freely. When Begum Zia waged people's movement, Hasina stationed dozens of trucks filled with sands and bricks to barricade the rented house of Begum Zia to confine her within her house and isolate her from the rest of the world. She was not even allowed to go to the party office or attend any meeting. When she decided to go to the party office on foot, hundreds of police thronged at the gate, locked it from outside and no one was allowed to come in or go out of the house. The Hasina government threatened to disconnect gas and water links to Begum Zia's residence. The BNP leaders and workers were also barred from visiting her.

When she was allowed to go to her Gulshan (political) office, Begum Zia was not allowed to go back to her rented residence. She was kept confined inside the office for months. No party leaders or workers were allowed to enter or get out of the office. All the walls of the office compound were raised much higher than they were before and then fitted with high barbed-wire fences, basically to deter her party leaders and workers from entering the office premises even jumping from outside.

Trucks filled with bricks and sands were kept standing in front of the office and heavy police guards and secret service personnel deployed round the clock. Electric lines were disconnected. The supply of food items was stopped. The cooked food that the common people, even celebrities such as Baby Naznin, brought for her was not allowed in.

Human history has no record of such atrocious cruelties. No political leaders, from Nelson Mandela to Aung San Suu Kyi, even the dissidents of the then Soviet Union, ever experienced such notorious barbarity.

The episode of imprisoning Begum Zia is more atrocious and shocking. The Moeen gang sued against Sheikh Hasina for misappropriating funds from the Bangabandhu Memorial Trust and for other reasons. She was accused of 15 cases including misappropriation and murder. After attaining power, she had dropped over eight thousand cases lodged against her and her party leaders and activists branding them as politically motivated. But none of the cases against Begum Zia and her party-men was withdrawn; rather Sheikh Hasina lodged more cases against them to crush and corner the BNP, though almost all of those cases were fake and false. This is enough to understand that the imprisonment of Begum Zia is completely politically motivated and preplanned.

The corruption charges against Begum Zia should have been dismissed on the very first day of the hearing, as identical charges against Sheikh Hasina and her party-men were earlier withdrawn. Therefore, the imprisonment of Begum Zia has many loopholes. No foreign attorneys were allowed to assist her case in the court. Even the common people know very well that the verdict against Begum Zia was preplanned and contrary to justice. Observers around the world believe that Sheikh Hasina imprisoned Begum Zia to keep her away from politics. She desired Begum Zia died in prison. She was kept in an abandoned unhealthy prison in such a room where there was no air conditioner, despite the unbearable heat. She was deprived of proper medical treatment in jail. When the matter was raised before the court, it decreed to form a medical board for her treatment. Sheikh Hasina formed a biased medical board comprising of the physicians who are actively affiliated to Hasina's party Awami League.

The most tragic and deceptive aspect of Hasina's revenge against Begum Zia was that she was brought from the hospital to attend a session of a court. But she was taken directly to prison from the court, instead of keeping her in a hospital room which was turned to a prison-cell. It was a cruel bluff.

In this regard, Advocate Ruhul Kabir Rizvi, Joint Secretary of BNP, said that Begum Zia was admitted to the BSMMU (Bangabandhu Sheikh Mujib Medical University) Hospital at the instruction of the court, but she was sent back to the prison without treatment at the instruction of the government. Advocate Rizvi alleged that, as a result, her "treatment is severely hampered and despite her extreme sickness she is deprived of therapy."

Meanwhile, Mirza Fakhrul Islam Alamgir, Secretary General of BNP, at a press conference on February 8, 2019, alleged that "Begum Zia was forcibly sent to the prison without any release letter supposed to be issued by the Medical Board. Instead, the release order was issued by the hospital authority" that belongs to the ruling Awami League. He said, "We visited Begum Zia. She is very sick, very sick. She cannot even properly sit on the wheelchair, still she was brought using a wheelchair. Under this situation, she was forcibly bound to be seated before the court for a long time. It is an act of extreme inhumanity. We condemn it and we demand her immediate release."

There was a popular demand at home and abroad to unconditionally release Begum Zia, at least on humanitarian grounds. Sheikh Hasina government paid no heed. The biggest question was how long would Begum Zia survive in an unhealthy jail-situation without proper treatment, care and nursing? Common people feared she might not survive if she remains in jail.

It is my studied conviction and perception that in whatever way Begum Zia dies, her sacrifice, especially her dedication and devotion to retrieve, revive and restore democracy will keep her immortal in the heart of the Bangladeshis. The inhuman atrocities and mental and psychological torture that has been let loose on her have already crowned her as an uncompromising, ever shining and immortal personality in Bangladesh history.

Begum Zia's firm belief in Allah, the Almighty, and her patriotism endowed her with mental strength and endurance to remain tenacious to serve her nation despite repeated tempests that she faced. Despite losing her beloved son amid the anti-Hasina movement, she did not retreat and relinquish the movement. She has already made her foes to believe that as long as she remains alive she will uphold the same spirit and never bow down for her personal gain and relief in the hope of a rosy life. She has told the court that it could punish her in whatever way it desired and suggested her followers to continue their struggle for democracy.

Such a painstaking, undeviating and punctilious lady is rare in the contemporary political arena. There is no such honest and patriotic political personality, either. She is an invaluable asset of and pride for Bangladesh. She taught the people how to love the motherland, protect its assets and existence, and stand up against evil power by sacrificing self-interest and comfort.

Begum Zia is totally innocent and free from corruption in the people's Court. Her zeal and struggle for democracy and human rights crowned her with an appropriate title, 'The Mother of Democracy' that paved the way for her to be a memorable personality in history. It is the steamroller of Sheikh Hasina's atrocities that established Begum Zia in history and in the hearts of the people of Bangladesh. Even an ordinary Bangladeshi can assume and imagine what a great and glorious position history has budgeted for her. They cannot express it out of fear of persecution. There is no room for Hasina in the hearts of the masses, but the same masses pray for the well-being of Begum Zia. It is her great asset and achievement that cannot be lost. Sheikh Hasina cannot snatch it away. We pray for Begum Zia`s full and complete well-being. May Allah, the Most Just and Most Compassionate, bless her in the world and the hereafter.

Part II: Is it too late for Bangladesh to allow its opposition leader to receive treatment?

Begum Zia, 74, an uncompromising nationalist and liberal politician, is hugely popular in Bangladesh. A Bangladesh court jailed her and three others for seven years in what is widely perceived as a fake Zia Charitable Trust corruption case on October 29, 2018. Zia supporters and independent jurists questioned Begum Zia's trial, alleging Sheikh Hasina influenced the court decision. Begum Zia, the ailing widow of the country's former President Ziaur Rahman, was released on March 25, 2020 on "humanitarian grounds" on condition that she would stay and take her treatment at home without leaving the country. Sources close to Begum Zia in Bangladesh say that she is virtually on deathbed. "She cannot move. She cannot walk. Her health is extremely bad," one source revealed.

Many in Bangladesh and abroad are questioning the timing the country's authoritarian government's choice to conditionally release the country's opposition leader Begum Khaleda Zia. Is the life of Bangladesh's former prime minister in any danger? Questions and curiosities float all around as to why Sheikh Hasina, Bangladesh's despotic prime minister, temporarily released from prison her arch-rival Begum Zia through an executive order. Many in Bangladesh and around the world are perplexed at the timing Hasina chose to let Mrs. Zia go home when the world is engulfed in the deadly COVID-19 pandemic.

Bangladesh watchers and analysts question Sheikh Hasina's choice of the timing of Begum Zia's release. Why did Hasina have a change of heart when the world was dealing with a killer pandemic? Why is Begum Zia being forced to seek treatment at home instead of letting her go for better medical help overseas?

The answer is in Sheikh Hasina's authoritarian style of governance. Those familiar with her vindictive nature alleged that she released Begum Zia because her life was in serious danger and might come to an end. Rumors have even been making the rounds in Bangladesh and overseas that Begum Zia might have been given 'slow poison' while in prison, which was pushing her towards death. "The government could not afford Begum Zia dying inside jail because that would bring the blame on the government and will have serious fallout," one source in Dhaka confided, adding: "So she (Hasina) released Begum Zia to escape the responsibility."

Multiple sources in Bangladesh said the condition that Begum Zia had to get treatment at home had political and legal reasons. They alleged such an abnormal precondition was imposed as the Hasina government apprehended that if Begum Zia was allowed to go out of Bangladesh, foreign physicians might find the 'wrongs,' if any, in her body, and that would prove Hasina government's crime. "Otherwise, there is no logic for such precondition."

The irony is that while Hasina has often been accused of forcing the Bangladesh courts to withdraw thousands of corruption cases against her, her family and party members, she is bringing new cases against all opposition members. Begum Zia, the only potent challenger to her authoritarian rule, was always her obvious target. Hasina's vindictive policies do not stop here.

Interestingly enough, Hasina herself went to London on parole for treatment while she was detained during the caretaker government. "She wants Begum Zia to die in her house without proper treatment, removing her biggest political challenger for the rest of her life," the source in Dhaka concluded.

The Hasina government has often been criticized by the international human rights groups of human rights abuses and stifling free speech. She and her family have been at the center of major corruption scandals since 2007. At least 15 cases of corruption against Hasina were quashed through political interference and abuse of power after she was elected in (late) 2008. In a damning statement, Human Rights Watch released a charge-sheet against Hasina's authoritarianism in January: "In Bangladesh, people who question the government's increasingly authoritarian rule fear they may be next in line to be killed or forcibly disappeared by security forces." When Human Rights Watch raised this with the Bangladesh authorities, they were quick to dismiss the reports as lies made up by the political opposition.

Yet extrajudicial killings have become so common in Bangladesh that some legislators openly recommended them as a way of dealing with the country's high level of rape when protesters mobilized over the recent rape of a 21-year-old student. For instance, according to media reports, one legislator told the parliament that "the only remedy is killing rapists 'in crossfire' after their confession."

Sheikh Hasina is known for instigating her supporters to violence, much of which is documented by independent sources. The tragic happenings of October 28, 2006 when 18 people were killed across Bangladesh are still fresh in Bangladesh's political history. The violence occurred after Hasina asked her cadres to march to Dhaka with oars and sticks. American Embassy in Dhaka in a report on the happenings of that black day reported:

> Sheikh Hasina, the President of Awami League, called her party activists to march to Dhaka with oars and sticks to take control of the streets of the capital. From a rally held on 18th September 2006 at the Paltan Ground in the capital, Sheikh Hasina instructed her party activists to come to Dhaka with oars, logs, and sticks: "You [the people] be ready and come to Dhaka from villages, upazillas and districts with oars, rowing poles and with whatever you have when I will call you." Hasina instructed her coalition activists urging to build a resistance against the caretaker government of the time. Following her call, her party activists gathered in the city sparking the violence of October 28.
>
> The activists of the then opposition alliance led by Awami League took to the streets, started setting fire in the markets, set vehicles ablaze and clashed with the BNP and Jamaat activists, and even with the law enforcers. Hundreds of Awami League activists carrying bamboo poles and oars paraded most city roads, chanting slogans against Khaleda Zia and Justice KM Hasan. The Awami League activists blocked almost all the city entry points in the morning and clashed with any procession of the BNP they saw. ... At least 18 people were killed throughout the country by the "oars and logs" attack of Awami League and its allies. At least 1,000 (throughout Bangladesh), were injured, many with bullets, in attacks by the activists of the AL led alliance.

In the same report the American Embassy suggested:

The government should ensure the proper and immediate trial of the offenses committed on 28 October 2006 in Dhaka and it must change its decision of withdrawal of the case filed by the victims in order to serve the people with the proper administration of justice. The illegal practice of using violence and torture to suppress the political opponents must be stopped immediately by Awami League and all other political parties. The law enforcing agencies should not tolerate such violent political activities.[1]

Bangladesh's interim government of the time filed a case mentioning Sheikh Hasina. The police investigated and charge-sheeted her after finding the accusations against her as true. She was also accused of many other cases of graft, misappropriation and other criminal charges. But after assuming power in early 2009 with the blessings of India-influenced army-led government, she withdrew over 8,500 cases against her and her party cadres, by branding them as "politically motivated." Those cases ranged from murder, arson, bombing, damaging private and public property, illegal occupation, vandalism, ransacking, etc. However, she used fake cases against Begum Zia that led to her arrest and jail. Resultantly, Begum Zia now faces 34 cases, while some of her party leaders and activists face over 150 cases each.

The allegations against Begum Zia and her subsequent imprisonment are the outcome of vindictiveness. For Hasina, jailing her political opponents is not very difficult because much of the Bangladesh's judiciary is compromised. Many judges in the lower and higher judiciary are her loyalists, as they are former cadres of the ruling party and have always failed to act impartially.

---

[1] https://www.jamaat-e-islami.org/en/pdf/99_28_october_report.pdf

Chapter 12

Begum Khaleda Zia: Never One of the "Two Begums" in Bangladesh Politics

Abid Bahar

Introduction

Begum Khaleda Zia would be wrongly understood if historians placed her as just one of the two "Begums" in Bangladesh politics, the other being highly notorious Sheikh Hasina. Unique as she is, Khaleda remains her own "Begum," exampled by herself, with her special virtues and qualities that far outweigh the vengeful and vindictive characteristics of her counterpart in Hasina. In fact, Khaleda Zia is the nemesis of Sheikh Hasina, who is arrogant and quarrelsome and who is ruling the country in an extremely dictatorial way. On the other hand, Khaleda Zia is known for her respect for the people of Bangladesh and their aspirations for democracy and democratic development. The most remarkable thing about her is that she is noble, virtuous and broad-and-open-minded; she listens to her people; she is charismatic and she practices what she preaches. As the title of a married Muslim lady of high rank, "Begum" (feminine of "Beg," like "Khanam" from "Khan") appropriately applies to the rarely great leader that Khaleda Zia is. She continues to be so even when she, at 75, is going through the terrible injustice venomously inflicted upon her by the selfish, self-centered and self-seeking Hasina, who, fascistically oriented, is bent upon getting divisively and destructively locked in a mean personal and political vendetta with the highly polished, polite and patriotic Khaleda.

In politics, particularly in South and Southeast Asia, most politicians are good at promising but short on delivering. Sheikh Mujibur

Rahman, the first Prime Minister of independent Bangladesh, promised a "Sonar Bangla" but in reality, he delivered a "bottomless Bangla." Hasina had been promising to deliver democracy, but with the help of the muscle men of her cadre groups in Chatro League, Jubo League, Sramik League, Shaschasevok League and other party groups, she delivered an "anti-democratic" authoritarian rule, even destroying the democratic institutions such as the judiciary, election commission and the existence of the opposition party in the country. This is Hasina's unethical contribution in the politics of Bangladesh.

What about Begum Khaleda Zia? Research on Khaleda Zia remained a neglected topic. It started getting attraction when people started to realize that Khaleda was not only a leader but also a stateswoman. Her leadership shows she is different from the rest of the leaders. She is a kind-hearted, respectful, and soft-spoken person, she is equally a person of great integrity and vision. She is resolute in the question of defending Bangladesh's sovereignty. Leaders at times try to model themselves conforming to the aspirations of their people and their societies. Begum Zia is one such leader who found her model, her ideology, her objective. It was the promotion of democracy and protection of the sovereignty of the country.

Historical Perspective: Where did Khaleda Zia get the inspiration?

It is an interesting story to tell. It was in 1995, when I went to Bangladesh to collect data for a major project I had undertaken: Leadership in Bangladesh politics. In this venture, I was researching mainly on the life of Maulana Abdul Hamid Khan Bhasani. At the same time, I was also trying to understand such leaders as Sheikh Mujibur Rahman, Ziaur Rahman, Begum Khaleda Zia and Sheikh Hasina Wazed. While in Dhaka, I was invited by the famous Bangladeshi writer Ahmed Sofa to have dinner with him at his Kalabagan residence. During our talks, he related a story which I still remember. It was about President Ziaur Rahman.

Several years before 1995, he went to India. While entering to Bangladesh through the Benapole border, he noticed something unusual.

He noticed the serenity and peacefulness in the Bangladesh side. He saw that the citizens voluntarily followed law and the order in the country that he had never seen in Bangladesh before. Upon his return to Dhaka, he told his colleagues that "they" would not tolerate President Ziaur Rahman's rule in Bangladesh. "They" would kill him. Someone among his colleagues asked, "they who?" His reply was, "the anti-Bangladeshi forces."

The next day, a story was published in a newspaper that "Sofa said Zia would be killed." The news reached Ziaur Rahman, who invited Sofa to his office and asked what the basis of the news was. "Was it from your dream?" asked the president. Sofa replied that India would not tolerate an independent-minded leader like him with a vision for a progressive and peaceful Bangladesh.

The fact is Indian hegemony on Bangladesh took shape even before Mujib landed in the newly independent country in January 1972. It created the MujibBadi group with Sheikh Fazlul Haq Moni, Mujib's powerful nephew, as its leader. The big neighbor continued to play dirty politics in the affairs of all its neighbors, more so in Bangladesh.

Strange but true, within a year after this prediction by Ahmed Sofa, Zia was killed by some ambitious anti-Bangladesh forces in the army in Chittagong Circuit House on 30 May 1981. He was killed in a coup allegedly masterminded by General H M Ershad, who was in close contact with Hasina and India (while overtly serving Ziaur Rahman loyally). In this act, he took the help of some pro-Indian elements in the army. Of the group directly involved in the assassination of Zia, one who shot at Zia at point blank was later killed, along with others, after the coup failed. Three of the plotters found shelter in India. One of them eventually went to the USA. (One of the accused of Zia's murder case, Captain (Rtd) Giasuddin Ahmed is now an Awami League member of Parliament from Gaffargaon Upazila, Mymensingh District.[1] Indeed, Indian hand in Zia's death was widely suspected because Zia brought the country to the path of order and prosperity.

Mujib was killed in August 1975, six years before Zia's own assassination. Mujib invited his own fall. His track record of misrule and maladministration tells all. People still shudder to talks of the torture and persecution of Rakkhi Bahini. The corruption in the administration and Awami League brought a man-mand famine that killed and displaced millions. The last nail of the virtual coffin of Bangladesh came in the form of one-party BAKSAL (Bangladesh Krishok Sramik Awami Leaque) dictatorship. Mujib's close associate, Khandaker Mostaque Ahmed led the coup brought an end to Mujib. Later, a pro-Awami faction led by Brigadier Khaled Mosharraf, removed Mostaque Ahmed in a conspiratorial putsch on November 3, 1975 when General Zia was also arrested.

Zia was a popular leader and his arrest was not liked in the military hierarchy, as well as in the ranks and files. On the night of November 6, 1975, soldiers revolted and came out in open making various demands of their own, mostly on socialist line. Retired Colonel Abu Taher played a role in fomenting dissatisfaction among the troops. Civilians, not happy with the pro-Indian, pro-Awami takeover by Khaled, also joined the soldiers in the revolt. It is known as the Sepoy-Jonota Biplob (Soldier-people Revolution), later termed as the BNP administration as the National Solidarity Day. The revolutionary soldiers rescued General Ziaur Rahman from house arrest and installed him back in the command of the army, as well as the nation on November 7, 1975. In 1977, Zia took over as the president when president Justice ASM Sayem resigned on health grounds. Through 5th Amendment to the Constitution in 1979, revived the multiparty democracy that was disbanded by Mujib. Zia allowed freedom of press, free speech, in addition to free market economy and administrative accountability. He also allowed Sheikh Hasina to return from her self-exile in India and resume the banned Awami politics.

The two models of leadership continued in the Bangladesh politics even after the death of Ziaur Rahman.

The Two Models of Leadership

1. Mujib's authoritarian leadership: One approach to leadership was known as Mujibbadi which is pro-Indian, pro-Bengali, BAKSAL authoritarian one-party dictatorship enshrined in Mujib's infamous 4th Amendment to the Constitution. This also asks for loyalty to Mujib's charismatic authority. MujibBad was

for populist politics. Mujib's BAKSAL allowed Awami party supremacy over the state.

Mujibbad has never been fully explained and the people remained totally vague about it. To the Mujib followers, it meant unflinching loyalty to Mujib's authoritarian leadership. One explanation was that it combined the four principles: Democracy, Nationalism, Socialism and Secularism, which were incorporated in the first Constitution framed in 1972. Many people remained confused how democracy and socialism could go together.

Mujib's politics was primarily based on Bengali Vs. Non-Bengali polarization which led to serious divisions in society. It appeared that this politics of division could by no means be conducive to a nation's progress.

2. Zia's Rational-Legal form of leadership: This was led by Zia's pro-Bangladesh, pro-democratic, independent-minded politics enshrined in the 5th Amendment of the Constitution. Zia allowed state supremacy over the party and the individual. In the words of German philosopher Max Weber, such measures always help state supremacy over the party and help to implement the principles of rational- legal form of authority.

Due to the above historical background, two models of leadership emerged in Bangladesh which also led to a country of a divided soul. Regrettably, starting from the 1990's two leaders emerged, Mujib's daughter Sheikh Hasina and Zia's wife Khaleda Zia. Khaleda followed the Zia model, also known as the "Zia Way." Hasina followed the Mujib model, also called the Mujib's "BAKSAL Way." History records Mujib's BAKSAL way was characterized by a "Bottomless Basket" and Zia's "Zia Way" was known as the "Basket of Hope."

As soon as Zia died, Gen Ershad was on his way to capture power to rule by his authoritarian style of politics. Hasina was also ready to capture power with Indian help. However, the nation called upon Khaleda Zia to take the leadership of the country to re-establish democracy. Hasina, the daughter of Mujib with her fake Islamic headwear gadgets was lurking in the dark to challenge Khaleda Zia.

Elections in Bangladesh

After the fall of dictator Ershad, elections were called. The following shows the elections in Bangladesh and the changing dynamics of politics in Bangladesh from 1991-2018 to present.

- Khelada Zia's first term in office was during 1991-96, after the fall of General Ershad through a democratic revolution.
- Khelada Zia was re-elected in 1996 but the parliament was dissolved under the pressure of the opposition Awami League leader Hasina, who created a situation in which Khaleda was compelled to install a Care-Taker Government (CTG) to monitor elections.
- Sheikh Hasina won the election in 1996 in alliance with the Jamati Islami and stayed in power until 2001.
- Khaleda Zia wins again in 2001 and was in power till 2006.
- Military backed Care-Taker government exceeding its constitutionally mandated 3 months term and stayed in power 2006-2008.
- Hasina was elected end of 2008 and removed the Care –Taker system that she forced Khaleda to establish in 1996.
- The BNP boycotted 2014 election in protest for removing the Care-Taker system.
- The Awami League continued to stay in power by using massive vote rigging end of 2018. Just before the election the opposition leader Khaleda Zia was put in jail along with many other BNP leaders. The ballot boxes were stamped the night before the election and the opposition voters were intimidated and forced by the police and secret service agents to leave voting centres or not to get out of home to vote. This authoritarian rule by Hasina has been the trend from 2009. Hasina continues to rule Bangladesh as the first woman dictator in the Muslim world.

Khaleda Zia, the Nemesis of Sheikh Hasina

In her first term, perhaps the most telling virtue Khaleda Zia demonstrated was courage, her respect for democratic institutions and endurance in political leadership. The great Greek philosopher Aristotle reiterated that for the common good, virtuous leader is preferable. He thought there was no split between ethics and effectiveness in politics. He says, "Virtue is something that you can only have if you practice it. Virtue requires habitation and, therefore, requires practice, not just theory."[2] Her effectiveness in promoting the policies by having honest and effective people in her cabinet and remaining ethical is truly praiseworthy.

If one is asked about some of the virtues of Khaleda Zia, they must be that she is (a) personally well-mannered leader; (b) she is an independent-minded, pro Bangladeshi patriot; (c) she is dutiful; (d) she is charismatic and courageous; (e) she is ready to suffer for the sake of the country; (f) she is personally honest; (g) she is democratic-minded; (h) she is a believer in stability and order; and (I) she practices what she preaches, which is, in the words of Aristotle, "habitation."

Khaleda Zia Practices What She Preaches

(A) Khaleda is ready to suffer for the sake of the country. She had personally suffered in captivity during the war. After her husband's death, she raised her two children as a single mother. Despite that her motto remained the same, to deliver the common good. For the sake of the country, it was not just herself but also her two children had to suffer torture caused by the regime of Indian puppet Moeen U Ahmed. Her first son Tarique Rahman was severely tortured in captivity by the same regime and, out of extreme hatred, forcefully evicted him out of the country. The family's only crime is that they love Bangladesh and they like to call themselves "Bangladeshis," which goes against the Hindu and Indian influenced Awami "Joy Bangla" politics, echoing in parallel with Indian "Jai Hind" slogan.

(B) Khaleda Zia Is No Other Begum. In politics, Khaled Zia is far above Hasina with no comparison with the latter. She is a kind-hearted, gentle, and charismatic personality. Many of her critics wrongly attributed her as being another Begum in Bangladesh politics. Such assertion is nothing but an uninformed understanding of Khaleda. The truth is that Khaleda Zia is the nemesis of Sheikh Hasina. She is a polite and courteous lady. In contrast, when several years ago I personally met Hasina with several of her Awami followers in her hotel room in Montreal, I saw her as a quarrelsome and irritating personality. Like Mujib she did not listen to her followers.

(C) Khaleda Zia, the Independent-Minded Patriot. During the Care-Taker government, she was pressured to leave Bangladesh. but she insisted on staying in the country. On the other hand, Hasina as an opportunist, instantly accepted the offer and left Bangladesh for India and then USA. One would notice in Khaleda Zia many more attributes but the one that stands out is her pro-Bangladesh nationalist politics. This alone makes her close to her famous husband Ziaur Rahman. While this is a great virtue, it led Zia to lose his life and Khaleda Zia to suffer in jail.

(D) Khaleda Zia's Struggle for Democracy. Khaleda Zia has been struggling to establish democracy since early 1980s. Her husband President Ziaur Rahman reinstated multi-party democracy by replacing the authoritarian BAKSALi rule established by Sheikh Mujib. Zia thus became the enemy of the Indian backed Awami League. After Zia's assassination, said to be at India's instruction, Ershad ran another autocratic rule similar to the previous Awami BAKSAL Khaleda Zia had to struggle for democracy against Ershad's dictatorship during 1980s. Now she is fighting against Hasina's authoritarian rule. Both Ziaur Rahman and Khaleda Zia struggled to establish democratic system in Bangladesh. Khaleda Zia does not just speak about democracy, she practices it as well. She fought for it and she suffered for it. This is called "habitation" by Aristotle.

(E) Devastating Farakka. For the benefit of Bangladesh, Khaleda took the case of the destructive Farakka dam to the United nations. While taking her stand against the Indian dam project, she quoted the famous saying, "Boishakh Mashe Tar Hatu Jol Thake" (In the dry season, the water level goes down as low as the knee).

(F) Khaleda Zia, the Suffering Leader. As the chairperson of the BNP, she was put under house arrest in 1983, 1984 and 1987 by Ershad administration. In 1987, police arrested her from a meeting at Hotel Purbani in Dhaka. Her challenge to the authorities while in police custody remains exemplary. During the military- backed Care-Taker Government, Khaleda Zia was taken to custody and put in jail. In 2014, Sheikh Hasina in her desperate attempt to stop Khaleda's democracy movement, the BNP office was looted and destroyed by the Awami goons. Live ammunition was used during the attack. They also attacked Khaleda's convoy of cars. On more than one occasion, Khaleda was put under house arrest with the Gopali police force blocking the entrance to her house by sand and brick and cement trucks, even stopping food supply to her residence. At one stage, basic utility services such as electricity and water were discontinued in violation of minimum human rights. This shows how dangerous Hasina could become and how low she could go. Despite all these, Khaleda never deviated from the path of democracy to fight the oppression.

(G) Dutiful Khaleda Zia: Country First. Khaleda Zia's distractors, such as pro-Awami people and media, at times tried to portray her on a negative light, but my personal experience is totally different. I made a few visits to the Prime Minister's Office and met a number of her ministers on various occasions. I found her administration disciplined and organized and everyone possessed a sense of purpose. Unlike Sheikh Hasina, who demanded personal loyalty from the people around her, Khaleda Zia preferred her ministers to show loyalty to the people and to the country. National duty came first to Begum Zia and her administration. She shunned unnecessary foreign trips that involved huge strain on the government exchequer. To the contrary, her nemesis Hasina is seen touring foreign countries with a planeload of her family members and her party men. Even a small cataract eye surgery—that is commonly done in Bangladesh-- took her to London for weeks at a time when the country was beset by natural disasters such as the devastating flooding from Cyclone Fana and dangerous Dengue attacks.

(H) Honest Khaleda Zia. Khaleda Zia was not found guilty in tax evasion, fraud, conflict of interest, diversion of resources, influence peddling, and conspiracy to defraud. Even the widespread propaganda against Tarique Rahman, her son, that he was a corrupt man was found to be unfounded. The corruption case against him, even though the Hasina government tried to influence the court, was dismissed as being baseless. Although Ziaur Rahman's high standards in honesty and dedication to the country remained a sought-after goal, evidence shows his family members tried to follow those standards as far as they could.

(I) Khaleda as a believer in order and stability. Like her late husband Ziaur Rahman, Khaleda is a believer in stability and peace. In the face of devastating hartals and work stoppages staged by Hasina, Khaleda did not hesitate to dissolve the elected government with a view to avoiding loss of lives and property that could be caused by the Awami thugs. Khaleda quickly held a fresh election within a few months.

(J) Virtue is something that one can only possess if one practices it. Aristotle says that "virtue is a habit." Khaleda Zia played as a role model of practicing what she preached. She believes virtue requires "habitation," and, therefore, requires practice, not just a theory.

State of Democracy: Like Father, Like Daughter

In today's Bangladesh, Sheikh Hasina is dangerously inflated with arrogance and confidence, which is reinforced and reassured by the Indian backing of her, as well as her belief in manipulative machinations of politics. Despite that, she seems to be losing her strategic focus and support from the people. Like her father Mujib, she is living in a self-spun cocoon of illusion losing touch with reality. She carries an extremely negative emotional baggage. She has no courage to face the voters in a fair election and so had to resort to the "midnight" robbery (vote rigging) to win. It is her father's BAKSAL model. Mujib had Rakkhi Bahini and Indian support.

Hasina has converted the administration, police and other law enforcing agencies into the model of her father's Rakkhi Bahini. In the footstep of her father, Hasina rules the country as a dictator. Her temptation of power with "voter less polls" and "midnight elections" destroyed the very fabric of democracy in Bangladesh. Learning from Mujib's failure, India is behind Hasina with full throttle, reducing hers to a puppet regime. The question that one raises is, "how long such a remote-control regime can survive without public support?" Frankenstein usually turns against its creator. In Bangladesh, will it? Time will tell.

Hasina is transformation of a monster from her father Sheikh Mujib's misrule and misdeeds. It seems she failed to learn anything good from her father's misrule. We know, history repeats itself, and the dictator will one day be removed from power, by force or by natural means. That is Hasina Way or BAKSAL Way. On the other hand, Khaleda Zia followed Zia's ideology, which was about Bangladesh, its sovereignty and development. The Zia Way is about patriotism, a sense of honor, stability and development of the country. In a country of divided souls, the Zia Way struggles against the BAKSAl Way. The former strives to glorify Bangladesh, the latter is of betrayal to the nation and to the people only to stay in power, and selling Bangladesh at a far less price than what we paid in blood for our independence.

Finally, Khaleda Zia would be wrongly placed in history books, if she is seen only as the wife of Ziaur Rahman. She would be wrongly understood if we place her as one of the other "Begums" in Bangladesh politics. That is erroneous. Also, many of her critics might think Khaleda failed with Hasina's dictatorship. To my understanding, Khaleda did not fail. Khaleda was and remains a democrat. Her fight was and is against a fascist regime. It is an unequal comparison, unequal fight. The failure, if any, was of democracy against fascism, freedom and rule of law against neo BAKSAL dictatorship.

Khaleda did win her fight against dictator Ershad. Presently, she is fighting against dictator Hasina. In all, due to her virtuous life in politics, she was elected 3 times as Prime Minister. Khaleda Zia has been unique in her own right. Her track record in the spare of economic development is also quite remarkable.

"When she became prime minister for the third time, the GDP growth rate of Bangladesh remained above 6 percent. The Bangladesh per capita national income rose to 482 dollars. Foreign exchange reserve of Bangladesh had crossed 3 billion dollars from the previous 1 billion dollars. The foreign direct investments of Bangladesh had risen to 2.5 billion dollars. The industrial sector of the GDP had exceeded 17 percent at the end of Zia's office."[3] That was no mean achievement of the time, given the various disturbances and obstacles created by the opposition Awami League under Sheikh Hasina.

Bangladeshi dictator Hasina is treating Khaleda Zia, a three-time Prime Minister, like a "common criminal." Question arises, why is an ex-prime minister being treated so shabbily and dishonorably before a national election under Hasina? People are increasingly upset at the display of arrogance and hatred on Hasina's part. Under the circumstances, people wonder if free and fair election will ever be allowed?[4] To make sure that Khaleda wouldn't have any chance to contest the election in 2018, Hasina government arrested Khelada on fake and false charges and sent her to jail. When people came to know about her serious illness, they were in pain and anguish but in solidarity with her. I saw many of them crying. It was as if Bangladesh democracy was bleeding through their eyes.

Conclusion

Khaleda Zia has been fighting against the most corrupt, vindictive and highly authoritarian regime of Bangladesh. In fighting for democracy against Hasina's dictatorship, Khaleda uses her cherished virtues of serving the aspirations of the people, and it shows she has not failed. Her struggle only continues, because the curtain has not dropped yet, it has just stuck requiring some much needed adjustments.

All told, to stand on guard for Bangladesh's sovereignty, the nation needs Khaleda Zia. No other leader of Bangladesh can match her on this. Khaleda's courage is a necessary virtue; it is needed to be on guard against Hasina's Indian puppet government that is slowly Indianizing Bangladesh and undermining Bangladesh's sovereignty.

In the end, the most remarkable aspect about Khaleda Zia is that she listens to the nationalists, patronizes the patriots, and, above all, she practices what she preaches. This is the strength of her character.

However, most patriots feel that it would be imperative on Begum Khaleda Zia to make room for BNP's young leadership with courage, dedication and determination like herself, to bring them in the forefront and send the old, aged, tattered leadership in the party to retirement, or at best to an Advisory Pool. This will certainly bring new vitality and dynamism in the party. The BNP needs to re-energize itself like it did when Khaleda began her political career in the early eighties. Such reorganization in the party is a rare commodity these days.

"It is not the strongest of the species that survives, nor the most intelligent, but the one most responsive to change," said Charles Darwin in 1809. Very true.

---

[1] https://en.wikipedia.org/wiki/Assassination_of_Ziaur_Rahman Among the attackers, Lt. Col. Matiur Rahman and Col. Mahbub were killed while trying to escape, Major Khaled and Major Mojaffar escaped, and Captain Moslehuddin was caught and sentenced to life in prison. However, as of 2010, he is in the United States." One of the accused of Ziaur Rahman's murder case, captain (Rtd.) Giasuddin Ahmed is now an Awami League member of Jatiya Sangshad from Gaffargaon Upazila, Mymensingh District.

[2] Joanne B. Ciulla, *The Ethics of Leadership* (2003).

[3] Khaleda Zia, Wikipedia.

[4] Jyoti Malhotra, Delhi supports 'dictator' Sheikh Hasina despite Khaleda Zia's entreaties, 12 June, 2018, https://theprint.in/opinion/global-print/delhi-supports-dictator-sheikh-hasina-despite-khaleda-zias-entreaties/69100/

Chapter 13

Begum Khaleda Zia: Personal Recollections and Beyond

R Chowdhury

Others Eclipsed

"Others finished, totally eclipsed," Captain Hafiz whispered, elbowing me as he was pointing at the regal entry of Begum Khaleda Zia by the side of her husband Colonel Ziaur Rahman.

It was a bright mid-morning in January 1972. We gathered to inaugurate a new Officers Club at the Dhaka Cantonment. Captain Hafizuddin Ahmed and I, both wartime comrades, sat next to each other in the front lawn. Bachelors, we screened and compared the beauties and styles of the ladies sitting in the sofas facing us in front. Being the first social gathering after a long and painful gap, the lady wives left little to chance to present themselves the best way they could. It was a fashion parade for most.

None came close to Begum Zia in beauty, elegance and personality. That was the first time I saw her from a close distance.

Ziaur Rahman was an instructor at the Pakistan Military Academy in the late sixties when I was a cadet. Though we rarely had the opportunity to meet the ladies, beauty of Mrs. Zia was known in the academy circle. One or two weekends, I had seen Major Zia accompanied by his wife driving down the road that passed through the cadets living area, to and from Abbotabad city.

"I don't know"

In the liberation war, I founded and commanded 2 Field Artillery under the Z Force of Colonel Ziaur Rahman. Our frequent operational interactions brought us close. One November afternoon, Zia and I stood on a high ground to oversee the passage of the truck convoy carrying 1 Bengal troops to Zakiganj and Atgram. The unit was to take up new operational positions in northeastern Sylhet. After the convoy cleared through the hilly tracks, we sat down and talked. I felt he wanted a little relaxation. I seized the informal moment to ask the reclusive commander about the whereabouts of his family. Silence descended. His gaze went far to the western horizon that met Bangladesh tree line.

"I don't know," was his quiet reply after a deep breath. Zia usually did not show emotion, but I noticed his soaked voice. I later learned that Begum Zia, with her two infant sons, was hiding from place to place after her husband revolted against Pakistan on the night of March 25, 1971 and two days later, making the risky but crucial and landmark declaration of the independence of Bangladesh. Following a lead, Begum Zia was arrested in April and remained in military confinement. Reportedly, Brigadier Janjua (not to be confused with Colonel Rashid Janjua of 8 Bengal), a former commander of Zia, treated the Zia family with respect and accommodated it with his family in the cantonment. She was freed after the surrender of the Pakistani forces in December 1971.

Insinuation!

In the nineties, a denigrating story was circulated by the detractors of the Zia family. It went like this. From the war front, Colonel Ziaur Rahman sent Captain Hafiz or someone to Dhaka with a message for his wife to come out of the cantonment and join him. She did not. After the war, a displeased Zia wanted to divorce his wife for her supposed betrayal and reported infidelity. Sheikh Mujibur Rahman intervened, and their marriage survived. A highly unlikely narrative. I find huge discrepancies in it.

Nobody heard of this story for more than two decades, certainly not during Mujib's or Zia's lifetime. I was close to Hafiz and he never talked about it, even if he may have been part of it. When the Zias were reunited after the war, nobody noticed or felt any dearth of love and respect between them. I have seen their close bond both in good times and bad times. Above event in January 1972 is a clear evidence. I have also seen how devastated Begum Zia was after the loss of her beloved husband in May 1981.

Fact Check

After hearing the announcement of independence by Major Ziaur Rahman, Captain Hafizuddin Ahmed of 1 Bengal, which was deployed away from its base in Jessore, went to his Commanding Officer, Colonel Rezaul Jalil, requesting him to join the liberation war. The CO chickened out but allowed Hafiz to do whatever he thought right. The young Captain revolted with whatever troops he could muster and gave a number of fights to Pakistani forces, including a fierce one at Roumari, Kurigram. In June, his group joined 11 Sector of Ziaur Rahman in northern Mymensingh, later becoming part of the Z Force. In August, the Z Force moved to the war hotspot in Sylhet, relinquishing the command of 11 Sector to newly arrived Major Abu Taher. Major Mohammad Ziauddin, co-escapee with Taher from Sialkot, took command of 1 Bengal. There is no record that Captain Hafiz went to Dhaka on any mission during the war. Nor was Ziaur Rahman the type of person to make such an attempt. In any case, how would it be possible for a woman with two kids to escape from strict military custody?

Sheikh Mujib had no love lost for Ziaur Rahman, who stole the show by declaring the independence of Bangladesh and leading the liberation war to victory, both of which Mujib missed. In an implied grudge, Zia was bypassed and his junior, K M Safiullah, a questionable character, was made the new Army Chief after General Osmany reverted to his political career. Zia was sent to Comilla to command 44 Brigade. But his war contribution, efficiency, and above all his popularity, could not be ignored. The post of Deputy Chief of Army Staff was created and Zia was accommodated there. It was a common knowledge that Safiullah was a figurehead and the real command of the Army lied with the DCAS.

Mujib patching up a misunderstanding between the Zias did not fit the bill. It was uncharacteristic of him.

I thought it was an Awami doing, specifically Sheikh Hasina's, aimed at killing two birds with one stone. First, to project Mujib's paternal magnanimity, which he lacked (Remember Dalim-Nimmi episode? The young couple was physically assaulted by the goons of Ghazi Gholam Mostafa in 1974. In wretched state, they came to "Mujib Chacha" for justice. The Chacha sided with GGM, even though the Dalims were like his family members). Second, to defame the Zia family. The Zias were the last people Hasina could stand. Zia out-shadowed her father. Hasina rarely leaves a session without hurling an insult or insinuation at the Zias. Even some neutral minds could also be infected with the false story. However, the story soon died its natural death, though still may be keeping a thin trail. The Zia family thought it was below their taste to even take it into cognizance.

Birthday Challenge

Also came Begum Zia's birthday controversy. All official records indicated the birthday of Khaleda Khanam, her maiden name, as August 15, the day Mujib fell. The Awami circle felt "insulted" when Begum Zia's birthday was celebrated on the day it mourned for its lost leader. Nobody challenged it for decades. But it became an issue when Sheikh Hasina came to be the Prime Minister. Mahfuz Ullah, in his book *Begum Khaleda Zia: Her Life, Her Story,* clearly and convincingly nullified the Awami concoction.

Interaction with Begum Zia

I next met Begum Zia when I visited them to introduce my newly married wife in 1973 at their Dhaka Cantonment residence. Brigadier Ziaur Rahman was the DCAS. I noticed that my wife could hardly take her eyes off from Begum Zia. "I thought I was looking at a *Protima* (beauty queen)," she told me on our way home. She noted another thing. Zia was wearing an ordinary sandal having repairs done on it.

Later, I met Begum Zia a number of times. A few stuck in my memory. In 1978 or 1979, President Ziaur Rahman was visiting an African country. On the way they stopped over in Jeddah for refueling the Biman, which was free for the Bangladesh VVIP flights. The old Jeddah airport was not equipped with today's aerobridges to connect gates with plane. Passengers were driven by buses/cars to the distant tarmac. The Saudi security and protocol took the President to the lounge but Begum Zia preferred to stay in the plane for the short stay. Working at the Embassy, and as in-charge of the VVIPs and protocol, I went to her to request if she would like to disembark and relax a bit at the lounge. She again politely declined, perhaps not wanting to cause trouble to others for her comforts. On my query if she needed anything, she asked me if I could get her a little moisturizing or cold cream. I was in trouble. Where could I get the cream in such a short time? Terminal building was far away and I was not sure if it had cosmetics. I came out, ran to my car at a distance and drove fast looking for a cosmetic store. When I found one, I didn't know what to choose. I thought I picked up Pond's, the best I could get. I rushed back and managed to hand it over to her before the plane door closed. The ADC wanted to pay but I declined; it was not much anyway.

During the return trip, they again halted for refueling but it was only for a few minutes and the passengers remained onboard. Ambassador Humayun Rasheed Choudhury and I went up the plane to greet the President and Begum Zia.

I had since been wondering why the wife of a President could not have a simple face cream with her? Maybe, she forgot it while packing, or she felt its need only at the hot and dry climate as it was in Jeddah. And, she would not like to ask a hostess who would be too happy to oblige. It was one of her first overseas trips.

In February 1994, I was travelling by Biman from Dhaka to New York (Biman MD, Muyeed Chowdhury, a friend, upgraded my seat to the Business Class, in addition to sending a message to NY and all halts to render VIP care, which I did not need. As then District Commissioner of Dhaka, Muyeed Chowdhury took the famous picture depicting a resting Zia in a vest after a canal digging). During the long flight, I had time to interact with a friendly air hostess. A girl from north Bengal, she traveled with Begum Zia a number of times and became her admirer. She said that "Madam" used minimum make up. Yet, almost magically, she always presented herself in the most elegant and graceful manner! "Few could match her styles," she said.

I Goofed Up

Two of my meetings with Begum Zia were important. One was in mid-1981, after the assassination of her husband President Ziaur Rahman. I had observed how sad and heartbroken she was, looking severely devastated. I noticed that one side of her fair cheek was blackened; couldn't understand why. I assumed it could be due to her prolonged mourning while keeping her head on one side. I could be wrong. Sad, she did not talk much but acknowledged receipt of my personal letter of condolence sent from abroad. But I goofed up on an important question. She wanted to know what I thought about the future of the country. Unprepared, I gave a blank look. Brigadier Mahtab, a family friend, was with us. He was a distant relative of the Zias. He explained what I thought about the future leadership of the country. I hadn't the faintest idea that Begum Zia was already being prompted by close circle to take a political role. I fumbled and failed to give the answer she looked for. In fact, I gave a totally wrong answer. I said I thought General Manzur could come close to President Zia in quality and leadership. Unfortunately, he was the one who committed such a betrayal. Begum Zia made no comment. Brigadier Mahtab later explained to me that she was trying to find out support for her political leadership. He also doubted that Begum Zia had minded my remarks, given my ignorance of the internal political dynamics of the time. Mahtab also took credit for pushing Khaleda into politics.

The Manzur Story

My assertion came from the fact that Zia and Manzur were very close. Major Mohammad Abul Manzur was known as the "Pundit" by his seniors in Pakistan for his superior knowledge, high intelligence and sound efficiency. When a re-installed Zia was finding difficulty to restore discipline in the army in the post-November 7 *Sepoy-Janata Biplob,* he recalled Brigadier Manzur from New Delhi, where he was the Defense Adviser at the Bangladesh High Commission. Together, they soon brought the unruly elements under control. In 1979, I had a long talk with General

Manzur in Chittagong where he commanded 24 Division. I found him extremely bitter about the rehabilitation of non-freedom fighters and Razakars in high civil and military positions. At the same time, perhaps trying to stay politically correct, he affirmed that it was the President who could fix the dichotomy.

Away from the epicenter, I was influenced by the official version of the gruesome act in Chittagong, even believed the White Paper published by General Hussain Muhammad Ershad. Subsequently, I came to know more than what people were made to believe. I learned some untold facts. It became clear that India masterminded the assassination of Zia with its local agents that included Ershad. Sheikh Hasina, whom President Zia allowed to come to Bangladesh just two weeks earlier, was in the loop. (Ref: Amar Fansi Chai by Matiur Rahman Rentu, onetime Hasina aide). During her six-year self-exile in India, the Research and Analysis Wing (RAW), India's External Intelligence, tutored her well to destroy Zia, who was not toeing the Indian line. Hasina had her own grudge against Ziaur Rahman, who outsmarted her father Sheikh Mujibur Rahman by declaring the Independence of Bangladesh and leading the liberation war to victory. Mujib failed on both counts.[1]

I learned some details from a few insiders. General Manzur was not in the plot in the beginning and tried to explain it to Dhaka but without much success. Nonetheless, he tried to own responsibility for what his officers did. He went round the units and attempted to make a case for his officers' action. But the troops' faces indicated they were not convinced. Manzur then frantically tried to contact Ershad, DGFI General Mohabbat Jan Chowdhury, and other senior officials in Dhaka but none came in line, perhaps realizing that the Chittagong plot backfired. They had underestimated Ziaur Rahman and his popularity. A shrewd Ershad quickly made an about face and became a hero by quelling the rebellion in Chittagong. Manzur with his family and two officers--Lieutenant Colonels Mahbubur Rahman (his nephew) and Matiur Rahman-- were on the run. They were caught in a tea garden at Fatikchari. After arrest Manzur insisted to be sent to civilian custody, but not to military hands, saying he had already resigned from the military service. He realized cunning Ershad would not spare him for his own sake. True, the General Officer

Commanding of Chittagong was made the scapegoat and was brutally gunned down, along with the two officers, at the gate of the garrison he commanded. His family was not hurt.

What, however, surprised me was why Begum Zia spared Ershad when she had the authority to deal with him? In fact, if his complicity could be proved, Ershad could have been hanged along with other plotters. Maybe, unlike her archrival, she was not vindictive. To me, it was another blunder (similar to Zia allowing Hasina's return and entry into politics) that Khaleda committed, for which she had to pay a heavy price.[2]

My assertion came from the fact that Zia and Manzur were very close. Mohammad Abul Manzur was known as the "Pundit" by his seniors for his superior knowledge, high intelligence and sound efficiency. When a re-installed Zia was finding difficulty to restore discipline in the army in the post-November 7 *Sepoy-Janata Biplob,* he recalled Brigadier Manzur from New Delhi, where he was the Defense Adviser at the Bangladesh High Commission. Together, they soon brought the unruly elements under control. In 1979, I had a long talk with General Manzur in Chittagong where he commanded the 24 Division. I found him extremely bitter about the rehabilitation of non-freedom fighters and Razakars in high civil and military positions. At the same time, perhaps trying to stay politically correct, he affirmed that it was the President who could fix the dichotomy.

Away from the epicenter, I was influenced by the official version of the gruesome act in Chittagong, even believed the White Paper published by General H M Ershad. Subsequently, I came to know more than what people were made to believe. I learned some untold facts. It became clear that India masterminded the assassination of Zia with its local agents that included Ershad. Sheikh Hasina, whom President Zia allowed to come to Bangladesh just two weeks earlier, was in the loop. (Ref: Amar Fansi Chai by Matiur Rahman Rentu, onetime Hasina aide). During her six-year self-exile in India, the Research and Analysis Wing (RAW), India's External Intelligence, tutored her well to destroy Zia, who was not toeing the Indian line. Hasina had her own grudge against Ziaur Rahman, who outsmarted her father Sheikh Mujibur Rahman by declaring the Independence of Bangladesh and leading the liberation war to victory. Mujib failed on both counts.

I learned some details from a few insiders. General Manzur was not in the plot in the beginning and tried to explain it to Dhaka but without much success. Nonetheless, he tried to own responsibility for what his officers did. He went round the units and attempted to make a case for his officers' action. But the troops' faces indicated they were not convinced. Manzur then frantically tried to contact Ershad, DGFI General Mohabbat Jan Chowdhury, and other senior officials in Dhaka but none came in line, perhaps realizing that the Chittagong plot backfired. They had underestimated Ziaur Rahman and his popularity. A shrewd Ershad quickly made an about face and became a hero by quelling the rebellion in Chittagong. Manzur with his family and two officers--Lieutenant Colonels Mahbub (his nephew) and Matiur Rahman-- were on the run. They were caught in a tea garden at Fatikchari. After arrest Manzur insisted to be sent to civilian custody, not to military hands, saying he had already resigned from the military service. He realized that the foxy Ershad would not spare him for his own sake. True, the General Officer Commanding of Chittagong (that is, Manzur) was made the scapegoat and was brutally gunned down, along with the two officers, at the gate of the garrison he commanded. His family was not hurt.[1]

What, however, surprised me was why Begum Zia spared Ershad when she had the authority to deal with him? In fact, if his complicity could be proved, Ershad could have been hanged along with other plotters. Maybe, unlike her archrival Hasina, Khaleda was not vindictive. To me, however, it was another blunder (similar to Zia allowing Hasina's return and entry into politics) that Khaleda committed, for which she had to pay a heavy price.[2]

The Hasina Factor

My last meeting with Begum Zia was in 1992 at her Secretariat Office. It was her first term as Prime Minister. After routine pleasantries, our discussion turned business. She assured me that she would look into the problems we faced in the Ministry of Foreign Affairs, such as held up promotions, postings to insignificant places and denial of routine benefits. I felt she was treading a thin line in the face of stiff and nasty opposition from her nemesis Sheikh Hasina, particularly with regard to the military officers absorbed in the Foreign Service. Colonel Mustafizur Rahman, Foreign Minister, later told me that the PM talked to him about my much awaited but deliberately blocked promotion (to Ambassador). He further confided to me that he had his own problems with the ministry, which was not suitably disposed towards the military. He even hinted that there was no dearth of pro-Awami elements in that outfit, and Hasina had her moles installed there.

One of Khaleda Zia's weaknesses, as most observers suspect, was that she was too soft on Hasina and she always tried to avoid confrontation with her adversary. Some people even went to the extent of claiming that she was afraid of the other woman. If so, it was not because the other Begum was any better but because she was nasty, uncouth and unscrupulous. Hasina exploited it to her best advantage. We have seen that day in and day out since her return to Bangladesh in 1981.

Khaleda perhaps had other reasons. Opposition Awami League commanded the loyalty of a sizeable section of the administration, media and intelligentsia. India, a reckoning factor for Bangladesh, was backing Hasina to suit its own agenda. Fighting Hasina meant fighting all these fronts, not an easy task for a first time Prime Minister, however strong her convictions be. Rumors had it that if one wanted something done from the Khaleda administration, one would go to Hasina. It would be promptly done. I saw the truth in it.

Khaleda is a "Time Bomb" for Hasina

Conversely, Hasina is equally, if not more, fearful of Khaleda when she is in power. In fact, Hasina was so scared of the hold on the nation of the Opposition Leader (Khaleda) by virtue of the latter's popularity that she had often confined her in office/residence cordoning it with armed Rapid Action Battalions (RAB) and Gopali forces (the loyal elements from Gopalganj, Hasina's home district). Trucks filled with sands and bricks surrounded Khaleda's living compounds and office premises. Those forces regularly used water cannons, tear gases, pepper sprays and other harmful objects, including gun fires to disperse Khaleda's supporting crowds. There were scores of fatalities in such police actions. To harass her archenemy, Hasina filed over thirty cases, all flimsy or fictitious. A law-abiding person, Begum Zia dutifully attended the hearings in the partisan or party affiliated courts and prosecution. None of the cases could be proved, yet the ailing and elderly Opposition Leader was sentenced to a 17-year prison term. Public disapproval and nationwide demonstrations to the mistrial and conviction were ruthlessly suppressed causing fatalities in hundreds. Khaleda's bail petitions and appeals against the sentence were routinely denied by a compliant judiciary.

"Khaleda is a Time-Bomb for Hasina," said a political observer living in the US. "The Opposition Leader (Khaleda) is not coming out of jail anytime soon. If Khaleda is out, Hasina will be in," he adds. Meanwhile, the Corona allowed Khaleda to breathe free air since March 25, 2020 "conditionally," as the Hasina administration prefers to term it. The Pandemic also seems to have put a hold on whatever little politics there was.

Hasina's Electoral Farce

In the first ever democratic election in 1991, Sheikh Hasina thought her Awami League would win handily. She was so confident of victory that she was said to have completed her cabinet nominations. But destiny had a different story to tell. Bangladesh Nationalist Party, founded by President Ziaur Rahman and now chaired by his wife Begum Zia, came out as the winner. An enraged Hasina could not absorb the defeat and continued blaming "subtle rigging" without substantiation. She openly challenged that she would not allow Khaleda to run the country peacefully, not even for a day. Indeed, she continued to create blockades and troubles at the slightest pretext. On the demand for a neutral Caretaker Government (CTG) to oversee national elections, her party and affiliates conducted a devastating run of *hartals* (work stoppage) for 173 days in 1995/96. Khaleda accepted the public demand and enacted the CTG. The next few elections were conducted under it with acceptable fairness and impartiality.

The CTG Discarded

Paradoxically, it was Hasina who did away with the CTG the soonest after reaping its full benefits. She regained power through a military-RAW stratagem in December 2008. But she soon saw her administration slipped to the lowest ebb in public esteem because of her various anti- state and anti-people actions. Her party Awami League would be washed away in any fair and participatory election. Taking advantage of her parliamentary majority, Hasina found it convenient to quash the CTG so that she could manage future elections. In fact, there has not been any election since. What happened in the name of elections in 2014 and 2018 were farce of the highest order and severely condemned at home and abroad. Additionally, the opposition BNP became targets of attacks, extra-judicial killings, police cases, harassments, abductions and oppressions. Begum Zia and her family members became the prime targets. "She had undergone insurmountable hardships," recounts Professor Asif Nazrul of Dhaka University. "I doubt if any other leader in Bangladesh ever suffered as much for the sake of the country and the people as did Begum Zia," adds the Law Professor.

Abandoning the Ladder After the Climb

Another grand failure of the Opposition Leader was her ineffective stand against the Repeal of the Indemnity Act, which allowed the Hasina administration to try and execute the August 15 coup leaders. Being the beneficiary of August 15 political change for more than two decades, most observers term it an abject failure, if not total betrayal, on the part of the BNP. Former BNP Law Minister Maudud Ahmed remarked that "justice was done" after the court verdict to hang the heroes of August 15. The BNP later clarified that it was his personal comment. When Khaleda became Prime Minister in 2001, she made no attempt to rescue the accused who were languishing in the prison cells. At the minimum, she could arrange a retrial to right the wrongs done in Hasina's Kangaroo Court. When the August 15 *Surja Santans* were paraded to the gallows in January 2010, the BNP remained a silent bystander. A shame!

As early as in 1976, noting the neglect of the August 15 leaders, Dr. Abdur Rashid, an Adviser under President Ziaur Rahman, commented of the administration he served, in his colloquial Bangla: "কার দোয়ারে শিন্নি খাছ মোল্লা চিনলি না" (You enjoy the benefits but forgot the provider). Begum Zia's

BNP conveniently and unceremoniously threw away the ladder it climbed to power!

Housewife to People's Leader

Khaleda entered politics carrying the sympathy of the assassinated and hugely popular President Ziaur Rahman. More than two million people gathered in Dhaka to mourn the death of the President, an unprecedented event in the history of Bangladesh. The bereaved lady converted her sorrow into strength and soon developed an image of her own. Professor Nazrul says at the launching of a book on Begum Zia authored by Dr. Mahfuz Ullah, "We now know her as Begum Khaleda Zia, not as the wife of Ziaur Rahman."

During the lifetime of Zia, Khaleda was largely a housewife. She was rarely seen in public during the initial days of Zia presidency. She did not accompany her husband in his first few foreign trips. She joined him in later day visits.

Born in Dinajpur, a north Bengal district, in August 1945, Khaleda was nicknamed Putul, meaning doll. Indeed, she was a doll to adore. She achieved double credit in 1960. First, she passed her Matric. Second, and the most important thing of her life, marriage to Captain Ziaur Rahman. Their lives remained largely separated for the first few years, as the husband mostly remained away on training assignments at home and abroad. Meanwhile, Khaleda attended Surendranath college in Dinajpur. In 1965, she moved to West Pakistan to live with her husband. The same year, Zia fought the Indo-Pak war with 1 Bengal in Khem Karan Sector and won Hilal-e-Jurat, the second highest award for gallantry. After a two-year tenure as instructor at the Pakistan Military Academy and later completion of the Staff College Course, Zia was posted to East Pakistan in 1969, first in 2 Bengal in Joydevpur and then to help raise 8 Bengal in Chittagong. In early 1971, 8 Bengal was ordered to move to Multan, West Pakistan, and a composite company had already moved there as Advance Party. The main body was to move shortly, but political situation overtook the routine activities. Zia sent his family to Dhaka for safety.

On March 25, 1971, Ziaur Rahman revolted when the Pakistan military attacked the Bengalis. Most political leaders fled or surrendered.

In that leadership vacuum, Major Ziaur Rahman made the declaration of independence on March 27, 1971. Bangladesh won victory after a bloody war for nine months.

A Polished Woman

Begum Khaleda Zia may not have advanced much in education but formal education is not always necessary for making a mark in national or even international arena. Examples are galore. Those who heard Khaleda Zia's speeches during political rallies agree that she spoke with considerable literary flare and fervor. Her speeches in the Parliament, both as Prime Minister and Opposition Leader, remain masterpieces. I have not heard her speak in English, but a former Attorney General told me that she spoke impeccable English. Begum Zia is a fast learner, as we can see from her meteoric transformation from a passive housewife to a fiery politician and highly successful and popular national leader. She must have mastered her English as the wife of a military officer interacting with others, mostly in English, as it was common in officers circle. Even her critics agree, Khaleda is a highly polished woman.

Among the Powerful Women

Little known is the fact that Khaleda Zia ranked among the 100 Most Powerful Women in the World, of the *Forbes* magazine rankings. She was number 14 in 2004, number 29 in 2005 and number 33 in 2006. Her slide in subsequent ranking was due the multifarious difficulties created by her nemesis Sheikh Hasina in administering the country. That also hampered her efforts in attending to a few national issues. Even then, Begum Zia's accomplishments were worth noting by any standard.

Before I conclude, let me quote again Dr.Asif Nazrul, the Law Professor. "As a Dhaka University student in 1987," said Nazrul, "I would look at a poster in which a lady under police custody throwing challenge to the authorities." It was Begum Khaleda Zia and "I was thrilled that such a great leader was born in Bangladesh...Begum Zia became a synonym of a Bangladesh of honor, dignity, self-respect and sovereignty. She became a symbol of Bangladesh." [3] Indeed, Khaleda Zia is an example of herself.

Despite all the sufferings she had to undergo, she she remains ever cheerful.

When Khaleda Zia was evicted from her 38-year living residence in the Dhaka Cantonment in 2010, Obaid Chowdhury (New York, USA) wrote the article "Eviction of Khaleda Zia: Latest in Hasina's Zia-Phobia," which was published in a number of media outlets. He said that Prime Minister Sheikh Hasina "was seen enjoying Nero's grin when her archenemy was publicly humiliated." Such was Hasina's vendetta against her political archenemy. But Begum Khaleda Zia continues to stand tall-- for her country, for her people.

---

[1] One may check the Daily Star, which published a report on the subject: https:// www. thedailystar.net / the – murder - of-major-general - abul-manzur-bir-uttam-12397.

[2] For more, read "Confusion Over A Killing" by Lawrence Lifschultz, Far Eastern Economic Review, July 10, 1981

[3] http://southasiajournal.net/bangladesh-dr-asif-nazruls-speech-on-mahfuz-ullahs-book-launching-begum-khaleda-zia-her-life-her-story/

Chapter 14

Begum Khaleda Zia: Her Long Walk, In and Out of Bondage and Freedom, to Save the Nation—No End in Sight

Q M Jalal Khan

Part I: Introduction

This chapter began from the idea that no amount of exposure is enough for Sheikh Hasina and her tyrannical rule since 2009. It is also since then that Begum Khaleda Zia'a present round of suffering began—hard, intense, prolonged, protracted--, not to mention her bitter, yet uncompromising and successful struggle against the military ruler H M Ershad in the 1980s. There are and will be tons of volumes written on Sheikh Hasina's recklessly evil deeds and actions, far worse than those of Gen Ershad and her own father Sheikh Mujibur Rahman during the post-independence years of 1972-1975 (despite the fact that during the macabre and merciless Mujib period, about 30,000 patriots were killed and nearly 1.5 million people died in the man-made famine of 1974). The way things have been unfolding every passing day for the last thirteen years or so concerning the fascist Hasina regime's continued corruption and oppression, literally every single day opens into a new chapter about her party's and her regime's terribly diabolical and devilish agenda constantly carried out in her police and prison state.

In fact, Hasina's politically dubious and diabolical days can be traced back to 1981 when she was allowed to return to Bangladesh from India by President Ziaur Rahman and when, within less than two weeks of her return, he was assassinated. It was during her stay in India that she became "close friends with Suvra Mukherjee, wife of the future Indian President Pranab Mukherjee." The destructive role of Pranab Mukherjee in the politics of Bangladesh since is widely known. The same is true about Gen Ershad and Gen Moeen who also fully exploited their close relationship with India to the detriment of their own country. It is, again, from the days of Hasina's return to Bangladesh that Freedom Fighter Matiur Rahman Rentu begins his most reliable record of Hasina's dastardly dubious activities in his classic book, আমার ফাঁসী চাই/Amar Fashi Chai (1999).[1] That she and her Awami League were involved in the planning of the assassination of President Zia is well documented by Rentu and other sources.[2]

Sheikh Hasina's reckless misdeeds and mistreatment of Begum Khaleda Zia beggar description. One's absolutely corrupt power and one's absolute powerlessness have been taking place simultaneously and contemporaneously, all due to the former's personal vendetta against the latter. One's vengeful aims and designs are the cause or source of another's miseries and adversities. Both are distinctly separate, mutually exclusive, yet inseparable from and to be juxtaposed with each other. If one may use an analogy, it is the same way that there is a mutuality between God's good and great and kind and compassionate role, on the one hand, and, on the other, Satan's evil temptations and operations. In fact, Begum Zia becomes more highlighted by way of contrast with her vindictive torturer Hasina, the way, to draw yet another analogy, Prometheus (meaning "forethought") becomes a prominent god in ancient Greek mythology due to his titanic sufferings, imposed on him by the jealous and repressive Zeus/Jupiter, for championing the cause of humanity by bringing fire from heaven for humans to develop their culture and civilization through arts and crafts.

This chapter begins and ends with Begum Zia, who comes into indirect focus by way of what she is and, especially, what she is not, compared with the fascist Hasina. Readers would remember her more as they read about her in the context of Hasina's horribly despotic reign. While the whole book is about Khaleda with Sheikh Mujib, Ziaur Rahman, Hasina, and Ershad in the background, in this chapter, however, it is Khaleda who appears to be in the background and her mortal enemy

Hasina, in the foreground only to be relegated into the pit down below. This structural organization of the chapter has been deliberately designed to demonstrate how low and scornful the Hasina regime can be to cause most unjust suffering to Khaleda.

Considering the fact that a paper could be comprehensive in its premises, consisting of broad outlines and perspectives, covering the main themes and aspects in question, Hasina has been foregrounded, which, however, does not mean that the main subject of the book—Khaleda--has been overshadowed. Not at all. Because it is all Hasina's nefarious negatives which bring Khaleda into the fore by way of contrast. Had it all been positives about Hasina (of which she has hardly any), one could have a reason to make an argument otherwise.

Instead of looking at the confines of a paper from traditional point of view, one can argue, as academics do in the classroom, that a thing can be defined by what it is and also by what it is not. For example, a chair is a piece of furniture that has four legs with a small flat surface to sit on, but a chair may also be defined by saying it is not a table, which also has four legs but which is higher than a chair with a bigger flat surface used for writing and reading. Similarly, a deer, a lovely and wounded deer, is neither a hungry hyena nor a feline ferocious tiger. This chapter defines and describes Begum Zia in both ways, putting her in her own virtues and accomplishments and also in the larger context of the predatory and perfidious Awami axis against which her role (or lack of role therefrom) plays out glaringly and without which her suffering and sacrifice cannot be gauged or even imagined. I think readers will be provided with the needed variety of its own in this chapter.

Part II: Sheikh Hasina's Horrible and Heinous Tyranny, As Opposed to the Patriotically Suffering and Sacrificing Khaleda Zia's Struggle for Democracy with Dignity and Determination

Let me begin by quoting from *The Rime of the Ancient Mariner* (1798) by Samuel Taylor Coleridge (who, by the way, along with Robert

Southey, wrote fragment poems and had plans to write long and narrative epics of adventure and heroic battles mostly in praise of Islam's Prophet Muhammad). The plight and predicament of the Ancient Mariner as described by Coleridge is, metaphorically, exactly the same facing the people of Bangladesh today, particulary Begum Khaleda Zia and her BNP-led popular opposition for no fault of theirs. Some of the relevant verses of the poem are as follows:

> And now the STORM-BLAST came, and he
> Was tyrannous and strong:
> He struck with his o'ertaking wings,
> And chased us south along. [....]

> The very deep did rot: O Christ!
> That ever this should be!
> Yea, slimy things did crawl with legs
> Upon the slimy sea. [....]

> And every tongue, through utter drought,
> Was withered at the root;
> We could not speak, no more than if
> We had been choked with soot. [....]

> There passed a weary time. Each throat
> Was parched, and glazed each eye.
> A weary time! a weary time!
> How glazed each weary eye, [....]

> Alone, alone, all, all alone,
> Alone on a wide wide sea!
> And never a saint took pity on
> My soul in agony.

Like Coleridge's Ancient Mariner, to use an analogy of suffering, Khaleda Zia and her BNP-led popular opposition also, for no faults of their own or no crimes committed by them, find themselves under the "tyrannous and strong storm blast" of Awami fascism. Most unjustly and unexpectedly, they find themselves landed in a state of intense and intolerable "agony." They cannot but tide through "a weary time," utterly lonely, with "parched throat," "glazed eye" and "withering tongue," with "slimy" and "crawling" and "rotting things" all around. Like the Mariner and his crew, the BNP men also see ice and ice only, "cracking," "howling," "roaring" and "growling" with no water to drink.

As the title of this chapter suggests, Begum Khaleda Zia's arduous travel began with the beginning of the birth pain of Bangladesh in 1971. When her husband Major Ziaur Rahman rebelled against the marauding Pakistan military in late March, she was picked up with her two infant kids from an hideout in Dhaka and was kept detained for the whole period of the war. Her perilous journey received another cruel shock when her husband, now President, was assassinated in 1981, ironically, in Chittagong where he, on March 26 or 27, exactly ten years ago, took the bold step to declare the Independence of Bangladesh.

With a series of ups and downs in between, her struggle continues to get bitter and burdensome under the ongoing fascism of Sheikh Hasina, the worst in the history of Bangladesh. To repeat, in its short history, Bangladesh has never experienced such oppression, such tyranny. Khaleda is still alive, if not well, during these jointly inflicted (Covid-19 and, worse, Sheikh Hasina) times, choking and suffocating, ominous and odious, beyond toleration.

Begum Zia followed the footprints of her husband. With his historic role, democratic leadership, hard work and unmixed patriotism, President Ziaur Rahman became the most successful and extremely popular leader Bangladesh had seen so far. By following the ideals and high standards of President Zia, Begum Zia too reached a high leadership position and stood out. She still does. Her elegance, her composed and stateswomanly personality, her loyalty to the people, her unflinching determination and her uncompromising stand on matters of national interest elevated her to the position of an unmatched popularity. By virtue of her excellent contribution to the nation, she created a legacy of her own, a lasting legacy for the nation to emulate.

Additionally, Begum Zia has become an icon of patriotic endurance and uncompromising struggle by courageously standing up to the unjust and inhuman victimization meted out to her. Of legendary proportions, her long and painful travail continues as the authoritarian Indian puppet regime and its sole supremo Sheikh Hasina are set on a conspiratorially collision course against her. Sheltered and shielded by the Hindutva nation of India in exchange for her social, political and economic capitulation to it, Sheikh Hasina's terrible rule of violence, unrest, oppression, repression, lies, untruths and fabrications knows no bounds.

On the other hand, Begum Zia's magnanimous and patriotic love for her country is unbounded that appears to have no limit. Her role, both in and out of power, has been one of unifying vision, peace, harmony, democratic fairness and equality. It has left, like the commanding and lighthouse role of her husband President Zia, a highly nonpartisan model of state building administration that the future generations would proudly cultivate with a sense of admiration and emulation.

Millions of Khaleda Zia's supporters do see the distinguishing factors why she is far different and way above her characteristically cruel and vindictive nemesis Sheikh Hasina.[3] They continue to underline her unique status as the wife of an already decorated Major Ziaur Rahman Rahman (Hilal-i-Jurat/Crescent of Courage, a gallantry award for the Indo-Pak War in 1965), who, most importantly, proclaimed the independence of Bangladesh at the most crucial moment of the beginning of its birth in 1971. Overwhelming millions of Bangladeshis love to underscore Begum Zia's status as the wife of an award-winning (Bir Uttam) freedom fighter, of a successful sector commander, of a deputy chief of the army, of the chief of the army, and, finally, of a most successful president with a track record of unprecedented contributions, including multiparty democracy, economic, industrial (especially garments), and agricultural liberalization, export of manpower and, most importantly, the befitting and comprehensive ideal of Bangladeshi Nationalism.[4]

Standing tall on her own, Khaleda Zia led the movement against the military dictator H M Ershad, became a three-time prime minister, two-time opposition leader, and the first woman prime minister (in Bangladesh, second in the Muslim world) with demonstrated patriotism and unbeatable popularity that made her never lose any electoral constituencies-- sometimes five, sometimes 1/11 military dictated three—that she contested from. By contrast, Sheikh Hasina is highly unpopular with the public. She is afraid of the people, afraid to face them in fair competition. As such, she keeps on resorting to election engineering, commonly known as "vote rigging" or "stealing the election," in her case, through "midnight vote dacoity," which only matches her or her rogue regime's massive financial scams and scandals, widespread corruption, and inhuman political persecution and discrimination since 2009.

In these farcical and fraudulent exercises, she uses her loyal but corrupt Election Commissions, administrative machinery, law enforcing agencies and local party activists. Her sponsor is the communal and fundamentalist Hindutva India, which is in league with her in her rogue planning. By all standards, local or international, Sheikh Hasina is holding on to power illegally at least since 2014, if not 2009 when also it was far from being a free, fair and clean election, as twisted and tainted as it was. Among the hissing and horrible hallmarks/trademarks of her fascist rule, there are her concoctions of fake and fabricated cases against Khaleda Zia and the BNP leaders, let alone her police-ridden addiction to power and large scale corruption everywhere every way and all the way.

Like the endless number of fraudulent practices, unlicensed vehicles, hospitals, centers, structures and entities in her country, Sheikh Hasina also has no mandate or license to rule the country. She can only hanker after and doze upon Khaleda Zia's popular support as a people's leader. Known as a great leader Asia-wide, as was her husband, Khaleda Zia is incomparably superior, beyond the reach of the divisive and Indian-installed Sheikh Hasina.[5] In jail or out of jail (five times, 3 times by Ershad, once by Moeen, once and for a longer time by Hasina) Khaleda Zia, unlike Sheikh Hasina, remained uncompromising on questions of national interest and democratic principles, so she has rightfully come to be regarded as "mother of democracy." In her struggle and steadfastness, she remains her own example, her own parallel. It is because of her--the Begum--and the BNP that Bangladesh can still afford to think big and dream big as the future unrolls and the horizon extends before it.

By recounting some of Begum Khaleda Zia's characteristic traits and virtues—political, personal and administrative, as noble, lofty, selfless, patriotic, nationalist and democratic as they are/were--this book, among many others available, thus, helps to offer a necessary counternarrative—credible and authentic—to the wildly inflated and exaggerated claims propagated by the fascist regime in its favor. It is a regime that, like Shelley's Ozymandias (who, as Pharaoh Ramses II, was once very powerful) is likely to be reduced to a shattered wreck, preserved in art or recorded in history; or, like Blake's sick rose, is rotting and worm-eaten from within through corruption; or, like Tennyson's Eagle (quoted below), forcibly clings to power before it is going to fall with a violent counter force:

> The Eagle by Alfred, Lord Tennyson
>
> He clasps the crag with crooked hands;
> Close to the sun in lonely lands,
> Ring'd with the azure world, he stands.
> The wrinkled sea beneath him crawls;
> He watches from his mountain walls,
> And like a thunderbolt he falls.

All the three poems alluded to, as deep in thoughts and ideas as short and simple they are, are about the sudden dissipation or slow withering away of tyrannical forces unleashed for a while. Such forces face their demise and destruction before it is too long. What follows is the broad context in brief in which Begum Khaleda Zia has faced untold suffering for the cause of the democratic goals and aspirations of her people.

Part III: Classification and Categorization of Sheikh Hasina In Chomskyan and Trumpish/Trumpsteinian Terms

In an Intercept interview, conducted by Mehdi Hasan, with the world famous political dissident, academic and linguist 91-year old Professor Noam Chomsky (formerly of MIT, currently at the University of Arizona), the latter describes the Trump administration as "malignancy," "madness," "destruction" and "devastating catastrophe" that America badly needed to get rid of.[6] He compares Donald Trump and his policies with those of Adolf Hitler in the 1930s when he (Hitler) fascistically tried to control every aspect of life. Hasan describes Trump as a "proto-fascist" and "sociopathic" President, "criminally incompetent" to run the country. The same description would very well apply to Sheikh Hasina, whom the Bangladesh Supreme Court once termed as a "wrong-headed" woman. The criminally obsessed, power-drunk Hasina runs her corruption-ridden regime with extremely harsh and brutal repression on the people.

Both Prof Chomsky and journalist Hasan argue that despite the Democratic candidate Joe Biden's "sins" or weaknesses, it is a time when even a small difference would make a big difference in short term and the progressive movement of Bernie Sanders would have a better opportunity to make a headway under a Biden presidency. For now, when America is not ready yet for Sanders' progressive views about healthcare and education, for example, a Sanders nomination would mean losing the party, which Chomsky thinks is far worse than losing the election. The message is clear: win or no win the White House, the party should first come together and remain united. Only then it should try to win the election. Once in the White House, the Democrats can take steps to move the progressive movement forward.

Similarly, from 2007 onwards under the burden of the Hasina-brand fascism, synonymous with Hitler's and that of other tyrants throughout history, it is one of those abnormally evil times when any difference, however small that may be (as represented by the BNP-led alliance, despite its shortcomings), would mean a big difference in terms of the Bangladeshi nation coming together. That unity is likely to tear down the sociopath and power-addict Hasina. That solidarity is likely to keep at bay the utterly odious opprobrium that Sheikh Hasina so garrulously harbors and gluttonously embodies. To bring about a downfall to the destructive Awami regime can only be in the patriotic and national interests of Bangladesh—its peace, harmony, independence, freedom, sovereignty, territorial integrity, equality, rule of law and social justice. The nation needs to be locking down and socially distancing from the disastrous "Bungalee"/Bengali and "Bango" Virus hostile to Muslim-majority Bangladesh under the banner of Bangladeshi Nationalism.

According to Chomsky, one thing that does emerge with considerable clarity is an effort to construct an international coalition of the most reactionary and oppressive states, led by the gangster in the White House—Trump. The world is facing a disaster and Trump is accelerating that disaster. The same argument fits in well with the gangster in the Ganabhaban, Dhaka—Sheikh Hasina, who has become a member of the coalition of similar states—her own Bangladesh, India under Narendra Modi, Israel under Benjamin Netanyahu, China under Xi Jinping and the USA under Trump. Both Trump and especially Modi and Hasina face a disastrous corona virus response for which Hasina deserves to get an IG NOBLE, as Modi already got, to be awarded by Nobel Laureates at Harvard.

Hasina should in fact get a double IG NOBLE (ignoble) as she is also engaged in criminalizing politics and politicizing crimes, adding high level state corruption and repression to her villainous agenda for more than an age now. Her sins, lies, mischiefs, and misdeeds, particularly in the form of her police and political persecutions, widespread and wholesale election riggings both by midnight and midday, and massive financial frauds, scams and scandals, are in thousands that would fill several volumes of *Arabian Nights* and Rentu's *Amar Fashi Chai*. Reigning over a system that has gone corrupt to the core under her watch, Hasina and her people loot and plunder the money of their own people, rape and kill their own people, abduct and murder their own people, imprison and intimidate their own people, and fiendishly and ferociously take away the political freedoms and human rights of their own people.

As the New York-based millionaire Dr Mina Farah (once a Hasina supporter, now rightly turned into a deep anti-Hasina mine fighting against her fascist mis/rule with the force and power of a warplane like an F-16 fighter jet, which is her (Mina Farah's) verbal assaults and rebuttals hurled over the social media and YouTube videos), argues that unless it was a criminal act, for no administrative lapses whatsoever, if there were any (perhaps hardly none), Begum Zia should have been sentenced by the lame and loony Hasina*ized* corrupt cronies and lackeys in judges and justices, who, including the passive and incompetent military, have made themselves a burdensome liability and a laughing stock of the nation, instead of being its proud assets.⁷

Being a country of extrajudicial killings, endless oppression, repression, persecution, unlawful lawsuits, kidnaps, unlimited loots and launderings, massive vote dacoity/rigging, and bootlicking of India (নির্বিচার হত্যা, নির্যাতন, নিষ্পেষণ, হামলা-মামলা, গুম-খুন, সীমাহীন লুটপাট, বিশাল ভোট ডাকাতি, ভারতের পদসেবা করা), Bangladesh is against Bangladesh, deeply divided, fractured and fissured. It is a frightening 'foreign' country to its own people. It is no country with Hasina's willful torture, terror, misconduct, negligence, sabotage, subversion, favoritism, nepotism, cronyism, mismanagement and maladministration going on uncontrolled and unabated (see Appendix B and the rest). Journalist Minar Rashid aptly describes this regime as a government of the *batpars* by the *batpars* for the *batpars* (গভর্নমেন্ট অব দা বাটপার বাই দা বাটপার এন্ড ফর দা বাটপার), the Bengali word *batpar* may mean anything – touts, cheats, deceivers, swindlers, conmen, scoundrels and mountebanks, so on.⁸

As just has been mentioned above, many observers compare Hasina's fascism with that of Hitler and other known tyrants in history. Dictators usually control the entire state apparatus, including the oppressive mechanisms, tools and tactics. Resistance and opposing groups do exist but are unable to surface for fear of arrest, torture or even elimination. In such a scenario, unity among the challengers, however small and insignificant they be, is of paramount importance, as emphasized by Chomsky. They cannot afford to quarrel among themselves or divide and discord on trifling matters.

The Bangladesh situation under the Hasina dictatorship is not any different. Chomsky's message is especially important for the opposition parties in Bangladesh. If they remain divided on small ideological issues, the dictator will have a field day and continue with her fascism. Also, one must remember that the fascists in history thrived on creating such division among their challengers. If they (the latter) succumb to such traps and manipulations, their position only gets further weakened. Solidly united under an organization and an able leadership, it may **not** be difficult for them to free themselves and the country by throwing off the yoke of the

Hasina dictatorship and tearing down the chains of its Hinduized police-led, jejune and jaundiced judiciary-led and rusted and roasted bureaucracy-led oppressive state apparatus and machinery.

Once the statecraft is under their control, their ideological differences, if any, can be adjusted, accommodated, or even be compromised to suit the general aspirations of the people. The bottom line is: Solid unity among the opposition ranks and files; no room for disagreement. The only task before them is to get rid of the fascist. Let the people decide about who should govern them in a free choice through a free election. As such, the opposition should have only one demand: Immediate handover of power to a neutral Caretaker Government to hold a fair and participatory election within the shortest possible time.

Trump created his own monster, the Fox News, which blindly and broadly supported him giving him 'a giant platform' during his 2016 campaign. Now, following his sore defeat in 2020, with the channel playing a neutral role and projecting Joe Biden the winner much ahead of the pro-Biden CNN and other channels, frustrated and disappointed Trump supporters chanted, "Fox News Sucks! Fox News Sucks!" Satirical comedian and journalist Dean Obeidallah comments: "This is akin to an updated version of Frankenstein -- perhaps called Trumpenstein -- where the 'monster' has now turned on his 'creator.' [...] But it was Fox's glowing coverage that has been credited with playing a significant role in helping him get elected in 2016."[9]

Hasina the Frankenstein's horrible and hideous monster consists of the entire state machinery: her *gopal* and gestapo police, RAB, Indian RAW, DGFI, judiciary, bureaucracy, Election Commission, and even the armed forces which have traded their true military and patriotic character for their Indianized Hasina-gifted mercantile, mercenary, and commercial identity.[10] For fear or favor of the fascist Hasina, the entire state apparatus, which, according to Dr Mina Farah, has become a 'criminal industry,' serves at her will and pleasure. She broke, bended and brought all state bodies and organs to their knees. Almost the entire Bangladesh media (most of the national dailies and TV channels) is her own Fox News, playing the role of her own 'propaganda' Goebbels, going garbled, full of yellow journalism in fear or favor of her majesty's voice (HMV). The brave and brilliant UK-exiled Col (Ret) Shahid Uddin Khan and many others would love to 'respectfully' award her a specially 'privileged' nomenclature, মাতারাণী 'Mother of Mafia', whose anti-state media is all a stuffed parrot garrulously gargling out, in a harsh and hoarse voice, what she wants to hear in a vein of gonorrheal flattery and sycophancy.[11]

The Hasina-controlled Bangladesh media abounds in the lesser quality likes of Fox News's Shawn Hannity, Radio personality Rush Limbaugh, and Trump's White House Advisers and Spokespersons (or Press Secretaries) such as Sarah Huckabee, Kellyanne Conway, and Kayleigh McEnany, who defamed the White House in an un-American way by American standard. They proved to be controversial in talking the talk in support of Trump only to be mocked at by Democrats and in their protest lyrics in the aftermath of his election defeat. Those American journalists are, however, still smart people of character, having great talent and merit, outstanding in their own virtues, far above the lower quality materials of Bangladesh's pro-Hindu pro-India media men and women, who are widely perceived to be dull, unimpressive, and unreliable in their nonstop insane and uncritical parroting about the authoritarian mafia-mother Hasina agenda and propaganda.

The superior media houses of Bangladesh—Amar Desh, Naya Diganta, Daily Sangram, Diganta TV, Islamic TV, Channel One, Bangla Vision, Ekushey TV—which were not tuned to HMV have either been shut down and taken off the air by the fascist regime or forced to find a way to compromise, change ownership and sing the same yellow song as the other pro-regime propaganda outlets do. The recently relaunched (since August 2020) and UK-registered Amar Desh (amardesh.co.uk) under the editorship of the Turkey-based intrepid and indefatigable Mahmudur Rahman is now the only major online outlet to provide the true picture of the autocratically run Bangladesh. Those journalists who had the guts not to be inclined to parroting and tried to uphold their honesty, integrity, neutrality, impartiality, objectivity, and freedom of expression in a patriotic and professional way have been removed from the scene (either killed or detained or tortured or abducted or exiled or somehow silenced under the threat of fake and false cases filed against them in the regime's kangaroo courts.

Mahmudur Rahman, Shafik Rehman, Shahidul Alam, Abul Asad, Mohammad Zainal Abedin, Shawkat Mahmud, Shagor-Runi, Tuhin Malik, Kazi Jesin, Nayeb Ali, Shafikul Islam Kajol, Ruhul Amin Gazi, Oliullah Noman, Kanak Sarwar, Mukhlesur Rahman Chowdhury, Shamsul Alam Liton, Monir Haider, Elias Husain, Abu Saleh Mohammad Nayeb Ali, Minar Rashid, Pinaki Bhattacharya, and Gautam Das are only a few of dozens of critics and journalists who are/were direct or indirect victims of the ferocious Hasina fascism. There are also many, such as, Kai Kaus and Noyon Chatterjee, who have been regularly exposing the Awami *Jahiliyya* (darkness/ignorance) and its violently and vindictively destructive and devastating nature by resorting to and renaming themselves under those pseudonyms. Perhaps the time is not far when one fine morning the blindly pro-Hindu and pro-Hasina channels such as BTV, Ekattor TV, DBC, Shomoy TV, Channel I and all the major dailies in the print media would turn fairly balanced to have the Hasina supporters shout at them, 'they suck, they suck,' as the Trump supporters did at the Fox News post 2020 election (also see Part VI below).

As has just been implied, part of Sheikh Hasina's monster lies in the handful of so-called fake and false চেতনাজীবি journalists, intellectuals and government and private sector officials with ties with the Hindu nationalist India. Secured by humongous amount of black money, nepotism, favoritism, patronage of Hasina and her surrogates, and connections with India's RAW sponsors, they are all fanatical and fundamentalist secularists with no love lost between them and Bangladesh. Of dangerously misleading ideas, they are as half-witted, half-enlightened, and shortsighted as they are thoughtless, God-less and religion-less (ধর্মহীন).

They are engaged in the business of propagating a suppression of the universal religion of Islam in their own soil, while advocating a promotion of Hindutva myth and Indian Hinduism. Supporters of their extremist Hindu allies and followers, they are like those of Zionist Judaism, far right Christian radicalism, and rightwing white supremacy.

Unlike the lockdown on the media in Hasina's fascist and other dictatorships, the West is a free world and America is a free country. Differences of opinion, freedom of expression, and the proposition of 'let's agree to disagree' are the bedrock or cornerstone of

American/Western democratic culture. It is characterized by a respect for the values of transparency, accountability, intellectual development, academic progress, creativity and innovation. Considering Trump's failures, Chomsky declared Trump not only a 'disaster' but also the 'worst criminal in human history'.[12]

Well, if Chomsky knew Hasina and did indeed care to dignify her with a comment, he would probably go further and declare her to be the worst of the worsts known from prehistoric times or the time immemorial. Former Trump's own White House chief of staff, retired Marine Gen. John Kelly, said that Trump was "the most flawed person" he has ever known and that "The depths of his dishonesty [was] just astounding," making him "more pathetic than anything else."[13] Is Sheikh Hasina any different from what has been described of Trump by Kelly? "Trump's dishonesty is getting worse. He made at least 66 false or misleading claims in three days. He has been reliably deceptive for his entire presidency, filling his speeches and tweets with lies and other false statements. The frequency and magnitude of his deception tends to accelerate, however, during campaign season -- when he complements his usual ad-libbed inaccuracy with a barrage of inaccurate statements that are written into his speech scripts."[14]

[Para break]Chomsky's starkly true and damaging views of Trump are supported not only by those mentioned above but also the senior journalist Bob Woodward as suggested by his 2018 book *Fear: Trump in the White House* and its sequel *Rage*. There are many others in light of what follows below. In early 2016, before Trump became the Republican nominee and then President, Jenna Ellis, a law professor and radio personality, who later became one of Trump's ardent supporters and legal advisers, was one of his toughest critics and deeply opposed his candidacy. Before she joined the Trump campaign, she repeatedly slammed him as an "idiot," who was "boorish and arrogant," and a "bully" whose words could not be trusted as factually accurate. She called comments he made about women "disgusting," and suggested he was not a "real Christian."

[Para break] Ellis said Trump's values were "not American," and called Trump an "American fascist." "Why should we rest our highest office in America, on a man who fundamentally goes back and forth and really cannot be trusted to be consistent or accurate in anything." She attacked Trump supporters for not caring that he was "unethical, corrupt, lying, criminal, dirtbag." "I could spend a full-time job just responding to the ridiculously illogical, inconsistent, and blatantly stupid arguments supporting Trump." "But here's the thing: his supporters DON'T CARE about facts or logic. They aren't seeking truth. Trump probably could shoot someone in the middle of NYC and not lose support. And this is the cumulative reason why this nation is in such terrible shape: We don't have truth seekers; we have narcissists."

Ellis, a conservative evangelical Christian, compared Trump to a "last days" bible verse and shared a post calling Trump "without love," "treacherous," "abusive" and "unholy." She contended that Trump was not a genuine Christian because he was incapable of seeking forgiveness or repentance. "Trump cannot handle criticism," she wrote. "This is insanely dangerous to the fundamental American value and inalienable right to freedom of speech." She reiterated that Trump was "one of the greatest threats to our liberty" by seeking stricter libel laws.[15] Had Ellis been in Bangladesh, she would never have changed her mind about the proven fascist Hasina whose treacheries, irregularities, and inconsistencies know no bounds, and who is known for being "boorish and arrogant," "unethical, corrupt, lying, criminal, dirtbag," to say the least.

While predicting Biden victory in post-election night analysis, filmmaker Michael Moore calls Trump 'bigot' and 'psychopath.'[16] In the book, *Donald Trump and His Assault on Truth: The President's Falsehoods, Misleading Claims and Flat-Out Lies* (June 2020), *The Washington Post*'s Fact Checker staff claims that "President Trump's flagrant disregard for the truth and his self-aggrandizing exaggerations, specious misstatements, and bald-faced lies have been rigorously documented and debunked since the first day of his presidency." Politicians, academics, journalists, and media personalities can perhaps write a series of similar books on Sheikh Hasina. Time is long overdue for them to investigate Hasina's complicity in innumerable crimes (only a few of them being the BDR massacre; logs, oars and poles (*logi-boitha* লগি বৈঠা) massacre; Hefazat-e-Islam massacre; Satkhira Jamaat massacre; public bus arson attack massacre near Sheraton Hotel; controversial ICT hangings; election riggings; hundreds of millions in black money, stolen, smuggled, looted and laundered; bank loots; share market loots, filing millions of fake and false and fabricated lawsuits against the opposition; and hundreds of enforced disappearances) as CNN's chief legal analyst Jeffrey Toobin did in his *True Crimes and Misdemeanors: The Investigation of Donald Trump* (August 2020).

There is Mary Lea Trump's scathing criticism of her uncle Donald Trump in her tell-all book, *Too Much and Never Enough: How My Family Created the World's Most Dangerous Man* (July 2020), which may be considered an equivalent to Matiur Rahman Rentu's similarly explosive book *Amar Fashi Chai* (I want/Wish To Be Hanged/Executed) about Bangladesh's most dangerous being called Sheikh Hasina. Freedom Fighter Rentu and his wife were like household members of the Hasina family for more than a decade. Reviewing Mary's book, Peter Conrad writes, "This blistering memoir by the president's niece reveals the twisted dynamic of America's 'malignantly dysfunctional' first family. Like America, Trump claims to be unique, exceptional, a shining self-creation. This book by his estranged niece demolishes that myth. Mary's ruthless memoir blames their family for creating him: she sees it as her patriotic mission to "take Donald down," and she does so by showing how derivative and dependent the ultimate self-made man has always been. Trump was bankrolled at first by an indulgent father, who paid him to be an idle show-off and proudly collected grubby tabloid reports on his antics; nowadays he is propped up by tougher, cannier men such as Vladimir Putin and Senator Mitch McConnell, for whom he is an easily manipulated stooge."[17]

Asking Trump to resign, Mary gives a "scathing criticism of the President, in which she accuses him of being a 'sociopath' and charges that his 'hubris and willful ignorance' dating back to his early days threatens the country."[18] "I saw firsthand," Mary claims, "what focusing on the wrong things, elevating the wrong people can do -- the collateral damage that can be created by allowing somebody to live their lives without accountability [....] If I can do anything to change the narrative and to tell the truth, I need to do it. Because I don't believe the American people had the entire truth four years ago." Such allegations are confirmed by Trump's own elder sister Maryanne Trump Barry, a retired federal appellate judge, who bitterly criticized her brother, saying that "Donald's out for Donald" and that he had a friend take his SATs to get into college. "His goddamned tweet and lying, oh my God…, The lack of preparation. The lying. Holy shit," she said, describing him as cruel and selfish.[19]

In much the same way, the people of Bangladesh did not have the entire truth about Hasina being so cruel and selfish. Part of the truth, as Rentu's book and her decades-long ill-motivated and ill-intentioned actions and measures demonstrate, is that she is a "sociopath," hubristically egotistical and willfully ignorant focusing on wrong or made-up things and living a life without responsibility and accountability. Members of her own family should come forward speaking up against her misrule and misdeeds the way those of Trump's did against him. In addition to the host of sick and suspicious, fake and fishy, and criminal and immoral things committed by Sheikh Hasina as recounted by Rentu in his amazing book, shouldn't the people of Bangladesh eternally remember her fascist deeds and policies since the allegedly Indian-and-Bangladesh-engineered BDR massacre of 2009? Besides, other black and brutish deeds and policies of Hasina are as follows:

> 1. systemic oppression of the opposition at every level, from the most popular leader of the country, *DeshNetri* and *DeshMata* Begum Khaleda Zia, (would-be) *DeshNayok* Tarique Rahman, national hero/conscience Mahmudur Rahman, and thousands of others ('আজকে প্রায় ৩৫ লক্ষ মানুষের বিরুদ্ধে মামলা, আজকে এক লক্ষের উপরে মামলা এবং মারা গেছেন ২৬'শ উপরে, আর ৬০৩ এর উপরে গুম হয়ে গেছে, ৮৪২ জন মারা গেছেনা এই সব তথ্য ডুকেমেন্টেড যারা রিপোর্ট করেছেন তাদের, আনডুকেমেন্টেড অনেক আছে এটা সম্পূর্ণ তথ্য নয়, অনেক তথ্য আছে যেটা আমাদের কাছে নেই।'),
>
> 2. snatching away the people's freedom of speech, thwarting and throttling the people's freedom of expression, and squeezing and strangulating the media hard,
>
> 3. countless abductions, enforced disappearances, extrajudicial killings, and deadly beatings (BUET's Abrar Fahad. Army Brigadier General Aman Azmi, BNP's Elias Ali and Chowdhury Alam and hundreds and thousands of others),[20]

4. Mir Jafar-and-Lendhup Dorji-type crippling capitulation of Hasina to India and placing the country by her at the colonial control and occupation by India,

5. letting the rogue RAW forces enter and infiltrate everywhere starting from the highest level of the state,

6. letting millions of Indian Hindus work, both legally and illegally, and, thereby, take away as many jobs from the local Muslim Bangladeshis, who are thus left disadvantaged and unemployed ("আজ স্বাধীনতার নাম দিয়েই ,বাংলাদেশের বুকচিরে এপ্রান্ত থেকে ওপ্রান্ত পর্যন্ত ভারতীয় ট্রাক বহর ছুটছে। বাংলাদেশের স্থলপথ, রেলপথ, নৌপথ ভারতের জন্য উন্মুক্ত হয়েছে। বাংলাদেশের নৌবন্দরে ভারতের একচেটিয়া প্রাধান্য। বাংলাদেশের প্রায় সবকটা নদী ভারত কর্তৃক নিয়ন্ত্রিত। Lader complex বস বসিয়ে ভারত; বাংলাদেশের উপকূলে নজরদারী করছে। ভারতের সাথে অসম সামরিক চুক্তি করতে হয়েছে। নিয়মিত সীমান্ত হত্যার মাধ্যমে ভারত,বাংলাদেশের জনসাধারণ কে আতঙ্কগ্রস্ত করে রেখেছে, বাংলাদেশের প্রতিবাদ করারও অধিকার নেই । দেশের সবকটা প্রচার মিডিয়ায় ভারতীয় আধিপত্য। ভারতের সাথে ৭.৩৫ বিলিয়ন ডলারের মত বানিজ্য ঘাটতি। চাল ডাল মরিচ মশলা ডিম মাছ মুরগী গরু আলু পেঁয়াজ এমনকি চা ও চানাচুরটা পর্যন্ত ভারত থেকে না আনলে বাংলাদেশের মানুষের চলছে না। স্বাধীনতার নাম নিয়ে বাংলাদেশের মানুষ যেন,ভারত নামক প্রভুর অতিথিশালায় নিষ্কর্মা বাসিন্দা হয়ে প্রভুনাম জপ তপ করছে । ৯০%মুসলমানের দেশে, সামরিক, আধাসামরিক, বেসামরিক, সরকারি, সকল বিভাগের উচ্চ পদগুলো একচেটিয়া ভারতপন্থিদের দখলে। দেশের মুসলমান যুবকদের চাকরী নেই , অথচ লক্ষ লক্ষ ভারতীয়, আইনি- বেআইনি ভাবে বাংলাদেশের কর ফাঁকি দিয়ে চাকরী করে ভারতে টাকা পাচার করছে। বর্তমান ভারত, বাংলাদেশ থেকে সবচেয়ে বশি ফরেন একচেঞ্জ উপার্জনকারি দেশ। আর সেই ফরেন একচেঞ্জের যোগান দিচ্ছে খেতে খামারে রক্ত পানি করা কৃষক, গার্মেন্টের হাড় জিরজিরে শ্রমিক, আর মরুভূমির উত্তপ্ত দেশে নিয়ত মৃত্যুর সাথে লড়াই করে বেঁচে থাকা কিছু শ্রমজীবী মানুষ। এই নাকি স্বাধীনতার সুখ! স্বাধীনতার নাম নিয়ে বাংলাদেশ ভারতের সাথে এ পর্যন্ত (১৯৭১ সাল থেকে২০২০সাল) ৯০ টিরও বেশি চুক্তি, সমঝোতা স্মারক সই করেছে। যেগুলো বিশ্লেষন করলে দেখা যাবে বেশির ভাগই দাসত্ব চুক্তির নামান্তর। যার মধ্যে মুজিব আমলে ১১টি, এবং তার মেয়ে হাসিনার আমলে ৭৭ টি চুক্তি তো দেশ বিক্রী করে দেয়া চুক্তির সমতুল্য। মুজিব আমলের ২৫বছর মেয়াদী চুক্তির ১২ টি দফা তো পলাশী যুদ্ধের পর, ক্লাইভ-মীরজাফর চুক্তির ১২ দফার কথা মনে করিয়ে দেয়। মুজিব কন্যা হাসিনা তো করেছে ৭৭ টি চুক্তি , যার মাধ্যমে দেশের বন্দর, সড়ক, রেলপথ,নৌপথ, এমনকি দেশের স্বাধীনসত্তা টকুও হিন্দুত্ববাদী ভারতের হাতে তুলে দিয়েছে । এদের চুক্তিগুলোর একটি মাত্র নমুনা পাঠকদের মনে করানোর জন্য তুলে ধরে এ লেখার ইতি টানতে চাই ।"-- Playwright Ariful Haque),

7. putting the small minority (8%) Hindu men and women everywhere in the administration at the expense of the Muslim majority,

8. cancellation of the care-taker government,

9. humongous corruption,

10. complete politicization of all levels and branches of the government, including the police and the judiciary, and, most importantly,

11. locust-type massive vote rigging by Hasina, day and night, not once but every time there was an election, local or national, for years, since 2008.

Like a crude, crabbed, and coarse-minded grower, manufacturer or industrialist with no empathy for their workers and employees, Hasina is full of "impenetrable ignorance and dull egoism," to borrow those two phrases from the short story "A Doctor's Visit" by Anton Chekhov set in the context of the 19th century Russian cotton factory. True and patriotic journalists, not the hilariously pro-fascist Hasina sycophants working for different media houses, should have the honest courage to expose her lies, disinformation and false claims the way Jonathan Swan, a reporter for Axios, does those of Trump's by way of basic follow-up questions of who, what and how.[21]

The Hasina regime has established all kinds of abnormal relationship with India, from 'blood' relationship to 'husband-wife' relationship to servile and slavish 'give away' political, economic, and security agreements. Similarly, to save her corrupt and cruel mismanagement and maladministration, she would spare no pains to let her ties with the Trump administration go deeper. According to the social media-active Canadian resident Maj (Ret) Delwar Hussain, Sheikh Hasina and her affiliates allegedly gave a huge sum of money to Trump's re-election campaign.[22] Just as for Trump, 'America First' means 'Trump First', for the atrociously authoritarian Hasina, the whole and wholesome spirit of the liberation struggle 'first' means the sick and split and divisive spirit 'first', and the autocratic Hasina-Awami League 'first'; for the hissing and conspiratorial Hasina, 'democracy first' means she and her Awami League 'first.' She secures her torn, tainted and tailored 'first' through the police-conducted farcical elections in an egregiously 'guided' and 'illiberal' democracy, much worse than her father's bloody BAKSALi-RakkhiBahini governance in 1972-1975 following the Pakistani army's mainly Dhaka-based genocide in 1971.

Besides Matiur Rahman Rentu, Trump's niece and sister also may be an inspiration for Sheikh Fazlul Karim Selim to write a similar book taking his cousin sister Hasina down (as he almost did at the time of Moeenuddin-Fakhruddin-Masududdin), as they should also be an inspiration for others close to her to write a book on Hasina whose ill and evil deeds are fantastically infinite. Whoever it is, anybody should have enough to mock and make fun of Hasina and her fat but fact-free propaganda tools and techniques the way CNN anchor Anderson Cooper does when he says: "Trump is like an 'obese turtle on his back flailing in the hot sun realizing his time is over.'[23]

Part IV: From "Bottomless" to "Topless"

Violence has been brutish; corruption chronic; oppression overwhelming. All has been as pandemic as COVID-19, more widely so, more crippling and cancerous, more constant and continuous. It has been so since 2008/09 when the devilishly fascist regime of Sheikh Hasina came to power through the Indian-conspired evil and stealthy means (not to speak of her first term, 1996-2000, when she was not that bad). Now, for the last many years, she has shrunk into an anarchically tyrannical and nihilistically despotic divider, instead of growing (unlike Khaleda Zia) into a dynamic democratic unifier. No words can describe the boundless violence, repression and corruption under dictator Sheikh Hasina, the worst in the history of Bangladesh. By all accounts, she is far worse than her father Sheikh Mujib (during his brutal BAKSAli period of 1972-1975) and H M Ershad (during his baneful 1980s).[24]

In terms of their mutual support and collaboration, both Hasina and the lesser evil JP-Ershad were and are still locked in a politically farcical hermaphrodite partnership since. If her father Sheikh Mujib turned Bangladesh into a "bottomless" basket, hers is a "topless" one, wide open, without a cover, so that the "rats" of the Sonali, Rupali, Agrani, Janata, Oriental, Farmers, Basic, and Bangladesh Banks and those of the Destiny, Hallmark, Bismillah, Rana Plaza, Titas, Panama Papers Benzirs, Regent,

JKG, and Health Ministry could easily enter from the top. There are hundreds and thousands of other Awami "rats" in the form of Josephs, Shaheds, Arifuls, Papuls, Papias, Somrats, Shamims, Sabrinas, Nasims, Hanifs, Sikders, Hyes, Hajis, Hazaris, Yaba Badis, Netaji Lilus, Lupas, Dubai Mitus, Teknaf Pradeeps, Tala Selims, golden Munirs, *ahammak* Anisuls, and Security Siddiquees (see Appendix B). The other name of the Hasina regime, therefore, is corruption and its another name is fascist oppression. Like Coleridge's "ice" and "water" tropes, one can also say that under Hasina, "corruption is here, corruption is there, corruption is all around; repression and discrimination are everywhere, persecution is all between."

"It is even more shocking," says even the Awami-allied daily Prothom Alo journalist Sohrab Hassan, "that whoever is being caught [on corruption charges], whether businesspersons, physicians, hospital owners or members of parliament, they are all somehow or other connected to the ruling party."[25] Hassan makes it clear that it is no more secret that Hasina who always depends on the police has lost her grip on people and politics. Her "topless" basket is open for the business of looting, laundering, bribing, and subverting through her gopali and gestapo police[26] beating the entire opposition with boots and batons and through remands and fabricated court cases. All these are abominably immoral and illegal subversive of the state and the people. There are so many allegations of fantastically humongous financial corruptions against Hasina herself and her family members![27]

According to Indian Panorama's We the People Report, Sheikh Hasina tops the list of the five worst dictators in the last 100 years.[28] According to Mahfuz Anam, editor of the largest English daily of Bangladesh, The Daily Star, hers is "An ornamental Sangsad," with her "own party, own government, own opposition and own parliament."[29] According to the prolific writer on socio-cultural and political issues, Dr Firoz Mahboob Kamal of the UK, Hasina with her fake elections, fraudulent practices and fictitious charges against the members of political dissent is an existential threat to Bangladesh.[30] In an interview with Dr Kanak Sarwar, Lt Gen (Ret) Chowdhury Hasan Sarwardy, initially pro-Hasina, now turned a patriotic general of true military character and integrity, exposes the Hasina regime's widespread misrule, terrorism, servility to India and anti-state subversive activities.[31] Major (Retd) Delwar Hussain also heroically exposes the rot and rat that is the present fascist Hasina regime.[32] In the view of William B. Milam, former American ambassador to Dhaka and Islamabad and currently a senior fellow at Woodrow Wilson Center, Bangladesh is on the march to authoritarianism (which is an understatement of a veteran diplomat).[33]

Ambassador Milam and Illinois State University Prof Ali Riaz describe the appalling Hasina pandemic of persecution in Bangladesh with her regime in the relentless pursuit of its own vested and vindictive interests, not the welfare of the people of Bangladesh.[34] Describing the regime as a rusty and nasty machine, eminent writer and researcher Prof Taj Hashmi of Canada/USA speaks about the moral, intellectual and economic corruption and degeneration that have eaten into the vitals of the society, from top to bottom, especially the state machinery that is down into deep devastation and decadence because of the terribly ruling Hasina.[35] Referring to Dr Hashmi, responds R Chowdhury of the USA, a former high ranking diplomat: "You have correctly diagnosed and exposed the decline and decadence of the society under Hasina, perhaps in the worst, direst and dirtiest stage in the history of Bangladesh. The Awami League might have done a few good things but their balance sheet of performance tilts overwhelmingly to the negative and to the destruction of values that the common Bangladeshis espouse and aspire for. The most hateful and obnoxious elements are the sponsored pseudo intellectuals that support the dangerous regime for a price. You exposed them effectively."

"Giving in to external (Indian) hegemony is an insult to Bangladesh's 160 million people. No amount of self-trumpeting economic growth can erase or obliterate those darkest spots," comments R Chowdhury. True, the Awami-BAKSALi-Indian conspiracies have been carrying out vicious propaganda against Bangladesh since the time of President Ziaur Rahman whose assassination in 1981 was supposedly triggered by those behind-the-scene secret plans and designs. From 1/11 of 2007, they have brought Bangladesh under the grip of Awami fascism and Indian hegemonism, as they did during the Mujib regime which killed 30 thousand patriots and caused the man-made famine of 1974-75, in which 1.5 million people died, directly or indirectly. A brief Bengali version of that devastating situation would be like this:

২৪ ফেব্রুয়ারি ১৯৭৫-এ বাকশাল বা বাংলাদেশ কৃষক শ্রমিক আওয়ামী লীগ বাংলাদেশ আওয়ামী লীগ নামের ফ্রন্ট গঠিত হয়েছিল বাংলাদেশ কমিউনিস্ট পার্টি, জাতীয় আওয়ামী পার্টি (মোজাফফর) এবং জাতীয় লীগ নিয়ে। বাকশাল ছিল একটি জাতীয় বিশ্বাসঘাতক ফ্রন্ট। মুজিব সরকার ৩০ হাজার দেশপ্রেমিক হত্যা করে। তাদের অপশাসনে দেশে নেমে আসে নির্বিচার হত্যা, নিপীড়ন, নির্যাতন, লুঠন, দখলবাজী, সীমান্ত পাচার ইত্যাদির বিভীষিকা। তাদের অপশাসন, লুঠন, কালোবাজারী, সীমান্তপাচারের ফলে দেশে যে মানবসৃষ্ট দুর্ভিক্ষ ঘটে তাতে সরাসরি মৃত্যু হয় ৫ লক্ষ মানুষের এবং পরোক্ষ ভাবে মৃত্যু হয় আরও ১০ লক্ষ মানুষের। অন্যদিকে, মুজিব নিজে ভারতপন্থী না হলেও, মুজিব সরকার পরিচালিত হয় মূলতঃ ভারতের নির্দেশে, যারা বাকশালতন্ত্র নামক চরম স্বৈরতন্ত্র ও ফ্যাসিবাদ সৃষ্টি করে।

There has been a counter narrative to heinous Awami-BAKSALi-Indian propaganda in Bangladesh. Apart from the vast material available in the social media, the print media counter narrative is effectively and convincingly developed in a number of books. These books collectively describe the army-people uprisings of 1975 as patriotic and glorious transitions and offer a counter argument to the Hasina/Awami regime, its wildly exaggerated partisan propaganda, and its horrible hyena hordes and hooligans (see Appendix A). Since 2009, the regime perpetrated indiscriminate killings, terror, plunder, oppression and repression. To cling to power, Hasina domestically resorted to widespread misrule and unscrupulously sold out Bangladesh's national interests to her sponsor India. By surrendering national sovereignty to the neighboring fundamentalist Hindu India, the fascist Hasina administration has consolidated Indian hegemonism in Bangladesh,

To repeat, Bangladesh has been under the grip of Indian hegemony and expansionism that abetted Sheikh Hasina to continue and strengthen her fascist rule since 2009. Starting with:

1. her declaration at a public meeting in Chittagong that she wanted ten of the other side dead for one of her side (একটার বদলে দশটা লাশ চাই);

2. her 173 days of hartals/total work stoppages during the first term of Begum Khaleda Zia (1991-1996);

3. the June 5, 2004 series of arson/gun powder attacks by her (and her Awami League) as a command (ordering) accused (হুকুমের আসামী) on public transport in Dhaka, especially the one on a double-decker bus in front of Sheraton Hotel, killing nine passengers, including a two-year-old girl and injuring fifteen; and,

4. the brutal and brutish লগি বৈঠা/logi-boitha (logs, oars, and poles) massacre of October 28, 200612, as directed by her, that left dozens beaten to death;

Sheikh Hasina further 'rewarded' Bangladesh with:

1. the boundlessly beastly (and nationally and internationally conspired) BDR (Bangladesh Rifles) massacre of February 25/26, 2009, which, based on a plethora of circumstantial evidence, is widely suspected to have been possible only with the premeditated complicity of the Hasina government together with the government of India (see Appendix F);

2. the gruesome Hefazat-e-Islam massacre of May 5/6, 2013 at Shapla Square, Motijheel, Dhaka;

3. the Shatkhira massacre of December 23, 2013, with hundreds of gory and grisly murders of the missing[36] and endless number of morally, socially and politically subversive misdeeds in between and those that followed and still counting; and,

4. the Bangladesh Bank cyber heist of close to US$1billion in February 2016, committed by the insiders (in collaboration with the outsiders--see the Hindus and Hindus section in Appendix B), preceded and followed by many other loots in similarly massive amounts from many other private and government banks, including the repeated share market scams and stealings in equally massive proportions.

The social, political and financial situation in Bangladesh under Sheikh Hasina is a total disaster—as disastrous as a tsunami, a whirlpool, totally engulfing and reeling. Unbearably choking, suffocating and burdensome as it is, the situation is tremendously bad, as bad as it could ever be or it should never have been.

Mahmudur Rahman, editor of the popular Bengali–daily Amar Desh (আমার দেশ), who was an adviser to the former Khaleda government and at present a most heroic political dissident, decries Sheikh Hasina, in a hard-hitting lambast of her totalitarian regime, as another Lucifer (Devil, Satan, Iblis), Hitler, Pinochet, Shah of Iran, Saddam, Kim of North Korea, perhaps even worse. He describes Bangladesh under Hasina as an utterly horrifying autocracy, an Orwellian state, a "ruthless police state" and "an extremely polarized and wounded nation [...], no better than a personal fiefdom," suffering from "the oppression of [a] fascist regime." Apart from being a recount of the historical past of Bangladesh, Rahman's book, *The Political History of Muslim Bengal: An Unfinished Battle of Faith*, also gives an authentic account of the high-handed iron-and-jungle rule of Sheikh Hasina: "The methods employed by the current rulers in Bangladesh are much simpler and more direct. They choke press freedom, resort to extrajudicial killings, practise enforced disappearances without any remorse, and imprison dissidents for indefinite periods without trial. India takes care on behalf of her client in Bangladesh [...] at this blatant disregard for human rights and democratic norms."[37]

Sheikh Hasina's horrible and horrendous one-party and one-person reign has turned Bangladesh into nothing less than a deeply divided police and prison state. Reaching its lowest ebb in reputation and deeply diminished in image and status, the country suffers from a deplorable situation where there is hardly any rule of law with justice or social justice conspicuous by its absence. If there is any law, it is the same discriminatory jungle law working either in favor of the men and women of Hasina, be they in politics, business, academia or administration, or against the opposition BNP or the BNP-led alliance. Members of all shades of political dissent, particularly the opposition BNP, are constantly being hounded by the hammer of injustice, while those of the autocratic ruling party walk away with the carrot of connivance or even cooperation from the regime and its kinky kangaroo courts.

Reduced to a country of wholesale economic looting and laundering and political repression, Bangladesh is caught in an evil axis of power and control wielded by one woman, Sheikh Hasina, with the help of the demoralized machinations of her party outfits and state affiliates.

All subversive and destructive mafia-style entities of the party and the state combined have formed a large conglomerate of an utterly corrupt corporate culture characterized by impunity, immorality, irresponsibility and unaccountability. The culture of looting, stealing and wasting has been operating not just in the dark and lurid underworld of casinos, but also in the banking sector, share market, health sector, environment sector, education sector, employment and public service sector, export and import sector, investment sector and construction and development sector, among others. While almost all sectors are infested with such corruptive mismanagement and malpractices, the police department stand out in the public eye.

According to the US-based Global Financial Integrity (GFI) report, the government sponsored entities and ruling Awami-affiliated people have amassed huge cash deposits in the Swiss banks, worth over US $82 billion since 2006. For 2018 and 2019, the deposits stood at US $625 million and US $605 million respectively:

> বাংলাদেশিদের আমানত : ২০১৯ সালে সুইস ব্যাংকে বাংলাদেশিদের আমানতের স্থিতি ছিল ৬০ কোটি ৩০ লাখ ফ্র্যাংক। আগের বছর অর্থাৎ ২০১৮ সালে যা ছিল ৬১ কোটি ৭৭ লাখ ফ্র্যাংক। ২০১৭ সালে ছিল ৪৮ কোটি ১৩ লাখ ফ্র্যাংক। ২০১৬ সালে ৬৬ কোটি ১৯ লাখ ফ্র্যাংক। ২০১৫ সালে ৫৫ কোটি ৮ লাখ ফ্র্যাংক। ২০১৪ সালে যা ছিল ৫০ কোটি ৬০ লাখ ফ্র্যাংক। ২০১৩ সালে ৩৭ কোটি ২০ লাখ ফ্র্যাংক স্থানীয় মুদ্রায় এর পরিমাণ ৩ হাজার ২৩৬ কোটি টাকা। ২০১২ সালে ছিল ২২ কোটি ৯০ লাখ ফ্র্যাংক। ২০১১ সালে ছিল ১৫ কোটি ২০ লাখ ফ্র্যাংক। প্রসঙ্গত, চলতি বছরের শুরুতে মার্কিন যুক্তরাষ্ট্রভিত্তিক গবেষণা প্রতিষ্ঠান গ্লোবাল ফাইন্যান্সিয়াল ইন্টেগ্রিটির (জিএফআই) রিপোর্ট প্রকাশ করা হয়। সেখানে বলা হয়েছে, ২০০৬-২০১৫ সাল পর্যন্ত দশ বছরে বাংলাদেশ থেকে সাড়ে ৪ লাখ কোটি টাকা পাচার হয়েছে, যা চলতি অর্থবছরের সংশোধিত বাজেটের প্রায় সমান। একক বছর হিসাবে ২০১৫ সালে বাংলাদেশ থেকে ১ হাজার ১৫১ কোটি ডলার পাচার হয়েছে। দেশীয় মুদ্রায় যা প্রায় ১ লাখ কোটি টাকা। এই পরিমাণ অর্থ দিয়ে ৪টি পদ্মা সেতু নির্মাণ করা সম্ভব। জিএফআইয়ের প্রতিবেদনে বলা হয়েছে, ৪টি প্রক্রিয়ায় এই অর্থ পাচার হয়েছে। এর মধ্যে রয়েছে বিদেশি পণ্যের আমদানিমূল্য বেশি দেখানো (ওভার ইনভয়েসিং), রফতানিমূল্য কম দেখানো (আন্ডার ইনভয়েসিং), হুন্ডি ও অন্য মাধ্যমে বিদেশে লেনদেন এবং ভিওআইপি ব্যবসা। এ ছাড়া টাকা পাচারে বিশ্বের শীর্ষ ৩০ দেশের তালিকায় রয়েছে বাংলাদেশের নাম।

The deposits by Bangladeshi citizens in Swiss banks stood at Tk 5,392 crore or 603.02 million Swiss francs in 2019, according to the Swiss National Bank data released on Thursday. The Bangladeshi deposits in the year, however, slightly fell — by around 2.30 per cent — compared with those of 617.72 million Swiss francs in 2018. The deposits from the country in the banks of Switzerland had increased by 28.33 per cent in 2018 from those of 481.32 million Swiss francs in the previous year[…]The Global Financial Integrity, a Washington-based watchdog, in its report released in 2019, said that a total of **$81.74 billion** was siphoned off from Bangladesh between **2006 and 2016**. According to the SNB [Swiss National Bank] data, the deposits by Bangladeshi citizens were 235.59 million Swiss francs in 2010 which declined to 152.31 million in 2011 and again increased to 228.86 million in 2012. The deposits went up to 371.88 million in 2013, to 506.05 million in 2014 and reached the highest-ever amount at 661.96 million Swiss francs in 2015. (See Appendix B)

Sheikh Hasina's Bangladesh has nearly $67 billion annual budget for 2020-2021. This includes, among the other across-the-board spendthrift expenditures, the staggering amount of wasteful daily overspend, in millions, on her own person, her immediate family and her personal office.[38] It also includes hundreds of thousands of dollars (allegedly as much as $500,000) paid for a week-long advertisement in the New York Times during her visit to the United Nations General Assembly meeting. What is funny is that when she addresses, the UN Assembly and other Committee Meetings go almost empty, because few are interested in the self-praising rubbish she delivers. To compensate in the audience, she usually takes a large delegation abroad. Official Bangladesh television focuses only on the Bangladehsi attendees in the audience. It is an ugly sight when the camera moves around, albeit by default.

A fact-free but not fat-free malafide budget dependent on high interest foreign loans and widening the budget deficit is deliberately intended to leave many loopholes in Pandora's box open for the Awami and Awami-aligned political and business vultures to loot and smuggle from. Engineer Rashed Anam of the USA compiles a brief black list of corrupt Awami wastebaskets full of what Shakespeare, in *The Merchant of Venice* (Act 1, Scene 3), would describe as rats, thieves and pirates (See Appendix C).

The above gives a clue to both the "bottomless" and "topless" Hasina's Bangladesh that has been designated and downgraded as a country of looters, plunderers, smugglers, launderers, swindlers, embezzlers, cheats, conmen, and so on. Despite being just a tip of the iceberg of their loot in cash (in addition to their existing corrupt businesses, tainted investments, and ill-gotten fixed properties in land and structures, at home and abroad), it is all as massive and overwhelming as Hasina's vampire vote riggings throughout her dictatorial reign since 2009. In the name of "election," the regime holds a farcical stage show in which the results are customarily a matter of foregone conclusion. All its candidates "win" a predetermined absolute majority of votes in their respective constituencies, sometimes even more than the total number of enlisted voters in a poll center.

It happens either through an outrageously stealthy mechanism of what has been reported as early morning ballot box stuffing, violently forcing the opposition voters away from polls, as in December 2018, or amid the opposition boycott of polls in the prearranged election engineering scam, as in January 2014. Massive vote rigging with the help of the gopali and gestapo police, party hooligans and loony lackeys in the administration has become a common practice in almost all the elections, thousands of them, held locally or nationally, over the past decade. The regime scares the opposition (BNP) voters away, often violently, for days and weeks leading up to the day of sham "election," just as it intimidates them away with beastly force from attending the public meetings, processions and demonstrations, which the BNP is hardly allowed to organize. Yet, occasional mammoth gatherings, few and far between, called on short notice show how popular the BNP remains with the public, and that is a scare for the ruling Awamis.

Rampant in Bangladesh are all forms of division, destruction, discrimination, misappropriation, oppression, suppression, persecution, incarceration, murder, maiming, mutilation, abduction and forced disappearances. Wild and widespread are torture and tyranny that have been let loose with no accountability. There are hundreds of thousands of people rotting in jail, abducted and/or killed, with all the opposition leaders carrying the burden of dozens of court cases each. It is a country where many political leaders have been hanged to death by the order of highly controversial kangaroo courts under the pressure and coercion of Sheikh Hasina (see Appendix G). The country has millions to seek justice for myriads of bleeding wounds—political, personal and physical. Known for its indescribable mafia notoriety for more than an age now, Bangladesh has become a country of bribes, yaba drugs, mosquito-infested drains, deadly dengue fever, boat capsizes, child labor and human traffickers; a country where deadly rapes and deadly extramarital affairs involving people of all ages, from teens and minors to adults and adolescents, are more common than the cycle of night and day every twenty four hours.

Like *Macbeth*, Bangladesh under the Hasina regime has grown to be a country of awfully weird beings where "fair is foul, foul is fair." Under the same regime, it has developed to be a country where the norm has become abnormal and the irregular regular, as common as everyday phenomenon. The same has been happening at all levels of Hasina's brutal and blindly loyal police, judiciary, bureaucracy, legislature, and DGFI intelligence, all becoming synonymously one and the same, indistinguishable from and interchangeable with each other, including the ubiquitous Hindutva RAW intelligence networks all across the country. In other words, the entire state machinery has lent itself to becoming most blindly and unpatriotically loyal to the hyena-style Hasina regime and its associates to the extent that it jocularly masquerades as nothing more than a joke or, worse, a jockey in the animal race.

The entire country is a politically tyrannical Circus Maximus and Colosseum, to refer to ancient Roman mass entertainment stadiums, with violent gladiatorial and venatio spectacles watched by "Her Majesty" Sheikh Hasina, herself riding a politically ferocious tiger, for her sado-masochistic fun and excitement. It is all that can happen in a regressive and retrograde administration of an out-and-out dictator, a top-to-toe tyrant. Surrounded by sycophants and flatterers, goons and gangs, cliques and crooks, loonies and lackeys, and hoodlums and hooligans, especially in the party and the brutishly biased and partisan police, the autocratic and authoritarian Hasina regime has brought the entire spectrum of the democratic and patriotic opposition led by the popular BNP to its knees. The cowardly opposition, completely cowed down, is trying to somehow survive and keep itself afloat by catching at a straw with its hands and feet tied. Besides, its own weak leadership under the hopeless, useless and unimpressive Mirza Fakhrul and many of the rest in the "Standing" and/or "Sitting" Committee (except the top two—Khaleda and Tarique) has greatly contributed to its failures leaving no impact either orally/verbally or in body language (see Appendix H).

Part V: The Regime's Misrule Is as Pandemic as COVID-19

Naturally, corruption is another name for the scheming Hasina and her development strategy that continues to remain highly dented and defective, more as a self-panegyrical and self-extolling political propaganda than an actual reality. In the name of development, corruption has been so caustic and eroding that the regime's hospitals and health sector completely failed to meet the challenge of COVID-19. Hasina's health ministry, immersed in outrageous corruption (as all other ministries, departments and directorates are), completely failed to take any effective measures to confront the corona pandemic (see Appendix D). At the onset of the deadly disease, many in Hasina's administration became so greedy and selfish that they could not resist the temptation to indulge in a huge "corona corruption," as if it was only a one-time plague, never to appear again for them to have another opportunity to steal at victims' expense.

Except for the rich and famous and their support staffs, most of the less fortunate victims die as quickly as they get infected, without any treatment. Many of the infected in towns and cities die like anything at home and outdoors in the streets. In remote areas and villages, such deaths remain unaccounted. There are also reports of people dying in the privacy of their own premises to avoid being known as casualty of corona, which has become a stigma due to discriminations by medical workers and even family/community negligence of the contagious disease.

Left abandoned and uncared for, with hardly any treatment available to corona patients, their actual number, reportedly, goes undisclosed for the regime's ulterior motive to show that the country under Hasina, who is acting like a faustian mafia don, was faring well with the number of the infected lying deceivingly low. According a report, the actual casualty figures could be four to eight times higher than what is being reported. Despite many patients dying of the deadly virus before or during the test or treatment or due to the lack of treatment, their death certificates are falsified, as alleged by DeshKonnya (দেশকন্যা) Syeda Ashifa Ashrafi Papia, showing the cause of their death to be some other diseases, not COVID-19.[39]

The corona numbers are "all politically manipulated and bureaucratically manufactured figures by the devil incarnates and he-and-she hyenas in the regime," says Engineer M Gani of the USA. "The numbers released have no connection with the real counts. People shall never know the actual numbers until the Day of Judgment." In the words of Zoglul Husain of the UK, "Hasina concocts statistics as they suit her, as she cooked 'bhapa ilish fish' (ভাপা ইলিশ) for Indian President Pranab Mukherjee. After all, she is the warden of a whole big prison called Bangladesh, the prison being created with the connivance of India, America, and Israel. But tyrants never learn from history. Fascism covered with fictions! Fascism digs its own grave."

As dysfunctional and corruption-ridden as all other institutions (due to criminalization and compartmentalization of politics), all hospitals, be they government or private, have proved to be equally greedy, selfish, inhuman, incompetent, incapable, underequipped and understaffed. In many cases, medical centers refuse treatment and mercilessly show exit doors to the patients. There are no adequate supplies and resources such as doctors, nurses, protective equipments, masks, gloves, test kits, ventilators, beds and intensive care units (ICUs). Some members of the staff go on leave or run away for fear of infection showing various excuses. Whatever facilities are there, those are far from being enough. Whatever scarce and scanty measures are in place, those have been politicized and monopolized by and for the fortunate few—money-wise or political connection wise. The paucity of measures, lack of treatment and the inhuman handling of the infected in a corrupt-to-the core country made the BNP Secretary General Mirza Fakhrul Islam Alamgir remind Hasina about the mainly man-made famine during her father Mujib's time in 1974. As he was talking about the country inevitably going to the dogs not only due to the corona crisis but mostly due to Awami loots and launderings, Mirza Alamgir said:

> 'দেশ রসাতলের দিকে' যাচ্ছে মন্তব্য করে মির্জা ফখরুল বলেছে, আমার মনে পড়ছে অনেক আগের কথা। ১৯৭৪ সালে ঠিক একইভাবে সেদিন অবহেলা করা হয়েছিলো সমস্যগুলোকে গুরুত্ব দেয়া হয়নি। ফলে কি হয়েছিলো খাদ্য থাকা সত্ত্বেও চরম দুর্ভিক্ষ হয়েছিলো। তৎকালীন অর্থনীতি সমিতির সভাপতি মাজহারুল ইসলাম সমিতির প্রথম অধিবেশনে তৎকালীন প্রধানমন্ত্রীকে সামনে বসিয়ে বলেছিলেন, বাংলাদেশ তীব্র গতিতে রসাতলে যাচ্ছে। আজকেও বাংলাদেশ রসাতলের দিকে যাচ্ছে। এখান থেকে টেনে তোলার দায়িত্ব সকলের। সরকার কোনো উদ্যোগ নেবেন না, উদ্যোগ নেয়ার মতো তাদের সেই মানসিকতাও নেই। জনগণকে এই ব্যবস্থা গ্রহণ করতে হবে। [40]

Eminent personality Dr Zafrullah Chowdhury also took the opportunity to remind Hasina of the same famine of her father's period when he was indicating that the country under COVID-19 was likely going to face another famine that may occur as two crores of people (20 million) could be in dire need of food shortly, mainly because of Awami misrule and mismanagement:

> আপনাকে আমি মনে করাতে চাচ্ছি ১৯৭৪ সালের দুর্ভিক্ষের কথা। তার ওপর ছোট একটা ডকুমেন্টারি আছে 'আনফ্যাশনাবল ফ্যামিন। গুদামে খাবার আছে তবু মানুষ অনাহারে ছিল। ঠিক আজকেও আপনাদের মন্ত্রী মহোদয়ের বক্তব্য, ১৬ লাখ টন খাদ্য এখনো আপনার গুদামে আছে। আপনাদের হিসাবে যাই থাক, এক কোটি পরিবার তারা অতি গরিব লোক, কাজ না থাকায় আরো এক কোটি পরিবার আছে - এই দুই কোটি পরিবারের খাবার দরকার। আপনার ইনসেনটিভ যাচ্ছে ধনীদের কাছে। কৃষকদের দুরবস্থার কথা উল্লেখ করে তাদের কাছ থেকে সরাসরি সরকারকে ধান ক্রয় করার দাবি জানান তিনি। [41]

"One can blame the US, blame the PL-480 or whatever," comments R Chowdhury in an email response to the 1974 famine, pointing fingers at some Awami pundits who blamed the US for stopping food shipment to Bangladesh thus causing the famine, "but the fact was there was no dearth of food supply and relief materials, coming from all sources, including the US. Reportedly, godowns were full but dispensed on political considerations, and much of it found way to black markets, even went across the border to India. Also, there were unprecedented corruption at all levels, and a total breakdown of the distribution system in the administration." During the said famine, many died of starvation looking for rotting crumbs in the public waste bins and landfills as many mothers, due to acute shortage of food, killed their own children by having them eat addoes/taros mixed with poison. Many women had to cover themselves with simple fishing net of cotton with no proper clothes, not even rags to wear.[42] "The question is," R Chowdhury continues,

> Why the poor and the common people had to die when the Sheikh family, Ghazi Gholam Mostafa (the Awami Chairman of the Red Cross) and the ruling party members remained as rich and healthy as before. Remember the royal style wedding of Mujib's two sons, Sheikh Kamal and Sheikh Jamal and Mujib's own birthday celebrations during those crisis days? Gholam Mostafa's dogs were said to be overweight feeding on the relief food. The US might have played a dirty game but our leaders of the time were not saints either.

To return to the deteriorating COVID-19 situation in Bangladesh, the Hasina regime has completely and criminally failed to face it. Her hordes and hooligans have stolen much of the relief goods and materials intended for the poor in these corona-caused difficult times. As mentioned above, hundreds are dying without treatment or even without being admitted to hospitals. Many have been turned away from seeking treatment as doctors and nurses showed their back to them. There are lots of treatment denial stories in the media.

To paraphrase what the New York-based Nazma Mustafa said in her blog (www.nazmamustafa.com), doctors are made OSD (officer on special duty, as a sort of penalty, with no active service/responsibility) when they raise personal safety questions. They are also forbidden to complain in the media. Authorities say they are made OSD due to illness or upon request. The question is why a doctor will face OSD if s/he gets positive. Instead, s/he should be placed on quarantine with a temporary suspension or exemption from active duty. Sometimes, they are sent OSD even if they test negative just because they raise questions about the whole failing procedure. The present government has always been unreliable in all its efforts. Despite so many irregularities, how did the highly controversial Hasina acquire a place in the Forbes magazine? Why "Banorer golai muktar har"/ বানরের গলায় মুক্তার হার (why a necklace of pearl on the neck of a monkey)? Seems to be cheating with the nation, just like stealing votes the night before, depriving Bangladeshis of their democracy again and again. The question arises whether Forbes is playing a game of deception with the ill-fated country.

While the New York-based Forbes magazine—a magazine of the few rich and famous--reports that countries with the best responses to the pandemic have all women leaders except the absolute authoritarian Shiekh Hasina, the same magazine is full of praise for her who is known for buying and bagging many low and light propaganda prizes with her ill-gotten money.[43] Doesn't the world know that many are dying of corona in Bangladesh with no treatment at all, that many patients are not even admitted to hospital and are left abandoned, that there is a dire shortage of everything related to test and treatment, that even the doctors and nurses run away from the ordinary patients, that there is an autocratic suppression of both facts and figures, that Hasina's Bangladesh is full of oppression and repression and persecution, that even the corona relief funds and provisions are being stolen away right and left by her goons and gangs, and that Hasina is a fascist vote dacoit/robber illegally holding on to power for years? Has the whole world gone blind? Doesn't it know what a horribly fascistic Hasina is?

"The world is blind to a great number of things;" observes the Bangladeshi-born American writer-columnist Sabria Chowdhury Balland, "it is full of sheeple, conditioned to believe all the lies they are being fed. The Hasina issue is no exception. In fact, she has an army of news outlets such as this one to immediately put her on a pedestal usually with false information, or as Trump calls it, 'fake news!' Even her ambassadors sit around and get paid to dispute every word written about her. The Forbes paragraph praising Hasina is just one more example of the ignorance going on about who Hasina truly is. It would be a service to the people of Bangladesh to call out Forbes on this fake news."

Part VI: No Freedom of Expression

As has been suggested above in the discussion how Hasina relates to Trump in her inhuman police brutalities, there are no press freedoms and freedom of speech whatsoever in Bangladesh (see Appendix E). The Hasina-imported RAW and the Hasina police have totally tightened the grip on the print, electronic and social media freedoms. Apart from the forced shutdowns of the popular dailies and TV channels, such as Amar Desh, Channel One, Diganta TV, Ekushey TV (under its former Chairman Abdus Salam), Islamic TV, and apart from the stories of the above named journalists and hundreds of others (who were either killed, imprisoned, exiled, disappeared, or intimidated for exercising their minimum freedom of expression in the print, social, or electronic media), there is no dearth of evidence and examples concerning the lack of press freedoms since 2009. Many of those exiled journalists and media personalities have recently been further harassed and humiliated by having their bank accounts brought under the surveillance of the fascist regime. It is yet another tactic to scare them and prevent them from their democratic right to freedom of speech and force them to refrain from doing what is indeed a bold and noble service to the nation currently under the fascist grip of Sheikh Hasina.

It is this total strangulation of people's voices that makes playwright Ariful Haque depict both Hasina's and her father's dangerous digital as well as analogue fascism in a concise, compact and convincing manner.[44] Even Dr Ahrar Ahmad (of Black Hills State University USA and Director General of Abdur Razzaq Foundation Dhaka), known to be a pro-Awami intellectual, is highly critical of the limits and restrictions imposed on free speech by the Hasina regime. Based on the Western idea of free speech that offers protection not only to the sweet and nice talk that does not really need any protection but to the otherwise that may sound negative to the ruling party, Dr Ahmad is of the view that debate, discussion, and criticism, be they humorous, satirical, or even offensive, should remain open, even be encouraged for the sake of democratic tolerance and understanding. Talking about Sheikh Hasina's Information, Communication and Technology Act (ICT, 2006, amended 2013), and the Digital Security Act (DSA, 2018), Dr Ahmad writes:

> Allowing the sweeping generalities and ambiguities inherent in these Acts as the basis for criminally prosecuting people would probably have embarrassed even Emperor Draco (from whom the word Draconian is derived). Moreover, giving police almost unlimited power of search, seizure and arrest without warrant, imposing severe punishment regimes, and making some offences non-bailable, made the Acts even more menacing ... it was hoped that these Acts were "ones for the book" and would not be used much. Jyotirmoy Barua indicated that between 2006 and 2013 no cases were prosecuted under Section 57. However, after that, the numbers began to increase exponentially and between 2013 and April 2018, Human Rights Watch calculated that 1,271 charge sheets had been submitted under this Section.
>
> Under the DSA, which superseded Section 57, The Daily Star reported that there were 34 cases filed in 2018, 63 in 2019, and by May 6 of 2020, almost 60 involving about 100 people. Newspapers regularly carry the names and pictures of people (some in handcuffs) charged under this Act.
>
> Politicians of the ruling party and the police have used these Acts primarily to file cases against editors, reporters, photographers, bloggers, baul/sufi artistes, writers and even cartoonists. It is noteworthy that, as Shahdin Malik has pointed out, while "spreading rumours" or "criticizng the government" are not specifically mentioned in the DSA, people ARE being arrested on those grounds.
>
> It would seem that the entire exercise was really intended to limit historical enquiry, critical thinking, political satire, policy disagreement, journalistic investigation or personal expression. More than a "chilling effect" on free speech, these laws hang like

the sword of Damocles over the population waiting to drop on any hapless citizen at the slightest provocation.[45]

Just as the "without fear or favor" oaths taken by Sheikh Hasina and others have become a joke, as much as the elections under her naked interventions have become a farce, journalism "without fear or favor" also under her notorious interference has become deplorably nonexistent. Like the opposition politicians, journalists also have become the target of terror and torture by the Hasina regime. They are either arrested or abducted for reporting the Awami corruption, misdeeds, scams and scandals, thefts of flood and corona relief goods, and all other kinds of Awami sponsored thuggery. Not only the journalists but also those who take to social media to protest against the Awami-engineered fake news, falsehoods and propaganda are detained, disappeared, and hounded and harassed. From teenage schoolboys to University teachers and students to people of all professions and walks of life, no one is spared from Hasina's horrible gopali and gestapo police. "We are hounded by fear, both within the law and extrajudicially too," writes Sohrab Hassan (as identified above as joint editor of what is perceived to be a pro-Awami daily, Prothom Alo). He goes on saying:

> The repressive Digital Security Act [DSA], enforced in 2018, is being used to suppress both the common citizens as well as journalists. [...] cases were filed against 180 journalists. Other than journalists, the arrested persons include writers, cartoonists and human rights activists. 114 were arrested immediately after the cases were filed. [...] The Digital Security Act has been used against many journalists for reporting on the theft and misappropriation of relief materials during the coronavirus pandemic. Some have gone into hiding and some, like Shafiqul [Islam alias Kajol, are behind bars. [...] Fearless and unbiased journalism is not possible in a country where such a repressive law exists. Fear is a constant companion for journalists. They are often forced to publish and air the government's one-sided views. They cannot publish the counter views. There are innumerable instances of this at present and in the recent past.[46]

Yet another pro-Awami intellectual Engineer Dr Habib Siddiquee of the USA writes:

> In the post-independent period, our political leadership has simply failed us. With much validity, one can even accuse them of betraying our national interest. It's an utterly disappointing, disgusting, embarrassing and humiliating experience for our nation! I also believe that the sad state of our nation may not become better tomorrow with merely the change of the guards, no matter how desirable one may imagine such to be. After all, leadership comes from the people and can't be separated from the population it has emerged from or pretends to represent. As the Prophet (S) famously said, "As you are, so will be your leaders." When we have good people that are willing to imitate Spartacus and Abu Dhar (RA), Allah's help will come In-sha-Allah as a blessing and the change will be desirable and beneficial for all. Our problem requires looking at things as they are in an unbiased manner without the borrowed lenses of partisanship from AL and BNP that, sadly, has contributed to sycophancy and a parasite culture and nothing helpful. [Author's Note: BNP's Zia did not fail us, nor did Khaleda in her first term, and the failures in her subsequent terms are only negligible and far outweighed by the countless and crippling faults and fissures of the fascist Awami League in its every term].
>
> The system today is corrupt to the core and oblivious of its accountability before God and people (or more properly 'ibad) for its monumental crimes and Pharaonic despotism. I don't see a God-fearing, people-caring and environmentally-concerned leadership emerging any time soon that knows and is mindful of the very meaning of being the trustee (Khalifah) of Allah on earth. Thus, sadly, our suffering continues and will continue for a foreseeable future. Let's all pray for better days ahead. Who knows the same Allah who has brought everyone to their knees, from Trump to Xi to Modi through Covid-19, may out of His Infinite Kindness and Grace take pity on our poor souls and make

our last days better than the days past! Surely, He is capable of everything. Let's also pray for the guidance of our temporal leaders -- whoever they are and wherever they are (Group e-mail of May 30, 2020).

Referring to Voltaire, John Stuart Mill, Amnesty International, Human Rights Watch (HRW), and even pro-Awami Regime Bangladesh journalists, Balland observes that the Hasina regime is fully exploiting DSA for what is in effect a zero tolerance for freedom of speech in Bangladesh, silencing the voices of constitutionally guaranteed democratic dissent. "The victims of these injustices," she writes, "simply want to talk about the corruption and irregularities they experience via the news, cartoons, photographs and social media posts. It is not as though their observations and comments are based on falsehoods. They are truthfully revealing the irregularities ... [but] wrongfully convicted on the false grounds of [...] criticizing the government (a fundamental right guaranteed in any nation which wants to be taken seriously as a democracy)."[47] Balland continues to accuse Hasina of gross and glaring human rights violations through extrajudicial crossfire killings and senseless deaths with impunity granted to the perpetrators.[48]

Under the regime's draconian laws aimed at stifling the freedom of speech, no one can exercise their right to print and social media freedoms. Below are a few recent examples of Sheikh Hasina's foolish and fascist intolerance even of minimum dissent:

> 1. In view of President Ziaur Rahman's incalculable state building measures and tremendous success providing forward looking lighthouse directions to the nation, Dr Morshed Hasan Khan described him as the incomparably luminous Zia (জ্যোতির্ময় জিয়া) in a Naya Diganta column of 26 March 2018, for which, by the order of the fascist regime, he lost his job as a professor of Marketing at Dhaka University on 9 September 2020.[49]
>
> 2. According to a reliable source, Neyamatullah Bhuiyan, who was retired as a joint secretary after being made an OSD, was arrested, jailed, and tortured for months for writing a poem circulated on Facebook. The poem truthfully parodied the conduct of voting in the fake elections under the regime. It had couplets

that meant something like this: "I will give my vote; I will also vote for you; so you don't have to go through the trouble of going to the voting center." Neyamatullah's FB page has since been taken down and he is a broken man, but grateful to be still alive.

3. Sirajam Munira, a lecturer at the Department of Bangla of Begum Rokeya University, was arrested following her FB status criticizing the Awami leader Mohammad Nasim who recently died and is alleged to have been extremely corrupt amassing and smuggling millions through his son in New York and full of foul and filthy language hurled at the opposition BNP.

4. Similar situation faced Mahir Chowdhury, a 4th year Economics student at ShahJalal University of Science and Technology Sylhet, who merely wanted to exercise his freedom of speech at the death of Nasim, widely perceived to have been utterly corrupt. There are hundreds and thousands who faced and are facing a similar fate for their right to freedom of speech even in the minimum.

Mahmudur Rahman, a national conscience/hero of Bangladesh, writes in an e-mail of June 9, 2020: "Bangladesh is a country under the fascist regime of Sheikh Hasina since 2009!!!...Hasn't Hasina closed down all the newspapers and television channels which she considered detrimental to her autocracy? Have we forgotten the torture, imprisonment and killing of scores of journalists in Bangladesh? How many of them have been forced to an uncertain life in exile? […] Shafik Rehman has a fabricated attempted murder case against her (Hasina's) son Joy? Incidentally, I am a co-accused in that case. We two allegedly conspired in Bangladesh to abduct Hasina's son who is living in the US. The charge is absolutely fantastic because I was in jail while the alleged conspiracy to abduct the crown prince was going on."[50]

In response to some pro-Awami intellectuals and academics somewhat critical of the lack of freedom of speech and tolerance of democratic dissent without directly finger-pointing at the root of all evil, that is, the Awami League and its leader Hasina, Engineer Rashed Anam of the USA observes:

> The flower of free speech does not bloom in the desert of autocracy. Expecting otherwise is disingenuous or at best naive. There are some Awami appeasers who want to be intellectuals by

faint-heartedly criticizing selective issues without criticizing the mandateless Awami dictatorship that is the mother ship of all evil in Bangladesh. They want it both ways--keeping mum on the existence and activities of this dictatorship but at the same trying to take moral authority by writing some innocuous pieces. There is no morality in tolerating and cheerleading dictatorship. We all see through the hypocrisy and fakeness. What do you think people would think if South Africa's aparthied Botha or his obedient supporters lecture on equal rights? Wouldn't that be ridiculous and laughable?

Asian Human Rights Commission claims that the lack of freedom of speech attended by government-sponsored police violence in a literally frightening and terrifying manner has surpassed the barbarism of the Dark Ages.[51] Hitler, Modi, Trump, Hasina (who was safe and secure in a comfort zone in Dhaka protected by Pakistani military, which was then engaged in committing a genocide just outside her comfort zone in 1971) and her *kaowa* and *murgi* and *ghora* and *ghadani* and yaba lieutenants[52] talking about racial, political and religious harmony in a disorganized pick-and-choose method are nothing more than a joking copartnery.

Some pro-Hasina intellectuals criticizing the lack of free speech mildly or moderately without directly challenging her illegal and illegitimate regime itself headed by the power grabber and vote rigger Hasina are also those who cowardly, yet cleverly help perpetuate her despotic regime. How could anybody, except the fair-weather sycophants and opportunists, be pro-Awami, even remotely, in these political dog days under the Goneril-type tigress in Hasina? Shoudn't the Awami leaders and whatever little following they may have among the people run away from Hasina the way they ran away from Mujib after his death and joined the other top Awami leader Khandoker Mustaque Ahmad, who masterminded the coup and succeeded as a popular President of Bangladesh with immediate effect?

Part VII: Like Father, Like Daughter

The regime would also like to force the people of Bangladesh to blindly accept and worship Sheikh Mujib as if he was an above criticism cult hero or a pagan deity. (The regime forces people to worship his daughter Hasina the same way, day in and day out, at every sitting and standing, as if she was a "Hazrat Sheikh Hasina," a title given to her, among her many other "collected," "purchased" and "accumulated" titles, by her supporters and flatterers—with "Hazrat," as many critics consider, being offensive to the religious sentiment of Muslims). It is by this forced demand that a great political personality and also one of the founding fathers that Mujib truly was has been reduced to a less admired figure, open to critical inquiry.

Mujib's status, like M K Gandhi of India accused of engaging in selective racism,[53] has become a subject of critical scrutiny. Critics condemn: (1) his controversial stand on the creation of Bangladesh; (2) his planned surrender to (the protection of) the Pakistani authorities for fear of treason on 25 March 1971, leaving his family in the safety of the Pakistani forces, but at the same time leaving the people of East Pakistan (soon to be Bangladesh) to be killed in the genocide committed by them; (3) his absence or being away for the entire 9-month period of the armed struggle that was going on for the liberation of Bangladesh; (4) his having no contribution at all to the creation of Bangladesh; (5) his feeling not so happy with the military role of India in splitting Pakistan (which broke his dream of premiership of the whole united Pakistan through constitutional means); and (6) his post-war dictatorial maladministration that saw the killing of democracy as a political system and thousands of political opponents and the creation of a man-made famine that caused hundreds of thousands to die of hunger.[54]

It was this intolerably bad administration that expedited his downfall with his own people turning against him, describing him as a tyrant Feraoun (Faraoh) and cheering on the streets at his demise with a sense of relief (readers may do the fact checking from the print media such as the Bangladesh Times and Ittefaq from 15/16 August 1975 onwards) and also the electronic media of the time available on blogs, YouTube and Facebook).[55] There is no denying there was a public euphoria and an outpouring of joy from all quarters at the 15 August change led by Mujib's own close partymen under the new President Khandoker Mustaque Ahmad.

Mujib promised to deliver a "Sonar Bangla" (a golden Bengal) but he delivered a "Bottomless Bangla." Indian writer-journalist Kuswant Singh wrote in the Illustrated Weekly of India:

> Within a couple of years, [Sheikh Mujib] had lost much of his charisma and lived in a cocoon of self-spun esteem. He came to regard honest critics as traitors and sycophants as loyal friends. It was a classic case of folio de grandeur. He was blissfully unaware that the very people who called him Bangabandhu to his face were behind his back called him Banga-Shatru.[56]

Writer and novelist Sunil Gangopaddhaya of West Bengal said that Mujib killed democracy for which he fought all his life. পশ্চিমবঙ্গের প্রখ্যাত সাহিত্যিক আওয়ামী লীগের প্রিয়পাত্র সুনীল গঙ্গোপাধ্যায় লিখেছেন, "যে গণতন্ত্রের নামে শেখ সাহেব সারাজীবন গলা ফাটালেন শেষে তিনি নিজেই হত্যা করতে গেলেন সেই গণতন্ত্রকে।[57] শেখ মুজিবুর রহমানকে হত্যা করা হয়েছে, রাস্তায় মিছিল বের হয়েছে। দুর্ভাগ্যজনকহলেও সত্যি, সেই মিছিল আনন্দ-মিছিল।"--কথা সাহিত্যিক হুমায়ুন আহমদ (Sheikh Mujib was killed, streets were filled with processions. The reality was that those were the jubilations of the people--Novelist Humayun Ahmed).

Even if the people of Bangladesh let bygones be bygones, it is Mujib's own daughter Hasina and his/her own party Awami League who are responsible, two decades later, for letting the nation treat Mujib with less than the great respect he deserves. Hasina and her people have had hundreds of things named indiscriminately after her father and her family members, herself included, rendering their style of narrow-minded dynastic nomenclature of structures and entities a matter of laughing stock as if political leadership was a collection of tribal totems. They do not mind spending hundreds of crores of taka in observance of what they shockingly call 2020 a Mujib Borso (Mujib Year) in a country where there are millions of poor people going without basic necessities such as food and medical treatment and suffering from flood-expedited famine. Selfishly, they took out the name of the most popular political figure of

Bangladesh, President Ziaur Rahman (Khaleda Zia's husband) from only a few deserving places or institutions that were called in memory of his name.[58]

Unfortunately, both Ziaur Rahman and Khaleda Zia were betrayed by their own men and the people they trusted, took in good faith and directly promoted. Hasina and Ershad (both locked up in political hermaphroditism), Manzoor, Moeen and Masud and Sayeed Iskandar—all are alleged to have complicity in the death of President Zia and near destruction of *DeshNetri* and *DeshMata* Khaleda Zia and (to be) *DeshNayok* Tarique.[59] In fact, starting from 1971 through the BDR massacre of February 2009, the history of Bangladesh is a history of betrayals, until the current betrayal of the political and economic interests of Bangladesh by Hasina to India and the countless looters ripping off the country.

Engineer-turned-politician-writer-journalist Mahmudur Rahman sheds light (in his Chapter in this book), as do many others, on the similarity that Bangladesh has with the 1757 Battle of Plassey in terms of palace coups and family betrayals.[60] Engineer M Gani of the USA comments: "Only Almighty Allah knows how many Mir Jafars of cunning tricks this gutter nation Bangladesh has so far produced; literally, Bangladesh has become a 'Mir Jafar infested land.'" As the so-called Syed Mir Jafar Ali Khan Bahadur (originally of Comilla Bangladesh and an ultimate symbol of betrayal/ "Namak Haram"), who was a close relative of the young Nawab Mirza Mohammad Sirajuddowla of Bengal, acted treacherously as a puppet of British East India Company's Robert Clive only to face a miserable and pathetic death by leprosy, Sheikh Hasina also has unfortunately been acting at the direction of Hindutva fundamentalist Muslim killer Narendra Modi of New Delhi. R Chowdhury, mentioned above, comments in a similar vein through a group email:

> There is no dearth of Mir Jaffors in Bangladesh today. The East Pakistanis fought in 1971 for independence, democracy, freedom and an exploit-free society. What they got in return under their chosen leader Mujib, who chose not to be in the war in the first place? Their aspirations were brutally trampled. Three and half years of Mujib rule still brings shudder to those who lived in the

period. Yet, it is surprising that some people worship Mujib as if he was a god. Yes, Mujib did have some contributions in raising hopes in the Bengalis against the Pakistani dictators and overlords, but his crimes in 1972-75 cannot be exonerated. Mujib was responsible for his own fall. People's reaction at Mujib's death on August 15 was tell all. We all know that. And the Hasina regime? Like father like daughter, in full steam. Hasina went over-the-top in one aspect: She sold herself and Bangladesh to her sponsor India. I wonder how can a person promote dictatorship, goom-khoon (forced disappearances-murders), jail-zulum (imprisonment, persecution and discrimination) and arrest of free voice in Bangladesh!... While the country is in the grasp of the menacing COVID-19 killing people on daily basis, Sheikh Hasina's own lust for blood and violence sees no end. May Allah (SWT) save Bangladesh from the blood suckers: Corona One and Corona Two.

Playwright Ariful Haque, one of those who can beautifully write in a historically-oriented manner, describe Hasina's puppetry and capitulation to Indian hegemony in the footseteps of the traitors Mir Jafar and Ghaseti Begum (who betrayed Nawab Sirajuddowla of independent Bengal), Mir Sadiq (who betrayed Tipu Sultan of independent Mysore), Munshi Govinda Das (who betrayed the last Mughal emperor Bahadur Shah Zafar in Delhi), and Al-Idrus (who helped the independent Hyderabad to fall). One of the almost biblical and inspirational articles by him covers the frustrations and disappointments at those tragic Muslim defeats in the subcontinent but ends with a note of hope at the poetic call to strike back hard:

বাংলার মুসলমানরা ১৭৫৭ সালে মীরজাফর-ঘসেটি বেগমদের প্রতারনা দেখেছে। ১৭৯২ সালে মীরসাদিকের প্রতারনায় টিপু সুলতানকে প্রান দিতে হয়েছে দেখেছে। ১৮৫৭ সালে সিপাহী বিপ্লবে, বাহাদুর শাহের সাথে প্রতারনাকারি, মুন্সী গোবিন্দ দাস, আগাজানদের চরিত্র দেখেছো ১৯৪৮ সালে ভারত কর্তৃক হায়দারাবাদ দখলের সময় হায়দারাবাদের সেনাপতি আল-ইদরুসের প্রতারনায় হায়দারাবাদের নাম নিশানা মিটে যেতে দেখেছো কিন্তু তাদের ইতিহাস থেকে কিছুই শিক্ষা নেয়নি বাংলাদেশের মানুষ। তাই আজ ছবি দেখছি , আর এক পলাশী পতনের ছবি, আর

এক মহীশূরের পতনের ছবি, আর এক দিল্লী পতনের ছবি, আর এক স্বাধীন হায়দারাবাদ পতনের ছবি ! ছবি দেখছি বাংলাদেশের ১৭ কোটি মুসলমান স্বেচ্ছামৃত্যুর ফাঁস গলায় আটকে কি নির্বিকার ভাবে দাঁড়িয়ে আছে । শেষজীবনের প্রান্তে দাঁড়িয়ে, তারপরও আশা ছাড়তে ইচ্ছে করেনা। আমার প্রিয় কবি কাজী নজরুল ইসলামের ভাষায় বলতে ইচ্ছে করছে-'সত্যমুক্তি স্বাধীন জীবন লক্ষ্য শুধু যাদের / খোদার রাহায় জান দিতে আজ ডাক পড়েছে তাদের।'[61]

Part VIII: Conclusion

Let me conclude with a hope too for the better future of Bangladesh free of betrayers, traitors, tyrants, autocrats, oppressors, dictators, fascists, flatterers, sycophants, looters, smugglers, thugs, hoodlums, hooligans, goons and gangs. Let us look forward to a Bangladesh free from the politically motivated bundles of fake and fabricated, false and frivolous, ludicrous and ridiculous court cases against almost each of the opposition leaders and activists. Let us expect Bangladesh to be free from weak and spineless "yes" election commissions acting at the direction of the regime; free from the evil forces in the police, judiciary and administration; free from enforced abductions and disappearances. Let us hope for free and fair elections—both local and national--where all voters can cast their votes in peace and harmony without fear, coercion, intimidation, police control and police beating.

Let us hope for a future when দুষ্টের পালন শিষ্টের দমন/The observance/promotion of evil and the suppression of decency/truth will be banished. Let us hope for a future when all can develop a sense of proud and patriotic belongingness to the country, not one of dictatorial disunity and divisiveness, full of frauds and scams. Let us hope for a morrow when the military of the country can have a chance to cultivate its professional military character with honor and dignity. Let us look forward to a military to play a truly selfless patriotic role, a military not turned into a greedy business community of corporate and consumer culture to profiteer from nearly 150 lucrative projects as it may allegedly be doing for years without caring to stop both the internal and external disturbances, encroachments and trespasses and thereby to ensure peace and harmony in the country in its own way.

Finally, let all political prisoners, including Begum Khaleda Zia, be free, totally and completely, from the politically cooked and judicially made up charges and bondages. Along with her husband President Ziaur Rahman before her, she is among the greatest political phenomena of Bangladesh. Let her come to light at the end of the long dark tunnel of suffering, sacrifice and struggle that she has been traversing for the sake of her people and the nation. Let her come to the end of her long walk in her efforts to save the nation and take it forward. Let the nation benefit, once again, from her great leadership as it did during her tenures in 1991-1996 and 2001-2006, as well as that of her husband President Zia in 1975-1981 and his key and crucial role in 1971.

To reiterate, the BNP is the largest and most popular party of Bangladesh. It is vastly popular and enormously superior to Bangladesh Awami League (the BAL). But, let the people decide. Time is overdue, as it was in 2014 and then in 2018, for the foolishly but ferociously repressive, vote-rigging and illegal Hasina regime, cut off from the people, to take a 180 degree turn for the sake of 180 million people of Bangladesh. They hardly support the threatening and throttling, and choking and suffocating Hasina regime but they can hardly say anything in her police and prison state—a frightening wonderland. As the plethora of evidence suggests, Hasina is people's anathema and, therefore, should go in no time through a peaceful transition so that those who are chosen by voters in a free, fair, clean and competitive general election held under a neutral caretaker administration can lead the nation out of internal bondage, domestic violence and bloodshed, and Indian chains and shackles.

The first seven points for such a democratically elected and people mandated patriotic government should be: (1) to trumpet, "Down with Fascist Hasina," or, to say, with Dr Hashmi, "Hell with Hasina's Fascism;" (2) to ditch and ban pro-Hindu and pro-India "Joy Bangla" and "Bungalee nationalism," both soaked in the Hindutva; (3) to throw out the existing stale, rotten, torn, tattered, loosely adhered to, conveniently tailored and re-tailored, and expediently and expeditiously made and re-made constitutional clauses and patchworks; (4) to remove the misused, misleading, and Hindutva-promoting and Islam-bashing term "secularism" from the constitution; (5) to draft a new and fresh and pro-people constitution, infused with the spirit of the inclusive Bangladeshi Nationalism, with the aim of establishing the rule of law and social justice on the land of Bangladesh; (6) to solemnly declare the fascist Hasina regime of 2009 onwards totally illegal and invalid; and (7) to hold all the culprits of the regime and their accomplices in the police, RAB, judiciary, and administration accountable and try them all on ICT for the fascist, black, brutal and brutish misdeeds they have committed since 2009 to suit the dark, dreary, and dull Awami BAKSALi-Hindutva-saturated Indian agenda.

---

[1] Matiur Rahman Rentu ("I Want/Wish to be Hanged/Executed," 1999), http://amarfashichai.blogspot.co.uk (in English); http://docshare01.docshare.tips/files/2977/29771574.pdf (English); https://mazams.weebly.com/uploads/4/8/2/6/48260335 / amar_fashi_chai_bangla.pdf (in Bangla); http: // amarfashichai.blogspot.co.uk /2013 / 07 / amar-fashi-chai-by-motiur-rahmanrentu.html (in English). Banned by Hasina, this book by her once very close aide for many years, from 1981-1997, is a detailed description of the notorious conduct and activities she was engaged in. Rentu's wife also was Hasina's close household aide for about ten years.

[2] bangla.bdnews24.com/politics/article808372.bdnews বোরকা পরে পালাচ্ছিলেন কেন: হাসিনাকে খালেদা; www.dailysangram.com/post/148087-জিয়ার-মৃত্যুর-দিন-শেখ--হাসিনা-বোরখা-পরে--ভারতে-পালাচ্ছিলেন---গয়েশ্বর; www.prothomalo.com/bangladesh/'কেন-আপনি-বাংলাদেশে-ঢোকার-১৩-দিনের-মাথায়-জিয়াউর Rizvi

[3] In a Facebook status Turiqul Islam Patowary writes: কে এই বেগম খালেদা জিয়া--নতুন প্রজন্মের জানা উচিত । এটা বহু সংগ্রামী মহীয়সী নারীর জীবনীকে হার মানায়।। তিনি একজন প্রাক্তন সেনাপ্রধানের স্ত্রী !তিনি একজন প্রাক্তন প্রেসিডেন্টের স্ত্রী !তিনি সার্ক এর প্রতিষ্ঠাতার স্ত্রী !তিনি একজন মুক্তিযোদ্ধার স্ত্রী তিনি স্বাধীনতার ঘোষকের স্ত্রী!তিনি একজন মুক্তিযুদ্ধের সেক্টর কমান্ডারের স্ত্রী!তিনি তিন তিন বারের প্রধানমন্ত্রী !তিনি দুইবার সংসদের প্রধান বিরোধীদলীয় নেত্রী !তিনি বাংলাদেশের প্রথম ফাস্টলেডি!যে রেকর্ড ভাঙার সাধ্য কারো নেই !তিনি বাংলাদেশের প্রথম নারী প্রধানমন্ত্রী!যে রেকর্ড ভাঙার সাধ্য কারো নেই ! তিনি মুসলিম বিশ্বের দ্বিতীয় নারী প্রধানমন্ত্রী। এই রেকর্ডও ভাঙার সাধ্য কারো নেই ! স্বামী ছিলেন প্রেসিডেন্ট আর স্ত্রী অর্থাৎ তিনি ছিলেন প্রধানমন্ত্রী এই double record বাংলাদেশে আর কারো নেই!এটা এখনো পর্যন্ত বেগম জিয়ার দখলে !তিনি ৯১, ৯৬ ও ২০০১ সালে প্রতিটি নির্বাচনে পাঁচটি করে সিটে দাঁড়িয়েছেন এবং প্রতিবার পাঁচটিতেই জিতেছেন! এই রেকর্ড এখনো কেউ ভাঙতে পারেনি !২০০৮ সালে মঈনুদ্দিন ফকরুদ্দিন সরকার বেগম জিয়াকে টার্গেট করে পাঁচ সিটে দাঁড়ানো যাবে না, সর্বোচ্চ তিন সিটে দাঁড়ানো যাবে আইন করলে বেগম জিয়া তিন সিটে দাঁড়ান এবং তিন সিটি জয় লাভ করেন। তিনি বাংলাদেশে একমাত্র আপোষহীন নেত্রী যিনি সেবা দাসী বা আপোষ কাকে বলে সেই শব্দ তাঁর অভিধানে নেই ! এই রেকর্ড বাংলাদেশে বেগম জিয়া আর ভাসানী ছাড়া আর কারো নেই !! অভিজাত্যের ছোঁয়ায় লালিত হয়েও তিনি ছিলেন গণমুখী ও দেশ দরদী তাঁর ব্যক্তি জনপ্রিয়তাসব সময়ই ছিল তুঙ্গে যার ধারে কাছে এখনো কেউ যেতে পারে নি একমাত্র শহীদ জিয়া ছাড়া !তিনিই বাংলাদেশে একমাত্র নারী প্রধানমন্ত্রী যিনি চার চার বার বন্দি হয়েছেন, একবার পাকিস্তান সরকার-দ্বিতীয়বার

এরশাদ সরকার তৃতীয়বার মঈনুদ্দিন / ফখরুদ্দিন সরকার চতুর্থবার হাসিনা সরকার যদি ২০১৪ সালের বালুর ট্রাক দ্বারা অঘোষিত গৃহ বন্দিত্ব ধরি তাহলে পাঁচবার হবে বন্দিত্ব জীবন এই বন্দিত্ব জীবনের রেকর্ডটিও বেগম জিয়ার দখলে!ম্যাডাম থেকে গণতন্ত্রের 'মা' হতে পারার রেকর্ডটি বিশ্বে একমাত্র বেগম জিয়ার দখলে.আজ আমরা গর্বিত।হাজার কোটি সালাম জানাই আমাদের প্রিয় নেত্রী ও গণতন্ত্রের মা বেগম খালেদা জিয়া কে, দেশ ও বিদেশে সকল জিয়া প্রেমিক, ও সর্বস্তরে নেতা কর্মী আল্লাহ তুমি আমদের গণতন্ত্রের মা বেগম খালেদা জিয়া কে হেফাজত করুন ও সুস্থ রাখেন ও দীর্ঘায়ু দান করুন আমিন!

[4] See this amazing article, www.eurovisionbd.com/শহীদ-জিয়ামিথ্যা-এবং-শত-মি/ by H Shahadat Suhrawardy; a great poem, www.eurovisionbd.com/কায়েদে-আজাদী-শাহাদাত-সুহ/

[5] This is from Anwar Hussen's FB: এশিয়া মহাদেশে দেশনেত্রী বেগম খালেদা জিয়ার মতো ত্যাগী নেত্রী খুঁজে পাওয়া যাবে না। এজন্যই তিনি দেশে এবং বিদেশে নিজেকে বাংলাদেশের গনতান্ত্রিক "মাতা" হিসাবে ভূষিত হয়েছেন। তিনি এইদেশ এবং এইদেশের জনগণের জন্য এবং এইদেশের গনতন্ত্রের জন্য যতটুকু অবদান রেখেছেন বিশ্বের ইতিহাসে এমন নজির খুবই বিরল।পক্ষান্তরে আওয়ামী লীগের সভানেত্রী গনতন্ত্র হত্যার জন্য এবং এইদেশের জনগণের মানবাধিকার, মত প্রকাশের স্বাধীনতা হরন করে নিজেকে গনতন্ত্র হত্যাকারী, এবং মহিলা স্বৈরশাসক শাসক হিসাবে ভূষিত হয়েছেন। বিএনপির চেয়ারপারসন বেগম খালেদা জিয়া সব সময় বাংলাদেশ এবং বাংলাদেশের জনগণের জন্য রাজনীতি করেন। এজন্য তিনি স্বৈরশাসনের বলি হয়ে মিথ্যা মামলায় বারংবার কারাবরণ করেছেন। তিনি কখনও অন্যায়ের সাথে আপোষ করেন নাই, ইতিমধ্যেই তিন তাঁর প্রমান দিয়েছেন। তিনি জেলখানায় অসুস্থ হয়ে মৃত্যুর সাথে পান্জা লড়েছেন কিন্তু অবৈধভাবে ক্ষমতা দখলকারদের সাথে আপোষ করেন নাই। এজন্য তিনি গনতান্ত্রিক ইতিহাসে আপোষহীন নেত্রী হিসাবেও দেশে এবং বিদেশে সমাদৃত।পক্ষান্তরে আওয়ামী লীগের সভানেত্রী শেখ হাসিনা তিনি নিজ এবং তাঁর বন্ধু দেশ ভারতের খুশির জন্য রাজনীতি করেন। তিনি বাংলাদেশের স্বার্থ জলান্জলী দিয়ে সবসময় ভারতের স্বার্থ রক্ষা করেন। এজন্য শেখ হাসিনা গর্ববোধ করে বলেন, "আমি ভারতের যা দিয়েছি, তারা সারা জীবন মনে রাখবেন। বিনিময়ে শেখ হাসিনা অবৈধভাবে ক্ষমতা ধরে রাখার জন্য ভারতের অনুকম্পা পেয়ে যাচ্ছেন। শেখ হাসিনার কাছে নিজ, তাঁর দল এবং ক্ষমতা ছাড়া জনগণের কথা কখনও চিন্তা করে না। তাঁর প্রমান জনগণ করোনা মহামারির চলাকালীন সময়ে হাড়ে হাড়ে টের পাচ্ছেন। বাংলাদেশের রাজনীতিতে বিএনপির চেয়ারপারসন বেগম খালেদা জিয়ার তুলনা তিনি নিজেই, অন্য কারও সাথে তুলনা করা যাবে না। কারণ তাঁর যোগ্য নেতা বা নেত্রী এই বাংলাদেশে এখনও জন্মগ্রহণ করে নাই। অ৩গামীতে জন্মগ্রহণ করবে কিনা, তা সন্দিহান।

[6] https://theintercept.com/2020/04 / 15 / biden-trump-noam-chomsky-mehdi-hasan; www.youtube.com/watch?v=zRvqkUoiKJo;www.youtube.com/watch?v=d-6EXZ7yM2E; www.youtube.com/watch?v=5BXtgq0Nhsc The Crimes of U.S. Presidents

[7] https://youtu.be/4jIZeJXTOjY
www.facebook.com/Minafarahofficial/videos/409438473420889/?sfnsn=wa
www.facebook.com/pg/Minafarahofficial/videos/
https://youtu.be/VtKtAGiLE1U জেনারেলরাই and judges যখন বিশ্বাষঘাতক

[8] amardesh.co.uk/গভর্নমেন্ট-অব-দা-বাটপার/

[9] www.cnn.com/2020/11/15/opinions/trump-election-war-fox-news-obeidallah/?hpt=ob_blogfooterold

[10] amardesh.co.uk/সেনাবাহিনী-ও-পুলিশে-চূড়া/ চূড়ান্ত ভারতীয়করণ?

buffalobangla.com/ভারতীয়-রএর-কজ্জায়-প্রিয়-স/ স্বদেশ
amardesh.co.uk/বর্তমানে-দেশের-সরকারি-কর/ কর্মকর্তাদের পোস্টিং দিল্লির কথার বাইরে হয় না-গয়েশ্বর চন্দ্র রায়

[11] Col Shahid Uddin Khan with Dr Kanak Sarwar:
https://youtu.be/V4z3F5hHXb4; https://youtu.be/Ol0vMwGOFSE;
https://youtu.be/Y8ih5GW3FJs

[12] www.alternet.org/2020/10/noam-chomsky-lays-out-a-variety-of-reasons-why-he-considers-trump-the-worst-criminal-in-human-history-interview/
Why Noam Chomsky is declaring Trump the 'worst criminal in human history'

[13] www.cnn.com/2020/10/16/politics/donald-trump-criticism-from-former-administration-officials/index.html

[14] www.cnn.com/2020/10/19/politics/fact-check-trump-dishonest-weekend-florida-michigan-georgia-wisconsin/index.html

[15] www.cnn.com/2020/11/18/politics/kfile-jenna-ellis-2016-trump-comments/index.html

[16] www.foxnews.com/entertainment/michael-moore-biden-victory-post-election-night-trump-bigot-psychopath

[17] www.theguardian.com/books/2020/jul/21/too-much-and-never-enough-by-mary-l-trump-review-donald-trump-niece; www.theguardian.com/us-news/2020/nov/08/mary-trump-on-the-end-of-uncle-donald-all-he-has-now-is-breaking-things

[18] www.cnn.com/2020/07/15/politics/mary-trump-donald-trump-resign.

[19] www.cnn.com/ 2020 / 08/ 22 / politics/maryanne-trump-barry-donald-trump-mary-trump/index.html

[20] See all my Appendices, particularly Appendix H (on abductions and enforced disappearances), in Sabria Chowdhury Balland (ed), *Bangladesh: A Suffering People Under State Terrorism* (New York: Peter Lang, April 2020). Also the following:
www.youtube.com/watch?v=sAAQCW9zhqE আমার বাবা গু'ম হয়েছে | অবুঝ শিশুর শাহবাগে বুকফাটা কান্না | আমার বাবাকে ফিরিয়ে দিন ??

www.dailynayadiganta.com/Incident-accident / 525118 / ১৩-বছরে-৬০৪-জন-গুম;-তারা-কোথায়?

www.jugantor.com/politics / 339901 / যারা-গুম-করেছে-একদিন-তাদের-ফাঁসির-কাষ্ঠে-ঝুলানো-হবে-ইশরাক

www.dailynayadiganta.com/Incident-accident/525113/'ছেলে-অপরাধ-করলে-বিচার-করেন-গুম-করতে-তো-পারেন-না' www.dailynayadiganta.com/politics/525095/গুম-বিচারবর্হিভূত-হত্যাকাণ্ডের-আন্তর্জাতিক-তদন্ত-চায়-বিএনপি

www.dailynayadiganta.com/politics/525099/গুম-খুন-ও-প্রতিহিংসা-পরিহার-করে-মূল্যবোধের-সমাজ-প্রতিষ্ঠা-করতে-হবে-বিচারপতি-আব্দুর-রউফ

http://southasiajournal.net/bangladesh-crime-and-law-the-killings-that-never-see-justice/

[21] www.cnn.com / 2020/08 / 04 / politics/fact-check-jonathan-swan-axios-hbo-interview-trump-coronavirus/index.html; www.cnn.com/2020/08/05/opinions/axios-interview-trump-presidency-filipovic/index.html

[22] www.youtube.com/watch?v=jdw3UWOeKIo; www.youtube.com/watch?v=i8jQQCcuv-4; amardesh.co.uk/ট্রাম্প-গেছে-ওর-বোন-কবে-যা/ ; www.youtube.com/watch?v=jwO2ZxlTeXc&feature=share

[23] Also refer to Part D, Pieces on Donald Trump: Lessons and Implications for Bangladesh" in my *Bangladesh Divided: Political and Literary Reflections on a Corrupt Police and Prison State*, pp. 353-378

[24] www.facebook.com/notes/kai-kaus/এরশাদ-বাঙালের-রাজনৈতিক-আয়না-০১/10 06206 149837227/

[25] http:// aequitasreview.org / bangladesh-the-awami-league-doesnt-seem-to-have-any-answers-by-sohrab-hassan/

[26] Loyal police recruited from Hasina's home district of Gopalganj and the greater Gopalganj and beyond. Gestapo was "the official secret police of Nazi Germany and German-occupied Europe. The force was created by Hermann Göring in 1933 by combining the various security police agencies of Prussia into one organisation." See Chapter 3, "The Role of the Police and the RAB (Rapid Action Battalion) in the 'Development Sans Democracy' Conversation and the Gopal/Gopali Parrots and Predators in the Police," in my *Bangladesh: Political and Literary Reflections on a Divided Country* (Peter Lang, 2018), pp. 97-135.

[27] See all my Appendices, particularly Appendix C (on the corruptions of the top Awami family) in Balland (ed), *Bangladesh: A Suffering People Under State Terrorism* (New York: Peter Lang, April 2020). Also, https://youtu.be/ufGXNDhCxwg "শেখ হাসিনার পুত্র জয়ের সকল দুর্নীতির তথ্য ফাঁস হল! প্রমানসহ দেখুন" Also,

https://en.prothomalo.com/bangladesh/BNP-blasts-govt-silence-about-300m-in-Joy-s-US

https:// thewire.in / south-asia / exclusive-us-court-dismissed-claim-of-plot-to-injure-bangladesh-pm-son (refers to Joy's US$300 m)

https://bdnews24.com / politics / 2016 / 05 / 02/khaleda-asks-hasina-to-get-joy-questioned-over-so-called-300-million-in-his-account

https://bdnews24.com/politics/2016/04/30/khaleda-wants-to-know-source-of-money-of-prime-ministers-son-joy

https://en.wikipedia.org/wiki/Sajeeb_Wazed In April 2016, an exclusive write-up by David Bergman in the Indian website The Wire revealed that a "Suspicious Activity Report" (SAR) covering a transaction of US$300 million recorded in a memo of the United States Federal Bureau of Investigation (FBI) was linked to

Wazed. But the court documents did not provide any further information about the reference to 'US$300 million

[28] www.theindianpanorama.news / wp-content / uploads/2018/06/TIP-June-8-NYC.pdf

[29] http://dhakadigest.net/en/2014/02/an-ornamental-sangsad

[30] http://dhakadigest.net/en / 2014 / 01 / the-fake-election-in-bangladesh-the-existential-threat/

[31] https:// medium.com / netranews/retired-lieutenant-general-in-hiding-after-criticising-army-chief-and-government-on-facebook-live-86043095e362; www.facebook.com/drkanaksarwarbd/videos/286106049170265; www. facebook.com/drkanaksarwarbd/videos/সাক্ষাৎকার-দেয়ায়-জেনারেল-সারওয়ার্দীকে-প্রাণনাশের-হুমকি/ 984030782047672/; www.justnewsbd.com/en/ special-report/news/10461 Lt Gen Sarwardy in hiding after criticising govt and the army chief www.facebook.com/560237674/videos/10157699847582675/
Both S K Sinha and Hasan Sarwardy used to be pro-Hasina, who is a fascist to the core, worse than a she-feraoun, a rogue heiress to her father, who, according to Awami leader Abdul Malek Ukil, was a he-feraoun. Now with the change of their mind and position, both of them belong to anti-Hasina boat, which, like Noah's Ark, is expected to be one of rescue and survival, renewal and regeneration. Acting like a horrible she-hyena, Hasina, according to Matiur Rahman Rentu's classic Amar Fashi Chai, wanted to have the great political phenomenon of Bangladesh, Begum KhaledaZia, drowned in the river Dharla in north Bengal. Traitor Ghaseti Begum of the palace coup during the Battle of Plassey is believed to have been drowned in the Buriganga (on the way to Murshidabad from Jinjira palace Dhaka by order of Mir Miron, son of Mir Jafar). It was by order of Miron that Mohammadi Beg killed the young Nawab Mirza Mohammad Sirajuddowla of Bengal, who was caught by traitor Danesh Fakir while fleeing away from Murshidabad by a boat. The wise and mysterious sage Hazrat Khidir (AS) caused a boat to sink because it was carrying evil people. For Rentu's immortal book, click:: http://amarfashichai.blogspot.co.uk (English); http://docshare01.docshare.tips/files/2977/29771574.pdf (in English); https://mazams.weebly.com/uploads/4/8/2/6/48260335/amar_fashi_chai_bangla.pdf (Bengali); http://amarfashichai.blogspot.co.uk/2013/07/amar-fashi-chai-by-motiur-rahmanrentu.html (Bengali). Also, see: www.ittefaq.com.bd/national/168210/চৌধুরী-হাসান-সারওয়ার্দী-সেনাবাহিনী-সম্পর্কে-মিথ্যাচার-করেছেন--আইএসপিআর

[32] https://youtu.be/fLpz5xvPf40; https://youtu.be/e76XmGPNBJU; https://youtu.be/WKR69ZwMJk4; www.youtube.com / watch?v = NZyfqRhnDIM; https://youtu.be/e1XTOU3zbY8; www.youtube.com/watch?v=hBVYSPOBnGA; www.youtube.com/watch?v=GSZZJNpPeTk

[33] http://dhakadigest.net/en/2014/01/bangladesh-on-the-march-to-authoritarianism/

[34] www.justnewsbd.com/interview/news/29057;

https://youtu.be/KEsi6kDvUX8;
www.youtube.com/watch?v=KEsi6kDvUX8&feature=youtu.be

[35] www.youtube.com/watch?v=PaGZq_VVQcM&feature=share&fbclid; Dr Taj Hashmi and Dr Asif Nazrul https://m.facebook.com/story.php?story_fbid=3256701811117339&id=100003326573022; www.facebook.com/drkanaksarwarbd/videos/1950205411769968; www.youtube.com/watch?v=mmf6dsjxqM8 "Face to Face with Dr Taj Hashmi"; https://ummid.com/news/2020/august/13.08.2020/china-has-replaced-india-in-bangladesh-expert.html; https://amardesh.co.uk/যারা-মনে-করেন-শেখ-হাসিনার/https://m.facebook.com / story .php? story_fbid=673192869954624&id=87183732864&sfnsn=wa&extid=L085hIucptRIaaz7&d=w&vh=e

[36] https://medium.com/netranews / new-uk-government-sanctions-regime-could-target-bangladesh-government-and-law-enforcement-d7a9aa3117e by David Bergman

[37] Mahmudur Rahman, *The Political History of Muslim Bengal: An Unfinished Battle of Faith* (UK: Cambridge Scholars Publishing, 2018), p. *xix*, xvii. Watch him speak: https://youtu.be/N0XPw9mPBLw Also Mahmudur Rahman and Asafuddowla, another great son of the soil: https://youtu.be/v9Zlv9gRl5Q; https://amardesh.co.uk/প্রবাসে-আমার-দেশ-এর-নব-অধ্/ ;

chintaa.com/index.php/chinta/showAerticle/445/ফরহাদ-মজহার/মাহমুদুর-রহমান-ও-'বাঙালি-মুসলমান'/bangla

www.dailynayadiganta.com/ampproject/miscellaneous/335940/সবচেয়ে-নির্ভীক-এবং-দৃঢ়-প্রতিরোধের-সম্মুখ-ফ্রন্টের-সৈনিক-মাহমুদুর-রহমান-ফরহাদ-মজহার

[38] https://bangla.bdnews24.com/politics/article636286.bdnews; https://probasnews24.com/2015/05/29/7364/; www.amadershomoy.com/bn/2018/06/09/571362.htm; www.facebook.com/230571253700625/photos/প্রধানমন্ত্রীর-আপ্যায়ন-খরচ-৮০-লাখ-থেকে-বেড়ে-৭-কোটি-৮০-লাখ-টাকা-একদিনেই-ব্যয়-হ/447664795324602/

[39] https://youtu.be/gtqqXlgu16I (Syeda Papia on Awami Hasina corruption); www.youtube.com/watch?v=VWYcDlcKWM8 (Syeda Papia); https://youtu.be/73zEUYgb3zU (Syeda Papia)

[40] www.jugantor.com/politics/bnp/312157/ করোনার-ভয়াবহ-পরিস্থিতির-দায়দায়িত্ব-সরকারকেই-বহন-করতে-হবে-ফখরুল; www.dailynayadiganta.com/politics/505663/ করোনায়-উদ্ভূত-পরিস্থিতির-দায়-সরকারের-মির্জা-ফখরুল; www.dailynayadiganta. com/politics/513172/দুর্নীতির-মাধ্যমে-স্বাস্থ্য-ব্যবস্থা-ভেঙ্গে-দিয়েছে-সরকার-ফখরুল

[41] www.dailynayadiganta.com / last-page/499720 / সঙ্কট-মোকাবেলায়-জাতীয়-পুনর্গঠন-কমিটি-করুন

[42] In a way, it reminds one of Charles Kingsley's "O Mary, go and call the cattle home," translated by great Indian Bengali poet-politician Humayun Kabir as

"মেঘনায় বান" which begins as follows: "শোন মা আমিনা রেখে দেরে কাজ ত্বরা করে মাঠে চল/এল মেঘনায় জোয়ারের বেলা এখনি নামিবে ঢল!"

[43] www.forbes.com/sites/avivahwittenbergcox/2020/04/13/what-do-countries-with-the-best-coronavirus-reponses-have-in-common-women-leaders; https://unb.com.bd/category/Bangladesh/covid-19-hasinas-efforts-lauded-in-forbes-article/50567; www.dhakatribune.com/bangladesh/2020/04/26/forbes-hails-sheikh-hasina-for-fighting-covid-19; https://bangladeshpost.net/posts/sheikh-hasina-shows-talents-in-virus-response-forbes-extols-32041

[44] amardesh.co.uk/ডিজিটাল-ফ্যাসিবাদ/; amardesh.co.uk /আমার-দেশ-এর-উপর-ফ্যাসিবাদ/

[45] www.thedailystar.net / in-focus / news / free-speech - and-the-imperatives-democracy-1907053

[46] http:// aequitasreview.org/so-whats-the-point-of-journalism-then-by-sohrab-hassan/

[47] http://aequitasreview.org/1158-2/Bangladesh: Silencing Voices With The Digital Security Act

[48] https://asiatimes.com /2020 / 09 /hasinas-broken-promises-and-death-with-impunity/

[49] www.justnewsbd.com/national/news/3693 জ্যোতির্ময় জিয়া ; https://pl-pl.facebook.com/zia.communications/photos/a.217369255490665/228909994336591/?type=3; www.facebook.com/notes/ashraful-islam/জ্যোতিময়-জিয়া/602343083450070/

[50] Mahmudur Rahman, however, continues: "I further appeal to you all not to mention the name of Mahfuz Anam, an agent of Delhi, in any discussion about press freedom. People like him wholeheartedly assisted in the cultural aggression of Bangladesh by India. Mahfuz Anam is no less important to Delhi's political and intelligence establishment than Sheikh Hasina herself. Mahfuz Anam, Motiur Rahman, Anisuzzaman, etc. have played the Trojan horse in the process of Indian colonization of Bangladesh. Any reference of these people in the discussion about freedom of expression in Bangladesh is insulting to those persecuted journalists who actually fought for press freedom and against Indian hegemony."

[51] amardesh.co.uk/বাংলাদেশের-গণমাধ্যম-অন্ধ/

[52] *Kaowa* means the black bird crow; *murgi* means chicken; *ghora* means horse; and *ghadani* means *Ghadak Dalal Nirmul* Committee. All terms are used in derogatory sense to describe some Awami elements, who either said there were some kaowas in the AL, or supplied chicken to the Pakistani soldiers in 1971 or received horses from India as a bribe (Moeen U Ahmad) or have been demanding the hanging of Bangladeshi citizens who once supported Pakistan as their lawful and rightful political right. Hasina MP Badi is norious for his Yaba drug empire.

[53] Gandhi was out and out a racist. Retired Justice Markandey Katju of India called Gandhi a British agent who did great harm to India. Katju wrote, "Ever since

Gandhi came to India from South Africa in 1915 or so till his death in 1948, in almost every speech or article he would emphasize Hindu religious ideas, e.g., Ramrajjya, Go Rakkhya (cow protection), Brahmacharya (celibacy), Varnashram (Caste System), etc. Thus Gandhi wrote in "Young India" on 10.6.1921, "I am a Sanatani Hindu. I believe in varnashram dharma. I believe in protection of the cow." Thus, not only Gandhi was a racist, he was a staunch supporter of Caste system, which needs to be banned and abolished as it tramples human rights through slavery and apartheid. In 1903, when Gandhi was in South Africa, he wrote that white people there should be "the predominating race." He also said black people "are troublesome, very dirty and live like animals." In his selective racism, Gandhi fought for his own Indians in South Africa, not the South African Blacks. Also, it was not Gandhi's "non-violence" movement that brought forth the independence of the subcontinent. It was Subas Bose's Azad Fouz that threatened the British fall in the WWII. The crook Brits promised to the subcontinental leaders that if they supported the Allied/British Forces against the German-Japanese, they would get independence etc. So, it was the counterforce of Subas Bose that expedited Indian independence. Gandhi fought for his own kinds and for Indian national independence. His movement had nothing to do with the equal rights and dignity of all minority races. The movement was based solely on the self interests of Indian race and Indian nationalism. His movement was about the rights of local Indians. By no means, Gandhi introduced non-violent resistance to the world. It was there since 470 BCE i.e. from before Alexander the Great, born in 356 BCE. Please see the history section of the Wikipedia article, https://en.wikipedia.org/wiki/Nonviolent_resistance. Was Mahatma Gandhi a racist? www.bbc.com/news/world-asia-india-34265882; www.npr.org/2019/ 10/02/766083651 / gandhi-is-deeply-revered-but-his-attitudes-on-race-and-sex-are - under-scrutiny; https:// timesofindia.indiatimes.com / india/Justice-Markandey- Katju-Gandhi-a-British-agent/articleshow/46517634.cms; www. prothomalo.com / opinion / article / 1663320/ বর্ণবাদবিরোধী-আন্দোলন-এবং-ক্লাইভ-চার্চিল-ও-গান্ধী

[54]http://southasiajournal.net/was-sheikh-mujib-for-an-unbroken-pakistan-or-independent-bangladesh-sensational-revelation-about-mujib-in-pakistan-in-1971-%EF%BB%BF/. Also see: Sharmin Ahmad, *Tajuddin Ahmad: Neta O Pita* (2014). See Chapter 5: The Untold Truth About Sheikh Mujib's Independence Stance in 1971 and How He Brought Bangladesh to the Brink of Collapse to Invite August 15, in *Bangladesh: A Suffering People UnderState Terrorism* (2020). এ কে খন্দকার তাঁর এই বইয়ে কতকগুলো বিষয়ে আলোকপাত করেছেন, যা নিয়ে ইতিপূর্বে আলোচনা হলেও তাতে নতুন মাত্রা যোগ করবে। স্বাধীনতার ঘোষণা: 'ধ্বংসযজ্ঞ শুরু হওয়ার ঠিক আগে শেখ সাহেব ইপিআরের বেতারযন্ত্রের মাধ্যমে চট্টগ্রামের জহুর আহমেদ চৌধুরীর কাছে স্বাধীনতার ঘোষণা পাঠিয়েছিলেন। এই তথ্যটি মোটেই বিশ্বাসযোগ্য নয়।'(পৃ. ৫৭) জনাব খন্দকার এ বিষয়ে প্রবাসী সরকারের প্রধানমন্ত্রী তাজউদ্দীন আহমদেরও উদ্ধৃতি দিয়েছেন: 'একদিন আমি তাঁকে জিজ্ঞেস করেছিলাম "স্যার, বঙ্গবন্ধু গ্রেপ্তার হওয়ার আগে আপনি কি তাঁর কাছ থেকে কোনো নির্দেশনা পেয়েছিলেন?" উত্তরে তিনি বলেছিলেন, "না, আমি কোনো নির্দেশ পাইনি"(পৃ. ৪৩)।

www.prothomalo.com/opinion/column/ইতিহাসের-এক-আকরগ্রন্থ এ বিষয়ে আমাদেরকে প্রাথমিকভাবেই নির্ভর করতে হয়েছে বিদেশি সংবাদপত্রের প্রতিবেদক ও বিদেশি রাষ্ট্রের গোপন নথির ওপর। যুক্তরাষ্ট্রের পররাষ্ট্র দপ্তর এবং নিরাপত্তাবিষয়ক দলিল-দস্তাবেজ যদিও এই সাক্ষ্য দেয় যে ২৬ মার্চ শেখ মুজিব স্বাধীনতা ঘোষণা করেছিলেন—এর কোনো দলিল আমরা এখনো দেখিনি।

[55] As Zoglul Husain of the UK recounts: "মুজিবকে বঙ্গশত্রু উপাধি দিয়েছিলেন মতিয়া। তিনি মুজিবের চামড়া দিয়ে ডুগডুগি বাজাতে চেয়েছিলেন এবং তার চামড়া দিয়ে জুতা বানাতে চেয়েছিলেন। মুজিবকে হত্যার পর ইনু সেনা ট্যাংকে উঠে উল্লাসে অস্ত্র উঁচিয়ে গুলি ছুড়ে আনন্দ করেন। মুজিব আমলের সেনাপ্রধান শফিউল্লাহ বলেন, শেখ মুজিব হত্যার সাথে হাসিনার ফুফাতো ভাই শেখ সেলিমও জড়িত আছে। শাহরিয়ার কবির লেখেন, মুজিব আর বঙ্গবন্ধু নয়, এখন থেকে মুজিব জনশত্রু। কর্নেল তাহের বলেন, মুজিবের লাশ বঙ্গোপসাগরে নিক্ষেপ করতে, কারণ বাংলাদেশে তার কবর হলে আ'লীগ তা মাজার বানাবে। মেননের দল বিবৃতি দেয়, 'মুজিবের মৃত্যুতে জনগণ উল্লসিত। তার মৃত্যু কারো মনে সামান্যতম সমবেদনা বা দুঃখ জাগায়নি, জাগাতে পারে না।' ১৫ আগস্ট ১৯৭৫ সেনা সদস্যরা মুজিবের বাড়িতে আসলে মুজিব সেনাপ্রধান শফিউল্লাহ, রক্ষীবাহিনীর রাজনৈতিক প্রধান তোফায়েল সহ অনেককেই ফোন করেছিলেন, কেউ আসেন নি, কর্নেল জামিল ছাড়া, কর্নেল জামিল নিহত হন। শফিউল্লাহ মুজিবকে বলেছিলেন পাচিল টপকিয়ে পালিয়ে যেতে। ১৫ আগস্ট ১৯৭৫ সেনা-জনতার অভ্যুত্থানে মুজিবের মৃত্যু হলে সেদিন তার মাগফিরাত কামনা করার জন্য লোক খুঁজে পাওয়া যায় নি। তার স্পীকার আব্দুল মালেক উকিল লন্ডনে বলেন, দেশ ফেরাউনের হাত থেকে মুক্ত হয়েছে। সাবেক স্পীকার ও সাবেক বিদেশ মন্ত্রী হুমায়ুন রশিদ চৌধুরী পরবর্তীতে বলেন, একশবার মুজিবের ফাঁসী হলেও তার পাপ মুক্তি হবেনা। তার মৃতদেহ যখন সিঁড়িতে পড়েছিল তখন ফনি ভূষণ মজুমদার ও মনরঞ্জন ধর সহ তার ১৮ মন্ত্রীর ১০ জন এবং ৯ জন প্রতি-মন্ত্রীর ৮ জন মোশতাক মন্ত্রী সভায় যোগ দেন, বাকিদের মধ্যে মুজিবের ৪ মন্ত্রীদের কারাগারে পাঠানো হয়, ৩ জন বিদেশে ছিলেন। শপথ অনুষ্ঠান পরিচালনা করেন এইচ টি ইমাম। মুজিবের জানাজায় উপস্থিত ছিলেন ১৮ জন, হাসিনা পরে বিবিসিকে বলেন, ১০-১৮ জন। ইত্যাদি, ইত্যাদি।"

[56] www.bangladeshchronicle.net/index.php/2013/01/august-15-know- the-facts-not-fiction; http:// newsfrombangladesh.net / new/index.php ? option=com_wrapper & view = wrapper&Itemid= 542; http://defence.pk/threads/august-15-1975-and-august-15-2011-the-contrast. 125607.

[57] সূত্রঃ পূর্ব-পশ্চিম, দ্বিতীয় খন্ডঃ আনন্দ পাবলিশার্স ০ঃ কলকাতা-৯, পৃষ্ঠা. ৫৭০

[58] See my *Bangladesh: Political and Literary Reflections on a Divided Country*, Chapter 10, "The Politics of the Past and the Honorifics of Titles," pp. 355-356; also see my *Bangladesh Divided: Political and Literary Reflections on a Corrupt Police and Prison State*, Chapter 5, "Sheikh hasina's egotistical and egregious personalization," pp. 114-116. Also see, www.bd-pratidin.com/first-page/2017/03/24/2173958; www.bd-pratidin.com/first-page/2016/03/27/134978; www.bd-pratidin.com/first page/2017/02/15/207991;www.amadershomoy.biz/beta/2017/02/25/818616; www.facebook.com/photo.php?fbid=10155212333839796& set=a.403462897 95.48054.632289795&type=3&theater;www.roshikhakim.com/2016/12/2010; www.thedailystar.net/parasites-feast-on-ruling-al-49542; http://dailyasianage. com / news/3383 / opportunists-belittling-mujib-floating-organizations-quader. Also add to the list: Bangabandhu Karnaphuli Tunnel Chittagong; Bangabandhu Sheikh Mujib University Kishoreganj; Sheikh Hasina International Cricket

Stadium; Sheikh Hasina University Netrakona; Sheikh Hasina Airport Road Chittagong. https://youtu.be/tW6iNB8iwjw Allama Sayedee on everything named after Bangabandhu.

[59] Retired Major Sayeed Iskandar was thought to be an indirect accomplice in 1/11 of 2007. Please see:

:https://defence.pk/pdf/threads/bangladeshis-demand-trial-of-gen-retd-moeen-u-ahmed.28297/page-11

The source of the above article is: General Moeen Purge 1/11 Key Players In Power Struggle To Regain Supremacy

By Saleem Samad, https://www.countercurrents.org/samad110608.htm (Saleem Samad is believed to be an operative of RAW. 1/11 was a conspiracy hatched by RAW). It is said that Moeen (a batch mate of Iskandar) would visit Iskandar almost daily and begged to be made the next Army Chief. And he became, superseding a number of seniors and deserving candidates. General Masud and Iskandar were Brothers-in-law. Masud is said to have helped Iskandar to escape to the US after the 1/11, later returned to die of cancer or something. It is likely the other members of the so called Khalifas may have taken advantage of Iskandar's influence. Iskandar may or may not have been a party to 1/11, but his beneficiaries went against him or his sister PM Khaleda. Major Iskandar died from lung cancer on 23 September 2012 in New York. He was buried in Banani military graveyard.

[60] See Chapter 6, "The Chiefs and Their *Uddinization* of the 2006–2008 Caretaker Government," pp. 215-241, in *Bangladesh: Political and Literary Reflections on a Divided Country*. The historic parallel is drawn specifically on p. 217 and Note#7.

[61] www.facebook.com/BNPPublicMediaOfficial/posts/367922267933029?__tn__=K-R; https://id-id.facebook.com / VOBIL / posts/737600223466431 ; amardesh.co.uk/ বাংলাদেশ-কি-হায়দারাবাদের/amardesh.co.uk/ডিজিটাল-ফ্যাসিবাদ/

Appendix A

(Authentic Counter Narrative to the Disturbingly Distorting Hasina-Awami Story)

Q M Jalal Khan

Apart from many other volumes (see the list of more than two hundred books in Appendix J in my *Bangladesh Divided: Political and Literary Reflections on a Corrupt Police and Prison State* (Peter Lang, 2019, p. 475), mention may be made of the following:

1. Matiur Rahman Rentu, আমার ফাঁসী চাই: Amar Fashi Chai/ I Want/Wish to be Hanged/Executed (1999), http://amarfashichai. blogspot.co.uk (in English);

    http://docshare01.docshare.tips / files / 2977 / 29771574.pdf (in English);

    https://mazams.weebly.com/uploads/4/8/2/6/48260335/amar_fashi_chai_bangla.pdf (in Bangla);

    http://amarfashichai.blogspot.co.uk/2013/07/amar-fashi-chai-by-motiur-rahmanrentu.html (in English).

    Banned by Hasina, this book by her once very close aide for many years, from 1981-1997, is a detailed description of the dubious, diabolical and notorious conduct and activities she was engaged in. Rentu's wife also was Hasina's close household aide for about ten years.

2. Air Vice Marshall A K Khandoker, ১৯৭১: ভেতরে বাইরে (Prothoma Prokashon, 2014)

3. মেজর জেনারেল মইনুল হোসেন চৌধুরী (অবঃ) বীরবিক্রম, 'এক জেনারেলের নীরব সাক্ষ্যঃ স্বাধীনতার প্রথম দশক' (Mowla Brothers, 2000)

4. Dr Pinaki Bhattacharya, "স্বাধীনতা উত্তর বাংলাদেশ" /Post Liberation Bangladesh, Volume I (Horoppa UK http://kck.st/3i22eLJ

_____, মুক্তিযুদ্ধের বয়ানে ইসলাম by পিনাকী ভট্টাচার্য (Guardian Publications, Dhaka)

_____, ইতিহাসের ধুলোকালি by পিনাকী ভট্টাচার্য (Guardian Publications, Dhaka)

5. Dr Khalifa Malik, *Bangladesher Rajniti: Mookh* O Mookhosh (Politics of Bangladesh: The Face and The Mask (Gyan Bitarani, Dhaka, 2003)

_____, *Challenges in Bangladesh Politics* (Adorn Publications, Dhaka, 2005)

_____, *War on Terror--A pretext for new colonization* (2005)

_____, Over fifty articles published in various outlets and countless speeches in various and TV talk shows, mostly in London.

6. Shafik Rehman (a well-known writer, journalist and media personality, who is a victim of the regime's false and fictitious cases against him) wrote many books of which the following deserve a mention: 1. সোনার হরিণ/ Golden Deer (1994); 2. গণতন্ত্র/Democracy (1999); 3. Democratic Leader Khaleda Zia (2012, in English); 4. সংগ্রামী নেত্রী খালেদা জিয়া (2012, Bengali version of the above); 5. Statesman Ziaur Rahman (2012, in English); 6. রাষ্ট্রনায়ক জিয়াউর রহমান (2012, in Bengali but different from the above); 7. নেড়িকুকুরের কাণ্ড/Slum Dog's Mess (2012); 8. নেড়িকুকুরের কীর্তি/Slum Dog's Misdeeds (2012); 9. বিদ্ধস্ত দেশ বিপন্ন মানুষ/ Devastated Country: People in Danger (2012); 10. We Revolt (2012); 11. চট্টগ্রাম পোলো গ্রাউন্ড লুঠন/Chittagong Polo Ground Loot (2015); 12. মৃত্যুদণ্ড: দেশে বিদেশে যুগে যুগে/ Death Sentence at Home and Abroad Throughout the Ages (2015)

7. Mahmudur Rahman (one of the best and most outspoken critics and columnists and one of the most tortured victims of the fascist Awami regime), *The Political History of Muslim Bengal: An unfinished battle of faith* (2018). www.cambridgescholars.com/ download/sample/65022 For all his more than ten books, visit: www.rokomari.com/book/author/5442/   মাহমুদুর-রহমান- (সাংবাদিক).

8. For Mahmudur Rahman speaking, watch:

https://youtu.be/rNBnSdlRYqE

www.youtube.com/watch?v=iI7nlfCx_N8;
www.youtube.com/watch?v=1DKBOIfiQMU;
www.youtube.com/watch?v=mDb56yhgTC0;
www.youtube.com/watch?v=mDb56yhgTC0;
www.youtube.com/watch?v=UcyGjlYL_zg;

www.youtube.com/watch?v=4cAdlHFsInQ;

www.youtube.com/watch?v=N9etWoRmj3I;

https://youtu.be/N0XPw9mPBLw;

https://youtu.be/0vd6OiToUdg

https://youtu.be/iQ0E6RKArsg

https://youtu.be/SEW3DIrwDpM

https://m.facebook.com/story.php?story_fbid=2814642208637655&id=100002757110915;

chintaa.com/index.php/chinta/showAerticle/445/ফরহাদ-মজহার/মাহমুদুর-রহমান-ও-'বাঙালি-মুসলমান'/bangla;

www.dailynayadiganta.com/ampproject/miscellaneous/335940/সব চেয়ে-নির্ভীক-এবং-দৃঢ়-প্রতিরোধের-সম্মুখ-ফ্রন্টের-সৈনিক-মাহমুদুর-রহমান-ফরহাদ-মজহার

9. For some of Mahmudur Rahman's recent articles, see:

"Islamophobia, Neo-BAKSAL Fascism, and Freedom Movement in Bangladesh," in *Bangladesh: A Suffering People Under State Terrorism* (Peter Lang, 2020, pp. 43-57).

http:// aequitasreview.org / sino-india-conflict-part-of-larger-geopolitics-by-mahmudur-rahman/

http:// aequitasreview.org / courting-the-fascist-in-bangladesh-by-mahmudur-rahman/

All his great editorials in Amar Desh (for example, amardesh.co.uk/প্রবাসে-আমার-দেশ-এর-নব-অধ্য/; amardesh.co.uk/ব্যক্তি-পূজার-অশ্লীলতা/);

amardesh.co.uk/শেখ-হাসিনার-মুনাফেকি-বচন/

10. Justice S K Sinha, *A Broken Dream*, jagaron.com/wp-content/uploads/2018/09/A-Broken-Dream_-Rule-of-Law-Human-Rights-Justice-Surendra-Kumar-Sinha.pdf;

http://southasiajournal.net / book-review-a-broken-dream-rule-of-law-human-rights-and-democracy-by-chief-justice-surendra-kumar-sinha/

Former Chief Justice Sinha, initially and highly controversially pro-Hasina, was ousted by the fascist Hasina just for two reasons: (1) for challenging her wishes to have the judiciary subject/accountable to her illegal parliament so that she could remove any judges/justices at will; (2) for indirectly claiming that her father Sheikh Mujib was not the only one behind the creation and independence of Bangladesh and that he was just one of the founding fathers like those of the USA; and for campaigning for the freedom of the judiciary.

11. Sabria Chowdhury Balland (ed), *Bangladesh: A Suffering People Under State Terrorism* (2020)

12. Col Rashed Chowdhury, *Facts, Not Fiction: Bangladesh in Perspective* (2018)

13. Dr Ali Riaz, *Voting in a Hybrid Regime Explaining the 2018 Bangladeshi Election* (2019)

14. Dr Q M Jalal Khan, *Bangladesh: Political and Literary Reflections on a Divided Country* (2018)

15. Dr Q M Jalal Khan, *Bangladesh Divided: Political and Literary Reflections on a Corrupt Police and Prison State* (2019)

16. Barrister MBI Munshi (ed), *The India Doctrine (1947-2007): A Contemporary Study on Indian Hegemony and Geo-Strategic Perspectives on South Asia* (2007, 2012)

17. Isha Khan, *RAW: An Instrument of Indian Hegemony: India's Intelligence Operations Unveiled* (2012):

    www.amazon.ca/RAW-Instrument-Hegemony-Intelligence-Operations/dp/3659239682;

    _____, http://themoroccantimes.com/2014/08/8421/indias-raw-operations-south-asian-countries

    _____, www.countercurrents.org/khan131007.htm RAW: An Instrument Of Indian Imperialism

18. Abu Rushd, *RAW in Bangladesh: Portrait of an Aggressive Intelligence* (2005)

19. Senior Journalist Mohammad Zainal Abedin

    In addition to several hundreds of his popular articles published in national and local dailies since the 1960s, some of his books are as follows:

    এক নদী রক্ত (A River of Blood, a play, 1971)

    রাজনীতিতে শ্রেনী সংকট (Class Crisis in Politics, 1973)

    জিয়া হত্যার নেপথ্যে (Secrets Behind the Killing of Zia, 1988)

India Needs Veto Power (1993)

RAW and Bangladesh (1995) won an award from London Institute of South Asia in 2007

পার্বত্য চট্টগ্রাম: স্বরূপ সন্ধান (*CHT: In Search of Its Own Reality* (1997)

The Chittagong Hill Tracts: A Victim of Indian Intervention (2003)

Human Rights Violation in CHT: Myth & Reality (2005)

Naga--A Cry for Freedom (2007)

BDR Massacre: Target Bangladesh (2009), and

ভারতীয় ধর্মনিরপেক্ষতার আসল চেহারা (*True Face of Indian Secularism*, 2011).

20. Dr Lawrence Ziring, *Bangladesh: From Mujib to Ershad, An Interpretive Study,* University Press Limited, Dhaka, 1992.
21. Kai Kaus, ইতিহাসের ছিন্নপত্র/Torn Leaves of History: From Colonial Rule to Independence Movement (Guardian Publications, Dhaka, 2020) www.rokomari.com/ book / 202698 / itihasher-chinnopotro--1st-part
22. একজন জিয়া by হেদায়েত হোসাইন মোরশেদ (1988)
23. S. Abdul Hakim, *Begum Khaleda Zia of Bangladesh: A Political Biography* (1992)
24. তারেক রহমান : অপেক্ষায় বাংলাদেশ by প্রফেসর ড. এমাজউদ্দীন আহমদ, ed. (2010)
25. জ্যোতির্ময় জিয়া এবং কালো মেঘের দল/Luminous Zia and the Black Clouds (2011) by Abdul Hye Sikder
26. রাষ্ট্রনায়ক জিয়া by ড. আবদুল লতিফ মাসুম (2012)
27. তারেক রহমান : তৃণমূল রাজনীতির প্রবক্তা by ড. কে. এ. এম. শাহাদত হোসেন মণ্ডল (2013)
28. Author, journalist Mahfuz Ullah, *Begum Khaleda Zia—Her Life, Her Story* (2018)

    _____, *President Zia of Bangladesh: A Political Biography* (2016)
29. Dr Emajuddin Ahmed and Abdul Hye Sikder (eds), 'খালেদা জিয়া-তৃতীয় বিশ্বের কণ্ঠস্বর' (2019)
30. Dr Q M Jalal Khan and Dr K M A Malik (eds), *Begum Khaleda Zia: Portrait of A People's Leader* of Bangladesh (November 2020)
31. Dr Q M Jalal Khan, et al (ed), India's Hegemonic Domination of Bangladesh

Appendix B

(Corruption and Awami BAKSAL Propaganda Development Under the Regime)

Q M Jalal Khan

For worse than Covid-19 virus--corruption, repression, rape, dengue, flood, and Indian Hindu RAW Control of Muslim Bangladesh under Hasina --, see:

(1) Chapter 2: Bangladesh Dented, Demoted and Demented Under Sheikh Hasina's Digital Carnival of Corruption and Ruthless Repression in my *Bangladesh Divided: Political and Literary Reflections on a Police and Prison State* (New York: Peter Lang, 2019), pp. 33-60;

(2) Chapter 2: Democracy and Development: Development with Corruption and Without Democracy, in my *Bangladesh: Political and Literary Reflections on a Divided Country* (New York: Peter Lang, 2018), pp. 55-96; and,

(3) Chapter 12: Sheikh Hasina's Brutal BNP-Phobia and Her Scandalous "Midnight" Power Grab through Vampire Vote Dacoity and Villainous S/Election Rigging with an All-Time High Record of Humongous White-Collar Corruption, pp. 145-216; and **all Appendices (A to I)**, in Sabria Chowdhury Balland (ed), *Bangladesh: A Suffering People Under State Terrorism* (New York: Peter Lang, April 2020). Appendix F (Corruption and Development), Appendix C (Top Awami Family) and Appendix I (Gambling and Casino).

Also visit the following as only some of the examples in context during the first few months of 2020:

"এই ষড়যন্ত্রের মূল ভিত্তি দুর্নীতি। ৭ হাজার কোটি টাকা দিয়ে যে পদ্মা ব্রিজ হতো সেটা ৫০ হাজার কোটিতে পৌঁছেছে। এই টাকা কোথায় যাবে, এর হাজারটা প্রমান আছে।" Dr Zafrullah Chowdhury শনিবার (৫ ডিসেম্বর) জাতীয় প্রেস ক্লাব

amardesh.co.uk/৭-বছরে-দেশ-থেকে-পাচার-চার-ল/ চার লাখ কোটি টাকা

amardesh.co.uk/২৩৬-কোটি-টাকা-পাচারের-অভি/

amardesh.co.uk/চাল-তেলের-বাজারেও-লুটপাট/ লুটপাটে চ্যাম্পিয়ন আওয়ামী সিন্ডিকেট

bonikbarta.net/home/news_description/241473/শতকোটি-টাকার-'ব্যর্থ'-প্রকল্প-শেষে-৫৫০-কোটি-টাকার-নতুন-প্রস্তাব-

amardesh.co.uk/এক-বছরে-ব্যাংক-ও-আর্থিক-প/

amardesh.co.uk/কক্সবাজারে-৭০-প্রকল্পে-ব/ ব্যাপক দুর্নীতির অভিযোগ

www.newagebd.net/article/115003/suffering-grows-as-crossing-padma-becomes-a-hurdle

amardesh.co.uk/লুটপাট-আর-বাহাদুরিতে-দশক/

www.prothomalo.com/opinion/editorial/দুর্নীতি-সব-মাত্রা-ছাড়িয়েছে

www.facebook.com/2106168432806604/posts/3214304091993027/?vh=e&d=n (Mina Farah and Pinaki Bhattacharya on Bangladesh's corruption and capitulation to India)

https://youtu.be/8G8kFI2UN40 (Mina Farah on Indian control of Bangladesh, BAL corruption, weaknesses of the ineffective Mirzas in the BNP and the strength of JI)

https://youtu.be/a44EGY4Dih0 Al Jazeera video on the Hasina regime's scandalous covid-19 corruption

www.somoynews.tv/pages/details/235810/খিচুড়ি-রান্না-শিখতে-বিদেশে-যাবেন-এক-হাজার-সরকারি-কর্মকর্তা www.youtube.com/watch?v=IwPK0LXjufk

http://aequitasreview.org/a-tale-of-misplaced-priorities-by-ali-riaz/

www.youtube.com/watch?v=a44EGY4Dih0&feature=youtu.be (all corruption video)

www.jugantor.com / todays-paper / first-page / 319688/সুইস-ব্যাংকে-বাংলাদেশিদের-টাকার-পাহাড়

www.thedailystar.net/frontpage/news/swiss-banks-deposits-bd-nationals-drop-1920613

www.newagebd.net/article / 109432 / tk-5392cr-bangladeshi-deposits-in-swiss-banks

www.jugantor.com/todays-paper/first-page/319690/দুর্নীতির-টাকাই-পাচার-হয়ে-সুইস-ব্যাংকে

www.newagebd.net/article/109455/coronavirus-exposes-al-dev-myth-bnp-mps

www.ittefaq.com.bd/wholecountry/167335/১৯-করোনা-রোগীর-চিকিৎসায়-৫-কোটি-৪১-লাখ-টাকা-বিল-দাখিল

Appendix B

www.banglanews24.com / international / news / bd / 800577.details বাংলাদেশে করোনার জাল সনদের রমরমা ব্যবসা: নিউ ইয়র্ক টাইমস

www.jaijaidinbd.com/todays-paper / first-page / 100583/১০-বছরে-ধনী-বাড়ার-শীর্ষে-বাংলাদেশ;

www.ittefaq.com.bd/national / 160992 / বাংলাদেশে-কোটিপতির-সংখ্যা-৮৪-হাজার;

www.jugantor.com/todays-paper/first-page/319983/গোপনে-বিদেশে-টাকা-যাচ্ছে-পাঁচ-কারণে-প্রভাবশালীরা-জড়িত-বাড়ছে-অর্থ-পাচার

www.dailynayadiganta.com/last-page/509661/দুর্নীতিগ্রস্ত-জনপ্রতিনিধিদের-তালিকা-দীর্ঘ-হচ্ছে

www.bd-pratidin.com/first-page/2020/06/14/538657 অর্থ পাচারের শীর্ষে গার্মেন্ট মালিকরা

www.bbc.com/bengali/news-47037982 অর্থ পাচার: বাংলাদেশ থেকে ৫০ হাজার কোটি টাকা বিদেশে পাচার হলো যেভাবে

www.kalerkantho.com/online/national/2020/07/14/934603একটি বাতি ৯৮ হাজার টাকা, খাল-নর্দমা-সড়ক ধরলেই চার কোটি!

www.bbc.com/bengali/news-42562225 বিদেশ থেকে যেভাবে বাংলাদেশের বিকাশ ব্যবহার করে অর্থ পাচার হচ্ছে

www.prothomalo.com/opinion/article/1621298/বাংলাদেশের-সর্বনাশ-হয়ে-গেছে

www.youtube.com/watch?v=NmiDjdMsvK4 গোপনে সেই আইন সংশোধন ,বড় বড় দুর্নীতি ধামাচাপার স্বার্থে !

http://bangladeshchronicle.net/mafia-syndicate-controls-bangladesh-bank/

www.newagebd.net/article/110438/13-banks-face-tk-25901-crore-capital-shortfall

www.thedailystar.net / bangla / শীর্ষ-খবর / পারিবারিক-ও-ব্যবসায়িক-সিন্ডিকেটের-দৌরাত্ম্যে-ব্যাংকিং-খাত-খাদের-কিনারায়-টিআইবি-174669

www.thedailystar.net/frontpage/news/swindle-pk-halder-so-far-it-tk-10200cr-1968125 Swindle by PK Halder: So far, it is Tk 10,200cr or $120.36 crore stolen by Prashanta Kumar Halder alias PK Halder

www.kalerkantho.com/print-edition/first-page/2020/09/25/959002 ডাক বিভাগের মহাপরিচালক (ডিজি) সুধাংশু শেখর ভদ্র , ডাক বিভাগের প্রায় ৫৪১ কোটি টাকা প্রাক্কলিত ব্যয়ের একটি প্রকল্পের ১৬০ কোটি টাকার কোনো হদিস পাওয়া যায়নি। প্রকল্পের ৩৮০ কোটি ৬৫ লাখ টাকা ব্যয়ের হিসাব পাওয়া গেলেও সেই টাকায় কেনা সরঞ্জাম অব্যবহৃত অবস্থায় পড়ে আছে৷

www.dailynayadiganta.com / miscellaneous / 509505 / দুর্নীতি-খেয়ে-ফেলছে-স্বাস্থ্যখাতকে

www.dailynayadiganta.com/miscellaneous / 529906 / স্বাস্থ্যের-সাবেক-ডিজির-গাড়ি-চালক-শত-কোটি-টাকার-মালিক

www.thedailystar.net/frontpage/news/dghs-official-wife-siphoned-tk-40cr-1964709

www.ittefaq.com.bd/national/164281/পিয়নের-ব্যাংক-অ্যাকাউন্টে-৩০-কোটি-টাকা

www.jugantor.com/country-news/328808/রিকশাচালক-থেকে-শতকোটি-টাকার-মালিক-এখলাছ-খান

www.pbc24.com/news/লেখক/উন্নয়নের-জোয়ার-ও-দুর্নীতি/ ;

www.pbc24.com/news/লেখক/দেশ-কী-হারিয়ে-যাবে-১-মোহাম/;

www.pbc24.com/news/লেখক/দেশ-কী-হারিয়ে-যাবে-২/;

www.prothomalo.com/economy/article/1661561/লাসভেগাসসহ-বড়-বড়-শহরে-সিকদার-পরিবারের-বিপুল-সম্পদ; https://youtu.be/A5_5dgQH2_Q "ট্রাক ড্রাইভার থেকে উথান জয়নুল শিকদারের; এই ১০ বছরেই সম্পদের পাহাড় বাড়তে শুরু করে;"

https://youtu.be/zNeRf5VcbBs Sikder family পেছনে কারা ? এটা কীভাবে সম্ভব?

https://youtu.be/KJZmCuGzGss "স্বাস্থ্যমন্ত্রী নাসিম-পুত্র 'তমালের' যুক্তরাষ্ট্রে মিলিয়ন ডলারের সম্পদ; উৎস কি?"

https://youtu.be/II5RNDXajrw নাসিম সাহেবের মৃত্যুতে এ কেমন উল্লাস! উনি কি স্বাস্থ্য অপরাধী ছিলেন??

www.youtube.com/watch?v=muwNggOC-3A ১৩ লাখ কোটি টাকা হাওয়া! মানবদেহ রপ্তানী ও মাননীয় পাচারকারী দম্পতি।

www.bd-pratidin.com/first-page/2020/08/27/560665 দেশের স্বাস্থ্য ব্যবস্থা ভেঙে পড়েছে

www.jugantor.com/todays-paper/sub-editorial/311230/ব্যাংকিং-খাতে-কোনো-কিছুই-আর-অবিশ্বাস্য-নয়

https://en.prothomalo.com/opinion/editorial/how-to-hide-such-shame MP Papul

www.newagebd.net/article/110699/human-trafficking-case-filed-against-lawmaker-papul

www.newagebd.net/article/109405/bangladeshi-mp-shahid-lands-in-kuwait-jail

www.newagebd.net/article/109007/kuwait-to-freeze-5-million-kd-of-mp-shahid The amount is equivalent to about 138 crore in Bangladeshi taka.

www.jugantor.com/national/others/317520/লস-অ্যাঞ্জেলেসে-কনস্যুলেট-ভবন-কেনায়-দুর্নীতি-ব্যবস্থা-নিতে-নোটিশ

https://asiatimes.com/2020/06/bangladesh-and-covid-19-disaster-within-a-disaster/

www.ittefaq.com.bd/national/161069/করোনায়-নতুন-করে-দরিদ্র-হলো-১-কোটি-৬৪-লাখ-মানুষ-বিআইডিএস

www.kalerkantho.com / online / country-news / 2020 / 03 / 03/881363 ঠাকুরগাঁও সুগারমিলে দুর্নীতি চার কোটি টাকার গাড়ির ক্রয়মূল্য দেখানো হয়েছে ৯০ কোটি!

www.facebook.com/20party/photos/a.712671395450115/3264507123599850/?type=3 সুপ্রিমকোর্টে বিচারকের নৈতিক চরিত্র ও স্মরণীয় স্মৃতি

https:// ca.finance.yahoo.com/photos / worlds-worst-countries-for-child-labor-082 701117/shipyard-workers-including-children-working-120234235.htm

www.ittefaq.com.bd / wholecountry / 153696 / জীবিত-আতরজানকে-মৃত-দেখিয়ে-চালের-তালিকা-থেকে-নাম-কাটলেন-ইউপি-সদস্য%C2%A0

www.facebook.com/jiblurahman78/posts/992946227384107/ ১৯৭৪ এর দুর্ভিক্ষ ও অর্থমন্ত্রী তাজউদ্দিনের বিদায়

www.amadershomoy.com/bn/2020/02/17/1083407.html গরু কচুরিপানা খেতে পারলে আমরা কেন পারবো না!' | M A Mannan | Cow Eats Water Hyacinth, Why Not Man? www.youtube.com/watch?v=7FWWVngynyw

www.jugantor.com / country-news / 339035 / গরিবের-ভাতার-দেড়-কোটি-টাকা-মেম্বারচেয়ারম্যানের-পকেটে

www.jugantor.com/country-news/339911 / বিদ্যুৎ-সংযোগ-নেই-তবু-বৃদ্ধার-১-লাখ-১৪-হাজার-টাকা-বিল

www.banglainsider.com/bangladesh/56129/ব্যর্থতা-ঢাকতে-ষড়যন্ত্র-তত্ত্ব

www.thedailystar.net/bangla / শীর্ষ-খবর / ১৪-শতাংশ-মানুষের-ঘরে-খাবার-নেই-চরম-দারিদ্র্য-বেড়েছে-৬০-শতাংশ-ব্র্যাক-143569

www.newagebd.net/article / 113317 / 70pc-bangladeshi-returnee-migrants-still-unemployed-iom

www.dailynayadiganta.com/first-page/536019/-কর্মসংস্থান-নেই-দারিদ্র্যসীমার-নিচে-নেমে-যাচ্ছে-অনেক-মানুষ

আওয়ামীলীগের ভোট চুরি করছে ভিডিও ফাঁস ⬤ নির্বাচনের নামে সত্যিকারের কি হচ্ছে এদেশে !

http://southasiajournal.net/bangladesh-mujib-borso-coronavirus-and-real-mujib/

www.facebook.com/notes/kai-kaus/চেতনায়-লুটপাট-০১/977979805993195/

www.facebook.com/notes/kai-kaus/চেতনায়-লুটপাট-০২/978706462587196/

www.facebook.com/notes/kai-kaus/চেতনায়-লুটপাট-০৩/979546735836502/

www.facebook.com/notes/kai-kaus/চেতনায়-লুটপাট-০৪/980346775756498/

www.facebook.com/notes/kai-kaus/ছফানামা/997993110658531/

www.somoynews.tv/pages/details/231823 রেললাইনে পাথরে বদলে ইটের খোয়া!

www.youtube.com/watch?v=b0dX0SznFyo বৃষ্টিতে ভেসে গেল উদ্বোধনের অপেক্ষায় Awami সেতু

www.bhorerkagoj.com/2020/06/14/খালে-দেয়াল-নিমার্ণ-দেখার/

www.dailyamaderkhobor.com/মানিকগঞ্জ-সিংগাইর-খাল-দখ/

www.jugantor.com/todays-paper/first-page/215732/হবিগঞ্জে-সায়হাম-গ্রুপের-দখল-বাণিজ্য-নদী-দখল-করে-উপজেলা-চেয়ারম্যানের-মার্কেট

www.prothomalo.com/bangladesh / district / নালাও-নেই-তবু-রাস্তা-খুঁড়ে-হচ্ছে-দুটি-কালভার্ট

www.dailynayadiganta.com / economics / 510881 / ১২১-উন্নয়ন-প্রকল্পে-ঘুমিয়েই-বছর-পার

www.jugantor.com/todays-paper / last-page / 323410 / ঝুঁকির-মুখে-হাজার-কোটি-টাকার-উন্নয়ন-কর্মকাণ্ড

www.jugantor.com/todays-paper/last-page/327182/নামমাত্র-কাজ-দেখিয়ে-প্রধানমন্ত্রীর-বিশেষ-প্রকল্পের-টাকা-নয়ছয়

www.mzamin.com/article.php?mzamin=235446 অন্যকে দিয়ে নিজের বোর্ড পরীক্ষা দেয়ার অভিযোগে আলোচনায় আসা সংসদ সদস্য তামান্না নুসরাত বুবলি এবার আলোচনায় এলেন কোটি টাকার গাড়ি কিনে

www.jugantor.com/country-news / 330584 / জালিয়াতিতে-বেদখল-হচ্ছে-কয়েকশ-কোটি-টাকার-অর্পিত-সম্পত্তি

www.newagebd.net/article / 112799 / another-shimulia-ferry-ghat-goes-under-padma-water

www.amadershomoy.com/bn/2020/07/31/1193032.html বাংলাদেশ থেকে ভারতে রেমডেসিভির চোরাচালান: ৮২ কোটি রুপি পাচার

ahmedabadmirror.indiatimes.com/ahmedabad/crime/gang-sells-covid-drug-smuggled-from-bdesh/articleshow/77157300.cms

www.newsbybd.net/newsdetail/detail/49/498944 'এই দেশে বিনিয়োগ করতে এসে হুহু করে কাঁদতে দেখেছি বিদেশিদের'

www.bd-pratidin.com/first-page/2020/08/27/560670 উন্নয়নের নামে বিনাশী প্রকল্প

www.voabangla.com/a/bd-04-১০-20/5367237.html বাংলাদেশ পাঁচটি আন্তর্জাতিক দাতা সংস্থার কাছে ঋণের আবেদন জানিয়েছে

www.newagebd.net/article/114937/pabna-bcl-leader-arrested-on-extortion-charge

www.kalerkantho.com/online/national/2020/07/09/932760 পাওনা টাকা চাইলে এভাবেই পেটাতো Awami Regent সাহেদ

www.newagebd.net/article/110750/bb-freezes-shaheds-accounts COVID-19 certificate forgery case; several thousand fake COVID-19 certificates and charging people for free tests

www.thedailystar.net/frontpage/news/fraudster-myriad-guises-1927977 Shahed

www.jugantor.com/national/government/330357/অনিয়মের-অভিযোগে-আরও-একটি-হাসপাতাল-বন্ধ

www.somoynews.tv/pages/details/226736/মসজিদের-টয়লেট-নির্মাণের-টাকা-আত্মসাতের-অভিযোগ-আ.লীগ-নেতার-বিরুদ্ধে

www.facebook.com/drkanaksarwarbd/videos/365998071069527 সাবেক আইন ও খাদ্য মন্ত্রী এডভোকেট কামরুল ইসলাম ওরফে 'গমরুল' এর চাঁদাবাজি রঅডিও ফাঁস

amardesh.co.uk/চাঁদাবাজ-কামরুল-অথচ-জেলে/

amardesh.co.uk/মিড-নাইট-সরকারের-মিড-ডে-হর/ মিড-নাইট সরকারের মিড-ডে হরিলুট

www.newagebd.net/article/113404/sirajganj-juba-league-leader-held-with-tk-1200cr-fake-cheques

www.bd-pratidin.com/country/2020/07/29/552822 ২০ লাখ টাকায় ছাত্রলীগের থানা সেক্রেটারির পদ বেচাকেনা!

www.prothomalo.com/bangladesh/article/1674005/সিগারেট-খাওয়ার-অপরাধে-গ্রেপ্তার-পরে-পুলিশকে-সাড়ে

www.dailynayadiganta.com/dhaka/525116/স্বাস্থ্য-কমপ্লেক্সের-রুমে-এবার-গরুর-খামার

www.jagonews24.com/country/news/607496 চারটি বাঁশের সাঁকো সংস্কারে ৯ কোটি টাকা বরাদ্দ

https://m.facebook.com/100024676380835/posts/786214798877726 Dr Taj Hashmi's Open Letter to Sheikh Hasina

amardesh.co.uk/শেখ-হাসিনাকে-খোলা-চিঠি/

https://youtu.be/Qy2NhI_dWuM "গনভবনের ভেতরে হাতেনাতে শেখ হাসিনার চাঁদাবাজির প্রমান || Mina Farah"

https://youtu.be/ufGXNDhCxwg "শেখ হাসিনার পুত্র জয়ের সকল দুর্নীতির তথ্য ফাঁস হল! প্রমানসহ দেখুন;"

www.facebook.com/143565626271113/posts/458793334748339/ মানি লন্ডারিংয়ের অভিযোগে হাসিনার মেয়ের জামাই মিতুর পাসপোর্ট আটক: বাসা তল্লাশি: কঠিন বিপদ আসন্ন!!

https://www.facebook.com/480751195648235/posts/1440758606314151/?vh=e&extid=NRdjQv1QHP9PyY1y&d=n চরম বিপাকে "রাজাকার বেয়াই মোশাররফ !! নিজের মেয়ে সায়মা ওয়াজেদ পুতুলকে রক্ষায় বেয়াই রাজাকার মোশাররফ এবং মেয়ে জামাই মাসরুরকে ফাঁসিয়ে দিচ্ছেন শেখ হাসিনা

দিপু মনির স্বামীর ৫৪১ কোটি টাকার অবৈধ সম্পদ জব্দ।

হাসিনার মন্ত্রী দীপুমনির স্বামী তৌফীক নাওয়াজের হোটেল, বাসভবন ও ব্যবসা প্রতিষ্ঠান জব্দ করার নির্দেশ দিয়েছে শারজাহের আদালত! ২শ ৫৬.৭ মিলিয়ন AED অবৈধ সম্পদ দিপুমনির স্বামী এ্যাডভোকেট তৌফিক নাওয়াজের মোট ২শ ৫৬.৭ মিলিয়ন AED অবৈধ সম্পদ জব্দ করেছে আরব আমিরাত সরকার! এগুলোর মধ্যে রয়েছে দুটি তিন তারকা হোটেল, তিনটি বিলাসবহুল বাড়ি, একটি কনস্ট্রাকশন কোম্পানি, ছয়টি ফ্ল্যাট, একটি রেস্টুরেন্ট। যেসব ফ্ল্যাটে ও বাড়িতে ভাড়াটিয়া রয়েছে তাদের এক মাসের মধ্যে খালি করার নির্দেশ দিয়েছে প্রশাসন।এডভোকেট তৌফিক নাওয়াজ সাহেব আবার ট্রান্সপারেন্সি ইন্টারন্যাশনাল বাংলাদেশ (TIB) এর একজন অতীব দায়িত্ববান সদস্য। জাতি এখন টিআইবির বক্তব্য শুনতে অধীর আগ্রহ নিয়ে অপেক্ষা করছে। উল্লেখ্য যে, দীপু মনির স্বামী তৌফিক নাওয়াজ মানি লন্ডারিং মামলায় শেখ হাসিনার মেয়ে পুতুলের সাবেক স্বামী মিতু'র সাথে আসামী ছিলেন। মিতু আরব আমিরাতের কারাগারে আটক থাকলেও তৌফিক কি পলাতক ? (collected from group e-mail messages).

www.facebook.com/photo.php?fbid=10160863479168636&set=a.10156163619918636&type=3

www.facebook.com/groups/313058046223567/?post_id=691821745013860

www.facebook.com/alampmobd/posts/10160847900938636

www.facebook.com/permalink.php?story_fbid=3368129983208261&id=1054197744601508

www.facebook.com/211138099280385/posts/1131130630614456/?app=fbl

www.facebook.com/12BNP/photos/a.251346672438997/614118946161766/ (www.facebook.com/12BNP/ কয়েকটা পোস্টিং নীচে যেতে হবে)

https://youtu.be/sW-Af1oAoe4 আল্লামা মামুনুল হক claims Awami শাহরিয়ার কবির was ... |

https://youtu.be/rKKmyr93E2s Awami শাহরিয়ার কবির সম্পর্কে একি বললেন Amir Hamza

www.facebook.com/muldharabd/posts/1637014336361883?__tn__=K-R ইতিহাসে শেখ সাহেবরে স্টেটসম্যান অইবার একটা সুযোগ দিছিল। তিনি এইডা কামে লাগাইবার পারলেন না।

https://www.facebook.com/photo.php?fbid=10216056063571820&set=a.10211401790937913&type=3&theater Bhutto and Sheikh Mujib friendship

www.facebook.com/753088635/posts/10160987688043636/?extid=0&d=n বাংলাদেশ সেনাবাহিনীর ভেতরকার গোপন কান্ডকীর্তির কথা ফাঁস করে দিয়েছেন অবসরপ্রাপ্ত কর্নেল শহীদ।

amardesh.co.uk/গুম-খুন-আর-লুটপাটের-হোতা-ব/ বাংলাদেশের শাসক পরিবার: সেনাপ্রধানের চাঞ্চল্যকর তথ্য

www.youtube.com/watch?v=tCq08zyEyFA সেনাপ্রধান জেনারেল আজিজ আহমেদ এর গোপন ফোনালাপ ফাঁস- গুম - খুনের মুল হোতা জেনারেল তারিক সিদ্দিক (অব)

https://www.jugantor.com/politics/367533/আওয়ামীতন্ত্র-প্রতিহত-না-করলে-গণমাধ্যমের-স্বাধীনতা-ফিরবে-না

amardesh.co.uk/শেখ-হাসিনার-মুনাফেকি-বচন/

amardesh.co.uk/গনতন্ত্রের-না%e2%80%8cমে-পেশীতন্/ গনতন্ত্রের নামে পেশীতন্ত্রের হাতে নির্বাচনের নির্বাসন যাত্রা

amardesh.co.uk/বর্তমান-প্রধানমন্ত্রীর-ক/ কথাবার্তা, আচার আচরণের মনে হয় তিনি পৈতৃকসূত্রে সবকিছুর মালিক—গয়েশ্বর চন্দ্র রায়

amardesh.co.uk/গুম-খুনের-হোতা-জিয়াউল-আহস/

https://youtu.be/f4EI6hR5e2U মেজর দেলোয়ারের সাক্ষাৎকার

www.youtube.com/watch?v=5l2Hio-u-eQ পিলখানা বিডিআর হত্যার আসল রহস্য ফাঁস, মেজর দেলোয়ার হোসেন

amardesh.co.uk/কিলিং-ইন্টেলেকচুয়ালস-আও/ আওয়ামী ফ্যাসিবাদের মৃত্যুভয়

amardesh.co.uk/ব্যক্তি-পূজার-অশ্লীলতা/ Mahmudur Rahman

amardesh.co.uk/আওয়ামী-জাহেলিয়াত-এবং-সাম/ Minar Rashid

www.ittefaq.com.bd/court/200394/ অর্থপাচার দেশটা কি মগের মুল্লুক ৩ হাজার ৫০০ কোটি টাকা পাচারে জড়িত পি কে হালদারকে ফিরিয়ে আনতে কী ব্যবস্থা নিয়েছে দুদক, ১০ দিনের মধ্যে জানানোর নির্দেশ

amardesh.co.uk/ডাকাতের-কবলে-দেশ/ Nazma Nustafa

amardesh.co.uk/বিদ্যুৎ-না-দিয়েই-এক-দশকে-স/ বিদ্যুৎ না দিয়েই এক দশকে সামিট লুটে নিলো ৮ হাজার ৯০০ কোটি টাকা

www.newagebd.net/article/121654/samrat-invested-tk-219cr-in-singapore-casinos-acc

www.newagebd.net/article/121109/mp-shahid-family-launder-tk-148cr

www.jugantor.com/todays-paper/first-page/356596/লোপাট-৬-হাজার-কোটি-টাকা

www.newagebd.net/article/109432/tk-5392cr-bangladeshi-deposits-in-swiss-banks

amardesh.co.uk/আওয়ামী-ব্যাংকে-জনগণের-অর/ আওয়ামী ব্যাংকে জনগণের অর্থ হরিলুট

amardesh.co.uk/ই-কমার্স-ব্যবসার-নামে-দশ-ম/ দশ মাসে ২২ লাখ গ্রাহকের ২৬৮ কোটি টাকা আত্মসাৎ

amardesh.co.uk/আন্তর্জাতিক-বাজারে-তেলের/ দাম তলানীতে কিন্তু বাংলাদেশে লুটপাট

www.ittefaq.com.bd/wholecountry/188984/% ২০ দিনও টিকলো না ১৯ কোটি টাকার পাকা রাস্তা

amardesh.co.uk/চুয়াডাঙ্গায়-দিনে-দুপুরে/ হেলমেট বাহিনীর ব্যাংক ডাকাতি

www.dailynayadiganta.com/dhaka/543502/মেঘনায়-চাঁদপুরগামী-লঞ্চে-ডাকাতি-৪০-জনের-মালামাল-লুট

AMARDESH.CO.UK/জাল-স্ট্যাম্পসহ-নারায়ণগঞ্জ/ ছাত্রলীগের সাংগঠনিক সম্পাদক গ্রেফতার

https://youtu.be/kenbA7iIHPk "বেরিয়ে আসছে হাজি সেলিমের অজানা কাহিনী!"

www.jugantor.com/todays-paper/last-page/356266/চাঁদাবাজিতে-কোটিপতি-কসাই-আতঙ্ক

amardesh.co.uk/৪৯-লাখ-জাল-নোট-ও-টাকা-তৈরির/

amardesh.co.uk/কোটি-টাকা-ভাগাভাগির-অভিয়/

www.dailynayadiganta.com/rangpur/543561/রংপুর-৫৮-লাখ-টাকার-নকল-ব্যান্ডরোলসহ-তিনজন-আটক

www.dailynayadiganta.com/last-page/499716/-চট্টগ্রাম-বন্দরে-কনটেইনার-থেকে-আমদানির-২৬-হাজার-টন-ফ্যাব্রিক-গায়েব

www.newagebd.net / article / 117682 / tk-17-lakh-robbed-in-jashore-in-broad-daylight

Hindutva India Controlled (Muslim) Bangladesh Under Hasina. It Is All Hindus And Only Hindus That Are All Over, and the High-Ranking Hindu Police Are Everywhere

In addition to my *Bangladesh: Political and Literary Reflections on a Divided Country*, see Appendix A in *Bangladesh Divided: Political and Literary Reflections on a Corrupt Police and Prison State*, and Appendix D and Appendix G in Sabria Chowdhury Balland (ed), *Bangladesh: A Suffering People Under State Terrorism* and the following:

www.dw.com/bn/বাংলাদেশের-চাকরির-বাজারে-বিদেশিরা/a-51876330

amardesh.co.uk/বাংলাদেশ-কি-রএর-শিকলে-ব/ বাংলাদেশ কি 'র'এর শিকলে বাঁধা পড়েছে ?

AMARDESH.CO.UK/সশস্ত্র-বাহিনীতে-বিজাতীয়/ সংস্কৃতির আগ্রাসন

amardesh.co.uk/বিএসএফ-এর-গুলি-চলছেই-প্রা/

amardesh.co.uk/বর্তমানে-দেশের-সরকারি-কর/ কর্মকর্তাদের পোস্টিং দিল্লির কথার বাইরে হয় না-গয়েশ্বর চন্দ্র রায়

amardesh.co.uk/সেনাবাহিনী-ও-পুলিশে-চূড়া/ চূড়ান্ত ভারতীয়করণ?

buffalobangla.com/ভারতীয়-রএর-কজায়-প্রিয়-স/ স্বদেশ

বাংলাদেশ-ভারত সীমান্তে বিএসএফের গুলি করে বাংলাদেশীদের হত্যা বন্ধ করতে হলে ভারতীয় সীমান্তরক্ষীদের দোষ দিয়ে লাভ নেই বলে মনে করেন **বাংলাদেশের খাদ্যমন্ত্রী সাধন চন্দ্র মজুমদার**।এক্ষেত্রে বাংলাদেশী নাগরিকদেই সতর্ক হতে হবে বলে তিনি মনে করেন।
www.bbc.com/bengali/news-51249303

www.bbc.com/bengali/news-51249303 সীমান্ত হত্যায় বিএসএফের দোষ দেখছেন না Indian stooge বাংলাদেশের Hindu খাদ্যমন্ত্রী

amardesh.co.uk/সরকারের-নিয়ন্ত্রণের-বাইর/ Police are beyond the control of Hasina Bangladesh University of Engineering & Technology (BUET) Vice Chancellor **Satya Prasad Majumder**, appointed in violation of the seniority of many other professors.

PG Medical Hospital and University (BSMMU) Vice Chancellor **Kanak Kanti Barua**

BSMMU former Vice Chancellor **Pran Gopal Datta**

http://bn.quora.com/বাংলাদেশ-পুলিশে-এতো-হিন্দু

www.boombd.com/fake-news/fake-posts-claim-bangladeshs-512-thana-has-hindu-officers-in-charge-9291

www.sheershakagoj24.com/District-News/details/100898/----

www.youtube.com/watch?v=mpMOHylSE6I Hindu audacities হঠাৎ! সংবিধান থেকে 'রাষ্ট্রধর্ম ইসলাম' বাদ দিতে আইনি নোটিশ! https://bit.ly/3249Qqy; https://bit.ly/2Ya4vgn;

৪২ কর্মকর্তাদের ডিঙিয়ে **সুভাষ কুমার দাশকে** সিনিয়র জেল সুপার পদে পদোন্নতি করা হয়েছে।

এমনকি মাদ্রাসার শিক্ষা বোর্ডের প্রশাসনিকের প্রধান নিয়োগ দিয়েছে **হিন্দু** জেগে উঠো বাংলাদেশ।

rupalibarta.com/বরিশালে-দাঁড়ি-রাখা-কর্মী/ বরিশালে দাঁড়ি রাখা কর্মীদের চাকরি খাচ্ছেন ড্রাগ ইন্টারন্যাশনালের **উত্তম কুমার শীল**

পুলিশের লালবাগ বিভাগের উপ-কমিশনার **বিপ্লব বিজয় তালুকদার**

amardesh.co.uk/ঢাকা-রেঞ্জের-এসপির-বিরুদ্/ ঢাকার প্রথম যুগ্ম জেলা জজ উৎপল ভট্টাচার্যের and সোর্স **প্রবাল বিশ্বাস** প্রায়ই ওই দোকানের মালামাল নিয়ে টাকা না দিয়ে চলে যেতেন।

রাষ্ট্রপক্ষের আইনজীবী (পিপি) **তাপস কুমার পাল**

https://bbc.in/3iPPecA; https://bit.ly/3h7S2RN অশোক কুমার ঘোষ www.facebook.com/ak.ghosh.58323

ডাক বিভাগের মহাপরিচালক (ডিজি) **সুধাংশু শেখর ভদ্র** ভারতে শত কোটি টাকা পাচার

Tk 10,200cr or $120.36 crore stolen by **Prashanta Kumar Halder alias PK Halder**

শুভঙ্কর সাহা যেভাবে ধ্বংস করছেন বাংলাদেশ ব্যাংক|: http://www.newsatbd.net/newsdetail/detail/200/391080. বাংলাদেশ ব্যাংক থেকে টাকা চুরির সময় ভারতীয় কর্মকর্তা

দীপক দাস হাতেনাতে আটক !https://bbcbengla.blogspot.com/ 2018/07/blog-post_20.html?m=1. www.amader shomoy.com/bn/2020/07/16/118 4361.html রাষ্ট্রায়ত্ত ব্যাংকগুলোর আইটি ভারতের দখলে : প্রতি বছর ৫০০ কোটি টাকা বিদেশে চলে যাচ্ছে For more Shahas and Dasas, see Chapter 2, "Democracy and Development: Development With Corruption and Without Democracy" in my *Bangladesh: Political and Literary Reflections on a Divided country*, pp. 77-79

"আপনি কোথায় যাবেন? বাংলাদেশে ব্যাংকে ? তার নির্বাহী পরিচালকের নাম শুভঙ্কর সাহা। পর্যটন কর্পোরেশনে যাবেন, তার চেয়ারম্যান অপরূপ চৌধুরী। 'একটি বাড়ি একটি খামার প্রকল্পে যাবেন, তার পরিচালক প্রশান্ত কুমার রায়, স্থলবন্দর কর্তৃপক্ষের কাছে যাবেন, তারও চেয়ারম্যান তপন কুমার চক্রবর্তী। পাওয়ার ডিস্ট্রিবিউশন (ডিপিডিসি) যাবেন, সেখানেও চেয়ারম্যান তাপস কুমার। জাতীয় বিজ্ঞান ও প্রযুক্তি যাদুঘরে যাবেন, তার মহাপরিচালক স্বপন কুমার রায়,পাবলিক লাইব্রেরী যাবেন, তারও মহাপরিচালক আশীষ কুমার সরকার। পাঠ্যপুস্তক বোর্ডে যাবেন, তারও চেয়ারম্যান নারায়ন চন্দ্র সাহা। প্রেস কাউন্সিলে যাবেন, তার প্রধানও শ্যামল চন্দ্র কর্মকার। সর্বত্রই এখন হিন্দুদের দাপট। বেছে বেছে সব উপরের পদগুলোতে বসানো হয়েছে হিন্দুদের। মুসলমানদেরকে করা হয়েছে হিন্দুদের অধিনস্ত। হিন্দু বস যা বলে, অধিনস্ত মুসলিমদের তাই মুখ বুজে মেনে নিতে হয়। তবে শুধু বস হিসেবে নয়, হিন্দু হওয়ার কারণে তাদের থাকে আলাদা দাপট, বিষয়টা এমন- তাদের অন্যায়ের বিরুদ্ধেও কিছু বলা যায় না। হিন্দুদের দ্বারা মুসলিম কর্মকর্তারা এখন পুরোপুরি কোনঠাসা এবং নির্যাতিত। সবাই বুঝতেছে, কিন্তু কিছুই যেন করার নেই। নিউইয়র্ক থেকে প্রকাশিত সর্বাধিক প্রচারিত বাংলা সাপ্তাহিকী 'ঠিকানা' ৩ জানুয়ারি (২০১৪) সংখ্যায় এক ভয়াবহ চিত্র তুলে ধরেছে। 'এক নজরে বাংলাদেশের সচিবালয়' হারিয়ে যাচ্ছে ইসলাম-মোহাম্মদরা, বাড়ছে রায়-বাবুদের আধিপত্য' শীর্ষক প্রতিবেদনের সূচনাতেই বলা হয়, 'সচিবালয়ে ঢুকে আপনি কনফিউজড বা বিভ্রান্ত হবেন না দয়া করে। হয়তো ভাবতে পারেন, কোথায় আসলাম? ঢাকা নাকি দিল্লির সিভিল সার্ভিস পাড়া এটা ! ৯৫ শতাংশ মুসলমানের দেশে সিভিল সার্ভিসে হিন্দু সম্প্রদায়ের আমলাদের আধিক্য দেখে আপনি অবাক হতেই পারেন। সাইনে লেখা রয়েছে, অমুক বোস বা অমুক রায়, কোনোটায় অমুক দত্ত, আবার কোনোটায় অমুক বিশ্বাস। এসব নেম সাইনের ভিড়ে হারিয়ে গেছে মোহাম্মদ বা ইসলাম নামের নেম সাইন। সচিবালয়ে এখন নাকি মুখে কথা হয় না, ভাব বিনিময় হয় ইশারায়। হিন্দু অফিসারদের দাপটে মুসলমানরা রয়েছেন কোণঠাসা অবস্থায়। চাকরি আছে কিন্তু চেয়ার টেবিল নাই, মুসলমান এমন কর্মকর্তার সংখ্যা সচিবালয়ে এতই বেড়েছে যে, লাইব্রেরিতে বা ক্যান্টিনেও এখন আর বসে সময় কাটানোর জায়গা নেই। নাম না প্রকাশ করার শর্তে কয়েকজন অফিসার বললেন, বর্তমান সরকারের শুরু থেকেই একটি চক্র তালিকাহাতে এ কাজটি করে আসছে। চিহ্নিত হিন্দু অফিসারদের গুরুত্বপূর্ণ কোথায় কোথায় বসাবে, তা আগে থেকেই নির্ধারিত। এমনকি কয়েকপদ ডিঙ্গিয়ে প্রমোশন দেয়া হিন্দু ওই কর্মকর্তাদের। ওএসডি থাকা একজন অতিরিক্ত সচিব বললেন, শুধু সচিবালয়েই নয়, প্রধানমন্ত্রীর কার্যালয়, বিচারালয়, টেলিকিমিউনিকেশন সেক্টর, পুলিশ-প্রশাসন, জেলা-উপজেলা প্রশাসনসহ সর্বত্র এখন দাপটে দায়িত্ব পালন করে যাচ্ছেন হিন্দু কর্মকর্তারা। তিনি জানালেন, এখন অনেকেই বলে থাকেন, খুব বেশি দূরে নয়, হয়তো দেখা যাবে পাকিস্তান আমলে 'পাঞ্জাবি খেদাও' অভিযানের মতো বাংলাদেশেও এ ধরনের কোনো অভিযান শুরু হয়ে যাবে। আমার দৃষ্টিতে, বর্তমান সময়টা ঠিক ব্রিটিশ আমলের মত। ব্রিটিশ পিরিয়ডের শুরুতে ইস্ট ইন্ডিয়া কোম্পানি নিজেদের প্রাধান্য বিস্তারের জন্য সকল মুসলিম কর্মকর্তা-কর্মচারিদের সরিয়ে শুধু হিন্দুদের নিয়োগ করেছিলো। বর্তমান আওয়ামী সরকার যেভাবে প্রকাশ্যে ঘোষণা দিয়ে (শেখ হাসিনার উপদেষ্টা এইচটি ইমাম বলেছে- - চাকুরীতে হিন্দুদের তুলনামূলক বেশি নিয়োগ দেওয়া হয়েছে) হিন্দুদের হাতে দেশ তুলে দিচ্ছে, তা দেখে মনে হচ্ছে নতুন করে পরাধীনতার শিকল এমনভাবে ঘিরে আছে, ধরছে বাংলাদেশকে তা থেকে বের হতে কত যুগ পেরিয়ে যায় !!!"

An alarming number of OCs (officers-in-charge) are Hindus all across the country

আরেকটা ইসকন সদস্য এসআই থেকে এখন এএসপি **ধীরেন মহাপাত্র। স্ত্রী সুজলা মহাপাত্র।** Has accumulated huge wealth.

www.youtube.com/watch?v=TAfrf_CT8ic Corrupt OC **Nandan Kanti Dhar**

www.prothomalo.com/home / article / 119980/ জ্যেষ্ঠতা লঙ্ঘন করে পুলিশে চলতি দায়িত্বনরসিংদীর বর্তমান পুলিশ সুপার **প্রলয় কুমার জোয়ারদার।**

www.priyo.com / articles / প্রধানমন্ত্রীর-নাম-ভাঙ্গিয়ে-একচ্ছত্র-আধিপত্য-এক-পুলিশ-কর্মকর্তার-ইনকিলাব/

www.kalerkantho.com/print-edition/last-page / 2014 / 08 / 20 / 119047 নরসিংদীর বর্তমান পুলিশ সুপার **প্রলয় কুমার জোয়ারদার।**

www.facebook.com/202647270140320/posts/811946032543771

www.facebook.com/photo.php?fbid=10220686380047638&set=a.1277775342723&type=3&theater

Noyon Chatterjee 6 ছবিতে দুইজন পুলিশ কর্মকর্তাকে দেখতে পাচ্ছেন, বামপাশের জন হলো- রংপুর রেঞ্জের ডিআইজি দেবদাস ভট্টাচার্য এবং ডানপাশের জন হলো- রংপুরের পুলিশ সুপার বিপ্লব কুমার সরকার। প্রথমে ডিআইজি দেবদাস ভট্টাচার্য সম্পর্কে কিছু বলি- ডিআইজি দেবদাস ভট্টাচার্য একজন পাক্কা ইসকন সদস্য। ছবি দেখতে- https://tinyurl.com/y5sdyha6)

২০১৬ সালে দেবদাস ভট্টাচার্য চট্রগ্রাম মহানগর পুলিশের অতিরিক্ত কমিশনার হিসেবে দায়িত্বরত ছিলো। ঐ সময় চট্রগ্রামে হিন্দু উগ্রবাদী এবং স্থানীয় মুক্তিযোদ্ধাদের মধ্যে জমি নিয়ে একটি দ্বন্দ্ব হয়। সে সময় হিন্দুরা মুক্তিযোদ্ধাদের বাড়িঘর আগুন দিয়ে জ্বালিয়ে দেয়ার স্লোগান দিয়ে মিছিল বের করে। (https://bit.ly/31zT8iB)। কিছু সাংবাদিক বিষয়টি নিউজ করলে উগ্রবাদী হিন্দুরা ক্ষেপে যায় এবং চট্রগ্রাম প্রেসক্লাবে হামলা করে (https://youtu.be/1D11lPWWHZ8)। এ ঘটনায় ৪ জন হিন্দু আটক হয়। মামলাটি প্রথম অবস্থায় গ্রহণ করা হয় 'দ্রুত বিচার আইন' এ, কিন্তু পরবর্তীতে দেবদাস ভট্টাচার্য এর নির্দেশে ওসি বাদীকে না জানিয়ে মামলাটিতে দুর্বল ধারা সংযুক্ত করে দেয়, এতে আসামীরা দ্রুত ছাড়া পেয়ে যায়। এ ঘটনাই চট্রগ্রামের সাংবাদিকরা সমাবেশ করে পুলিশ কর্মকর্তা দেবদাস ভট্টাচার্য এর অপসরণ দাবি করে। (https://archive.is/7q0fa) এরপর আসুন রংপুরের পুলিশ সুপার **বিপ্লব কুমার সরকারকে** নিয়ে কিছু বলি-বিপ্লব কুমার সরকারের বিরুদ্ধে অনেক অভিযোগ। তবে তার বিরুদ্ধে একটা উল্লেখযোগ্য অভিযোগ হলো- ২০১৩ সালে পুলিশের দেড় হাজার এসআই নিয়োগ হয়েছিলো। ঐ সময় তেজগাঁও জোনের ডিসি থাকা অবস্থায় বিপ্লব কুমার সরকার ৫০০ হিন্দু প্রার্থীর একটি তালিকা দিয়ে তদবির করে। বিষয়টিকে সমন্বয় করে তৎকালীন সচিব ও পুলিশ সমন্বয়ক (আইজিপি সমতুল্য) **ফণীভূষণ চৌধুরী।** এ খবরটি ঐ সময় অনেক জাতীয় দৈনিকে ছাপা হয়। তবে লিঙ্কগুলো ডিলিট করে দেয়া হয়। তবে ফেসবুকে অনেক পেইজে এখনও খবরটি রয়ে গেছে (https://bit.ly/3a9OWtM) কথা হচ্ছে, অসাম্প্রদায়িকতার কথা বলে হয়ত বাংলাদেশে বড় বড় পদে অনেক হিন্দু ধর্মাবলম্বীকে নিয়োগ দেয়া হয়, কিন্তু তারা ক্ষমতায় পেয়ে কিন্তু মোটেও অসাম্প্রদায়িক ভূমিকায় থাকেনি, বরং নিজ সম্প্রদায়ের পক্ষে কট্টর সাম্প্রদায়িক পক্ষপাতিত্ব করে।

রূপক চন্দ্র দাশ of Barisal

www.sheershakagoj24.com/District-News/details/100880/---- অস্ট্রেলিয়ায় বাড়ি, চট্রগ্রাম-কক্সবাজারে বাড়ি-ফ্ল্যাট-হোটেলসহ অঢেল সম্পদের মালিক **ওসি প্রদীপ**

www.jugantor.com/ todays-paper / last-page/332970/প্রদীপের-স্ত্রীর-নামে-বাড়ি-গাড়ি-অঢেল-টাকা

www.newagebd.net / article / 111386 / teenager-commits-suicide-after-police-assault-si-suspended

amardesh.co.uk / ঢাকা-রেঞ্জের-এসপির-বিরুদ্ধ / বিরুদ্ধে ৫ কোটি টাকা ক্ষতিপূরণ চেয়ে মামলা

https://paathok.news/89933 টাকা না দিলেই ক্রসফায়ার! ভয়ঙ্কর এক ওসির নাম **প্রদীপ কুমার দাশ**

www.dainikamadershomoy.com / post / 270262 মেরিন ড্রাইভকে ডেথ জোন বানিয়েছিলেন **ওসি প্রদীপ**

www.sheershakagoj24.com/politics/details/103906/প্রদীপ-সম্পর্কিত-বিস্ময়কর-তথ্য-যা-বললেন-আসিফ-নজরুল

www.bd-pratidin.com/chittagong-pratidin/2020/08/07/554616 শুধু টাকাই হাতিয়ে নেননি, ক্ষমতার জোরে স্বর্ণালংকারও আদায় করতেন **ওসি প্রদীপ**

www.dailynayadiganta.com/law-and-justice/522403/ওসি-প্রদীপের-বিরুদ্ধে-আরো-একটি-হত্যা-মামলা

www.youtube.com/watch?v=Ul6T38r0ouU সিনহাকে আর পাবো না -গণতন্ত্র চাই-দাঁতভাঙ্গা জবাব দিলেন -মেজর সিনহার মা -এই মাত্র ।

www.youtube.com/watch?v=ejXu_85guuY মুখে লা থি মেরে বলে শালা রে শেষ কইরা দিছি - ৪ টি গুলি খেয়েও দৌড়ে বাঁচতে চেয়েছিলেন মেজর সিনহা

www.ittefaq.com.bd/national/172605/পুলিশ-সদস্যরা-বিপথে-যায়-কীভাবে

www.youtube.com/watch?v=Vr1-fBYyMSo ; www.youtube.com/watch?v=Vr1-fBYyMSo ঐ ঘটনার সাক্ষী ছিলেন মেজর সিনহা -ফোনে বড় বোন শারমিনকে জানিয়েছিলেন ৪ দিন আগে, গত ২৬ জুলাই।

www.somoynews.tv/pages/details/227079/গাইবান্ধায়-পুলিশ-পরিচয়ে-গরু-চুরি

www.newagebd.net / article / 116749 / cop-arrested-on-charge-of-snatching-in-gazipur

<u>amardesh.co.uk/সোহরাওয়ার্দী-হাসপাতালের/</u> পরিচালক উত্তম কুমার বড়ুয়ার বিরুদ্ধে মামলা

amardesh.co.uk/হিন্দু-বৌদ্ধ-খ্রিস্টান-ঐ/

বাংলাদেশের হিন্দু সংগঠনগুলো কুরুক্ষেত্রের ঘোষণা দিচ্ছে, মানে তারা হিন্দুদের মধ্যে জঙ্গীবাদের বিস্তার ঘটাতে চায়৷ হিন্দুদেরকে তারা উগ্র সন্ত্রাসবাদী বানাতে চায়৷ কতিপয় হিন্দুনেতা প্রকাশ্যে বাংলাদেশের হিন্দুদেরকে বাড়িতে অস্ত্র মজুদ করার আহবান জানিয়েছে। অর্থাৎ তাদের লক্ষ্য বাংলাদেশের হিন্দুদেরকে একটি সশস্ত্র সংগ্রামের দিকে এগিয়ে নিয়ে যাওয়া, ধর্মীয় টার্গেট অখণ্ড ভারত প্রতিষ্ঠা করা, যা খুবই বিপজ্জনক একটি বিষয়। এ অবস্থায় তাহলে কি করা উচিত ? আসলে বাংলাদেশের সংখ্যাগরিষ্ঠ ধর্মের মানুষ হিন্দুবিরোধী নয়,তারা সাম্প্রদায়িক সম্প্রীতিতে বিশ্বাসী।তারা সংখ্যালঘু হিন্দুদের সর্বপ্রকার অধিকার দিতে আগ্রহী।কিন্তু এর মানে এই নয়, তারা কোন প্রকারজঙ্গীবাদ, উগ্রবাদ বা সন্ত্রাসবাদ মেনে নেবে। অথচ সে বিষয়টি করে যাচ্ছে কিছু হিন্দু নামধারী সংগঠন, যারা হিন্দুদের মধ্যে উগ্রবাদ ও

জঙ্গীবাদের বিস্তার ঘটাচ্ছে। তাই অবিলম্বে সেই হিন্দু নামধারী সংগঠনগুলোর কার্যক্রম থামানো জরুরী। সংগঠনগুলোকে কালো তালিকাভূক্ত তথা ব্ল্যাক লিস্টেড করা উচিত। জঙ্গীবাদী ও উগ্রবাদী সংগঠন হিসেবে দেশে তাদের সব ধরনের কার্যক্রম নিষিদ্ধ করা উচিত। এ রকম কয়েকটি উগ্র সন্ত্রাসবাদী জঙ্গী সংগঠন হচ্ছে -- ১) হিন্দু বৌদ্ধ খ্রিস্টান ঐক্য পরিষদ ২) বাংলাদেশ জাতীয় হিন্দু মহাজোট ৩) হিন্দু সমাজ সংস্কার সমিতি ৪) বিশ্ব হিন্দু পরিষদ, বাংলাদেশ ৫) আন্তর্জাতিক কৃষ্ণ ভাবনামৃত সংঘ (ইসকন) ৬) শারদাঞ্জলী ফোরাম ৭) সনাতন বিদ্যার্থী সংসদ ৮) সনাতন মৈত্রী সংঘ ৯) জাগো হিন্দু ১০) বাংলাদেশ হিন্দু যুব উন্নয়ন সংগঠন ১১) জাতীয় সমাজ সংস্কার সমিতি ১২) শ্রীশ্রী ভোলাগিরি আশ্রম ১৩) প্রণব মঠ ১৪) মহানাম সম্প্রদায় ১৫) হিন্দু ল'ইয়ার্স অর্গানাইজেশন ১৬) মাইনো‌রিটি জনতা পার্টি ১৭) বাংলাদেশ হিন্দুলীগ ১৮) বাংলাদেশ ব্রাহ্মন সমাজ ১৯) পতঞ্জলী যোগ সংঘ ২০) বাংলাদেশ সংখ্যালঘু অধিকার ঐক্য ২১) বাংলাদেশ মাইনোরিটি ওয়াচ ২২) সনাতন ইন্টারন্যাশনাল ফাউন্ডেশন ২৩) বাংলাদেশ জনতা পার্টি (বিজেপি) ২৪) বাংলাদেশ মাইনরিটি জনতা পার্টি (বিএমজেপি)২৫) বাংলাদেশ মাইনোরিটি পরিষদ ২৬ বাংলাদেশ মাইনোরিটি কোয়ালিশন ২৭) সংখ্যালঘু স্বার্থ সংরক্ষণ ও অধিকার বাস্তবায়ন পরিষদ, ২৮) বাংলাদেশ সনাতনী সেবক সংঘ ২৯) হিন্দু সেনা বাংলাদেশ ৩০) বাংলাদেশ হিন্দু জাতীয়তাবাদী সংগঠন আমার মনে হয়, এসব হিন্দু সন্ত্রাসবাদী সংগঠনগুলোর জন্য সাধারণ ও নিরীহ হিন্দুদের বদনাম হচ্ছে, হিন্দুদের সম্পর্কে সাধারণ মানুষ খারাপ ধারণা করছে। অনেক সাধারণ হিন্দু এদের সংস্পর্শে এসে অপরাধ প্রবণ হয়ে উঠেছে, উগ্রবাদী ও সন্ত্রাসী লক্ষণ প্রকাশ করছে। তাই দেশের সংখ্যালঘু হিন্দু জনগোষ্ঠীর মঙ্গল ও নিরাপত্তার জন্যই দ্রুত এসব সংগঠনগুলোকে কালো তালিকাভূক্ত তথা জঙ্গী সংগঠন হিসেবে নিষিদ্ধ করা জরুরী। দেশের কতটা গভীরে নিজেদের শেকড় স্থাপন করতে পারলে হিন্দুরা প্রকাশ্যে রাস্তায় এমন শ্লোগান দিতে পারে? শিবিরের আস্তানা ভেঙে দাও "হেফাজতের আস্তানা ভেঙে দাও গুড়িয়ে দাও" "চরমোনাইয়ের আস্তানা ভেঙে দাও গুড়িয়ে দাও" হিন্দু বৌদ্ধ খ্রিস্টান বাংলাদেশে এক হয়ে কাজ করতে পারলেও আমরা একই ধর্মের দুই ভাই এক হতে পারছি না। যার ফল অবশ্যই আমরা ভোগ করবো। এই শ্লোগানগুলো শুনে রেডি হতে থাকেন ভয়াবহ সময়েরা। আজ হয়তো লিখতে কিংবা বলতে পারছি। কাল হয়তো লিখা বা বলার আগেই আমার আপনার লাশ অচেনা কোনো জায়গায় পড়ে থাকবে। চট্টগ্রামের বুকে দাড়িয়ে "জয় শ্রীরাম" শ্লোগান দিয়ে হেফাজত ও চরমোনাইয়ের আস্তানা জালিয়ে দেয়ার হুমকিদাতা মাস্টার মাইন্ড শীর্ষ হিন্দু সন্ত্রাসী কুশল চক্রবর্তীকে সবাই চিনে রাখুন। এইগুলো এখন কি উস্কানিমূলক বক্তব্য হয় না !কোথায় আজ বাঁকশালী হাসিনার ডিজিটাল আইন!

Hindutva India Lover Obaidul Quader's "developed" Road Communication

See my Appendix F in Sabria Chowdhury Balland (ed), *Bangladesh: A Suffering People Under State Terrorism* (New York: Peter Lang, April 2020), and the following:

www.dailynayadiganta.com/chattagram/545189/কুমিল্লায়-কাভার্ডভ্যানচাপায়-২-মোটরসাইকেল-আরোহী-নিহত

www.dailynayadiganta.com/chattagram/545144/নোয়াখালীতে-সড়ক-দুর্ঘটনায়-যুবকের-মৃত্যু

amardesh.co.uk/নভেম্বরে-৪১৭-সড়ক-দুর্ঘটন/ ৪৩৯ জন নিহত

amardesh.co.uk/নাতনিকে-হাসপাতালে-নেওয়ার/

www.newagebd.net/article/119619/road-safety-still-far-off

www.facebook.com/shibirlohagara.official / posts / 960373987787078 বাংলাদেশ জয় বাংলা রোড!!

www.google.com/search?source=univ&tbm=isch&q=কাদার+রাস্তা&sa (click to see the Hasina Awami fake, false and propaganda development)

www.bd-pratidin.com/chayer-desh/2020/06/04/535763 ৬ মাসেই ধসে পড়ল ২৯ লাখ টাকায় নির্মিত সড়ক!; www.dainikamadershomoy.com/post/260288 কোটি টাকা ব্যয়ে নির্মিত রাস্তা, টান দিলেই উঠে যাচ্ছে কার্পেটিং

www.earki.co / news / article / 4760/আবিষ্কৃত-হলো-বিশ্বখ্যাত-নায়াগ্রা-জলপ্রপাতের in Hasina's "Switzerland"

www.facebook.com/photo.php?fbid=10160696292458636&set=a.276673213635&type=3&theater নতুন ধরনের একটা ব্রীজ in Hasina's Bangladesh

www.thedailystar.net/bangla / শীর্ষ-খবর/গায়েবি-সেতু-মেরামতে-৪৬-কোটি-টাকার-দরপত্র-তদন্ত-শুরু-171805

www.bd-pratidin.com/last-page/2020/09/23/569494 বেহাল ঢাকার সড়ক

www.bd-pratidin.com/country/2020/09/21/569001 টানলেই উঠে যাচ্ছে তিনদিন আগে নির্মিত হওয়া সড়কের পিচ

www.dailynayadiganta.com/chattagram / 529783 / পটিয়ায়-সড়ক-দুর্ঘনায়-মাদ্রাসা-শিক্ষক-নিহত

www.dailynayadiganta.com / sylhet / 526761 / হবিগঞ্জে-সড়ক-দুর্ঘটনায়-উপজেলা-চেয়ারম্যানসহ-চারজনের-মৃত্যু

amardesh.co.uk/সড়ক-দুর্ঘনায়-২সহোদরসহ-৩-জ/

www.jugantor.com/country-news / 339924 / সড়ক-দুর্ঘটনায়-প্রাণ-হারালেন-কিশোরগঞ্জের-প্রসিদ্ধ-চারুকলা-শিল্পী

www.newagebd.net/article/114938/three-university-students-killed-as-covered-van-rams-motorcycle-in-coxs-bazar

www.bd-pratidin.com/country/2020/08/30/561835 চকরিয়ায় কাভার্ড ভ্যানের চাপায় দুই ভাইসহ নিহত ৩

www.dailynayadiganta.com / chattagram / 529722/সীতাকুণ্ডে-সড়ক-দুর্ঘটনায়-পুলিশ-সদস্য-নিহত

www.bd-pratidin.com/city-news/2020/08/30/561837 রাজধানীর জুরাইনে প্রাইভেট কারের ধাক্কায় যুবক নিহত

www.newagebd.net/article/112550/14-killed-in-road-mishaps-in-bangladesh

www.newagebd.net/article/110795/113-killed-in-railway-accidents-in-6-months

www.dailynayadiganta.com/miscellaneous / 499610 / লকডাউনের-একমাসে-সড়ক-দুর্ঘটনায়-নিহত-২১১

www.newagebd.net/article/109675/at-least-3-killed-in-tangail-road-accident

www.newagebd.net/article/112067/four-people-killed-in-bogra-road-accident

www.newagebd.net/article/109675/at-least-3-killed-in-tangail-road-accident

www.newagebd.net / article / 112465 / three-of-a-family-die-in-gopalganj-road-accident

www.dainikamadershomoy.com/post/269924 বাসচাপায় দুই মোটরসাইকেল আরোহী নিহত

www.newagebd.net/article/113310/two-students-killed-in-jashore-road-accident

www.newagebd.net/article/113391/four-including-three-of-a-family-killed-in-kurigram-accident

www.dailynayadiganta.com/sylhet/521498/সিলেটে-বাসচাপায়-অটোরিকশার-৪-যাত্রী-নিহত

Bangladesh is an Awami "Singapore," Awami "Hong Kong" and Awami "Switzerland":

www.thedailystar.net/bangla/শীর্ষ-খবর/বাংলাদেশে-মোবাইল-ডাটার-গতি-নেপাল-শ্রীলঙ্কা-পাকিস্তানের-চেয়েও-কম-182269

www.jugantor.com/capital/305580/দূষিত-বাতাসের-নগরীতে-ফের-শীর্ষে-ঢাকা

http://dhakadigest.net/en/2014/08/welcome-to-the-traffic-capital-of-the-world/

www.thedailystar.net/business/news/mobile-internet-slowest-bangladesh-among-42-countries-1892761

www.breakingnews.com.bd/science-technology/article/154485 ব্রডব্যান্ডের গতিতে তলানিতে বাংলাদেশ, বিশ্বে ১৮৪তম

www.newagebd.net/article/112468/bangladesh-4th-worst-hit-in-terms-of-child-deaths-by-lead-exposure

Abducted, Disappeared, and Killed:

In addition to my *Bangladesh Divided: Political and Literary Reflections on a Police and Prison State* and *Bangladesh: Political and Literary Reflections on a Divided Country*, see my Appendix H in Sabria Chowdhury Balland (ed), *Bangladesh: A Suffering People Under State Terrorism* and the following:

https://youtu.be/DLfcoM3tots সেনাবাহিনীর লে.কর্নেল তারেক ফাঁস করলেন কিভাবে গুম ও ক্রসফায়ার করা হতো

amardesh.co.uk/অস্ট্রেলিয়ার-সংসদে-বাংলা/ বাংলাদেশকে মানবাধিকার লঙ্ঘনের হটস্পট হিসাবে আখ্যায়িত করলেন একজন সিনেটর

www.foreign.senate.gov/press/ranking/release/bipartisan-letter-calls-for-sanctions-on-bangladeshi-battalion-for-extrajudicial-killings-enforced-disappearances-torture

http://southasiajournal.net/an-open-letter-to-us-congressmen/

www.jugantor.com / country-news / 293280 / থানায়-যবককে-নির্যাতন-করে-হত্যা-আমতলীর-সেই-ওসি-প্রত্যাহার

www.mzamin.com/article.php?mzamin=229286 যুবলীগ নেতার হাতে অমানবিক নির্যাতনের শিকার বৃদ্ধ, ভিডিও ভাইরাল

www.dailynayadiganta.com/dhaka/523495/ফরিদপুরের-২১-রাউন্ড-কার্তুজসহ-আলীগ-নেতা-বাদশা-গ্রেফতার

www.newagebd.net/article/109754/juba-league-leader-hacks-youth-to-death

www.dailynayadiganta.com/dhaka/514541/যুবলীগ-নেত্রীর-টর্চার-সেল-নিয়ে-টঙ্গীতে-তোলপাড়-

www.thedailycampus.com/higher-education/49782/বাড়ি-থেকে-ডিবি-তুলে-নেয়ার-পর-ঢাবি-ছাত্র-নিখোঁজ

www.facebook.com/photo.php?fbid=3504638329643894&set=pcb.3504638566310537&type=3&theater police league bribe

amardesh.co.uk/দানবরূপে-ফিরেছে-বাংলাদেশ/

amardesh.co.uk/ব্যবসায়ীকে-ইয়াবায়-ফাঁসান/ ফাঁসানোর হুমকি দিয়ে চাঁদা দাবি: ঢাকার কোতয়ালী থানার ৫ পুলিশের বিরুদ্ধে মামলা

amardesh.co.uk/র%e2%80%8cযাবের-বিরুদ্ধে-মার্কি/ "এতে বলা হয় ২০১৫ সালের পর থেকে ৪০০ জনেরও বেশি মানুষকে বিনা বিচারে খুন করেছেন র্যাবের শীর্ষ কর্মকর্তারা"

https://youtu.be/bUO5m3H0nMk "মাদকাসক্ত পুলিশ সদস্যদের বেশিরভাগই ইয়াবা ও ফেনসিডিল সেবন করেন"

WWW.DAILYNAYADIGANTA.COM/DHAKA/536475/মুন্সীগঞ্জে-অস্ত্র-ও-মাদকসহ-আলীগের-নেতাসহ-তিনজন-গ্রেফতার

www.dailynayadiganta.com/chattagram/535473/এসআই-আকবরের-বিলাসবহুল-জীবন-এবং-রায়হান-হত্যা-

AMARDESH.CO.UK/সংঘবদ্ধভাবে-এক-স্কুল-ছাত্/ সংঘবদ্ধভাবে এক স্কুল ছাত্রীকে ধর্ষণের অভিযোগে পুলিশের এএসআই আটক

www.newagebd.net/article/119600/journalist-ruhul-amin-gazi-arrested

www.newagebd.net/article/119592/juba-odhikar-leader-picked-up

amardesh.co.uk/পুলিশের-বাঁধায়-নবীনগর-যু/

amardesh.co.uk/যশোরে-বিএনপি-কার্যালয়-ও-ন/

amardesh.co.uk/ময়মনসিংহে-আওয়ামী-সন্ত্রা/

amardesh.co.uk/আবারো-হেফাজতে-মৃত্যুর-ঘট/

amardesh.co.uk/দুই-অজ্ঞাত-সহ-তিন-লাশ-উদ্ধ/

amardesh.co.uk/যশোরে-প্রকাশ্যে-গুলি-করে/

www.dailynayadiganta.com/dhaka/538849/কিশোরগঞ্জে-এক-পরিবারের-তিনজনকে-হত্যার-পর-মাটিচাপা

www.dailynayadiganta.com/dhaka/543564/বরিশিতে-মাছ-ধরেছে-ভেবে-পানিতে-নেমে-মিলল-কিশোরীর-লাশ

www.dailynayadiganta.com/first-page/536014/চট্টগ্রামে-ছেলের-সামনে-কুপিয়ে-বাবাকে-হত্যা-

amardesh.co.uk/পাহাড়ের-ঝরনায়-মিলল-নিখোঁ/

www.dailynayadiganta.com/dhaka/536467/গাজীপুরে-রিসোর্টের-পাশ-থেকে-যুবকের-অর্ধগলিত-গলাকাটা-লাশ-উদ্ধার

www.newagebd.net/article/121111/police-probe-finds-raihan-tortured-in-custody

amardesh.co.uk/তিস্তার-বালুচরে-মিললো-হা/

amardesh.co.uk/ছাত্রদল-নেতা-টিপুকে-পিটি/

www.newagebd.net/article/37987/mans-sliced-body-parts-found-in-buriganaga

www.newagebd.net/article/37913/man-stabbed-dead-by-nephew-in-sylhet

amardesh.co.uk/নিখোঁজের-৪-দিন-পর-কলেজছাত্/ নিখোঁজের ৪ দিন পর কলেজছাত্রের লাশ উদ্ধার

www.dailynayadiganta.com/miscellaneous/525117/রাজধানীতে-কিশোরকে-হত্যা-করে-মোটরসাইকেল-ছিনতাই

amardesh.co.uk/সাভারে-গভীর-রাতে-স্কুলছা/

amardesh.co.uk/নিজ-ঘরে-খুন-হলে-গৃহবধূ/

amardesh.co.uk/গৃহকর্মী-নির্যাতন-আওয়াম/ আওয়ামী লীগ নেতার স্ত্রী গ্রেফতার

www.somewhereinblog.net/blog/noshtos/29801668 শেখ ফজলুল হক মনির মুজিব বাহিনীর হাতে যে সকল মুক্তিযোদ্ধা নিহত হয়েছে তাদের বিচার কবে হবে?

www.somewhereinblog.net / blog / noshtos / 29802024 আওয়ামীলীগের আবার রক্ষীবাহিনী তৈরী করা দরকার।

www.youtube.com/watch?v=RYZycgGTfgk বাংলাদেশের বেশ কিছু রাজনীতিবিদ, মিডিয়া ব্যক্তিত্ব এবং বুদ্ধীজীবীদের পৃথিবী থেকে মুছে দেয়ার উদ্দেশ্যে কঠোর গোপনীয়তার মধ্য দিয়ে বাছাই করা ক্ষমতাশীন আওয়ামী লীগের ১০০জন সশস্ত্র ক্যাডার ভারতীয় গোয়েন্দা সংস্থা রিসার্চ এ্যান্ড এনালাইসিস উইং 'র' এর প্রত্যক্ষ তত্ত্বাবধানে ভারতের দেরাদুনে সুদীর্ঘ ৬ মাস

https://defence.pk/pdf/threads/raw-trained-crusader-100-in-action-in-bangladesh.174858/

http://www.srilankaguardian.org/2012/04/bengal-tigers-in-r-cage.html R&AW trained Crusader 100 in action in Bangladesh

www.kalerkantho.com/online/national/2020/08/05/942219 প্রদীপ আর লিয়াকতের নেতৃত্বেই ১৬১ 'ক্রসফায়ার'

www.dailynayadiganta.com/politics/521293/প্রায়-৩০০০-মানুষ-বিচারবহির্ভূত-হত্যাকাণ্ডের-শিকার-ফখরুল-

www.prothomalo.com/bangladesh/ছয়-মাসে-বিচারবহির্ভূত-হত্যাকাণ্ডের-শিকার-১৬৭

www.kalerkantho.com / print-edition / first-page / 2020/08 /05/942160 'ক্রসফায়ার' ঘিরে লোমহর্ষক বাণিজ্য

www.newagebd.net / article / 113832 /mother-of-gunfight-victim-sues-ex-teknaf-oc-**pradeep**-27-others

www.newagebd.net/article/113143/dhaka-kotwali-oc-4-cops-sued-for-extortion-crossfire-threat

www.thedailystar.net/bangla/শীর্ষ-খবর/গত-২-বছরে-সারা-দেশেই-বেড়েছে-বন্দুকযুদ্ধ-ক্রসফায়ার-168941

www.thedailystar.net/frontpage/news/crossfires-gunfights-last-2-yrs-body-count-high-not-just-teknaf-1948877

হাসিনা সরকারের নৃশংস সন্ত্রাস গুম-খুন লুটপাট, **একজন প্রদীপ ওসি প্রদীপের ২২ মাসে ১৪৪ ক্রসফায়ারে ২০৪ জন নিহত**

https://nazmamustafa.wordpress.com/2020/08/21/সিরাজ-সিকদার-থেকে-সিনহা-র/

https://thediplomat.com / 2020/09 / bangladeshs-crossfire-culture-hits-home / by Brad Adams

https:// asiatimes.com / 2020 / 09 / hasinas-broken-promises-and-death-with-impunity/

https://medium.com / netranews / retired-lieutenant-general-in-hiding-after-criticising-army-chief-and-government-on-facebook-live-86043095e362;

www.facebook.com/drkanaksarwarbd/videos/286106049170265 (Retd) Lt Gen Chowdhury Hasan Sarwardy on the Hasina misrule;

www.facebook.com / drkanaksarwarbd / videos / সাক্ষাত্কার-দেয়ায়-জেনারেল-সারওয়ার্দীকে-প্রাণনাশের-হুমকি/ 984030782047672 /; www.justnewsbd.com/en/ special-report/news/10461 Lt Gen Sarwardy in hiding after criticizing govt, army chief; www.facebook.com/560237674/videos/10157699847582675/

www.facebook.com/drkanaksarwarbd/videos/সাক্ষাত্কার-দেয়ায়-জেনারেল-সারওয়ার্দীকে-প্রাণনাশের-হুমকি/984030782047672/

Heroic Major Delwar Hussain and Dr Kanak Sarwar

www.youtube.com/watch?v=e1XTOU3zbY8 ব্রিগেডিয়ার আমান আযমী কে তুলে নিয়ে যাওয়ার চার বছর এবং মেজর (অব) সিনহা হত্যাকাণ্ড বিশ্লেষণ

Maj Delwar on the rot and rats of the Hasina regime:

https://youtu.be/fLpz5xvPf40;

https://youtu.be/e76XmGPNBJU;

https://youtu.be/WKR69ZwMJk4;

www.youtube.com/watch?v=NZyfqRhnDIM

www.youtube.com/watch?v=sAAQCW9zhqE আমার বাবা গু'ম হয়েছে | অবুঝ শিশুর শাহবাগে বুকফাটা কান্না | আমার বাবাকে ফিরিয়ে দিন ??

Bangladeshi security forces have allegedly extrajudicially killed over 2,400 people during Sheikh Hasina's decade in power.

www.newagebd.net/article/117607/youth-dead-in-police-custody-torture-alleged

www.thedailystar.net/bangla/শীর্ষ-খবর/ঢাবি-থেকে-জিনিয়াকে-অপহরণ-ও-বহুরূপী-লুপা-172421

www.ppbd.news/crime / 172976 / কে এই লুপা তালুকদার?

www.ppbd.news/crime / 173049 / রাজনীতি-ও-সাংবাদিকতার-আড়ালে-বহুরূপী-লুপার-নানা-অপরাধ

www.newagebd.net/article/116750/one-held-for-killing-2-teenage-cousins

www.jugantor.com/capital / 331934 /আশুলিয়ায়-ঘরে-ঢুকে-দুই-ভাইকে-কুপিয়ে-হত্যার-চেষ্টা

www.dailynayadiganta.com / chattagram / 529610 / বড়-ভাইয়ের-আঘাতে-ছোট-ভাইয়ের-মৃত্যু

www.dailynayadiganta.com/chattagram/514322/কুমিল্লায়-ব্যবসায়ীকে-পিটিয়ে-হত্যা

www.jugantor.com / country-news / 327774 / কুমিল্লায়-কিশোর-গ্যাংয়ের-হামলায়-তরুণের-মৃত্যু

amardesh.co.uk/নির্মাণাধীন-ভবন-থেকে-পড়ে/

www.newagebd.net/article/117523/three-workers-die-falling-off-under-construction-building

www.jugantor.com/country-news/367606/কাপড়-কাটা-কাঁচি-দিয়ে-ছোট-ভাইকে-খুন

www.jugantor.com/country-news/367256/মোবাইল-ফোন-ছিনিয়ে-নিতে-বন্ধুকে-হত্যা-করে-সজীব

amardesh.co.uk/পৃথক-দুই-রুমে-ঝুলে-ছিল-পিত/

amardesh.co.uk/বিয়ের-৫২-দিনের-মাথায়-তালা/

Hasina's Bangladesh is a Rape, Yaba Drug, and Dengue country:

In addition to my *Bangladesh Divided: Political and Literary Reflections on a Police and Prison State* and *Bangladesh: Political and Literary Reflections on a Divided Country*, see my Appendix A (Rape and Kill) and Appendix E (Dengue) in Sabria Chowdhury Balland (ed), *Bangladesh: A Suffering People Under State Terrorism*, see the following:

শায়খ আহমদুল্লাহ (collected by Cap. Razzak Syed)

কর্ম:

টিভিভর্তি যৌনতা? সে তো সিনেমা!

কাগজভর্তি যৌনতা? সে তো কবিতা!

ক্যাসেটভর্তি যৌনতা? সে তো সঙ্গীত!

বিলবোর্ডভর্তি যৌনতা? সে তো বিজ্ঞাপন!

ক্যানভাসভর্তি যৌনতা? সে তো পেইন্টিং!

পাথরভর্তি যৌনতা? সে তো ভাস্কর্য!

স্টেজভর্তি যৌনতা? সে তো বিনোদন!

সমগ্র পৃথিবীর খাঁজে-ভাঁজে মাংসে-অংশে পাহাড়ে-নহরে উদ্যানে-বিদ্যানে যৌনতাই যৌনতা!!

ফল:

বাসে ধর্ষণ-বাসায় ধর্ষণ,

রেলে ধর্ষণ-রেল স্টেশনে ধর্ষণ,

খেলায় ধর্ষণ-মেলায় ধর্ষণ,

মাঠে ধর্ষণ-পাঠশালায় ধর্ষণ

ক্ষেতে ধর্ষণ-খামারে ধর্ষণ,

গাঁয়ে ধর্ষণ-শহরে ধর্ষণ,

শিশু ধর্ষণ-কিশোরী ধর্ষণ,

মধ্যা ধর্ষণ-বৃদ্ধা ধর্ষণ,

কুমারী ধর্ষণ, বিবাহিতা ধর্ষণ

কোচিংয়ের নামে ধর্ষণ-পড়ানোর নামে ধর্ষণ,

রাজনীতির নামে ধর্ষণ-নেত্রী বানানোর নামে ধর্ষণ,

মডেলিংয়ের নামে ধর্ষণ-অভিনয়ের নামে ধর্ষণ....

মানুষ তো ধর্ষণ; এমনকি পশুও ধর্ষণ!

www.prothomalo.com/opinion/column/স্মরণকালের-মধ্যে-সবচেয়ে-বেশি-ধর্ষণ-এবং

amardesh.co.uk/গত-১০-মাসে-১০৮৬-জন-নারী-শিশ/

ww.dailynayadiganta.com/first-page/545335/বিয়ের-প্রলোভনে-স্কুলছাত্রীকে-ধর্ষণ

http://rtnbd.net/opinion/40663 ধর্ষণ করে উল্টো চাঁদাবাজি মামলা করতে এসে ধরা বৃদ্ধ

amardesh.co.uk/নারী-নির্যাতনে-ছাত্রলীগে/ নারী নির্যাতনে ছাত্রলীগের রেকর্ড

www.ittefaq.com.bd/education/185875/এমসি-কলেজ-ছাত্রাবাসে-স্বামীকে-বেঁধে-স্ত্রীকে-গণধর্ষণ%C2%A0

www.sylhettoday24.news/news/details/Sylhet/107283 তরুণীকে গণধর্ষণ: মধ্যরাতে এমসি কলেজ ছাত্রাবাসে অভিযান, অস্ত্র উদ্ধার

www.sylhettoday24.news/news/details/Sylhet/107278 এমসি কলেজ ছাত্রাবাসে গণধর্ষণ: ধাপাচাপা দেওয়ার চেষ্টা করেছিলেন আ.লীগ নেতারা

shomoyershongbad.com/এমসি-কলেজ-ছাত্রাবাসে-গণধ-2/

shomoyershongbad.com/এমসি-কলেজের-ছাত্রাবাসে-ধ/

www.channelionline.com/মাকে-বেঁধে-মেয়েকে-ধর্ষণে/

www.newagebd.net/article/117490/7-confess-to-khagrachari-rape

amardesh.co.uk/মুমূর্ষু-স্বামীর-জন্য-রক/ মুমূর্ষু স্বামীর জন্য রক্ত সংগ্রহ করতে গিয়ে ধর্ষণের শিকার হন এক নারী

amardesh.co.uk/খাগড়াছড়িতে-স্কুলছাত্রীক/ ধর্ষণ

www.jugantor.com/country-news/367241/বিয়ে-থেকে-ফিরে-বাকপ্রতিবন্ধী-নারী-ধর্ষণের-শিকার

www.jugantor.com/country-news/367230/স্বামীকে-গাছে-বেঁধে-স্ত্রীকে-গণধর্ষণ

amardesh.co.uk/১১-বছরের-জমজ-দুই-বোনকে-ধর/

amardesh.co.uk/ধর্ষণের-পর-মেয়েটিকে-হত্য/

www.prothomalo.com/bangladesh/স্বামীকে-বেঁধে-স্ত্রীকে-ধর্ষণ-ছাত্রলীগ-নেতাসহ

www.somoynews.tv/pages/details/238077 এমসি কলেজ ছাত্রাবাসে স্বামীকে আটকে রেখে তরুণীকে গণধর্ষণ

www.somoynews.tv/pages/details / 226667 / বাবাকে-জখম-করে-মাকে-বেঁধে-রেখে-মেয়েকে-তুলে-নিয়ে-ধর্ষণ

bangla.dhakatribune.com/bangladesh/2020 /07/ 28 / 25751/বাবা-মাকে-মারধর-করে-কিশোরীকে-ধর্ষণের-ঘটনা-'পরিকল্পিত'

www.ittefaq.com.bd/wholecountry / 72480 /রামগড়ে-বাবার-বিরুদ্ধে-মেয়েকে-ধর্ষণের-অভিযোগ-সহযোগিতা-করত-মা

www.bd-pratidin.com/country/2020/09/24/569899 নারী পাচার ও ধর্ষণের অভিযোগে ৩ যুবক আটক

www.dailynayadiganta.com / dhaka / 530226 / ঘিওরে-পানি-আনতে-গিয়ে-ধর্ষণের-শিকার-৮ম-শ্রেণির-ছাত্রী

www.dailynayadiganta.com/chattagram/530221/বাসে-সংঘবদ্ধ-ধর্ষণ-চালক-হেলপার-রিমান্ডে-অধরা-সুপারভাইজার

amardesh.co.uk/রাজধানীতে-ধর্ষণের-শিকার/

amardesh.co.uk/পাঁচ-বছরের-শিশুকে-ধর্ষণে/

amardesh.co.uk/রংপুরে-জেলা-ছাত্রলীগ-সভা/ সভাপতির বিরুদ্ধে ধর্ষণের অভিযোগ মামলা

amardesh.co.uk/স্বামীকে-বেধে-রেখে-স্ত্র/

amardesh.co.uk/চট্টগ্রামে-বিধবাকে-ধর্ষণ/

www.prothomalo.com/bangladesh/article/1674003/সাত-মাসে-১৬৮৬-নারী-ও-কন্যাশিশু-নির্যাতের-শিকার

www.dailynayadiganta.com/sylhet/519509/নবীগঞ্জে-দুলাভাইয়ের-সাথে-শারিরীক-সম্পর্ক-দেখে-ফেলায়-মাকে-হত্যা

www.kalerkantho.com/online/country-news/2020/03/29/892090 ধর্ষণ ও হত্যা, প্রধান আসামি মুয়াজ্জিন আশিক গ্রেপ্তার http://www.dainikamadershomoy.com/post/248335 তাকমীনকে ধর্ষণের পর হত্যায় অংশ নেয় তিন বন্ধু লাশ ঝুলিয়ে মসজিদে গিয়ে নামাজ পড়ায় আশিক

www.dailynayadiganta.com / dhaka / 529521 /মুন্সীগঞ্জে-বিয়ের-প্রলোভন-দেখিয়ে-ধর্ষণ-যুবক-গ্রেফতার

www.jugantor.com/country-news / 330401 / ছোট-ভাইয়ের-অবৈধ-সম্পর্কে-প্রাণ-গেল-বড়-ভাইয়ের

Appendix B

https://youtu.be/nkP1DdLgRp0 "এমপি এনামুল হক আমাকেও নষ্ট করছে আমার বাচ্চাকেও নষ্ট করছে!"

dbcnews.tv/news/ভাতিজিকে-ধর্ষণ-করে-ফুলের-মালা-গলায়-চাচার-শোডাউন-উল্লাস

www.dailynayadiganta.com/dhaka/523484/তিন-বছর-ধরে-ছাত্রীকে-ধর্ষণ-ছাত্রীর-আত্মহত্যা-শিক্ষকের-বিরুদ্ধে-মামলা

www.ittefaq.com.bd/wholecountry/ 140507 / পরকীয়ায় মত্ত প্রবাসীর স্ত্রী প্রাণে মেরে ফেলল শিশু কন্যাকে

www.dailynayadiganta.com / dhaka / 511379 / প্রেমিকের-সামনে-প্রেমিকাকে-ধর্ষণ-অপমানে-আত্মহত্যা

www.thedailycampus.com/crime-and-discipline/49811/নতুন-জামার-লোভ-দেখিয়ে-১০-বছরের-শিশুকে-ধর্ষণ

www.newagebd.net/article/113833/man-lands-in-jail-for-raping-teenager

www.dailynayadiganta.com/more-news/509669/বড়াইগ্রামে-শিশু-ধর্ষণ-চেষ্টা-দোকান-ভাঙচুর

www.newagebd.net/article/109758/girl-killed-after-rape

www.newagebd.net/article/ 111735/girl-stabbed-dead-by-colleague-for-refusing-marriage-proposal

WWW.JUGANTOR.COM/COUNTRY-NEWS/364346/বাস-থেকে-নামিয়ে-জঙ্গলে-নিয়ে-হোটেল-শ্রমিককে-গণধর্ষণ

www.newagebd.net/article/120769/asi-rayhanul-placed-on-5-day-remand-in-rape-case

www.hrw.org/news/2020/10/29/bangladesh-pivotal-moment-stop-violence-against-women

www.jugantor.com/politics/others/353195 বাংলাদেশ এখন যে পরিস্থিতি তা পাকিস্তান আমলেও ছিল না: মান্না

https://mzamin.com/article.php?mzamin=245335&cat=3 সাড়ে চার বছরে ৪৫০০ ধর্ষণ

AMARDESH.CO.UK/পোশাক-শ্রমিক-ধর্ষণসহ-একা/ পোশাক শ্রমিক ধর্ষণসহ একাধিক মামলায় আ'লীগ নেতা লিয়াকত গ্রেফতার

WWW.NEWAGEBD.NET/ARTICLE/119513/UNSTOPPABLE-RAPE-INCIDENTS-COUNTRYWIDE

AMARDESH.CO.UK/ধর্ষণের-অভিযোগে-ছাত্রলীগ/

AMARDESH.CO.UK/টাঙ্গাইলের-গোপালপুরে-কলে/

AMARDESH.CO.UK/সংঘবদ্ধভাবে-এক-স্কুল-ছাত্র/ সংঘবদ্ধভাবে এক স্কুল ছাত্রীকে ধর্ষণের অভিযোগে পুলিশের এএসআই আটক

AMARDESH.CO.UK/বাংলাদেশে-৯-মাসে-৯৭৫-নারী/

AMARDESH.CO.UK/গাজিপুরে-চলন্ত-বাসে-নারী/

AMARDESH.CO.UK/স্বামীকে-আটকে-রেখে-গৃহবধূ/

WWW.NEWAGEBD.NET/ARTICLE/121112/TEENAGE-GIRL-RAPED-IN-MOVING-BUS

WWW.DAILYNAYADIGANTA.COM/CHATTAGRAM/536626/ফেনীতে-বেড়াতে-এসে-ধর্ষণের-শিকার-উপজাতি-কিশোরী

WWW.JUGANTOR.COM/COUNTRY-NEWS/359505/দেড়-বছরের-মেয়ের-গলায়-ছুরি-ঠেকিয়ে-মাকে-ধর্ষণ

WWW.JUGANTOR.COM/COUNTRY-NEWS/359533/প্রতিবন্ধী-গৃহবধূকে-গণধর্ষণ-থানায়-যেতে-বাধা

WWW.JUGANTOR.COM/COUNTRY-NEWS/359534/বোয়ালমারীতে-ধর্ষণের-অভিযোগে-৩-জন-গ্রেফতার

AMARDESH.CO.UK/নারীর-প্রতি-ভয়ঙ্কর-সহিংস/

AMARDESH.CO.UK/চার-জেলায়-চার-ধর্ষণ-ও-দুই-ব/

WWW.NEWAGEBD.NET/ARTICLE/72764/BANGLADESH-SEES-NEARLY-13-RAPES-EVERY-DAY

WWW.KALERKANTHO.COM/PRINT-EDITION/FIRST-PAGE/2020/10/06/962697 ধর্ষণ বর্বরতায় স্তম্ভিত দেশ

AMARDESH.CO.UK/ধর্ষণ-এক-আবহমান-আওয়ামী-ঐত/ ঐতিহ্য সেই একাত্তর থেকে শুরু

AMARDESH.CO.UK/কুলাঙ্গারদের-কবলে-উলঙ্গ/

AMARDESH.CO.UK/মুজিববর্ষ-নাকি-নারী-নির্/ নির্যাতন বর্ষ

AMARDESH.CO.UK/বাংলাদেশে-ধর্ষণের-সংস্কৃ/

AMARDESH.CO.UK/বাড়ি-থেকে-তুলে-নিয়ে-স্কুল/ স্কুলছাত্রীকে ধর্ষণের অভিযোগ

WWW.DAILYNAYADIGANTA.COM/RANGPUR/537973/রংপুরে-এসআইয়ের-নেতৃত্বে-নবম-শ্রেণির-ছাত্রীকে-গণধর্ষণের-অভিযোগ

WWW.DAILYNAYADIGANTA.COM/CHATTAGRAM/536626/ফেনীতে-বেড়াতে-এসে-ধর্ষণের-শিকার-উপজাতি-কিশোরী

WWW.JUGANTOR.COM/COUNTRY-NEWS/356246/তরুণীকে-৫-দিন-আটকে-রেখে-ধর্ষণ-মাথার-চুল-কেটে-নির্যাতন

WWW.JUGANTOR.COM/COUNTRY-NEWS/356245/শেরপুরে-কলেজছাত্রীকে-অটোরিকশায়-যৌন-হয়রানি

www.jugantor.com/country-news/356189/বরগুনায়-কলেজছাত্রীকে-তিন-দিন-আটক-রেখে-ধর্ষণভিডিও-ধারণ

www.dailynayadiganta.com/rangpur/536164/স্কুলছাত্রীকে-ধর্ষণের-অভিযোগে-ফায়ারম্যান-গ্রেফতার-স্ত্রীর-দাবি-ষড়যন্ত্র

www.dailynayadiganta.com/first-page/536018/সিলেটে-বিয়ের-আশ্বাসে-তরুণী-ধর্ষণ-যুবক-গ্রেফতার

www.dailynayadiganta.com/dhaka/542356/শিশুকে-রাতভর-ধর্ষণ-আটক-চটপটি-বিক্রেতা

www.jugantor.com/country-news/356592/অসুস্থ-বাবাকে-দেখতে-গিয়ে-গণধর্ষণের-শিকার-নাচের-প্রশিক্ষক-হেলপার-গ্রেফতার

amardesh.co.uk/আওয়ামী-লীগ-ক্ষমতায়-এলে-ধর্ ধর্ষণ বেড়ে যায় কেন?

https://youtu.be/URKxWxKMOwY আমাকে ও আমার মেয়েকে চেয়ারম্যান ধর্ষন করেছে

AMARDESH.CO.UK/আশুলিয়ায়-আবারও-তরুণীকে-ধ/

WWW.JUGANTOR.COM/COUNTRY-NEWS/356590/বন্ধুর-স্ত্রীকে-ধর্ষণ-করে-ভারতে-পালানোর-সময়-যুবক-গ্রেফতার

AMARDESH.CO.UK/বরিশাল-থেকে-অপহরণ-করে-ঢাক/

AMARDESH.CO.UK/এক-তরুণীকে-আটকে-রেখে-নির্/

AMARDESH.CO.UK/পরিচ্ছন্নতাকর্মীর-মেয়েক/

WWW.ITTEFAQ.COM.BD/WHOLECOUNTRY/188886/বরিশালে-অষ্টম-শ্রেণির-ছাত্রী-ধর্ষণের-শিকার-আটক-১ WWW.ITTEFAQ.COM.BD/NATIONAL/188616/ স্বামীকে বেঁধে রেখে গৃহবধূকে নিজের বাসায় সংঘবদ্ধভাবে বিবস্ত্র করে মুখমণ্ডলে লাথি মারাসহ নির্যাতনের যে ফুটেজটি সোশ্যাল মিডিয়ায় এসেছে তা চোখে দেখা যায় না। যেভাবে একজন নারীকে নির্যাতন করা যায়? তা যেন চিন্তার অতীত। ধর্ষণের পরে পৈশাচিক নির্যাতন করতে দেখা যায় সেই নির্যাতন দেখে এদের কাউকে কাউকে আনন্দ প্রকাশ করতে দেখা যায়। মানসিক বিকারগ্রস্ততার কোন পর্যায়ে রয়েছি আমরা! বেশ কিছুদিন ধর্ষণ এতটাই বেড়েছে যে, বিশ্লেষকরা বলছেন, দেশে 'ধর্ষণের সংস্কৃতি' গড়ে উঠেছে। বিচারহীনতার কারণে নারীরা দেশ জুড়েই ধর্ষণ, শ্লীলতাহানিসহ পুরুষের নানামুখী অত্যাচারের মুখোমুখি হচ্ছে। অপরাধী যখন শাস্তি পাচ্ছে না সেই সুযোগে ধর্ষণ দেশে মহামারির মতো ছড়িয়ে পড়েছে। সাম্প্রতিক সময়ে সিলেট এমসি কলেজে, সাভারে নারীশ্রমিক, খাগড়াছড়িতে ধর্ষণের ভয়াবহ ঘটনার কথা আমরা জানতে পেরেছি। বেশকিছু ধর্ষণের ঘটনা থানায় মামলার পর আদালতেও গড়ায়। কিন্তু শেষ পর্যন্ত

ধর্ষকরা শাস্তি পায় খুব কম। এই বিচারহীনতা, শাস্তি নিশ্চিত করতে না পারার ব্যর্থতা বিকারগ্রস্ত পুরুষদের আরো বেপরোয়া করে তুলছে। জানোয়ারের চেয়ে নিকৃষ্ট আচরণ করছে তারা। পশুও কী এতটা বর্বর হয় কখনো? ধর্ষকের লোলুপ দৃষ্টি থেকে বাদ যাচ্ছে না শিশু ও বৃদ্ধারাও। এমনকি রেহাই পাচ্ছেন না বাকপ্রতিবন্ধী বা ভবঘুরে পাগলও। শুধু ধর্ষণ করেই রেহাই পাচ্ছে না নারীরা। সেই ধর্ষণের ভিডিও ধারণ করে তা সামাজিক যোগাযোগ মাধ্যমে ছেড়ে দিচ্ছে বিকারগ্রস্ত তরুণরা। এমনকি, ধর্ষণ করে সেই মেয়েটিকে নির্যাতন করা, হত্যা করা, আগুনে পুড়িয়ে হত্যা করা হচ্ছে। মানুষ এক বীভৎস রূপ নিয়ে হাজির হচ্ছে শিশু-কিশোর নারীদের ওপরে। এসবের পাশাপাশি অপসংস্কৃতি, আকাশ সংস্কৃতির বেসামাল প্রভাব, অশ্লীলতা, ঘুষ, দুর্নীতিসহ নানা কারণে দিনে দিনে সামাজিক অবক্ষয় আর অস্থিরতা চরম আকার ধারণ করেছে। পাশাপাশি অশ্লীলতার আগ্রাসনে মানুষের নৈতিক মূল্যবোধের অভাব ও সামাজিক অবক্ষয়ে ধর্ষণের ঘটনা আশঙ্কাজনক হারে বাড়ছে। বিশ্লেষকরা বলছেন, ধর্ষণের ঘটনা বৃদ্ধির পেছনে রয়েছে চরম নৈতিক অবক্ষয়, আকাশ সংস্কৃতির বিরূপ প্রভাব, মাদকের বিস্তার, বিচারহীনতা, বিচার প্রক্রিয়ায় প্রতিবন্ধকতা ও বিচারের দীর্ঘসূত্রিতা।

Yaba Virus Under Sheikh Hasina

In addition to Note# 53, p.208, and Appendix I in Sabria Chowdhury Balland (ed), *Bangladesh: A Suffering People Under State Terrorism*, see the following:

www.jugantor.com/capital / 324441 / ১০-হাজার-পিস-ইয়াবাসহ-মাদক-ব্যবসায়ী-গ্রেফতার

www.dailynayadiganta.com/chattagram/529777/কক্সবাজারে-৫-লাখ-ইয়াবাসহ-৭-কারবারি-আটক

www.jugantor.com / todays-paper / last-page / 327179 / কক্সবাজারে-এক-কোটি-ইয়াবা-চালান-লুটকারী-আটক

www.bd-pratidin.com/first-page/2020/09/24/569828 ইয়াবা ব্যবসা করে মা-ছেলে করেছেন বাড়ি-গাড়ি

www.bd-pratidin.com/country/2020/09/24/569906 উখিয়ায় ইয়াবাসহ দুই রোহিঙ্গা মাদক ব্যবসায়ী আটক

www.dailynayadiganta.com/chattagram/544979/হাতিয়ায়-ইয়াবা-কারবারি-আটক

Flood and Boat Capsize Under the Hasina Development

www.deshergarjan.net/ফটো-গ্যালারী/ (Hasina's "developed" Bangladesh alias Singapore)

twitter.com / hashtag / FloodinBangladesh? src=hashtag_click (Hasina's "developed" Bangladesh alias Switzerland)

www.thedailystar.net / frontpage / news / flood-engulfs-over-third-bangladesh-1938449

www.newagebd.net / article / 112438 / bangladesh-faces-longest-flooding-in-2-decades

www.newagebd.net/article/113360/rivers-in-north-swell-again-as-india-opens-3-barrages

www.newagebd.net / article / 117681 / thousands-driven-out-of-home-again-as-flood-worsens-in-north

www.newagebd.net/article/112718/17-die-in-netrokona-trawler-capsize

www.newagebd.net/article/115785/netrakona-boat-capsize-kills-10

www.facebook.com/rajuahmeddipu/photos/a.837516189606347/3383463985011542/?type=3&theater&ifg=1 dire poverty in Hasina's "Singapore"

www.ittefaq.com.bd / national / 170384 / বন্যাকে-সঙ্গী-করেই-চলছে-বাংলাদেশ (Hasina's "Hong Kong")

studentjournalbd.com/স্বয়ং-আল্লাহ-এসেও-কিছু-কর/ স্বয়ং আল্লাহ এসেও কিছু করতে পারবেন না: পানিসম্পদ প্রতিমন্ত্রী

Appendix C

(More Corruption Under the Regime)

In addition to: (1) Chapter 2: Bangladesh Dented, Demoted and Demented Under Sheikh Hasina's Digital Carnival of Corruption and Ruthless Repression in my *Bangladesh Divided: Political and Literary Reflections on a Police and Prison State* (New York: Peter Lang, 2019), pp. 33-60;

(2) Chapter 2: Democracy and Development: Development with Corruption and Without Democracy, in my *Bangladesh: Political and Literary Reflections on a Divided Country* (New York: Peter Lang, 2018), pp. 55-96; and,

(3) Chapter 12: Sheikh Hasina's Brutal BNP-Phobia and Her Scandalous "Midnight" Power Grab through Vampire Vote Dacoity and Villainous S/Election Rigging with an All-Time High Record of Humongous White-Collar Corruption, pp. 145-216; and **all Appendices (A to I)**, in Sabria Chowdhury Balland (ed), *Bangladesh: A Suffering People Under State Terrorism* (New York: Peter Lang, April 2020), see the following:

Engineer Rashed Anam About Corruption Under Hasina:

যে দেশে ৪০০কোটি টাকা বাজেট মৃত [Sheikh Mujib] মানুষের নামে, সেখানে জিবীত মানুষের অবস্থা কেমন?

যেই দেশে প্রতি সংসদের ৯৩ লাখ টাকার গাড়ি কেনার টাকা আছে, যেখানে ওবায়দুল কাদেররা হাতে নতুন নতুন মডেলের ৫০ লাখ টাকার রোলেক্স ঘড়ি পড়তে পারে, দেশে যেই চোখের ছানি কাটে বিনা পয়সায় হয় সেই চোখের ছানি কাটতে পোন্দান মন্ত্রী যদি লন্ডনে সাঙ্গপাঙ্গ নিয়ে হাজার হাজার কোটি টাকা খরচ করতে পারে, যেখানে প্রেসিডেন্ট সামান্য রুটিন স্বাস্থ্য চেকাপ করতে কথায় কথায় সিংগাপুরে কোটি কোটি টাকা খরচ করতে পারে, যেখানে মন্ত্রীরা তাদের চিকিৎসার জন্য জনগণের টাকাতে সিঙ্গাপুর থেকে এয়ার এম্বুলেন্স আনতে পারে, যেখানে মন্ত্রীরা মিলিয়ন ডলার মাস ব্যাপী মাউন্ট এলিজাবেথ হসপিটালে থাকতে পারে, যেখানে আর্মি অফিসার , সরকারি আমলা এদের কারীকারী কোটি কোটি টাকার ফ্রি জমি , বাড়ি, গাড়ি , বোনাস, দ্বিগুন তিনগুন বেতন বৃদ্ধি করতে পারে, যেখানে আওয়ামী প্রথম , দ্বিতীয়, তৃতীয় থেকে শুরু করে চতুর্থ শ্রেণীর সম্রাট , জি কে শামীম , পাপিয়ারা হাজর কোটি টাকার ক্যাশই রাখে, যেখানে আওয়ামী জি কে শামীম, পাপিয়ারা হোটেলের বিলই দেয়া লক্ষ লক্ষ টাকা ! প্রতিদিনের মদের বিলই আসে কয়েক লক্ষ, যেখানে সজীব ওয়াজেদ জয় ভিওআইপি বেবসা সহ কমিশন বাণিজ্যে আমেরিকাতে ৮/৯টা বাড়ি কিনতে পারে, এবিবিআই পায় $৩০০ মিলিয়ন ডলার সেই ২০১২ তেই, যেই দেশে দুর্নীতির চোটে রাস্তা বানানোর খরচ বিশ্বের সর্বোচ্চ, যেই দেশ দুর্নীতির চোটে

অর্থপাচারের ও অতিধনি বৃদ্ধি তালিকার শীর্ষে, যেই দেশ নাকি সিংগাপুরে হয়ে গেছে উন্নয়নের জোয়ারে, যেখানে মুজিববর্ষের নামে ভারত থেকে কোটি কোটি খরচ করে ৭ টন আতশবাজি আনতে পারে, সেই দেশে জনগেনৰ ভাইরাস টেস্ট করার সামান্য $১০ দামের টেস্ট কীট নাই ? সেই দেশে ডাক্তারদের প্রটেকশন সরঞ্জাম নাই? সেই দেশে জনগণ কোনো হাসপাতালেই যেতে পারে না চিকিৎসার জন্য ? কোনো আইসিউ নাই ? সেই দেশে বাপকে কুত্তার মতো এক হাসপাতাল থেকে আরেক হাসপাতাল থেকেই টানাটানি চিকিৎসার জন্য ? সেই দেশে মানুষ কুত্তার মতো মরে ? অবশ্যই !! দোষতো জনগেনৰই ! জনগণ যদি গুমখুনি , ভোটডাকাত , দুর্নীতিবাজ স্বৈরাচারকে মেনে নিতে পারে, তাহলে সেই স্বৈরাচারীর অপশাসনের সব পরিনিতিও মেনে নেয়া উচিত !! জনগনের অভিযোগ করার কোনো অধিকার নাই , কারণ জনগণ সেই অধিকার হারিয়েছে যখন তারা এই স্বৈরাচার অপশক্তিৰ বিরুদ্ধে প্রতিবাদ করার কর্তব্য পালন করনি ! নো ফ্রি লাঞ্চ ! এই অপশক্তিকে লাথি দিয়ে বেৰ করে কবর দেয়াই একমাত্র মুক্তির উপায় ! সেটা জন্যগণকেই করতে হবে ! অথবা এই রকম কুত্তার মতো মরতে হবে ! এই স্বাধীনতা দিবসে জনগণ দেখেছে যে আজ তার গণতান্ত্রিক স্বাধীনতা নাই , ভোট অধিকার নাই , কথা বলার স্বাধীনতা নাই, সংবাদ মাদ্ধমের স্বাধীনতা নাই, গুমখুন থেকে জীবনের নিরাপত্তা নাই ! গণতান্ত্রিক সম্মেলন মিটিং মিছিল ইত্যাদি অধিকার গেছে অনেক আগেই ! ফেসবুকে মন্তব্যের জন্যও পিটিয়ে হত্যা হতে হয় ! আর হরিলুটের বাকশালী স্বৈরাচার রাজ্যে এখন মহামারী ভাইরাস টেস্ট করার উপায় নাই , হাসপাতালে চিকিৎসা নেয়ার কোনো উপায় নাই ! চেতনার বাকশাল একদলীয় স্বৈরাচার রাজ্যে মৌলিক অধিকার গুলো গেছে অনেক আগেই ! এখন জীবন , রুজি , সামান্য নুন্নতম চিকিৎসার অধিকার সেগুলোও গেছে !! এই অবৈধ স্বৈরাচার নিজেদের বাপের মুজিববর্ষ নিয়েই ছিল ব্যস্ত ! কোনো টেস্ট কীটের বেবস্থা করে নাই ! ডাক্তারদের প্রটেকশনের সরঞ্জাম/মাস্ক/কাপড় বেবস্থা করে নাই ! সাড়া দেশে একটা মাত্র টেস্ট সেন্টার , তাও আবার এখন নামমাত্র ২০০০ এর মতো টেস্টকীট ছিল ! তামশা ! পরিণাম হচ্ছে জনগণ কোনো টেস্ট করতে পারছে না , কোনো হাসপাতালে চিকিৎসা করতে পারছে না ! কেউ নিচ্ছে না ! কারণ তাদের প্রটেকশনের সরঞ্জাম/মাস্ক/কাপড় ইত্যাদি সরকার বেবস্থা করে নাই ! জনগণ এক হাসপাতাল থেকে আরেক হাসপাতালে মরিয়া হয়ে ছুটছে ! আরো সংক্রমিত করেছে ! প্রতিটা হাসপাতাল এখন কোরোনা প্রজনন কেন্দ্রেতে পরিনিত করেছে সরকার ! কোনো কন্ট্রোল নাই ! একটা ভয়াবহ অবস্থার সৃষ্টি করে জাতিকে আতকংক্ষিত করে রেখেছে ! রুগীরা চিকিৎসার অভাবে বাসাতেই , অলিতে গলিতে মরছে !! জয় বাংলা ! মন্ত্রীরা হাতে রোলেক্স লাগিয়ে , মিরজাদি শাহজাদীরা ২৪ দিনে ২৪ শাড়ীর ফ্যাশন শো করে, গলাবাজি, মিথ্যাবাজি করেই যাচ্ছে !! আরো বলেছে দেশ সিঙ্গাপুর হয়ে গেছে , আমেরিকা ইউরোপ বাংলাদেশে ধন্যা দিচ্ছে সরঞ্জামের জন্য! শুধু দেশের মানুষরাই কিছু পাচ্ছে না ! চিকিৎসার অভাবে যত্রতত্র মরছে ! গুমখুন হয়ে মরার উপর এখন মরছে চিকিৎসার অভাবে !! যেই জাতি যেই রকম অত্যাচারী, লুটেরা স্বৈরাচার সরকার মেনে নিয়েছে সেই রকম পরিণীতি এখন ভোগ করছে !!

Appendix D

(The regime's failure to face the corona virus disease)

Q M Jalal Khan

www.thedailystar.net/frontpage/news/dhaka-slums-where-covid-curiously-quiet-1936293

www.newagebd.net / article / 111956/coronavirus-scams-on-rise-as-no-effective-action-yet

www.dailynayadiganta.com / Incident-accident / 517024 / করোনা-পরীক্ষায়-অনিয়ম-আরো-একটি-হাসপাতাল-বন্ধ

www.dainikamadershomoy.com/post/266503 অধিকাংশ হাসপাতালের লাইসেন্সই নেই

www.bbc.com/bengali/news-53048395 করোনা ভাইরাস: সরকারি কার্যক্রমে অনিয়ম, দুর্নীতি ও অযোগ্যতা কোভিড-১৯ পরিস্থিতিকে প্রকট করেছে - টিআইবি

www.thedailystar.net/frontpage/news/fraudster-myriad-guises-1927977 Shahed

www.jugantor.com / national / government / 330357 / অনিয়মের-অভিযোগে-আরও-একটি-হাসপাতাল-বন্ধ

www.newagebd.net / article / 112063 / du-official-sharmin-put-on-three-day-remand

www.newagebd.net/article/109455/coronavirus-exposes-al-dev-myth-bnp-mps

www.ittefaq.com.bd/wholecountry / 167335/১৯-করোনা-রোগীর-চিকিৎসায়-৫-কোটি-৪১-লাখ-টাকা-বিল-দাখিল

www.newagebd.net / article / 110750 / bb-freezes-shaheds-accounts COVID-19 certificate forgery case; several thousand fake COVID-19 certificates and charging people for free tests

www.thedailystar.net/editorial/news / fake-certificates-giving-false-sense-safety-1927785

www.thedailystar.net / backpage/news/covid-test-khulna-long-wait-and-backlog-1927913

www.thedailystar.net / frontpage / news / denied-treatment-own-hospital-young-nurse-dies-1914525 www.ittefaq.com.bd / national / 156136 / শুধু-ঢাকাতেই-করোনা-আক্রান্ত-সাড়ে-৭-লাখের-বেশি%C2%A0

www.dailynayadiganta.com / disaster / 506165 / আইসিইউ-পেতে-হাসপাতালে-ঘুরছেন-রোগীরা

www.dailynayadiganta.com / khulna / 506152 / শরীরে-করোনা-উপসর্গ-ভর্তি-নিল-না-কেউ-স্ত্রীর-কোলে-ছটফট-করে-স্বামীর-মৃত্যু

www.dailynayadiganta.com/chattagram / 510717 / হাসপাতালে-ভর্তি-হতে-না-পেরে-সড়কেই-প্রাণ-গেল-নারীর

www.thedailystar.net / bangla / মতামত / হাসপাতাল-থেকে-হাসপাতাল-মর্মান্তিক-অমানবিক-151903

www.dw.com / bn / ট্রলি-নেই-হাসপাতালে-কোলে-নিয়ে-যেতে-গিয়ে-রোগীর-মৃত্যু / a-53445326

www.ittefaq.com.bd / capital / 154365/বিনা-চিকিৎসায়-কলেজছাত্রের-মৃত্যুর-পর-ডেথ-সাটিফিকেট-পেতে-৫শ-টাকা

www.dailynayadiganta.com / dhaka / 514338 / করোনা-সন্দেহে-কাছে-আসেনি-কেউ-লাশ-পড়ে-রইল-রাস্তায়

www.newagebd.net/article / 106705 / covid-19-claims-21-infects-1602-in-a-day-in-bangladesh কোভিড-১৯ টেস্ট করবেন বলে ফুটপাতে শুয়ে বসে অপেক্ষা করছেন ভোর রাত থেকে

www.banglainsider.com/bangladesh/55964/দেশে-করোনার-ভয়ঙ্কর-আতঙ্কের-৫-তথ্য

www.banglainsider.com/bangladesh/55961/দুর্নীতির-বাধাহীন-উৎসব-চলছে-করোনাকালে

www.youtube.com/watch?v = TXDvaEZhWEU&feature = youtu.be জাফরুল্লাহর কিট না নেয়ার আসল কাহিনী ফাঁস করলেন মাহমুদুর রহমান মান্না!

bd.dailynewslive24.com/282/15/ তথ্য গোপন করতে করোনা রোগীদের লা*শ নদীতে ফেলা হচ্ছে!

https://asiatimes.com/2020/06/bangladesh-and-covid-19-disaster-within-a-disaster/

www.dailynayadiganta.com/diplomacy/499740/সঙ্কটকে-গভীর-করছে-অস্বচ্ছতা-অব্যবস্থাপনা-ও-সমন্বয়হীনতা

Www.banglainsider.com/politics/55155/বাংলাদেশকে-বিশ্বে-একঘরে-করবে-করোনা

www.newsbybd.net/newsdetail / detail / 31 / 496034 করোনায় সুস্থতার হার বাড়াতেই একলাফে বেড়ে সহস্রাধিক!

www.ittefaq.com.bd/national/151369/এশিয়ায় সর্বোচ্চ ঝুঁকির দিকে বাংলাদেশ

www.newsbybd.net/newsdetail/detail/49/489820 বাবার চিকিৎসার জন্য দ্বারে দ্বারে ঘুরেছি: করোনায় মৃত অধ্যক্ষের ছেলের স্ট্যাটাস

www.jugantor.com/todays-paper/first-page/319691/৫-হাসপাতাল-ঘুরে-চিকিৎসা-না-পেয়ে-দম্পতির-মৃত্যু

BBC on Hasina's failure on Covid https://www.youtube.com/watch?v =AxCw IEyi5U8

www.youtube.com/watch?v=QP3Juo0k8DA

https://jamuna.tv/news/159579 ফাইভ পাস মাছ ব্যবসায়ীর নিজের ক্লিনিক, নিজেই করেন সিজার অপারেশন!

https://vertex.news/mothers-death-and-facebook-post-of-zia-hyder/

www.bbc.com/bengali/bbc_bangla_radio/w172xdwh68z3362

https://youtu.be/In09xibm7ZQ করোনা নিয়ে আইইডিসিআর এর গোপন তথ্য ফাঁস করে দিলেন ডাক্তার পিনাকি ভট্টাচার্য !

www.jugantor.com/todays-paper / first-page / 303610 / নমুনা-সংগ্রহ-ও-ফল-দেয়ায়-অসঙ্গতি

www.dailynayadiganta.com/disaster/502608/-মধ্যরাতে-এসেও-করোনা-টেস্টের-কোয়ার্টার-কিলোমিটার-লাইন-ভোগান্তি-চরমে

সর্বনাশ সরকারের সব গোপনীয়তায় ফাঁস●যে গোপনীয়তার কারনে দেশের মানুষ বিপদে পরবে।bangla news news24 bangla

প্রবাহ - BBC News বাংলা=https://www.bbc.com/bengali/bbc_bangla_radio/w172x dwh68z6035

www.ittefaq.com.bd / national / 148009 কোভিড-১৯ প্রতিরোধে বিশ্বের বিভিন্ন দেশের মতো বাংলাদেশেও লকডাউন চলছে। লকডাউনের ফলে মানুষ ক্ষতির মুখে পড়েছে। এজন্য সরকারের পক্ষ থেকে চালসহ খাবার সরবরাহ করা হচ্ছে। তবে এরই মধ্যে ২ লাখ ৭২ হাজার কেজি চালের কোনো হিসাব পাওয়া যাচ্ছে না।

www.thedailystar.net/bangla / মতামত/ধর্ষক-চোর-ও-ঘুষখোরের-দেশে-করোনা-143443

www.prothomalo.com / bangladesh / article / 1647749 / অ্যাম্বুলেন্সে-১৬-ঘণ্টায়-৬-হাসপাতালে-ছোটাছুটি

www.bd-pratidin.com / first-page / 2020 / 04 / 26 / 524384 করোনা সংকটেও থেমে নেই স্বাস্থ্য খাতের দুর্নীতি

চিকিৎসাসামগ্রী কেনায় ২২ কোটি টাকার গরমিলের ব্যাখ্যা দিতে ব্যর্থ স্বাস্থ্য অধিদফতর, এন-৯৫ মাস্কেও কেলেঙ্কারি

www.somoynews.tv/pages/details/210867 নারায়ণগঞ্জে যুবলীগ নেতার গুদাম থেকে ১২শ' বস্তা চাল জব্দ

www.dailynayadiganta.com / dhaka / 496710 / চেয়ারম্যানের-গোডাউনে-মিলল-১৩৪-বস্তা-চাল-আটক-১

www.dailynayadiganta.com / mymensingh / 496685/জামালপুরে-৯৮-বস্তা-ত্রাণের-চাল-উদ্ধার

www.dailynayadiganta.com / rajshahi / 496763 / রাজশাহীতে-চাল-চুরির-মামলায়-কারাগারে-আওয়ামীলীগ-নেতা

www.dailynayadiganta.com / dhaka / 496317 / কটিয়াদীতে-সরকারী-চাল-আত্মসাতের-অভিযোগে-আওয়ামীলীগ-নেতা-আটক

www.dailynayadiganta.com / barishal / 496314 / বরিশালে-৭৬৮০-কেজি-চাল-জব্দ-আ'লীগ-নেতার-কারাদণ্ড

https://jamuna.tv/news/137338 ট্রাক আটকিয়ে ত্রাণ সামগ্রী লুট করে নিলো এলাকাবাসী

www.dailynayadiganta.com/sylhet/496842/ইউপি-চেয়ারম্যানের-বিরুদ্ধে-চাল-আত্মসাতের-লিখিত-অভিযোগ

www.dailynayadiganta.com / dhaka / 496736 / ত্রাণ-আত্মসাতের-অভিযোগে-আরো-১২-জনপ্রতিনিধিকে-বরখাস্ত

ww.dailynayadiganta.com/administration/496849/ত্রাণসামগ্রী-চুরি-বরখাস্ত-হয়েছেন-যেসব-জনপ্রতিনিধি

www.kalerkantho.com/ online / miscellaneous /2020/04/12/898119 'দেশ যখন মৃত্যুপুরী চোরায় তখন করে চুরি' (ভিডিও)

www.analysisbd.net/archives/15992১৩ দিনে ৩৩০০ বস্তা চাল চুরি করেছে আ.লীগ নেতারা!

www.banglatribune.com/country/news/618294/ইউপি-সদস্যের-ঘরের-মেঝে-খুঁড়ে-মিললো-চাল

www.kalerkantho.com / online / country-news / 2020 / 04/10/896999 করোনাতেও ২২৬৪ বস্তা সরকারি ত্রাণের চাল চুরি!

www.jugantor.com/covid-19/303903/ময়মনসিংহে-সরকারি-১১-বস্তা-চালসহ-ভ্যানচালক-গ্রেফতার

www.bd-pratidin.com/country/2020/04/22/523178 নোয়াখালীতে সরকারি ৪৫০ কেজি চালসহ আওয়ামী লীগ নেতা আটক

www.thedailystar.net/business/news/more-crore-no-job-and-hope-1898554

https://jamuna.tv/news/136398 বগুড়ায় হতদরিদ্রদের ৫০ বস্তা চালসহ কৃষক লীগ নেতা আটক

https://youtu.be/qmxWdqzYy-k "চাল চুরি করতে গিয়ে ধরা খেল আ'লীগ নেতা,জনগনের মাল লুট করে খাচ্ছে নেতারা"

www.dailynayadiganta.com / rajshahi / 504456/গাবতলীতে-৩শ-বস্তা-চাল-অবৈধভাবে-বিক্রিকালে-ট্রাকসহ-৭-জন-আটক

www.dailynayadiganta.com/rajshahi/504415/বগুড়ায়-১৫-টন-চালসহ-গম-আমজাদ-গ্রেফতার

www.jugantor.com/country-news/328469/দুইবার-বন্যা-হইল-এক-ছটাক-চাউলও-পাইলং-না ক র নার অজুহাতে দেশ কোন পথে !! পিনাকী ভট্টাচার্য শেখ হাসিনা খালেদা জিয়া আর ক র না নিয়ে যা বলল

www.drfirozmahboobkamal.com/blog/বাংলাদেশে-করোনা-ভাইরাস-৩/

www.newagebd.net/article/112198/spread-of-dengue-feared-as-many-patients-go-unreported

www.ittefaq.com.bd/covid19-update / 141483 / করোনার-মধ্যে-ডেঙ্গুর-ঝুঁকি-কার্যকর-পদক্ষেপ-নেই-সিটি-করপোরেশনের

Appendix E

(There Is No Freedom of Speech Under the Regime)

Q M Jalal Khan

In addition to Chapter 4, "Politics Bangladesh Style: All Sick and Rotten to the Core" in my *Bangladesh: Political and Literary Reflections on a Divided Country* (Peter Lang, 2018), pp. 137-178; and also my *Bangladesh Divided: Political and Literary Reflections on a Corrupt Police and Prison State* (Peter Lang, 2019), see the following for the total lack of press freedoms over the course of the last few months alone, not to speak of the last 12 years since 2009:

amardesh.co.uk/বাংলাদেশের-গণমাধ্যম-অন্ধ/ Asian Human Rights Commission

amardesh.co.uk/আবুল-আসাদ-প্রবীণ-সম্পাদক/

amardesh.co.uk/আমার-দেশ-ইউকে-অনলাইন-১২-ঘন/

http://aequitasreview.org/so-whats-the-point-of-journalism-then-by-sohrab-hassan/

www.justice.gov/eoir/page/file/967766/download ATTACKS ON FREEDOM OF EXPRESSION IN BANGLADESH

www.dailynayadiganta.com/more-news/509666/১০-সাংবাদিককে-পুলিশের-তলবে-ডিইউজের-নিন্দা-ও-প্রতিবাদ

www.justnewsbd.com/sylhet/news/29777 নাসিম ও ইনুকে নিয়ে আপত্তিকর মন্তব্য করায় গ্রেপ্তার

www.newagebd.net/article/108391/rokeya-university-teacher-held-over-fb-post

http://southasiajournal.net/the-prosecution-in-bangladesh-of-11-individuals-is-not-only-a-serious–infringement-of-freedom-of-speech-but-a-travesty-in-the-use-of-the-criminal-law/

সাংবাদিক কাজলের ছেলের মর্মস্পর্শী চিঠি: ৫৩ দিন গুমের পর ৫৪ ধারায় মামলা | Voice Bangla

www.dailynayadiganta.com/miscellaneous/500475/ফেসবুকে-সরকারবিরোধী-পোস্ট-ডিএসই-পরিচালক-ও-রাষ্ট্রচিন্তার-সমন্বয়ক-কারাগারে

www. dailynayadiganta.com / sylhet / 500319 / ফেসবুকে-এমপিকে-নিয়ে-পোস্ট-ডিজিটাল-নিরাপত্তা-আইনে-সাংবাদিক-গ্রেফতার

www.hrw.org/news/2020/05/07/bangladesh-mass-arrests-over-cartoons-posts

www.thedailystar.net/frontpage/news/digital-security-act-11-sued-two-sent-jail-1900228

www.thedailystar.net / frontpage/news / its-now-gag-the-media-free-speech-1900231

www.thedailystar.net / country / news/cartoonist-writer-arrested-under-digital-security-act-1899973

www.dailynayadiganta.com / law-and-justice / 496711 / চাল-চুরির-প্রতিবেদন-বিডিনিউজ-ও-জাগো-নিউজ-সম্পাদকের-নামে-মামলা

https:// rsf.org / en / news/bangladeshi-journalists-cartoonist-arrested-covid-19-coverage

www.dailynayadiganta.com / politics / 496745/সত্য-প্রকাশ-বাধাগ্রস্ত-করতেই-দুই-সম্পাদকের-বিরুদ্ধে-মামলা-মির্জা-ফখরুল

www.newagebd.net/article / 111914 / cartoonist-kishore-writer-mushtaq-denied-bail-again

www.thedailystar.net / in-focus / news / free-speech-and-the-imperatives-democracy-1907053

http://aequitasreview.org/1158-2/Bangladesh: Silencing Voices With The Digital Security Act

www.dailynayadiganta.com/rajshahi/496473/বঙ্গবন্ধুকে-নিয়ে-কটুক্তি-করায়-বগুড়ায়-এক-যুবক-গ্রেপ্তার

www.dailynayadiganta.com / miscellaneous / 499632 / মুখ-বন্ধ-করে-দেয়া-হলো-বঙ্গবন্ধু-মেডিক্যাল-বিশ্ববিদ্যালয়ের-চিকিৎসকদের

www.prothombangladesh.net / 2020 / 06/06/news/30852 শেখ হাসিনাকে নিয়ে ফেসবুকে কটুক্তির অপরাধে পলি আক্তার গ্রেফতার।

https:// news.yahoo.com / bangladesh-boy-15 - arrested-facebook - criticism-pm-130243620.html

www.dailynayadiganta.com / rajshahi/511354/নাসিমকে-কটুক্তির-অভিযোগে-রাবি-শিক্ষক-সাময়িক-বহিষ্কার

www.newagebd.net/article/109589/inqilab-editor-bahauddin-sued-under-digital-security-act

www.newagebd.net/article/109545/digital-security-act-cases-on-rise

www.dailynayadiganta.com/politics/514254/সাবেক-ছাত্রদল-সম্পাদক-আকরাম-গ্রেফতার-ফখরুলের-নিন্দা

Appendix F

(Conspiracies Behind the BDR Massacre)

Q M Jalal Khan

For the alleged "bilateral" (insider-outsider) conspiracies behind the BDR massacre, see Appendix B in *Bangladesh Divided: Political and Literary Reflections on a Corrupt Police and Prison State* (July 2019), pp. 419–421.

In addition, for the images, reports, and background stories of the BDR massacre, click:

- www.facebook.com/drkanaksarwarbd/videos/286106049170265   Lt Gen Chowdhury Hasan Suhrawardy
- www.youtube.com/watch?v=pCh_WDEBrdY BDR tragedy : Pilkhana GENOCIDE ! Sheikh Hasina : Mutiny ? A very real CONSPIRACY ::::: Episode 1
- https://youtu.be/dxujWslJc_k "BDR tragedy : Pilkhana GENOCIDE ! Sheikh Hasina : Mutiny ? A very real CONSPIRACY ::::: episode 2"
- amjonotablog.wordpress.com/2014/02/25/bdr-হত্যাকাণ্ডের-আসল-রহস্য-১/
- www.sangbad247.net/2019/02/25/20236 শেখ হাসিনা ও RAW এর যৌথ ষড়যন্ত্রে রক্তাক্ত পিলখানা
- https: // bangladesh2075.wordpress.com / 2011 / 02 / 23/bdr/ "বিডিআর হত্যাকান্ডের সেই গোপনীয় অধ্যায়গুলো," [A complete online references] ২.৫ সংস্করণ
- http://bdfact.blogspot.com/search/label/BDR%20tragedy
- http://bdfact.blogspot.com/search/label/BDR%20Probe%20Report
- http://bdfact.blogspot.com/search/label/BDR
- www.jagonews24.com/national/news/381043 ফিরে দেখা পিলখানা ট্র্যাজেডি
- https:// youtu.be/ZQ70y2FjK80
- www.youtube.com/watch?v=ZQ70y2FjK80&feature=youtu.be পিলখানা ট্র্যাজেডির হত্যার দায় হাছিনা জয় এক দিন না এক দিন দিতেই হবে।।
- https://youtu.be/FNKoDpsmKKg প্রতিশোধের আগুনে সেনাবাহিনী, সেনাবাহীনির অফিসার হত্যায় জড়িত ছিল তাপস,গোপন নথি ফাঁস
- www.facebook.com/photo.php?fbid=2558273840915477&set=a .223276921081859&type=1&theater (Barrister Taposh)

- www.somewhereinblog.net/blog/morubalok/29717705 আমাকে যদি জাতির জনকের নাতনি জামাই করেও পাঠাতে
- amjonotablog.wordpress.com/2014/02/25/bdr-হত্যাকাণ্ডের-আসল-রহস্য-১/
- www.google.com/search?q=bdr+massacre&espv=2&biw=1024&bih=634&source = lnms& tbm=isch&sa = X&ved=0ahUKEwiu3ZqCrKHLAhUECI4KHc16BcAQ_AUIBigB&dpr= 1
- https://bangladesh2075.files.wordpress.com/2011/02/bdr4.pdf; https://bangladesh2075. files.wordpress.com/2011/02/bdr4.pdf; CLICK FOR DOWNLOAD [19MB] Confidential
- Report on the Pilkhana tragedy and the aftermath; www.google.ca/search?q=Confidential+ Report+on+the+Pilkhana+ tragedy+and+the +aftermath&oq=Confidential+Report+on+ the+ Pilkhana+tragedy+and +the+aftermath&aqs=chrome..69i57.3790j0j7&sourceid= chrome&ie= UTF-8
- www.youtube.com/watch?v=Wpmr4gKFHww&list=PLIHKbOV-zIeJ M9xynUhH1mruUD5sclmx
- www.newsfrombangladesh.net/view.php? hidRecord=249918
- www.sonarbangladesh.com/article.php?ID=607
- www.amardeshbd.com/dailynews/detail_news_index.php?NewsID=214019&NewsType= bistarito&SectionID=home&HSD=VZOXOEOC&oldIssueID=2009/03/02
- http://www. zimbio.com/World+Politics/articles/3218/2009/03/02
- http://rupeenews.com/2009/03/02/ bangladesh-peelkhana-massacre-another-raw-commando-operation-to-destabilize- country-create-civil-war/
- www.thefinancialexpress-bd.com/2009/03/04/60316.html
- http://bdfact.blogspot.com/2009/03/bdr-massacre-act-of-revenge-or-foreign.html
- www.defence.pk/forums/world-affairs/22931-bangladesh-peelkhana-massacre- another-raw-commando-operation.html
- http://pakistanpal.blogspot.com / 2009 / 03 / bangladesh-peelkhana-massacre-another.html
- http://bdosintmonitors.blogspot.com/ 2009/03/peelkhana-massacre-act-of-revenge-or.html
- www.telegraph.co.uk/news/worldnews/asia/bangladesh/4982518/Bangladeshi- army-officers-blame-prime-minister-for-mutiny.html
- www.telegraphindia.com/ 1090227/jsp/frontpage/story_10599074.jsp
- www.telegraphindia. com/1090301/jsp/frontpage/story_10608500.jsp
- http://www.southasiaanalysis.org/papers 31/paper3072.html
- http://bdnews24.com/details.php?cid=2&id=77494
- http://blackfebruary25.blogspot.com/2009/04/article-published-in-weekly-holiday.html

- http://blackfebruary25.blogspot.com/2009/04/another-article-of-sunita-paul.html
- www.americanchronicle.com/articles/view/96420
- http://blackfebruary25.blogspot.com/2009/03/article-published-in-american-chronicle. html
- www.americanchronicle.com/articles/view/95135
- https://groups.yahoo.com/neo/groups/BUET_91/conversations/messages/2448
- http://blackfebruary25.blogspot.com/2009/03/
- www.weeklyblitz.net/index.php?id=428
- www.weeklyblitz.net/index.php?id=432
- www.weeklyblitz.net/index.php?id=453
- http://blackfebruary25.blogspot.com/2009/03/article-from-newsfrombangladeshnet.html
- http://newsfrombangladesh.net/view.php?hidRecord=251688
- www.newsforbd.net/blog/blogdetail/detail/11169/bartakedra/74690;
- www. facebook.com/photo.php?fbid=1569825790003543&set=a.1410 694752583315. 1073741828.100009284122418&type=3
- http://blackfebruary25.blogspot.com/2009/03/mail-from-army-officer.html

Appendix G

(The Regime's Controversial ICT)

In addition to Chapter 8 (on the cruel otherization in the murderous proceedings of the questionable International Crime Tribunal under the direction of the fascist Sheikh Hasina) in Q M Jalal Khan's *Bangladesh: Political and Literary Reflections on a Divided Country* (Peter Lang, 2018), pp. 276-308, see the following:

www.justsecurity.org/52854/toby-cadman-rejoinder-government-bangladesh/

http://bangladeshwarcrimes.blogspot.com/2012/12/comment-from-toby-cadman-on-economist.html.

http://www.theaustralian.com.au/media/the-economist-accused-of-hacking-bangladesh-war-crime-tribunal-judge/story-e6frg996-1226533435427.

SKYPE DIALOGUE (Bangla audio):

http://www.youtube.com/watch?v=MdgbrfS9ck4.বিচারপতির স্কাইপি সংলাপ: 'ড. কামাল ক্রিমিনাল বোঝে না, আমীর উল গ্যানজাম করে ওয়ালিউর চোর':

http://www.youtube.com/watch?v=yOChrbD5W7U.

http://www.youtube.com/watch?feature=player_embedded&v=MdgbrfS9ck4#!.

http://www.amardeshonline.com/pages/details/2012/12/09/177212.

https://www.facebook.com/photo.php?v=417605868310828.

https://www.facebook.com/photo.php?v=421012137972727.
https://www.facebook.com/photo.php?v=421013811305893.
https://www.facebook.com/photo.php?v=421020267971914.
https://www.facebook.com/photo.php?v=421008207973120.
https://www.facebook.com/photo.php?v=421002287973712.

http://www.youtube.com/watch?v=MdgbrfS9ck4&feature=endscreen&NR=1v.

http://www.youtube.com/watch?v=0sKq1KXRq4U.

http://www.youtube.com/watch?v=yOChrbD5W7U.

http://www.youtube.com/channel/UCFk6OTpBF1MhVhIcSrQHvZw.

http://www.youtube.com/watch?feature=player_embedded&v=MdgbrfS9ck4#!.

CRITICAL ANALYSES & CONCERNS:

A TV talk show by Dr. Pias Karim, a political analyst, on the Skype dialog:

https://www.facebook.com/photo.php?v=112617882239329&set=vb.109460289217516&type=2&theater.

https://www.facebook.com/photo.php?v=112617882239329&set=vb.109460289217516&type=2&theater.

Eminent author and journalist Mahfuz Ullah and Prof Pias Karim comment on the Skype Scandal:

https://www.facebook.com/photo.php?v=112609422240175&set=vb.109460289217516&type=2&theater.

Resignation & Punishment Demanded for Skype Scandal:

http://www.thedailystar.net/newDesign/news-details.php?nid=260763.

PROSECUTION'S action against the daily Amar Desh:

http://www.thedailystar.net/newDesign/news-details.php?nid=260764.

http://www.kalerkantho.com/?view=details&type=gold&data=Cricket&pub_no=1087&cat_id=1&menu_id=0&news_type_id=3&news_id=306646.

Journalist David Bergman on Prosecution Witnesses in Safe House and the Whole Episode of Drama:

http://bangladeshwarcrimes.blogspot.com/2012/12/sayedee-trial-analysis-safe-house.html.

Journalist David Bergman on the Abduction of Witness by the Government Authorities from the Tribunal Premises:

http://bangladeshwarcrimes.blogspot.com/search/label/Abduction%20of%20witness.

Journalist David Bergman on Evidence of Abduction of Witness:

http://bangladeshwarcrimes.blogspot.com/2012/11/evidence-of-abduction-look-at-tribunal.html.

Journalist David Bergman's interview of the Wife of the Abducted Witness:

http://bangladeshwarcrimes.blogspot.com/2012/11/exclusive-wife-of-abducted-witness.html.

Journalist David Bergman on Arbitrarily Limiting the Defense Witnesses:

http://bangladeshwarcrimes.blogspot.com/2012/11/sayedee-trial-analysis-limiting-defense.html.

Appendix H

(New and reconstituted BNP under the leadership of the Zia family)

Q M Jalal Khan

It is the people like the following who should move up to the front row of the BNP under the leadership of *DeshNetri* and *DeshMata* Begum Khaleda Zia and (would-be) *DeshNayo*k Tarique Rahman, who should discard and distance from the weak and unimpressive Mirza Fakhrul and the majority of the cold and current Sitting-cum-Standing Committee members. Fakhrul is hopeless and worthless. His statements are boring and boorish; his words do not fly; he is dull and dumb in his body language which lack gesture, expression and demonstration. Most of the most senior leaders are not only incompetent but also lack courage and confidence. Their speeches do not create any stir; their statements do not leave any impact. They look out for a supply of ideas from others, including the Awami League, but cannot find any new ideas for themselves. Lacking in patriotic and nationalist ideas, they cannot and do not act; they rather only react, and that is also in a feeble and futile manner. Regardless of how old and controversial the past of some of the following leaders may be, they still seem to be far better and more effective than many on the present highest committee --hopelessly lame and lethargic as it is.

Except President Ziaur Rahman and Begum Khaleda Zia, both of them being of incredibly selfless and successful credentials (to the extent of achieving legendary status), hardly anyone is without controversy and free from errors, blunders, missteps and miscalculations in Bangladesh politics. Most of the political figures are opportunistically dual faced. That is, many of them are myopically and maliciously corrupt and mischievous, full of dubious intentions and diabolical misdemeanors. All are on-again and off-again in their turns, counter turns and about-turns, morally inane and insane for power and position. Some have their nadirs or the lowest points as when they joined the horribly ruling Hasina at different times;

but they started getting back on track by leaving the evil Hasina regime after their realization not long after. Time to time, some were said to have been tempted by the Awamis to unseat the phenomenally and fantastically popular Begum Zia when she was in power.

If Matiur Rahman Rentu's book is authentic, which millions believe it surely is, Hasina and her Awami League are full of ill designs and evil engineering since 1981. It is their hallmark to engage in dubious and suspicious activities as their entire political careers throughout demonstrate. Their nefarious nepotism and favoritism and their fascist suppression of the opposition are an incontrovertible fact never to be forgotten and forgiven. That many opposition figures have been tempted to get into the Awami trap at different times, such as in 1991 and before the January 2014 farce, is true. Fortunately, some of those who were extended such Awami baits with the devilish intention of breaking the BNP or the BNP-led alliance were able to reject and rise above the lavish and lucrative Awami offers. Those few remain their own persons of independence and integrity; they remain loyal to Zia and Begum Zia in their own honest and candid way. They score high on this matter of honesty and integrity alone. If all of them are not directly under the banner of the BNP yet, they should honorably be invited to re-join or return to the BNP.

There are some who tend to take credit without doing anything, but there are those who do something and, more justifiably, take credit. There are some who are too simple and too innocent to be proactive, and, being people of inaction and non-action, they are also gullible. There are some who are people of controversy, but they are also men of action with sacrifice, commitment and dedication. They are the ones the BNP as a political party badly needs. Some of them need to be inducted and induced with proper and politically, not necessarily morally correct invitation to return to or join/rejoin the BNP. In this respect, Tarique Rahman (who has, however, enhanced his leaderlike image with wise and mature reflection and realization of his past and a demonstration of honor and respect for those who are capable, competent and energetic leaders of the party, be they senior or younger) should take a meaningful initiative to invite the likeminded leaders to come under the BNP banner. The new crop of people to lead the BNP under Khaleda Zia and Tarique Rahman should be (among many others):

1. Shah Muazzem Hossain (no matter how old, still a firebrand heavyweight, but to be removed from this list following his recent

foolish and stupid nonsensical criticism of the great and glorious Begum Zia)
2. Gayeshwar Chandra Roy (honest, sincere, loyal and committed)
3. Abdullah Al Noman (despite some past 1/11 related controversy, still great and better than many)
4. Maj Hafizuddin Ahmad (despite his past 1/11 controversy, still eloquent, forceful and articulate)
5. Author, journalist, and former adviser/minister Mahmudur Rahman
6. Author, journalist and media personality Shafik Rehman
7. Col Oli Ahmad (despite his past and present controversies, should still be invited back)
8. Maj Gen (Retd) Syed Mohammad Ibrahim (may bring more "Kollyan" to the BNP)
9. Ruhul Kabir Rizvi
10. Muazzem Hussein Alal, ex-MP
11. Engr Ishrak Hossein (bold, active and energetic)
12. VP Mahmudur Rahman Manna (despite 'Nagorik,' maybe a diehard 'Nationalist')
13. Junaid Saki (despite 'Janashanghati,' maybe an excellent 'Jatiyotabadi')
14. VP Nurul Haq Noor
15. Barrister Andaleeve Partho (should be invited to move from 'Jatiyo' to 'Jatiyotabadi')
16. Dr Tuhin Malik
17. Zainal Abedin Farook, ex-MP
18. Dr Ehsanul Haque Milon, ex-MP and State Minister
19. Dr Sakhawat Hussein Shayanta
20. Shamsuzzaman Dudu, former MP
21. Habibur Rahman Habib
22. Sheikh Rabiul Alam
23. Maj Akhtaruzzaman, ex-MP
24. Mahbubuddin Khokon, ex-MP
25. Harunur Rashid, MP
26. Fazlur Rahman
27. Zainul Abedin Farook, ex-MP
28. Dr Asaduzzaman Ripon, ex-MP
29. VP Amanullah Aman, exMP
30. Golam Mowla Roni, and,

All the following fantastic and fabulous DeshKonnyas (দেশকন্যাগণ)—

31. Barrister Rumin Farhana, MP
32. Syeda Ashifa Ashrafi Papia, ex-MP
33. Nilufar Chowdhury Moni, ex-MP
34. Afroza Abbas
35. Shama Obaid

36. Nipun Roy Chowdhury
37. Sultana Ahmed
38. Fahima Nasrin Munni
39. Shammi Akhter, ex-MP, and
40. Rehana Renu, ex-MP--, among many others, both male and female; and,
41. The BNP should remain in alliance with the Islamic parties, such as the Jamaat and the Hefazat-e-Islam under Maulana Junaid Babunagari.

At the same time, due recognition with state honors should be extended to patriotic politicians, writers, thinkers, artists, poets, intellectuals, cultural and media personalities, bloggers, and journalists, dead or alive, at home, abroad, and in exile, including those who may be pro-Awami but highly critical of the Indian loyalist and fascist Hasina brand Awami League. They are:

1. Sher-e-Bangla A K Fazlul Haq (posthumous)
2. Nawab Sir Khwaja Salimullah Bahadur (posthumous)
3. Maulana Abdul Hamid Khan Bhasani (posthumous)
4. Fazlul Quader Chowdhury (posthumous)
5. President Ziaur Rahman (posthumous)
6. Ex-Prime Minister Shah Azizur Rahman (posthumous)
7. Author, journalist Oli Ahad (posthumous)
8. M A G Osmani (posthumous)
9. M K Anwar (posthumous)
10. Elias Ali (posthumous)
11. Advocate Mumtaz Uddin Ahmed (posthumous)
12. Chowdhury Alam (posthumous)
13. Salahuddin Quader Chowdhury (posthumous)
14. Group Captain Saiful Azam (posthumous)
15. Prof Emajuddin Ahmed (posthumous)
16. Prof Pias Karim (posthumous)
17. Journalist Ataus Samad (posthumous)
18. Journalist Sadeq Khan (posthumous)
19. Poet Al Mahmud (posthumous)
20. Journalist, Author Mahfuz Ullah (posthumous)
21. Film maker Chashi Nazrul Islam (posthumous)
22. Film maker Amjad Hossain (posthumous)
23. Shafiul Alam Pradhan (posthumous)
24. Dr Aftab Ahmed (posthumous)
25. Singer and vocal artist Shahnaz Rahmatullah (posthumous)
26. Journalist Sanjeeb Chowdhury of Amar Desh (posthumous)
27. Novelist Humayun Ahmed (posthumous)
28. Prime Minister Begum Khaleda Zia
29. Maj Gen (Ret) Rezzakul Haider Chowdhury (rotting in jail)

~~30.~~ Maj Gen (Ret) Imamuzzaman
31. Brig Gen (Ret) Abdur Rahim (rotting in jail)
32. Former State Home Minister Lutfuzzaman Babar (rotting in jail)
33. Author, journalist, and media personality Mahmudur Rahman
34. Writer, journalist and media personality Shafik Rehman
35. Writer, intellectual Farhad Mazhar
36. Maulana Delwar Husain Saidee
37. Maulana Junaid Babunagari
38. Maulana Mamunul Haq
39. Maulana Abdur Rahim al-Madani
40. Poet and writer Abdul Hye Sikder
41. Cultural personality and columnist Ariful Haque
42. Dr Morshed Hasan Khan of DU
43. Photojournalist Shahidul Alam
44. Journalist Abul Asad
45. Journalist Shawkat Mahmud
46. Journalist Mahmud Bin Feisal of SATV
47. Singer and vocal artist Baby Naznin
48. Singer and vocal artist Monir Khan
49. Singer and vocal artist Nazmun Munira Nancy
50. Singer and vocal artist Nokul Kumar Biswas
51. Dr Khalifa Malik (UK)
52. Social media activist Zoglul Husain (UK)
53. Social media activist Dr Mina Farah (USA)
54. Author and essayist R Chowdhury (USA)
55. Journalist Mohammad Zainal Abedin (USA)
56. Journalist Elias Khan
57. Journalist Kanak Sarwar (USA)
58. Journalist Monir Haider (USA)
59. Journalist Oliullah Noman (UK)
60. Journalist Minar Rashid
61. Author and social media activist Pinaki Bhattacharya (France)
62. Author and social media activist Kai Kaus
63. Author and social media activist Isha Khan
64. Journalist Goutam Das
65. Writer and social media activist Noyon Chatterjee
66. Journalist Shamsul Alam Liton (UK)
67. Journalist Elias Hossain (USA)
68. Journalist Shafiqul Islam Kajol
69. Social media activist Abu Saleh Nayeb Ali (USA)
70. Blogger Nazma Mustafa (USA)
71. Social media activist Kajol Mirza (USA)
72. Lt Gen (Ret) Hasan Sarwardy
73. Maj (Ret) Abu Bakar Siddique (UK)
74. Maj (Ret) Delwar Hussain

75. Col (Ret) Shahid Uddin Khan
76. Journalist Amirul Momenin Manik
77. Journalist M A Aziz of New Age
78. Reazuddin Ahmed of Bangladesh Today
79. Barrister Mainul Hussein
80. Architect Mubassher Husain
81. Barrister Amirul Islam
82. Nur-e-Alam Siddiquee, and,
83. Hundreds of thousands of others, known and unknown, who became victims of Awami fascism in Bangladesh, especially since the fascist Hasina regime grabbed the state power in late 2008, again in early 2014, and then again in late 2018, every time stealing the elections and robbing the people of their right to vote in a more and more abject, abominable, reprehensible and unlawful manner with the help of the *gopal* and gestapo Awami police league, who, along with Hasina, has engineered a devastating harm in all sectors and sections, all around the country and in every nook and corner of the country.

Authors' Short Bios

Mohammad Zainal **Abedin** is journalist of great credentials. An MA in Sociology, he was associated with many major dailies and weeklies in Bangladesh before moving to the USA where he is currently editor of a New York-based bilingual weekly, the *Runner News*. Apart from hundreds of newspaper articles on national and international issues, particularly on India's hegemonic designs in the neighboring South Asian countries, he published over a dozen books, both in Bengali and English (see Appendix A Counter Narrative). Detained twice for over a year during 1968-69, Abedin, an activist of East Pakistan Student League, was an elected Vice-President of Noakhali Government College Students Union in 1970. He is a liberation war veteran who trained under 'Mujib Bahini' at Halflong India in 1971 when he wrote a full-fledged drama about Bangladesh's fight for freedom and independence. The play was staged in the training center mentioned, attended by dignitaries such as Maj. Gen. S. S. Uban of Indian Army and Serajul Alam Khan, then an active political thinker.

Dr Jasim Uddin **Ahmad** is former Vice Chancellor, Jahangirnagar University, Bangladesh. He has a PhD in Chemistry from Cairo University, Egypt with post-doctoral studies at Bradford University UK. A former Fellow of Royal Society of Chemistry, London, Dr Ahmad is a past President of Federation of Asian Chemical Societies and Bangladesh Chemical Society; and he is President Bangladesh Farakka Committee. Dr Ahmad has published and/or presented hundreds of research papers and popular articles and received the National award of Ekushey Gold Medal for his contribution in Education in 2006. He was co-editor with the late Professor Emajuddin Ahmad of the 12 volumes of Sectors-and-Brigade-based history of the great liberation war of Bangladesh, published by Ministry of Freedom Fighters, Government of Bangladesh.

Dr Abid **Bahar** is a Concordia University graduate. He teaches Ethics in Leadership at Dawson College Montreal, Canada. A strong critic of the authoritarian Awami regimes under Sheikh Mujib and currently his daughter Sheikh Hasina, he writes on social and political issues mostly related to Bangladesh and Myanmar. He has two chapters, "Understanding Sheikh Mujib's Surrender on March 25, 1971 and Its Repercussions in the Post- Liberation

Bangladesh" and "Sheikh Hasina Imposing Shackles on Bangladesh: Annihilating the Normal and Normalizing the Abnormal" in Sabria Chowdhury Balland (ed), *Bangladesh: A Suffering People Under State Terrorism* (Peter Lang, 2020).

R **Chowdhury** is a former soldier and diplomat, currently enjoying his retired life reading, writing, and growing vegetable in his backyard, among other passions. He has published a number of books: *A Soldier's Debt* (2015) deals with his escape from Pakistan and participation in the liberation war of Bangladesh in 1971; *Village Boy to Accidental Soldier* (2017) recounts his childhood struggles, military life, and glimpses into his family; and *FACTS, NOT FICTION: Bangladesh in Perspective* (2018) compiles some of his published articles. A regular contributor of excellent articles in online outlets, he has two chapters, "Ziaur Rahman's Legacy: Sheikh Hasina's Nightmare!" and "The Untold Truth About Sheikh Mujib's Stance on Independence in 1971 and How He Brought Bangladesh to the Brink of Collapse to Invite August 15 About Three and a Half Years Later" in Sabria Chowdhury Balland (ed), *Bangladesh: A Suffering People Under State Terrorism* (Peter Lang, 2020). Chowdhury is now working on a compilation of all his published articles since *Facts, Not Fiction*, possibly as FNF-II.

Dr A N M Ehasanul **Hoque** Milan is former State Minister of Education, Government of Bangladesh. He was a two-term elected Member of Parliament (1996-2000; 2001-2005). Twice elected as vice president of Fazlul Haq Hall at Dhaka University from where he graduated with a BSc (Hons) in Chemistry, followed by an MBA from New York Institute of Technology, New York, Dr Milan completed his PhD from International Islamic University Malaysia. An accomplished volleyball player, he has a good athletic background to be proud of.

Zoglul **Husain** is a London-based political commentator and a former activist and columnist relentlessly campaigning for Freedom, Democracy, Justice, Human Rights and Harmonious Development in Bangladesh. He appeared many times on Bengali-medium TV talk shows in London speaking on the political affairs of Bangladesh. A retired computer consultant with a Master's in Mathematics, he left his PhD studies in the UK to travel to Kolkata, India, in 1971 to join the Independence War of Bangladesh. He has a chapter, "A Brief Outline of Indian Hegemony in Bangladesh" in Sabria Chowdhury Balland (ed), *Bangladesh: A Suffering People Under State Terrorism* (Peter Lang, 2020). Forthcoming is his "Geopolitics of India Since 1947: Its Interactions with the Geopolitics of the World, and Its Adverse Effects on Bangladesh."

Dr Syed Serajul **Islam** is Distinguished Professor and former Chair of Political Science, Lakehead University, Canada. Graduated from Dhaka, Brock, and McGill Universities with an MA and a PhD respectively, he had taught at Dhaka University, McGill, and IIU Malaysia before joining Lakehead in 2000. Dr Islam has over a hundred publications in books and articles related to Bangladesh and South Asia with many conference papers to his credit. Two of his relevant articles stand out in context: "The Relative State Autonomy and the Development Strategy Under Zia" (Pacific Affairs) and "The State in Bangladesh Under Zia" (Asian Survey).

Dr Q M Jalal **Khan** is author of *Bangladesh: Political and Literary Reflections on a Divided Country* (Peter Lang, 2018) and *Bangladesh Divided: Political and Literary Reflections on a Corrupt Police and Prison State* (Peter Lang, 2019). Those are in addition to American-educated Dr Khan's dozens of other political articles published in online portals and numerous other publications in literary criticism. After disengaging from many years of teaching abroad, he is currently on the adjunct faculty at an institution of higher learning in North America. Prior to his works in this book, he wrote, *"Sheikh Hasina's Brutal BNP-Phobia and Her Scandalous 'Midnight' Power Grab Through Vampire Vote Dacoity and Villainous 'S/Election' Rigging With an All-Time High Record of Humongous White-Collar Corruption"* that has appeared in Sabria Chowdhury Balland (ed), *Bangladesh: A Suffering People Under State Terrorism* (Peter Lang, 2020). His co-edited *India's Hegemonic Domination of Bangladesh* is due out soon.

Dr K M A **Malik** has published several books on socio-political and strategic issues related to Bangladesh and the Middle East. These books include: (1) *Bangladesher Rajniti: Mookh O Mookhosh* (Politics of Bangladesh: The Face and The Mask (Gyan Bitarani, Dhaka, 2003; (2) *Challenges in Bangladesh Politics* (Adorn Publications, Dhaka, 2005); and (3) *War on Terror--A pretext for new colonization* (2005). Since then, while he wrote over fifty articles on contemporary socio-political themes for various outlets in London and Dhaka (all to be collected and published in book form in the near future), he has spent quite a bit of his energy and time in organizing seminars, meetings and campaigns on various issues of national and humanitarian interests. His involvement with several UK-based political and intellectual organizations concerning Bangladesh and the Middle East has made him regularly appear on TV talk shows and discussion forums. Dr Malik is Convenor of *Shatonagorik* (Hundred Citizens') UK Committee; *Mukta Mancha* (Open Forum); Bangladesh *Sammilito Peshajibi* (Combined Professionals') Parishad, UK; and Forum for Democracy, Human

Rights and Security. A retired Professor of Chemistry, Dr Malik taught at the University of Dhaka before leaving for the University of Wales Cardiff where he worked as a Lecturer and Researcher in Structural Chemistry. Following his MSc from the University of Dhaka in 1968, he completed his PhD from Birkbeck (University of London) and did post-doctoral research at Queen Mary University when he also taught at Hackney Technical College, London. He has published nearly 375 research articles on Chemistry and Chemical Crystallography. For his excellent academic performance and contribution to education and research, Dr Malik received several awards: Crown College Award (London), Third World Academy of Sciences Gold Medal (Italy), Bangladesh Academy of Sciences Gold Medal (Dhaka), Justice Ibrahim Gold Medal (Dhaka), Hari Prasanna Roy Gold Medal (Dhaka), all the way back to Mithapur High School Gold Medal, Faridpur owing to his standing 10th in the entire East Pakistan Secondary Education Board, Dhaka.

Nazma **Mustafa** is a writer, poet, and blogger. She published many books and articles in various Bengali dailies and weeklies in Bangladesh and New York. An MPhil in Islamic History and Culture from Dhaka University, she lives in New York and maintains a blog (www.nazmamustafa.com) where she regularly posts her essays and columns, mostly in Bengali, on current social, political, cultural and religious issues. Some of her writings are still unpublished. She loves teaching at school, sewing, and growing vegetable gardens in her backyard.

Dr Asif **Nazrul** is Professor of Law, University of Dhaka, Bangladesh. He is a columnist, civil society and social media activist and a prominent media personality. Dr Nazrul completed his PhD from SOAS, University of London in 1999, and later did his post-doctoral fellowship at Environmental Law Center, Bonn, Germany. His speech (https://www.youtube.com/watch?v=jPSJ_Uoe-rU) has been translated from original Bangla by Ahmad U Shihab, who is a US resident.

Mahmudur **Rahman** is former Energy Adviser and Investment Board Executive Chairman, Government of Bangladesh, and Editor, Daily Amar Desh (https://amardesh.co.uk/). Prior, he was a Managing Director at Beximco, Bangladesh's largest conglomerate, among the other positions he held earlier (with British Oxygen, Duncan Brothers Bangladesh, and Monno Ceramics). Rahman, who is currently living in exile in Turkey, is a renowned author who wrote more than ten books and hundreds of amazing editorial columns (see Appendix A Counter Narrative). A regular contributor to print as well as electronic media, Rahman is the foremost dissident voice against the current autocratic Hasina regime in Bangladesh. He suffered long imprisonment (for more than five years on two occasions combined) and endured inhuman physical torture by the Awami goons even in the court premises for his principled stand on human rights, press freedom and independence of judiciary. By academic training, a Chemical Engineer of BUET, an MBA from IBA, Dhaka, a post graduate diploma holder in Ceramic Engineering from Japan and a recipient of the highest award from the Institution of Engineers Bangladesh (IEB) for professional excellence in 2003.

Abdul Hye **Sikder** is a modern Bangladeshi poet, eminent journalist, Nazrul researcher, essayist, biographer, and travel writer. He is well known for his commitment to democracy, justice, and media freedom. With a long career as a journalist (Weekly Bichitra, Daily Inqilab, Daily Amar Desh, Bangladesh Sangbad Sangstha), Sikder has also served as Executive Director of Nazrul Academy/Nazrul Institute, Dhaka and Vice President of Jatiya Nazrul Samaj. A graduate of Rajshahi University, he taught as an Associate Professor at the University of Development Alternative, Dhaka; and is currently teaching as a Professor of Bangla Language and Literature at the Islamic University, Dhaka. Sikder published over eighty books in different genres, including children's literature and filmography. He published two books on (late) President Ziaur Rahman, one of which is জ্যোতির্ময় জিয়া এবং কালো মেঘের দল/Luminous Zia and the Black Clouds (2011). He won dozens of national awards, including the Bangla Academy Award in 2003. For his uncompromising stand against Indian hegemonism and Awami League fascism, some unknown assailants made a near death attempt on Sikder's life in 1996 and still, as of today, he continues to be hounded and harassed.

www.ingramcontent.com/pod-product-compliance
Lightning Source LLC
Chambersburg PA
CBHW070823250426
43671CB00036B/1834